CONTROLLING THE MESSAGE

Controlling the Message

New Media in American Political Campaigns

Edited by Victoria A. Farrar-Myers and Justin S. Vaughn

NEW YORK UNIVERSITY PRESS
New York and London

NEW YORK UNIVERSITY PRESS
New York and London
www.nyupress.org

© 2015 by New York University
All rights reserved

References to Internet websites (URLs) were accurate at the time of writing.
Neither the author nor New York University Press is responsible for URLs
that may have expired or changed since the manuscript was prepared.

ISBN: 978-1-4798-8635-7 (hardback)
ISBN: 978-1-4798-6759-2 (paper)

For Library of Congress Cataloging-in-Publication data, please contact
the Library of Congress.

New York University Press books are printed on acid-free paper,
and their binding materials are chosen for strength and durability.
We strive to use environmentally responsible suppliers and materials
to the greatest extent possible in publishing our books.

Manufactured in the United States of America

10 9 8 7 6 5 4 3 2 1

Also available as an ebook

CONTENTS

Acknowledgments — vii

Introduction: Controlling the Message in the Social Media Marketplace of Ideas — 1
Victoria A. Farrar-Myers and Justin S. Vaughn

PART 1: ELITE UTILIZATION

1. Strategic Communication in a Networked Age — 13
Daniel Kreiss and Creighton Welch

2. Congressional Campaigns' Motivations for Social Media Adoption — 32
Girish J. Gulati and Christine B. Williams

3. Surrogates or Competitors? Social Media Use by Independent Political Actors — 53
Julia R. Azari and Benjamin A. Stewart

4. The Competition to Control Campaign Messages on YouTube — 74
Robert J. Klotz

PART 2: MESSAGE CONTROL IN THE NEW MEDIA ENVIRONMENT

5. Campaign News in the Time of Twitter — 93
Regina G. Lawrence

6. New and Traditional Media Reportage on Electoral Campaign Controversies — 113
Mike Gruszczynski

7. Traditional Media, Social Media, and Different Presidential Campaign Messages — 136
Matthew Eshbaugh-Soha

PART 3: SOCIAL MEDIA'S IMPACT ON CAMPAIGN POLITICS

8. The Influence of User-Controlled Messages on Candidate Evaluations — 155
Joshua Hawthorne and Benjamin R. Warner

9. Terms of Engagement: Online Political Participation and the Impact on Offline Political Participation — 181
Meredith Conroy, Jessica T. Feezell, and Mario Guerrero

10. Is Laughter the Best Medicine for Politics? Commercial versus
    Noncommercial YouTube Videos   200
    Todd L. Belt

PART 4: SOCIAL MEDIA AND CIVIC RELATIONS

11. Comment Forum Speech as a Mirror of Mainstream Discourse   221
    Karen S. Hoffman

12. Sparking Debate: Campaigns, Social Media, and Political Incivility 245
    Daniel J. Coffey, Michael Kohler, and Douglas M. Granger

13. Flaming and Blaming: The Political Effect of Internet News and
    Reader "Comments"   270
    Brian R. Calfano

    Conclusion: Message Control at the Margins   302
    Victoria A. Farrar-Myers and Justin S. Vaughn

    About the Contributors   307
    Index   311

ACKNOWLEDGMENTS

The conversation that set the wheels in motion for this book occurred in the lobby of the Marriott Waterfront Hotel in Portland, Oregon, where we both were attending the Western Political Science Association's annual meeting. In the many months since, we have watched as the idea first discussed there turned into the volume you now hold in your hands (or, perhaps more relevant to the subject matter enclosed within, read on your laptop or tablet). Throughout the process, we have been gifted with the cooperation, wisdom, and patience of our chapter authors, the professionalism of the staff at NYU Press, and the insight of four anonymous reviewers. We are particularly indebted to Caelyn Cobb, whose ideas and guidance made this a much better book and whose enthusiasm renewed us throughout the process from proposal to publication.

Each of us would also like to give thanks to special people in our lives. Victoria thanks her husband, Jason; son, Kyle; and Anne Tego, whose collective love and constant devotion give her the inspiration to pursue her dreams. Justin thanks his wife, Elena, to whom he was engaged that same fortuitous Portland weekend, and the four dogs and two kitties who help make the Western Puggle Dome a place of love and joy.

Introduction

Controlling the Message in the Social Media Marketplace of Ideas

VICTORIA A. FARRAR-MYERS AND JUSTIN S. VAUGHN

The presidential candidate's campaign faced the threat of being derailed following a scathing depiction of him posted by an individual citizen. Regardless of whether the claims made against the candidate were truthful, the message already had gone viral, and the candidate's campaign flailed in its efforts to respond. Finally, one of the candidate's supporters not affiliated with his campaign repackaged the critic's depiction into a new theme, one that resonated positively with voters. The repackaged message itself continued well beyond its original posting as it was replicated in different forums time and time again.

The presidential campaign from which this vignette was drawn was not the 2012 contest between former Massachusetts governor Mitt Romney and incumbent President Barack Obama, where the use of social media was an indispensable tool in advancing positive narratives and beating back criticism. Nor was it the 2008 election, when Obama's first campaign for the presidency demonstrated the potential that the embryonic social media could have in the race for the White House (Germany 2009; Gulati 2010), or even in 2000, when Howard Dean demonstrated the effectiveness of the Internet as a fundraising tool (Kreiss 2012). Instead, the incident actually took place during the 1828 election between John Quincy Adams and Andrew Jackson and involved the "Coffin Handbill," a poster that depicted Jackson not as a military hero but instead as a murderer for his handling of six militia men whom Jackson ordered to be executed as their sentence for desertion (see figure I.1), and a subsequent newspaper editorial that recast the charges levied against Jackson in a positive light. Although the technology of printing presses and reliance on partisan-oriented newspapers may be antiquated in the world of modern political campaigns, the lesson behind this historical episode is timeless: candidates and their campaigns must worry about who controls the message affecting their campaigns.

Information, the Internet, and the 2012 Election

The volume of information produced and consumed in today's political world is immense. Furthermore, the outlets and mechanisms that producers of information use to provide, share, and communicate this information have proliferated

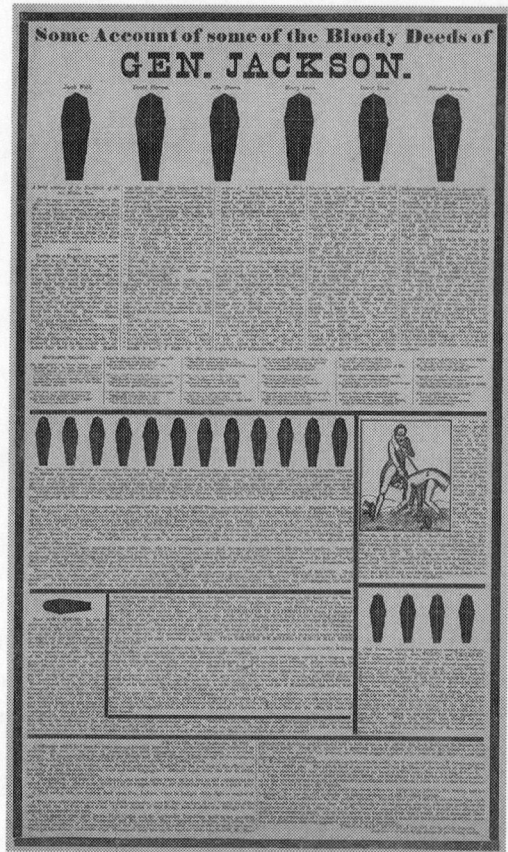

Figure I.1. The Coffin Handbill (Courtesy of the Tennessee State Library and Archives)

as new and social media have become fully infused into daily political life and contemporary election campaigns (Howard 2006; Gainous and Wagner 2011). The low-cost use of the Internet has already and will continue to have a dramatic and likely long-lasting effect on American politics. In the battle waged in the marketplace of ideas for supremacy of one's viewpoint, an uploaded video that goes viral or a simple 140-character tweet can potentially be more effective than reliance on more traditional forms of communication. Moreover, the low barriers of entry into the marketplace of ideas resulting from the technological innovations of new and social media not only create a "social media marketplace of ideas" but also promise—or threaten, depending on one's perspective—to make the nature of political discourse more democratic and less filtered. Indeed, we have reached the point where having a social media presence via a website, Facebook page, and Twitter account is a necessary means to be an effective political communicator. At the same time, however, merely having such a presence is hardly sufficient to ensure that one's message is reaching its intended audience, not being drowned out—or, worse, distorted—by competing messages.

Yet, despite all the focus on the use of new and social media in the political context, much of this phenomenon remains mysterious, if not misunderstood, by both practitioners and scholars of the political process. In order to realize the full power of new and social media in contemporary politics, one must first analyze and evaluate the implications that the corresponding free flow of ideas and information has for the American political system (see Farrell 2012; Dimitroval et al. 2014).

Such analysis and evaluation is the objective of this book. We utilize the context of the 2012 elections to study the phenomena of new and social media in American politics, with a particular focus on who controls the political message. For example, with this approach, one could examine the interaction between incumbency and using new and social media in the context of the 2012 presidential election. President Obama, as the incumbent, faced several structural advantages compared to Republican challenger Mitt Romney: no primary challengers, the ability to fundraise and spend resources solely with an eye toward the general election, and a longer lead time to dedicate to building campaign infrastructure. As a result, one would expect that Obama's campaign (and, more broadly, most incumbents) would develop more effective and innovative means to incorporate social media into the campaign as a means of controlling the campaign's message and reaching voters, as compared to the challenger. Obama's structural advantage should be kept in mind when evaluating the comparisons between the two presidential campaigns' use of new and social media in this volume, but it also highlights the reason for choosing to study the use of such media in an electoral cycle. The 2012 election context offers a time when the amount of political discourse was naturally heightened, the number of participants involved in or at least paying active attention to the political process increased, and the perceived importance of the discourse and its impact on the future and course of the nation grew.

That said, the planning and preparation for this volume started well before the general election season in 2012. Accordingly, the data and observations used in this volume were all intentionally captured and collected on a real-time basis during the 2012 election season. Interviews were conducted as interviewees were enmeshed in the political process and not trying to reconstruct their thoughts after the fact, online comments were monitored as they were posted, and video clips were viewed just as anyone in the nation with access to YouTube could have viewed them.

With the benefit of hindsight, one could wish that a certain topic was addressed in this volume or that certain methodological or substantive decisions were made differently. The benefit of the real-time research that is a foundation of this volume, however, far outweighs the trade-offs incurred by forgoing an after-the-fact analysis. The "raw" data for the studies that follow is just that—information collected truly in its most authentic form as it was contemporaneously being disseminated and consumed by participants in the political process. The result of our strategic preparation for this volume allows the analyses included to turn the context of the 2012 elections into a more comprehensive and methodologically rigorous examination of new media's true impact.

The holistic approach of this volume was by design, for just as politicos are trying to understand the impact of new media, scholars are still searching out how best to study the phenomenon. The chapters in this book dissect the multifaceted nature of this phenomenon from similarly diverse perspectives, as scholars across disciplinary borders and analytical boundaries provide unique contributions. Importantly, the chapters in this volume offer a balanced range of methodological approaches, yet bound together by the shared context of the 2012 elections, the lessons learned from each chapter build on each other to develop a more comprehensive picture of the true impact of new and social media than the simple sum of their parts would allow.

Furthermore, this collection of studies provides us with valuable insight into several key questions. Some of these questions are process oriented, such as whether and how the communication process between candidates (and the parties and interest groups active in their campaigns) and attentive members of the mass public is different in the new media age than what we know about traditional political communication. Other questions in this vein include the following: How can candidates and campaigns leverage social and other new media to promote or at least control their message? What information is processed and retained by the audiences of the various messages? Is the impact of social media usage limited to the governing and attentive publics, who would be attuned to the messages being delivered, or do the low barriers to entry in the social media marketplace of ideas facilitate the mass public's engagement at levels not found with traditional forms of communication? What are the implications for more traditional media outlets in the era of new and social media competition? In other words, the process-oriented questions can be more finely stated as concerning who controls the message, who consumes the message, and what impact (if any) these processes have for election outcomes.

More broadly, however, the emergence of new and social media challenges us to make sense of and derive meaning from the increased speed, breadth, depth, number of messengers, choice of outlets, and diversity of viewpoints that fill the political space each day. Along these lines, one has to consider whether, in a system in which any person can share his or her viewpoint given the low entry cost into the social media marketplace of ideas, too much information can be detrimental to the American form of democracy. In many ways, the abundance of information, ideas, and outlets creates "white noise" or a "cacophony of voices" (Farrar-Myers and Skinner 2012, 116; Hartnett and Mercieca 2007) where a constant heterogeneous mixture of sounds drowns out any individual sound or voice. Considering this, one might ask whether the increasingly democratic nature of political communication increases an individual's ability to contribute to the discourse or simply renders almost all citizens effectively voiceless. Also, can civic engagement and political participation be enhanced or even damaged by social media? What about citizen knowledge and political discourse (see Oxley 2012; Jones 2012)? Further, do and should the effects of new and social media in the political process apply differently among the governing public, the attentive public, and the mass public? To assess the true impact of these media developments fully, one must be willing to engage in a discussion of the normative implications such media bring.

Operating in the Social-Media-Driven Political Environment

This volume proceeds by engaging a number of distinct, but interrelated, themes that respond to the key questions discussed previously in this introduction. The first key theme concerns how various political actors use new and social media as they seek to control the political message in certain contexts. For example, building off interviews conducted with practitioners on Democratic presidential campaigns spanning the 2000 to the 2012 cycles and drawing on public accounts of the 2012 cycle, Daniel Kreiss and Creighton Welch's work in chapter 1 looks closely at the two presidential campaigns' use of data to model voters, the new platforms available for targeting communication, and the tailoring of communications in accordance with defined electoral goals. Their analysis yields significant insights about the relative success of these efforts, while also identifying the limits of social media usage as a means of fully controlling a campaign's information context.

Similarly, in chapter 2, Girish Gulati and Christine Williams complement Kreiss and Welch's emphasis on presidential campaigns with an analysis of underlying explanations for congressional campaign adoption of social media tools. Observing that by 2012 nearly all major party candidates for the U.S. Congress had adopted tools such as Facebook, they move the scope of analysis to examine not only how congressional candidates use social media but also which candidate characteristics explain differences in usage. Further, making use of a unique set of data gleaned from dozens of interviews with congressional campaign elites, Gulati and Williams are able to determine the strategic intentions of social media adoption. The conclusions offered in chapters 1 and 2, when juxtaposed with each other, reflect a seeming disconnect between the impact that social media could have as a campaign tool and campaigns' understanding of how to use social media to maximize their effects. Nevertheless, taken together, chapters 1 and 2 demonstrate how new and social media can, and in the current political environment perhaps must, be strategically and wholly integrated into a candidate's entire campaign effort as a tool to proactively promote and shape his or her political message, identity, and brand.

Although politicians and other participants in the process strive hard to control the political message, an increasingly democratic political discourse resulting from social media usage ensures that no public figures will be able to fully do so. Jan Kietzmann et al. (2011, 242) discuss in the business context the detrimental results that can occur when a business is not adequately prepared to protect its brand and products in the social media environment. They note that "firms regularly ignore or mismanage the opportunities and threats presented by creative consumers" (see also Berthon et al. 2007). The same can be said about candidates and other elite participants in the political process.

Several chapters in this volume address some of the "creative consumers" who could challenge candidates' efforts to establish and control the political message of their election. For example, in chapter 3, Julia Azari and Ben Stewart examine whether independent political actors (i.e., conservative and liberal groups not officially affiliated with parties or campaigns, such as interest groups, independent political action committees, and ideologically oriented media) use social media to perform a campaign surrogacy role in the twenty-first century or, alternatively, whether these groups act as campaign competitors, issuing messages that serve their own agendas rather than those of the official parties and candidates. Azari and Stewart conclude that, although independent organizations as a whole tend not to focus on a campaign surrogacy role, conservative organizations have shown a greater willingness to act as competitors to the campaigns.

In chapter 4, Robert Klotz studies candidate efforts to control the message via online videos on YouTube. His analysis indicates that campaign elites maintain a privileged position on YouTube, although even as the online video source offers a way for campaigns to bypass the traditional news media, it also provides an interactive venue for ordinary citizens to make substantive contributions to the political message. The results of Klotz's research show that the biggest losers in the rise of online video dissemination are the traditional media, whose most popular clips are those that exhibit the least journalistic control, and especially independent political actors (namely, interest groups), who spend millions of dollars yet are rarely among the most viewed clips. What these chapters help clarify is that when candidates lose control of their message—a near certainty in the social-media-driven political environment—the important matter is to be prepared to mitigate the loss of control to protect the candidate's brand and message to the extent possible.

A second theme throughout this volume is a consideration of continuities and differences across traditional forms of media and social media outlets. For all the focus on the revolutionary nature of new and social media, there is a remarkable amount of overlap and continuity with previous media forms (see Tewksbury and Rittenberg 2012; Williams and Delli Carpini 2011; Hershey 2014). Chapters 5 through 7 address from different perspectives these continuities and differences. Although each essay tackles the subject from a unique perspective and examines a different type of social media, each also demonstrates a remarkable amount of overlap and continuity with previous media forms.

For example, in chapter 5, Regina Lawrence reports findings from a broad range of interviews with political journalists as she examines the impact that the rise of Twitter has had on news reporting, noting that the way news is reported has not changed so much as it has been shifted into overdrive. Alternatively, Mike Gruszczynski analyzes the role of negative campaign elements—specifically campaign controversies—in chapter 6. Examining the persistence of key campaign controversies during the 2012 presidential campaign through a large-scale text analysis of mainstream and new media content (namely, blogs), Gruszczynski finds that new media do not generally differ from the mainstream media in their coverage of this aspect of electoral politics. Similarly, in chapter 7, Matthew Eshbaugh-Soha investigates the differences between traditional and social media coverage of the 2012 election across a range of dimensions, including volume and tone. In his analysis—which encompasses online news, newspapers, network newscasts, cable news, talk radio, Twitter, Facebook, and blogs—he demonstrates that although social media are generally more negative than more traditional sources, the coverage patterns follow those of traditional media.

A third theme that weaves its way through this volume examines the political consequences of social media usage. As will be discussed later in this volume, successful social media usage requires a continued reliance on fundamental political techniques of generating support that will drive interest in the message being disseminated via social media and on populating social media communications with meaningful content. If these two conditions are met, does social media usage sway such things as perceptions held by information consumers about actors in the political process or the consumers' own political participation? In chapter 8, Joshua Hawthorne and Benjamin Warner investigate the extent to which social media communication influenced the way candidates in 2012 were perceived. Examining the relationship between social media communication and candidate perception across two case studies—focusing on the first presidential debate and Mitt Romney's infamous leaked comments about "the 47%"—they find that social media does indeed have consequences for candidate perceptions, though these effects were limited, context dependent, and driven by partisan factors. Work by Meredith Conroy, Jessica Feezell, and Mario Guerrero presented in chapter 9 also shows a limited and conditional social media effect, in this case on political participation. Rooting their analysis in theoretical work on citizenship norms, Conroy, Feezell, and Guerrero show that political activity on Facebook was a predictor of several forms of offline political activity but that the linkage between online and offline behaviors was conditioned by individual attitudes about citizenship in general.

In chapter 10, Todd Belt's innovative examination of the differences between commercial and noncommercial humor-driven viral videos further illuminates the importance of generating interest and having meaningful content. Belt shows not only that noncommercial videos reach a significantly larger audience than do commercial videos (a finding that dovetails with Robert Klotz's own analysis in chapter 4) but also that these noncommercial videos are far more likely to contain identifiable political messages that reject value neutrality and are considerably more likely to encourage political action and comment on the potential consequences of the election. The lesson from Belt's work for political consultants and campaign managers is that they might well consider finding a way to give their commercial videos the look, feel, and content of noncommercial humor-driven videos, although the challenge of doing so would be balancing that goal with maintaining a professional, "serious" campaign message.

The final major theme of this volume concerns the broader questions addressed earlier and the implications that social media usage holds for the core tenets of democracy. The reduction in the entry costs into the social media marketplace of ideas enables ordinary citizens to take advantage of the burgeoning social media environment. Although promoting access and opportunity for more individuals to engage in political discourse is an indisputably worthy goal in democratic theory, what about the realities of the alleged dark side of this development: the perceived negativity and hostility on the part of the mass public that the information-technology-driven democratization of campaign communication has supposedly increased and even engendered?

To get a sense of the nature of this type of political discourse, two essays in the final section of this book directly examine, with surprising and thought-provoking results, online comment forums, often considered ground zero for democratically sourced negativity and often staggeringly hostile and offensive civic rhetoric. In chapter 11, Karen Hoffman utilizes content analysis to compare the discourse of these comment forums to mainstream media discourse, challenging the assumption that the rhetoric employed by political elites is meaningfully different from what the masses produce. Hoffman shows that comment forum discourse mirrors that of mainstream elite discourse, observing that the difference is less in what is said than in the status of who is saying it, an observation that could potentially reflect the unease of many people about the growing role of the masses in online discourse and the concomitant decline of elite power to control the message. Daniel Coffey, Michael Kohler, and Doug Granger take contemporary perceptions of mass incivility online as their point of departure and, like Hoffman, find that empirical analysis yields results inconsistent with widespread allegations of damaging civic rhetoric. Attempting to analyze the roots of this phenomenon by comparing differences in discourse in competitive and noncompetitive states during the 2012 election, Coffey, Kohler, and Granger find that campaign spillover explains the relative negativity of comment forum rhetoric, indicating that the nature of mass discourse is affected (and generally in a negative manner) by more vigorous campaign efforts by elites.

Finally, Brian Calfano extends the focus on democratically generated political messages by investigating the consequences of citizen exposure to negative comment forum rhetoric. Utilizing an Internet-based experimental research design, Calfano examines how individuals exposed to "flaming and blaming" rhetoric (i.e., discourse that negatively targets outgroups) alter their media consumption, showing that they have statistically higher rates of "hard" news consumption, selective exposure to specific media sources, reports of anger, and expressions of intolerance toward key outgroups. The analyses presented in this final section by Hoffman, Coffey et al., and Calfano provide readers with an informed foundation from which they can start to address for themselves their views of the normative questions raised in this introduction and throughout the remainder of this volume.

References

Berthon, Pierre R., Leyland Pitt, Ian P. McCarthy, and Steven M. Kates. 2007. "When Customers Get Clever: Managerial Approaches to Dealing with Creative Consumers." *Business Horizons* 50:39–47.
Dimitroval, Daniela V., Adam Shehata, Jesper Stromback, and Lars W. Nord. 2014. "The Effects of Digital Media on Political Knowledge and Participation in Election Campaigns: Evidence from Panel Data." *Communication Research* 41:95–118.
Farrar-Myers, Victoria A., and Richard Skinner. 2012. "Super PACs and the 2012 Elections." *The Forum* 10:105–118.
Farrell, Henry. 2012. "The Consequences of the Internet for Politics." *Annual Review of Political Science* 15:35–52.
Gainous, Jason, and Kevin M. Wagner. 2011. *Rebooting American Politics: The Internet Revolution*. Lanham, MD: Rowman and Littlefield.
Germany, Julie Barko. 2009. "The Online Revolution." In *Campaigning for President 2008: Strategy and Tactics, New Voices and New Techniques*, ed. Dennis W. Johnson, 147–159. New York: Routledge.
Gulati, Girish J. 2010. "No Laughing Matter: The Role of New Media in the 2008 Election." In *The Year of Obama: How Barack Obama Won the White House*, ed. Larry J. Sabato, 187–203. New York: Longman.
Hartnett, Stephen John, and Jennifer Rose Mercieca. 2007. "'A Discovered Dissembler Can Achieve Nothing Great'; or, Four Theses on the Death of Presidential Rhetoric in an Age of Empire." *Presidential Studies Quarterly* 37 (4): 599–621.
Hershey, Marjorie Randon. 2014. "The Media: Different Audiences Saw Different Campaigns." In *The Elections of 2012*, ed. Michael Nelson, 97–118. Thousand Oaks, CA: CQ.
Howard, Philip N. 2006. *New Media Campaigns and the Managed Citizen*. Cambridge: Cambridge University Press.
Jones, Jeffrey. 2012. "Rethinking Television's Relationship to Politics in the Post-Network Era." In *iPolitics: Citizens, Elections, and Governing in the New Media Era*, ed. Richard L. Fox and Jennifer M. Ramos, 48–75. Cambridge: Cambridge University Press.
Kietzmann, Jan H., Kristopher Hermkens, Ian P. McCarthy, and Bruno S. Silvestre. 2011. "Social Media? Get Serious! Understanding the Functional Building Blocks of Social Media." *Business Horizons* 54:241–251.

Kreiss, Daniel. 2012. *Taking Our Country Back: The Crafting of Networked Politics from Howard Dean to Barack Obama*. Oxford: Oxford University Press.

Oxley, Zoe M. 2012. "More Sources, Better Informed Public? New Media and Political Knowledge." In *iPolitics: Citizens, Elections, and Governing in the New Media Era*, ed. Richard L. Fox and Jennifer M. Ramos, 25–47. Cambridge: Cambridge University Press.

Tewksbury, David, and Jason Rittenberg. 2012. *News on the Internet: Information and Citizenship in the 21st Century*. Oxford: Oxford University Press.

Williams, Bruce A., and Michael X. Delli Carpini. 2011. *After Broadcast News: Media Regimes, Democracy, and the New Information Environment*. Cambridge: Cambridge University Press.

PART 1

Elite Utilization

1

Strategic Communication in a Networked Age

DANIEL KREISS AND CREIGHTON WELCH

In the weeks before the 2012 election, President Barack Obama's supporters using the campaign's Facebook application received messages asking them to urge select friends in key swing states to vote, register, or volunteer. An estimated 5 million voters responded positively to the requests of their friends, many of them 18- to 29-year-olds who could not be reached by phone (Judd 2012d). On quick glance, it may appear that there is not much new here. The 2008 Obama campaign notably pioneered the use of social media platforms for political organizing, leveraging Facebook to mobilize and coordinate supporters for electoral ends (Kreiss 2012a). What was different in 2012 lay in the campaign asking its supporters to contact only select members of their social network. The campaign matched parts of its massive voter databases, including one managed by the Democratic Party and encompassing more than 500 points of data on every member of the electorate, to data on the social networks of its supporters on Facebook to help it contact priority voters.

This social media targeting was premised on voter modeling, which entails assigning numerical scores representing likely political attitudes and behavior to every member of the electorate. These scores are the outgrowth of an enormous proliferation of data about the electorate over the past decade and, as importantly, new analytical techniques that render data meaningful. The Obama campaign used four scores that on a scale of 1 to 100 estimated the probability of voters' likelihood of supporting Obama, turning out to vote, being persuaded to turn out, and being persuaded to support Obama on the basis of specific appeals (Beckett 2012a). The campaign and the consulting firms it hired calculated these scores by continually surveying the electorate and looking for patterns within the massive databases of political data they had access to. These modeling scores, in turn, became the basis for the entire voter-contact operation, which ranged from making "personalized" voter contacts on the doorsteps (Nielsen 2012) and through the social media accounts of voters to running advertisements on the cable television screens of swing voters (Rutenberg 2012).

Although the use of political data for electoral advantage has a long history dating back to at least the middle to late 1800s (McGerr 1986; Kazin 2007), there is both qualitatively new data and new means of using it as the basis for targeted strategic communications in contemporary campaigning. Data lies behind the extraordinary growth in online advertising, which allows campaigns to target specific groups and even individual voters with highly tailored appeals. Data is also the foundation of the targeted outreach on social media platforms that both support widespread citizen social and symbolic participation in electoral politics and provide campaigns with new ways to subtly influence the electorate. These practices enable campaigns to create "individualized information flows" (Barnard and Kreiss 2013) to members of the electorate that are difficult, if not impossible in many cases, to open up to public scrutiny.

In this chapter, we take an in-depth look at the data practices of contemporary campaigns and the new forms of targeted communications they support, through the lens of the 2012 electoral cycle. We focus on President Obama's reelection bid given that practitioners on both sides of the aisle cite the campaign as the most advanced application of data and analytics to strategic communications in electoral politics to date and as the standard that Republicans are currently striving to meet (Confessore 2013). We first discuss the history of political data, placing particular emphasis on the rise of the sophisticated forms of voter modeling that underpinned the 2012 electoral success of the Obama campaign. We then show how data and modeling work in online advertising and strategic communications using social media. We conclude with a discussion of the implications for democratic practice, detailing the interplay between the decentering of political communication and the ways that campaigns have adopted new means of finding and appealing to members of the electorate. The data presented in this chapter is drawn primarily from a survey and analysis of journalistic articles, as well as open-ended qualitative interviews with campaign staffers active during the 2012 cycle.

In sum, we argue that the explosion of data on the electorate has provided campaigns with new ways to control their message in a networked media environment, from targeting and tailoring online advertising to using supporters as the implements of campaign communications on platforms such as Facebook and the doorsteps of voters. Data and analysis lie at the center of all aspects of contemporary campaigning—from the voter modeling that probabilistically determines who a candidate's supporters are and who is undecided to the continual tracking of the outcomes of voter contacts and behavior online in order to optimize messages. And yet this is far from complete professionalized control of the message of candidates such as Obama, as social media also provide unprecedented opportunities for political discourse by nonelites (Chadwick 2013). This chapter explores the contours of contemporary political communication in the context of presidential campaigning, revealing both new capacities for controlling the message and the limits to this control in an age of digital social networks.

The Long History of Big Data

Data has increasingly become central to political campaigns, but it is deeply ahistorical to posit that this change originated with the 2012 cycle, as many popular accounts suggest (Scherer 2012; Sifry 2011).[1] There is a gap in the scholarly literature as well when it comes to historical analysis of contemporary forms of mediated politics. The dominant approach to considering the effects of the Internet, and new media more generally, has failed to account for the fact that the Internet of 2012 does not look like the Internet of 2008 and even less so like the Internet of 2004 (for this argument, see Bimber, Flanagin, and Stohl 2012; Karpf 2012). Meanwhile, a body of literature compares campaigning across electoral cycles to account for technological change but offers few explanatory accounts of *why* and *how* practices and technologies change or grow more sophisticated.

Scholars need to take a historical approach to understand the particular arrangement of tools, practices, and techniques campaigns used during the 2012 cycle. Indeed, the accumulation of data by political parties, the specific systems that make this accumulation possible, the practices of analyzing and using data, and the forms of strategic communications that data supports all have a history (Kreiss 2012a). The two presidential campaigns' specific techniques and tools, and differing capacities, for gathering, storing, maintaining, and analyzing data were the product of the shifting configurations and work of different "party-networks" over the preceding decade. In recent years, scholars have reconceptualized political parties as "decentralized, nonhierarchical, fluid systems with porous boundaries among a wide array of actors" that "include interest groups, social movements, media, political consultants, and advocacy organizations, in addition to the usual suspects of elected officials, party officials, and citizen-activists" (Masket et al. 2009).

Following perspectives that conceptualize technologies as social actors (Latour 2006), we add to the party-network conceptualization technical artifacts such as the party-maintained databases candidates use.[2] Party-networks form a large part of the infrastructure candidates have at their disposal as they organize campaigns for office (Star 1999), although they must assemble and coordinate particular configurations of component parts effectively in order to maximize their chances for success (Nielsen 2012). In essence, party-networks are historically specific arrangements of human, organizational, technical, and knowledge resources that campaigns can draw on. Party-networks shape the background capacities campaigns have to act strategically during an electoral cycle, providing much of the technologies and staffers available for electoral runs. The advantages that Obama had over Mitt Romney in terms of campaign capacity cannot be fully explained by the differing strategies of the two campaigns, as some recent work suggests (Alter 2013), although they certainly played a role. The comparative Democratic advantage in voter data, analytic technologies, and electoral tools was built up over a decade at the level of an extended party-network. In short, the Obama campaign had better voter data, more robust databases, a deeper talent pool of technically skilled staffers, and more field-tested tools in its party network to draw on than the Romney campaign did.

The contemporary history of data utilization for electoral purposes begins in the 1970s, when political campaigns and consultants began to take advantage of technological advances to gather and leverage data for success at the polls (Howard 2006; Sabato 1981; Whitman and Perkins 2003). Driven by Republican innovations in the 1980s, consultants began using data to target specific categories of voters and households with tailored messages using direct mail. With this early work as a foundation, the Republican Party had a strong advantage in voter data, microtargeting, and data systems through the 2004 cycle. For instance, the party developed an extensive national voter file in the early 2000s, called Voter Vault, which provided the core of its infrastructure through the middle of the decade. There is no systematic research into Republican database efforts past Voter Vault, although a number of journalistic reports suggest both that much of the party's data infrastructure is handled by third parties (Judd 2012a) and that the Romney campaign in 2012 relied on extensive financial marketing databases (Gillum 2012) and in-house data on the electorate in at least some key primary states (Issenberg 2012b).

Practitioners and scholars alike agree that the Democratic Party is now far ahead of its Republican counterpart in voter data, database technology, and the analytic practices that render information actionable. This is the result in part of massive infrastructure projects launched by Howard Dean when he became chair of the party in 2005, a position he achieved in no small part on the basis of the party's valuing of the technological prowess of his presidential campaign (Kreiss 2012a). Throughout much of the 1990s and early 2000s, the Democratic Party's voter data management was "largely a haphazard affair, coordinated mostly by state parties or the stewards of local precincts" (Kreiss and Howard 2010). As chair, Dean created the party's first national voter file and online interface system, called VoteBuilder. As a key piece of infrastructure for Democratic campaigning, VoteBuilder extended the capacity of the party and its candidates to contest elections and target the electorate. It enabled Democratic candidates for offices from state senate to president to share data across campaigns and election cycles, while ensuring that the voter file was continuously updated with quality data from voter contacts. This system was first tested during the 2006 election cycle and provided the data infrastructure for all party candidates in 2008 and for the Obama campaign and the rest of the party's candidates in 2012.

The sources of this data are varied. The data includes public data collected from local, state, and federal records that detail party registration, voting history, political donations, vehicle registration, and real estate records. Credit histories, magazine subscription lists, and even drugstore discount cards provide the commercial data that campaigns use. The parties update this data through the millions of contacts generated by campaigns and carry their databases across election cycles, offering them to campaigns at all levels of office.

Analytic firms use this data to model the electorate and to generate the various scores (which are common in consumer marketing), detailed earlier. Data only become meaningful through this modeling, which distills hundreds of data points into simpler categories of voters: likely supporters, those who are likely to be undecided, and those who are likely to support the other candidate. In addition, there are further gradations of these categories, such as modeling supporters' likelihood of turning out and undecided voters' likelihood of being persuaded. To generate scores for these categories, firms servicing the Obama campaign began by surveying random, representative samples of the electorate and then looked for correlated data points (shared demographic, psychographic, attitudinal, and behavioral characteristics, etc.) among voters in the listed categories. Voter models entail particular combinations of correlated data, which are then layered onto the voter file to generate those composite scores on a 0–100 scale for every member of the electorate.

If in 2008 Republicans were marginally behind in voter data, analytics, field campaigning, and infrastructure, the 2012 election revealed the party to be a full cycle behind the Democrats in some of these domains (Kreiss 2012c).[3] This was apparent in the differing infrastructural capacities of the two parties and their candidates. In 2012, the Romney campaign launched Project ORCA, what campaign sources referred to as a "massive, state-of-the-art poll monitoring effort" (Terkel 2012). ORCA was supposed to entail thousands of volunteers across the country updating a central database as voters went to the polls so that campaign staffers could monitor returns and direct field resources efficiently toward those who had not yet voted. The system was both an organizational (Ekdahl 2012) and technical failure (Gallagher 2012).[4]

Project ORCA was similar to the 2008 Obama campaign's Houdini system, which staffers and volunteers used briefly until it crashed (Kreiss 2012b). After the election cycle, Obama's campaign operatives systematically assessed the failures of 2008 and made considerable investments to correct for them. Former campaigners realized that data integration was a significant problem during the 2008 campaign, Project Houdini lacked the basic capacity to support thousands of simultaneous updates to its database, and the campaign lacked many tools and work practices for integrating new media and field efforts. As a result, former campaign staffers working for Organizing for America, party operatives, and a network of Democratic-affiliated firms and interest groups spent the next three years attempting to solve these problems for the reelection effort. For example, through developing and field testing new systems during the 2010 midterm elections, the campaign and party operatives fine-tuned organizational structures and technical systems (Issenberg 2012a; Madrigal 2012). All this meant that when the campaign's programmers came on board during the Republican primaries, they could focus on using technology as a "force multiplier" for ground efforts (Lohr 2012) and to overcome problems of scale (Harris 2012)—instead of engaging in basic technical development.

This change mattered given that the effort to reelect Obama occurred in a radically different electoral context than 2008. As one senior staffer on the 2012 campaign stated (personal communication with the first author, September 22, 2012), "if in 2008 enthusiasm is 100%, our organization only captured 60%. If in 2012 enthusiasm is 80%, our organization can capture 90%." At the center of this organization was data gathering, management, and analysis, the planning and building of the infrastructure for which began early. "We are going to measure every single thing in this campaign," campaign manager Jim Messina said after taking the job, noting that the analytics department would be five times as large as it was during the 2008 campaign (Scherer 2012). This approach to measurement extended the 2008 campaign's development of "computational management" practices, which refers to the "delegation of managerial, allocative, messaging, and design decisions to analysis of users' actions made visible in the form of data as they interacted with the campaign's media" (Kreiss 2012a, 144). In 2012, the Obama campaign hired a "chief scientist" as well as dozens of software designers and developers, engineers, and scientists to work with the massive amount of available data (Judd 2012c).

All of this reveals both that data practices have a specific history and that the 2012 Obama campaign enjoyed a significant party-network advantage in terms of having data infrastructure and practices that were built up and tested during previous election cycles. For example, although it built a number of social media and other applications in-house, the Obama campaign also relied on outside vendors, such as Blue State Digital and NGP VAN, which served the 2008 campaign and the party since 2004 and had the accrued experience and robust technical systems that come from working across election cycles. In addition, the Obama reelection campaign started with the decidedly new incumbent advantage of more than 13 million email addresses it had already gathered during the previous campaign, as well as an established social media presence with millions of Facebook supporters and Twitter followers that provided ample amounts of data and messaging vehicles. Although more systematic research on the Republican Party's history over the past decade needs to be conducted, by contrast, the Romney campaign had a much more limited set of infrastructural resources within the Republican Party to draw on.

Although various streams of voter data lay at the foundation of much of the 2012 Obama campaign and modeling shaped its electoral strategy, these aspects of the campaign were generally invisible until postelection accounts emerged (for a summary of these accounts through the eyes of a campaign staffer, see Ecker 2012). Voters experienced these aspects of the campaign directly, however, through its strategic communications. In the pages that follow, we look closely at new practices of online advertising and social media targeting, areas of campaign practice premised on extensive use of data. We focus on online advertising and social media here because they are areas of significant and growing investment, likely to become even more central areas of campaigning during future presidential cycles.

Online Advertising

Commercial firms ran their first online advertisements in 1994 (Kaye and Medoff 2001), but digital political advertising came much later. Online political advertising was in its infancy during the 2000 cycle, being limited to banner ads on sites such as America Online (Barnard and Kreiss 2013). During the 2004 cycle, campaigns began running more interactive advertising and gathering user data to measure the effectiveness of ads, and a network of consultants specializing in online advertising and aligned with the two parties began to develop (ibid.). Both Barack Obama and John McCain devoted considerable resources to online advertising during the 2008 election, spending a combined $22.8 million during the cycle, with the vast majority of that spending ($16 million) coming from the Obama campaign (Stampler 2012), which is the focus of the findings presented here.

The 2008 Obama campaign had three primary objectives for its online advertising: to build a robust supporter base, to mobilize those supporters to become volunteers and donors, and to persuade undecided members of the electorate (Barnard and Kreiss 2013). These objectives were tied into electoral strategy and had associated metrics that tracked the effectiveness of ads toward meeting them. Even more, the campaign's online advertising involved tailoring different content to various targeted demographic groups and individuals on the basis of the voter modeling detailed earlier. In other words, the campaign used online advertising to send specific appeals to specific groups of people. In terms of building a robust supporter base, the metrics for success included sign-ups to the campaign's email list and online fundraising. Mobilization entailed a cluster of related advertising appeals around voter registration, early voting, polling and caucus location lookups, get-out-the-vote operations, and volunteer recruitment. The third objective, persuasion, accounted for the majority of the campaign's online advertising expenditures and involved advertising that delivered information designed to appeal to groups of individuals whom the campaign profiled as undecided. The campaign continuously measured its progress toward meeting these goals through the real-time gathering and analyzing of data about user interactions with online ads (Barnard and Kreiss 2013).

The growing emphasis on online advertising continued during the 2012 election cycle, with the two presidential campaigns combining to spend an estimated

$78 million. Again, Obama outspent his opponent by a considerable margin, devoting $52 million toward online advertising, compared with Romney's $26 million (Stampler 2012). Although expenditures on online advertising still pale in comparison to broadcast and cable television advertising (Miller 2008), online spending is growing far more rapidly (Bachman 2012). The online video platform Hulu, for instance, reported that the number of political ads aired in 2012 represents a 700% increase from the past two federal elections and that 80% of its users voted in both the 2008 and 2010 elections (Blumenthal 2012).

There are a number of reasons for the growth in online advertising. For one, campaigns cite a rapid decline in the consumption of live television (Johnson 2012). In addition, as the Hulu example suggests, online platforms and commercial advertising networks have an extraordinary amount of data about users. This means that campaigns have new opportunities to deliver specific messages to specific voters, affording the targeting and tailoring of information to individuals with greater ease, lower costs, and greater accuracy (Bennett 2008; Bennett and Manheim 2006; Kreiss and Howard 2010). As the earlier discussion of the 2008 election cycle suggests, the ability to use online ads to target specific voters, to tailor messages to their preferences and behaviors, and to track their responses has made online advertising a uniquely powerful tool for strategic communications.

During the 2012 cycle, the targeting of voters and tailoring of communications took shape on multiple levels as campaigns accessed new sources of data on the electorate. Both presidential campaigns used behavioral, demographic, interest, and "look-alike" targeting (matching voters on the basis of the characteristics they share with others with known political preferences), and also matched IP addresses with party voter files, to target ads to priority voters. Extending practices from 2008, the 2012 campaigns again used this targeting to deliver online ads for the purposes of list building, mobilizing supporters to get involved, and persuading undecideds. The presidential campaigns, for instance, served ads to voters they modeled as undecided. The content of those ads included information about particular issues the campaigns believed these voters would be responsive to on the basis of polling and focus groups with similar voters. Even more, while Travis Ridout et al. (2012) show how audience fragmentation also allows for targeted mass-media advertising on cable, online advertising has qualitatively different affordances that facilitate more precise targeting and interactivity. These qualities of the medium enable campaigns to ask specific individuals and groups (designated through the modeling detailed earlier), such as unregistered likely Obama supporters, to take specific actions such as registering to vote online. Campaigns ask others, such as committed, politically engaged supporters, to take actions such as donating or volunteering online.

For example, both presidential campaigns targeted communications to specific groups of voters and even individuals such as Democrats who voted in the previous election, Latinos living in swing states (Kaye 2012a), and voters who purchased certain luxury goods (Delany 2012a). They did so by targeting ads on the basis of behavioral data gleaned from users' browsing habits as well as what is known as "voter matching," in which the browsing histories of known supporters of a candidate or political party are used to find other computer users with similar behaviors (Beckett 2012b; Delany 2012b). Both campaigns looked at what known voters read online, what content they shared, and where they left comments in order to find and target other users like them. The idea is that similar browsing behaviors may predict similar voting behaviors. During the primaries, for instance, the Romney campaign used online survey data to identify voters in Wisconsin who were politically conservative but not yet convinced to vote for Romney, and then it narrowed this universe down to a specific target (18 years old, Republican leaning, dissatisfied with Obama). It then used these individuals' browsing histories to find others with similar web histories to target (Peters 2012).

The biggest change in online political advertising in 2012 was campaigns' increased ability to match the online and offline identities of voters. Campaigns (and the firms that service them) matched their voter records to the IP addresses assigned to the computers of targeted voters (Issenberg 2012b). For example, firms and campaigns on both sides of the aisle have actively matched party (and commercial-firm-maintained) voter databases to the online registration data of sites such as Yahoo!. This allows campaigns to deliver video, display, and search advertising to targeted segments of, and even individual, voters. This practice is not new, but it was much more widespread and sophisticated in 2012 than in earlier cycles. In 2008, for example, the Obama campaign took the first steps toward merging voter file data with the purchased registration data of America Online and Yahoo! (Barnard and Kreiss 2013). By 2012, however, this practice was far more expansive, with candidates matching voter files with data from an array of commercial advertising firms that track the online behavior of consumers with anywhere from 60% to 80% accuracy (Delany 2012b).

Campaigns also increased their advertising on social media, online video, and mobile platforms. The two presidential campaigns spent record amounts on Facebook advertising during the 2012 cycle (Kaye 2012c). Campaigns used Facebook and other social media to serve geotargeted ads to do things such as help increase event attendance (Shepherd 2012). Campaigns also sought to design advertisements that their supporters would share on these platforms. Strategists argued that when a person shares campaign information, such as online video advertisements, with friends on a site such as Facebook, that person's endorsement adds credibility to the campaigns' messages (Naylor 2012; Peters 2012). Campaigns also expanded video advertising during the 2012 cycle, running videos embedded in rich-media banner advertisements (Johnson 2012) and streamed before and after select content on news sites and video sites such as

Hulu and YouTube (Barnard and Kreiss 2013). The Obama campaign expanded its video-game advertising during the 2012 election cycle, running ads in online games such as Scrabble, Tetris, Madden NFL 13, and Battleship. Trade reporting suggests that gamers who saw political ads were 120% more likely to react positively to the candidate and 50% more likely to consider voting for the candidate than if they encountered the ad somewhere else (Ashburn 2012). All of these online advertising practices are premised on the voter modeling detailed earlier that allows campaigns to focus on niche voters and to find them, given the fragmentation of audiences across different media platforms. Or, as NPR put it, "campaigns that want to reach young males in Ohio might do better buying space in *Madden* than during *The Ellen DeGeneres Show*" (Yenigun 2012).

Although campaigns are clearly embracing the ability to target and tailor online advertising, there are persistent concerns that these practices might be harmful to the electoral process. For one, voters reject this widespread campaign practice. A national survey by Joseph Turow et al. (2012) revealed that 86% of Americans do not want "political advertising tailored to your interests," which is a far higher percentage of voters than those who reject other forms of tailored advertising for products and services (61%), news articles (56%), and discounts and coupons (46%). The public is not alone in its concern. Scholars fear that microtargeting might cause campaigns to completely ignore or tune out portions of the electorate (Howard 2006). Even more, scholars and commentators have called for increased public scrutiny of targeted political advertising, including modifying Federal Election Commission regulations to make these ads visible to everyone (Peha 2012). Ironically, legislators have proposed restrictions on commercial practices routinely used in politics. As Kate Kaye notes (2012c), legislators have proposed bills to restrict commercial tracking and ad targeting; however, their campaigns routinely use these technologies.

Social Media

Aside from advertising, the 2012 campaigns used social media extensively as a tool for strategic communications with the general public, journalists, undecided voters, and supporters, as well as providing the latter with opportunities to volunteer outside formal campaign structures. The growing role of social media in campaigning is a reflection of changing media habits more generally. Whereas Facebook played a key role in 2008, notably with the Obama campaign using the platform to organize supporters in contested primary and swing states (Kreiss 2012a), the scale of social media use has dramatically grown in four years. On the evening of the 2012 election, nearly 67 million people watched coverage on network television—while 306 million people consumed and produced political content on Facebook and more than 11 million used Twitter for similar purposes, according to the research firm Experian Hitwise (Guynn and Chmielewski

2012). And although Facebook, Twitter, and YouTube are the most popular, and most talked about, social media platforms, campaigns have developed a diverse social media communications strategy to keep pace with rapidly changing media contexts. For example, both 2012 campaigns shared song lists on Spotify, swapped recipes on Pinterest, posted pictures on Instagram, and had staffers spend time on Google Hangouts—*none of which existed in U.S. markets during the 2008 election.*

Although campaigns use social media for a variety of reasons, two developments in strategic communications during the 2012 cycle are of particular interest in the context of how campaigns seek to control their message. First, both campaigns used Twitter in the hope of amplifying messages from the campaign trail and setting the press agenda. These practices reflect the uniquely public nature of the platform. Second, both campaigns used Twitter and Facebook as platforms to mobilize and leverage the social networks of supporters for strategic communications purposes.

With a growing user base, Twitter emerged as a key medium for campaign communications during the 2012 cycle. To provide a sense of scale, the Obama campaign's tweet announcing his victory in 2008 was retweeted (or shared) 157 times, and on election day, users sent 1.8 million tweets about the presidential election. Now, Twitter gets that many tweets every eight minutes (Fouhy 2012). In 2012, the Obama campaign's tweeted photograph of the president embracing the first lady after networks announced his reelection became social media's most shared image ever at the time (Guynn and Chmielewski 2012), receiving more than 800,000 retweets in less than three days.

Twitter emerged as a significant platform for campaign activity, as staffers on both campaigns sought to leverage the medium to amplify communications, to set the press agenda, and to mobilize supporters. The Obama and Romney campaigns used Twitter to amplify messages that were in the press and to circulate communications from the campaign trail. For instance, the confusing syntax of Obama's 2012 campaign speech regarding transportation and infrastructure led to the quote, "If you've got a business—you didn't build that. Somebody else made that happen" (C-SPAN 2012). The Romney campaign repackaged and repurposed the "you didn't build that" phrase into a campaign slogan used in advertisements, on the trail, on placards and signs, and on Twitter. The Romney campaign promoted user-generated mashups of this phrase on sites such as YouTube and Twitter, helping to amplify this message to wider audiences.

Twitter also served as a forum for user-generated political content more generally. For example, in responding to a question about fair pay for women during a presidential debate, Romney discussed measures he took as governor of Massachusetts to ensure that more women were represented in his administration, saying, "I went to a number of women's groups and said, 'Can you help us find folks?' and they brought us whole binders full of women" (Commission on

Presidential Debates 2012). The meme "binders full of women" took off almost immediately in viral fashion through the efforts of a number of Twitter and Facebook users, including one post that generated more than 300,000 likes.[5]

In addition to pushing out campaign communications over Twitter and disseminating supporters' user-generated messages, both campaigns used the platform strategically to try and shape conversations in social media and to set the press agenda. For example, both campaigns purchased promoted trends (tweets and hashtags that Twitter makes highly visible to users) at a cost of well over $100,000 per day (Kaye 2012b). The goal, equivalent to a national advertising buy in a sense, was to put a particular message in front of Twitter users. Promoted trends are also designed to encourage user-generated responses to these messages. This often came with considerable risk, as messages such as #Areyoubetteroff? (Romney) and #Forward2012 (Obama) were repurposed and subverted by the campaign's opponents. Campaigns aim to reach not only a large, mass Twitter audience through a promoted trend but, as importantly, the journalists who write about that topic. During the 2012 campaign, promoting trends and pushing messages out through Twitter more generally were new techniques of setting the press agenda and speaking to the political influentials who are heavy users of the platform (Rainie et al. 2012). Although it is too soon for systematic research to be published from the 2012 cycle, anecdotally it is clear that a number of stories from the campaign cycle originated in, or were kept alive by, journalistic reporting on Twitter, such as the reaction to Romney's comments about Big Bird during the first presidential debate.

Both campaigns viewed supporters' digital social networks on Twitter and Facebook as channels of strategic communications. In keeping with a decade-long practice of campaigns attempting to leverage the social networks of supporters as conduits for strategic communications (Kreiss 2012a), both campaigns circulated messages on social platforms in the hope that supporters would be the vehicles for their dissemination to their friends and family, as well as wider social networks. This happened on a number of levels, the simplest being campaigns using Twitter and Facebook in the hope that strategic messages would spread virally through the networks of supporters.

With Facebook, however, strategic communications can be more targeted than Twitter. The Obama campaign, the lead innovator in the 2012 election cycle in social media strategy, integrated parts of its voter databases with supporter data culled from the profiles of individuals signing up for the campaign's Facebook application. This enabled the campaign to access a supporter's friends list and then target members of his or her social network on the basis of characteristics such as where they lived. This then enabled the campaign to engage in what technology journalist Nick Judd (2012b) calls "targeted sharing," which entailed sharing certain content with the supporter in ways that it would end up in the feeds of targets in that supporter's social network. Recent research in political communication suggests that this can be persuasive and have a positive impact on voter turnout (Bond et al. 2012). Even more, the targeted sharing of content turned into very specific appeals in the final weeks of the campaign. As Judd (2012b) details,

> Obama for America asked its supporters who had been signed up for the OfA Facebook application to pick potential voters from among their friends in swing states and urge them to get to the ballot box or register to vote. In the final days before the election and on election day, the application flooded its users with notifications asking them to reach out on the campaign's behalf. Officials told *Time*'s Michael Scherer that a staggering 20 percent of people asked by their friends to register, vote or take another activity went ahead and did it. While the campaign hasn't shared how many people elected to press the case for Obama on Facebook in this way, and this is only remarkable if enough people participated to help close the distance for OfA in voter registrations and turnout where it had those goals, the success rate is high enough to raise eyebrows. Behind the Facebook application driving get out the vote was the same targeted sharing code.

As detailed earlier, all of this is premised on voter data—knowing who a campaign's supporters are, identifying priority targets in their social networks, and being able to track the outcomes of voter contacts to measure effectiveness in terms of electoral strategy. These activities now lie at the foundation of contemporary campaigning and have made electoral politics an increasingly data-driven enterprise, shaping everything from which voters are contacted by a candidate's supporters to what they hear and see online, on their doorsteps, and in their social networks. For example, during the 2012 cycle, the Obama campaign leveraged its data to achieve a much more seamless integration of voter contacts across various platforms according to the dictates of its electoral strategy. Coordinating voter contacts on doorsteps and on Facebook is a massive organizational challenge, one facilitated in the 2012 cycle by the Obama campaign's social organizing tool, Dashboard. Dashboard was a platform that helped organize the numerous applications of the campaign and streamline canvassing, resulting in the more effective coordination of the activities of thousands of volunteers. The Obama Dashboard volunteer platform created volunteer teams based on location, achieved a degree of integration between the campaign's databases and supporters' contacts on Facebook, and displayed local voter contact targets and scripts for supporters' canvass efforts. This platform allowed the campaign to "break down the distinction between online and offline organizing, giving every supporter the same opportunities to get involved that they would find in a field office," according to the deputy campaign manager for Obama for America

Stephanie Cutter (Calderon 2012). Meanwhile, Dashboard was integrated with a mobile application that allowed volunteers to more effectively support the field effort (Lohr 2012). The Obama for America mobile app allowed voters to find local events, to report potential voter fraud, to find nearby houses to canvass and enter data about the results, and to donate directly to the campaign. In addition, the app was synced with Facebook, Twitter, email, and text messages so that the campaign could integrate data and users could share information on their activities as widely as possible (Tau 2012).

Conclusion

The 2012 campaign cycle featured a dynamic tension between the possibilities for control and disruption of campaign messages. On the one hand, campaigns over the past decade—particularly on the Democratic side of the aisle—have invested heavily in the infrastructure for gathering, managing, analyzing, and acting on data so as to better coordinate strategic communications across a variety of platforms, including the television screens, front porches, and social media accounts of voters. The Obama campaign leveraged these infrastructural investments, using data to model voters, to discover their issues of concern, and to target groups and even individual voters with tailored and social messages. Through increasingly computational managerial practices, which entail leveraging data and analysis to shape messaging and resource flows, campaigns attempt to better know and more efficiently and strategically communicate with the electorate.

At the same time, however, as the discussion of Twitter suggests, this is far from the professionally managed polity that some commentators have suggested. Hashtags become vehicles for supporters, and opponents, to creatively repurpose campaign content. Journalists remain the intermediaries for much political communication, and setting the agenda for voters is as much premised on journalistic buy-in as a campaign's ability to speak directly to the electorate. Finally, the social targeting and volunteer enthusiasm on Facebook and Dashboard is dependent on the ultimate buy-in of the supporters who devote their social identities and hours to the cause. In this sense, while big data, voter modeling, and targeting were at the forefront of the 2012 election, campaigning was still premised on the old-fashioned attempts to generate interest, enthusiasm, and political desire among the electorate.

What is clear is that scholars must be attentive to the actual, data-driven practices of campaigns in the study of contemporary strategic political communication. In order to understand the effects of negative advertising, for instance, scholars need to understand how these messages are crafted and increasingly targeted in very specific ways. At the same time, as the foregoing discussion reveals, much of what scholars take to be the organic or viral processes of social media can often be subtly engineered and managed, at least probabilistically.

Notes

1. Portions of this section have been adapted from Kreiss 2012b, 2012d.
2. The technical and institutional histories of the voter files, databases, and interface systems the two parties and their candidates use vary. For an in-depth discussion of these differences, see Kreiss 2012a and Nielsen 2012.
3. In numerous interviews conducted by the first author for an in-progress book project, Republican campaign staffers and party operatives active over the past decade cited a growing gap between the two parties in voter data and field infrastructure. Republicans even cite how their party has lost ground since 2004, when George W. Bush's reelection campaign fielded ground and Internet operations that were superior to those of the Democrats. Indeed, neither John McCain nor Mitt Romney could match the number of votes cast for President Bush in 2004.
4. Pending future research, it is impossible to state with any degree of certainty what failed with Project ORCA, although it appears that it was ultimately a problem of technical capacity, organization, and execution. First, like Project Houdini (discussed later in the chapter), ORCA was not able to handle large-scale database updates. Second, ORCA was poorly integrated with the larger field effort, including the structures the campaign had in place to train and manage volunteers. Finally, the implementation of ORCA failed to take account of the needs and practices of field staffers and volunteers.
5. See "Binders Full of Women," Facebook, https://www.facebook.com/romneybindersfull ofwomen.

References

Alter, Jonathan. 2013. *The Center Holds: Obama and His Enemies*. New York: Simon and Schuster.
Ashburn, Lauren. 2012. "Barack Obama's Campaign Scoring Points with Video Gamers." *The Daily Beast*, September 28. http://www.thedailybeast.com/articles/2012/09/28/barack-obama-s-campaign-scoring-points-with-video-gamers.html.
Bachman, Katy. 2012. "Forecast: Online Political Ad Spend Still Tiny: Only 1.5% of Total Spending, but a Spike from 2008 Election." *AdWeek*, March 8. http://www.adweek.com/news/online/forecast-online-political-still-tiny-138810.
Barnard, Lisa, and Daniel Kreiss. 2013. "A Research Agenda for the Effects of Online Political Advertising: Surveying Campaign Practice 2000–2012." *International Journal of Communication* 7:2046–2066.
Beckett, Lois. 2012a. "Everything We Know (So Far) about Obama's Big Data Tactics." *ProPublica*, November 29. http://www.propublica.org/article/everything-we-know-so-far-about-obamas-big-data-operation.
———. 2012b. "How Microsoft and Yahoo! Are Selling Politicians Access to You." *ProPublica*, June 11. http://www.propublica.org/article/how-microsoft-and-yahoo-are-selling-politicians-access-to-you.
Bennett, W. Lance. 2008. "Engineering Consent: The Persistence of a Problematic Communication Regime." In *Domestic Perspectives on Contemporary Democracy*, edited by Peter Nardulli, 131–154. Urbana: University of Illinois Press.

Bennett, W. Lance, and Jarol B. Manheim. 2006. "The One-Step Flow of Communication." *Annals of the American Academy of Political and Social Science* 608:213–232.

Bimber, Bruce, Andrew Flanagin, and Cynthia Stohl. 2012. *Collective Action in Organizations: Interaction and Engagement in an Era of Technological Change*. Cambridge: Cambridge University Press.

Blumenthal, Paul. 2012. "Hulu Political Advertising Jumped 700 Percent in 2012." Huffington Post, October 5. http://www.huffingtonpost.com/2012/10/05/hulu-political-advertising_n_1943111.html?utm_hp_ref=elections-2012.

Bond, Robert M., Christopher J. Fariss, Jason J. Jones, Adam D. I. Kramer, Cameron Marlow, Jaime E. Settle, and James H. Fowler. 2012. "A 61-Million-Person Experiment in Social Influence and Political Mobilization." *Nature* 489:295–298.

Calderon, Sara Ines. 2012. "Obama Campaign Releases Mobile Voter Engagement App." *TechCrunch*, July 31. http://techcrunch.com/2012/07/31/obama-campaign-releases-mobile-voter-engagement-app/.

Chadwick, Andrew. 2013. *The Hybrid Media System: Politics and Power*. Oxford: Oxford University Press.

Commission on Presidential Debates. 2012. "October 16, 2012 Debate Transcript." http://www.debates.org/index.php?page=october-1-2012-the-second-obama-romney-presidential-debate.

Confessore, Nicholas. 2013. "Groups Mobilize to Aid Democrats in '14 Data Race." *New York Times*, November 14. http://www.nytimes.com/2013/11/15/us/politics/groups-mobilize-to-aid-democrats.html?smid=tw-share.

C-SPAN. 2012. "President Obama Campaign Rally in Roanoke." July 13. http://www.c-spanvideo.org/program/307056-2.

Delany, Colin. 2012a. "Cookie-Based, Voter-File Ad Targeting: From Exotic to Expected in Six Months." *Epolitics*, May 6. http://www.epolitics.com/2012/05/06/cookie-based-voter-file-ad-targeting-from-exotic-to-expected-in-six-months/.

———. 2012b. "Voter File Digital Ad Targeting." *Campaigns & Elections*, July 18. http://www.campaignsandelections.com/magazine/us-edition/324582/voter-file-digital-ad-targeting-reality-vs-hype.thtml.

Ecker, Clint. 2012. "What I Spent the Last 14 Months Doing at Obama for America." *Officially Lucky* (blog), November 13. http://blog.clintecker.com/post/35666821967/what-clint-ecker-did-at-obama-for-america-narwhal-dashbo.

Ekdahl, John. 2012. "Mitt Romney's 'Project ORCA' Was a Disaster, and It May Have Cost Him the Election." *Business Insider*, November 8. http://www.businessinsider.com/romney-project-orca-disaster-2012-11.

Fouhy, Beth. 2012. "Twitter Plays Outsize Role in 2012 Campaign." Associated Press, May 7. http://www.wxyz.com/dpp/news/science_tech/twitter-plays-outsize-role-in-2012-campaign-wcp01336415661507.

Gallagher, Sean. 2012. "Which Consultants Built Romney's 'Project Orca'? None of Them." *Ars Technica*, November 15. http://arstechnica.com/information-technology/2012/11/which-consultants-built-romneys-project-orca-none-of-them/.

Gillum, Jack. 2012. "Romney Uses Secretive Data-Mining." Associated Press, August 24. http://bigstory.ap.org/article/ap-exclusive-romney-uses-secretive-data-mining.

Guynn, Jessica, and Dawn C. Chmielewski. 2012. "Social Media Turn Election Night into a Conversation." *Los Angeles Times*, November 8. http://www.latimes.com/news/nationworld/nation/la-fi-election-social-media-20121108,0,1020964.story.

Harris, Derrick. 2012. "How Obama's Tech Team Helped Deliver the 2012 Election." *GigaOm*, November 12. http://gigaom.com/cloud/how-obamas-tech-team-helped-deliver-the-2012-election/.

Howard, Philip N. 2006. *New Media Campaigns and the Managed Citizen*. New York: Cambridge University Press.
Issenberg, Sasha. 2012a. "A More Perfect Union: How President Obama's Campaign Used Big Data to Rally Individual Voters." *Technology Review* 18 (2012). http://www.technologyreview.com/featuredstory/508836/how-obama-used-big-data-to-rally-voters-part-1/.
———. 2012b. "The Romney Campaign's Data Strategy." *Slate*, July 17. http://www.slate.com/articles/news_and_politics/victory_lab/2012/07/the_romney_campaign_s_data_strategy_they_re_outsourcing_.html.
Johnson, Rebecca. 2012. "Online Advertising Heats Up for 2012 Election Cycle." WPP, May 8. http://www.wpp.com/wpp/marketing/digital/online-advertising-heats-up.htm.
Judd, Nick. 2012a. "For Romney's Digital Campaign, a Second-Place Finish." *TechPresident*, November 7. http://techpresident.com/news/23106/romneys-digital-campaign-second-place-finish.
———. 2012b. "How Obama for America Made Its Facebook Friends into Effective Advocates." *TechPresident*, November 19. http://techpresident.com/news/23159/how-obama-america-made-its-facebook-friends-effective-advocates.
———. 2012c. "Meet the Newest Tech Start-Up: The Obama Campaign." *The Ticket* (blog), *Yahoo! News*, April 6. http://news.yahoo.com/blogs/ticket/meet-newest-tech-start-obama-campaign-212401654.html.
———. 2012d. "Obama's Targeted GOTV on Facebook Reached 5 Million Voters, Goff Says." *TechPresident*, November 30. http://techpresident.com/news/23202/obamas-targeted-gotv-facebook-reached-5-million-voters-goff-says.
Karpf, David. 2012. "Social Science Research Methods in Internet Time." *Information, Communication & Society* 15:639–661.
Kaye, Barbara K., and Norman Medoff. 2001. *The World Wide Web: A Mass Communication Perspective*. Mountain View, CA: Mayfield.
Kaye, Kate. 2012a. "Romney Ad Firm Partners for Big Data on Hispanics." ClickZ, April 30. http://www.clickz.com/clickz/news/2171497/romney-firm-partners-hispanics.
———. 2012b. "Romney Camp Runs #BelieveInAmerica Promo Trend on Twitter." ClickZ, August 30. http://www.clickz.com/clickz/news/2201827/romney-camp-runs-believeinamerica-promo-trend-on-twitter.
———. 2012c. "The State of Online Political Advertising." ClickZ, May 8. http://www.law.yale.edu/documents/pdf/ISP/Kate_Kaye.pdf.
Kazin, Michael. 2007. *A Godly Hero: The Life of William Jennings Bryan*. New York: Knopf.
Kreiss, Daniel. 2012a. *Taking Our Country Back: The Crafting of Networked Politics from Howard Dean to Barack Obama*. New York: Oxford University Press.
———. 2012b. "The 2012 Campaign: Infrastructure, Organization, and Technical Failure." *OrgTheory.net*, November 20. http://orgtheory.wordpress.com/2012/11/20/the-2012-campaign-infrastructure-organization-and-technical-failure/.
———. 2012c. "The 2012 Obama Campaign in Historical Context." *OrgTheory.net*, November 11. http://orgtheory.wordpress.com/2012/11/11/the-2012-obama-campaign-in-historical-context/.
———. 2012d. "Yes We Can (Profile You): A Brief Primer on Campaigns and Political Data." *Stanford Law Review* 64: 70.
Kreiss, Daniel, and Philip N. Howard. 2010. "New Challenges to Political Privacy: Lessons from the First U.S. Presidential Race in the Web 2.0 Era." *International Journal of Communication* 4:1032–1050.
Latour, Bruno. 2006. *Reassembling the Social: An Introduction to Actor-Network-Theory*. New York: Oxford University Press.

Lohr, Steve. 2012. "The Obama Campaign's Technology Is a Force Multiplier." *Bits* (blog), *New York Times*, November 8. http://bits.blogs.nytimes.com/2012/11/08/the-obama-campaigns-technology-the-force-multiplier/.

Madrigal, Alexis. 2012. "When the Nerds Go Marching In." *Atlantic*, November 16. http://www.theatlantic.com/technology/archive/2012/11/when-the-nerds-go-marching-in/265325/?single_page=true.

Masket, Seth E., Michael T. Heaney, Joanne M. Miller, and Dara Z. Strolovitch. 2009. "Networking the Parties: A Comparative Study of Democratic and Republican National Convention Delegates in 2008." Paper presented at the annual meeting of the American Political Science Association, Toronto, September 3–6.

McGerr, Michael E. 1986. *The Decline of Popular Politics: The American North, 1865–1928*. New York: Oxford University Press.

Miller, Toby. 2009. "My Green Crush." *Journal of Visual Culture* 8:154–158.

Naylor, Brian. 2012. "That New Friend You Made on Facebook? He Might Be Named Mitt or Barack." *It's All Politics* (blog), NPR Online, May 3. http://www.npr.org/blogs/itsallpolitics/2012/05/03/151879422/that-new-friend-you-made-on-facebook-he-might-be-named-mitt-or-barack.

Nielsen, Rasmus. K. 2012. *Ground Wars: Personalized Communication in Political Campaigns*. Princeton: Princeton University Press.

Peha, Jon. 2012. "Making Political Ads Personal." *Politico*, September 11. http://www.politico.com/news/stories/0912/81022.html.

Peters, Jeremy W. 2012. "As TV Viewing Habits Change, Political Ads Adapt." *New York Times*, April 1. http://www.nytimes.com/2012/04/02/us/politics/as-tv-viewing-habits-change-political-ads-adapt.html.

Rainie, Lee, Aaron Smith, Kay L. Schlozman, Henry Brady, and Sidney Verba. 2012. "Social Media and Political Engagement." Pew Internet and American Life Project, October 19. http://pewinternet.org/Reports/2012/Political-engagement.aspx.

Ridout, Travis N., Michael M. Franz, Kenneth M. Goldstein, and William J. Feltus. 2012. "Separation by Television Program: Understanding the Targeting of Political Advertising in Presidential Elections." *Political Communication* 29:1–23.

Rutenberg, Jim. 2012. "Secret of the Obama Victory? Rerun Watchers, for One Thing." *New York Times*, November 12. http://www.nytimes.com/2012/11/13/us/politics/obama-data-system-targeted-tv-viewers-for-support.html?smid=tw-share.

Sabato, Larry J. 1981. *The Rise of Political Consultants: New Ways of Winning Elections*. New York: Basic Books.

Scherer, Michael. 2012. "Inside the Secret World of the Data Crunchers Who Helped Obama Win." *Swampland* (blog), *Time*, November 7. http://swampland.time.com/2012/11/07/inside-the-secret-world-of-quants-and-data-crunchers-who-helped-obama-win/.

Shepherd, Shawna. 2012. "Gingrich Pins Hopes on Hashtags." CNN.com, March 11. http://www.cnn.com/2012/03/10/politics/gingrich-social-media/index.html.

Sifry, Micah L. 2011. "Election 2012: It's Not Facebook. It's the Data, Stupid." *TechPresident* (blog), April 20. http://techpresident.com/blog-entry/election-2012-its-not-facebook-its-data-stupid.

Stampler, Laura. 2012. "Obama Spent More on Online Ads than It Cost to Build the Lincoln Memorial." *Business Insider*, November 5. http://www.businessinsider.com/infographic-obama-romney-final-ad-spend-2012-11.

Star, Susan L. 1999. "The Ethnography of Infrastructure." *American Behavioral Scientist* 43: 377–391.

Tau, Byron. 2012. "Obama Campaign Launches Mobile App." *Politico*, July 3. http://www.politico.com/politico44/2012/07/obama-campaign-launches-mobile-app-130576.html.

Terkel, Amanda. 2012. "Project ORCA: Mitt Romney Campaign Plans Massive, State-of-the-Art Poll Monitoring Effort." Huffington Post, November 1. http://www.huffingtonpost.com/2012/11/01/project-orca-mitt-romney_n_2052861.html?utm_hp_ref=elections-2012.

Turow, Joseph, Michael D. Carpini, Nora Draper, and Rowan Howard-Williams. 2012. "Americans Roundly Reject Tailored Political Advertising at a Time When Political Campaigns Are Embracing It." Annenberg School for Communication at University of Pennsylvania, July 24. http://www.asc.upenn.edu/news/Turow_Tailored_Political_Advertising.pdf.

Whitman, Joshua M., and Joseph W. Perkins. 2003. "The Technological Evolution of Campaigns: A Look at New and Emerging Practices." In *Campaigns and Elections: Issues, Concepts, and Cases*, edited by Robert P. Watson and Colton C. Campbell, 47–56. Washington, DC: Lynne Rienner.

Yenigun, Sami. 2012. "Presidential Campaigns Rock the Gamer Vote." NPR Online, October 1. http://www.npr.org/2012/10/01/162103528/presidential-campaigns-rock-the-gamer-vote.

2

Congressional Campaigns' Motivations for Social Media Adoption

GIRISH J. GULATI AND CHRISTINE B. WILLIAMS

The 2006 midterm elections ushered in a Democratic majority to the House of Representatives for the first time in 12 years amid the backdrop of an unpopular war, an unpopular incumbent president, and evidence of a culture of corruption permeating the Republican-led Congress. The campaign season also was memorable for its media spectacles surrounding Mark Foley, Jack Abramoff, Tom DeLay's smiling mug shot, and the "macaca" moment. A more significant long-term development in how campaigns are waged, however, was the debut of the popular social networking site Facebook as a campaign tool. Almost one-third of the candidates running for the United States Senate (32%) and about one of every ten candidates running for the House of Representatives (13%) had active Facebook profiles during the fall campaign. Even a few prominent senators who were not up for reelection but were exploring presidential bids in 2008 began experimenting with Facebook with the hope of building an online network of supporters (Gulati and Williams 2009).

By 2010, candidates for Congress had made significant strides integrating websites, Facebook, and social media into their larger communication strategy: 92% of the major-party candidates for the House had created a campaign website, and 82% had a presence on Facebook (Gulati and Williams 2011). The candidates were poised to build on these gains in the next election cycle and make the adoption of social media a near-universal campaign practice.

This embrace of social media by a large majority of candidates running for Congress is changing the way that campaigns are managed, how money is raised, how resources are allocated, and the means candidates use to communicate with the electorate and with their supporters and staff. This study seeks to understand who has embraced this new technology, to what extent, and for what purposes. Are social media changing the nature of the relationship between candidates and voters, to reach out to different groups, to mobilize and engage citizens in different kinds of activities? Do these practices and their consequences differ from what was possible using traditional media for campaign communications? If so, we are seeing both a new medium and a new message with potentially transformative implications for elections and democracy.

To understand these changes and their potential implications, a growing body of research has begun investigating which candidates are more likely and least likely to adopt Facebook and other social media. But now that adoption has become near universal and nonadopters are exhibiting idiosyncratic characteristics and circumstances that do not fit a common profile, there is little new to be gained from estimating Facebook adoption models. This chapter moves beyond a simple model of adoption to investigate which candidates were more likely and less likely *to use* Facebook during their campaigns and then explores *how* the candidates tried to use Facebook as a campaign communication tool. That latter question leads us to advance the existing literature by supplementing statistical models with over 90 interviews of candidates and staff from the 2012 campaigns. The motivation behind candidates' decisions to adopt Facebook and other social media provides insight into whether and how this new communication platform is changing candidates' relationship with voters and expanding voters' opportunities to interact with campaigns.

Social Media Adoption in Congressional Campaigns

Social networking sites are now widely accessible to the general public and rank among the top visited sites on the web. Launched in February 2004, Facebook is estimated to receive 800 million unique visitors a month and placed third in Compete's ranking of the most popular websites nine years later in December 2013.[1]

Facebook was an absent player in congressional elections in 2004 and began the 2006 campaign season mostly on the fringes because it was not compatible for Internet campaigning and restricted to users with the .edu domain. Some candidates overcame these obstacles by using alumni email accounts to create their own personal profiles that could include biographical information and personal tidbits, photos, and links to videos archived on other sites. Although creating a personal profile provided many candidates access to the Facebook community, the structural limits of the site made it ineffective for a candidate to use it as a tool for mobilizing a larger number of supporters. Each member was limited to having only 5,000 friends, which was inadequate for a candidate running for the presidency or statewide office.[2]

Facebook was aware that its site was growing in popularity as a space where candidates and voters could interact and recognized its potential as a vehicle for enriching the democratic process. In response, Facebook created a complementary section within the main site that provided generic profiles to candidates running for a congressional or gubernatorial seat, with the candidate's name, office, state, and party affiliation already posted to the profile.[3] Candidates already on Facebook were able to have their personal profiles converted into a candidate page within the election pages and were free to personalize their profiles in the same way open to any member. Facebook users who wanted to show their support for a candidate or just observe did not need to do so by requesting to be a "friend" and depending on the candidate's approval. Instead, supporters could simply click a "Support" button and then were able to receive updates and authorization to post comments and materials to the site. Facebook provided a listing of candidate profiles grouped by states and congressional districts so that specific candidates could be easily located by users.

Since Facebook took the initiative in creating profiles for all major-party candidates, identifying who were the earliest adopters of Facebook required a more precise definition of adoption. Adoption must mean more than simply "purchasing" or "owning" the technology but also should mean that the adopter actually is using the technology. By conceptualizing adoption in this way and identifying which candidates utilized their profiles in some way (e.g., at least posted a profile picture), we found in a previous study (Williams and Gulati 2013) that only 32% of the candidates running for the Senate and 13% of the candidates running for the House activated their account by updating it in some way. Early adopters were challengers, better financed candidates, and candidates running competitive races. Constituency factors had no impact, and there were no differences by party.

Facebook opened membership to people outside the .edu domain in September 2007 and made some modifications for the 2008 elections. Political candidates had fan pages instead of profiles. These pages were similar to personal profiles but offered the candidates greater capability to post various kinds of campaign material. Another change was that current elected officials and candidates for all levels of office in any country were eligible for fan pages as long as an official representative of the politician created the page. These changes contributed to a large majority of both Democratic and Republican candidates establishing a presence on Facebook. Among major-party House candidates, 50% had a Politicians page, and about half of those candidates seemed to have updated it in some way. Constituency factors in the form of education, age, and race had a significant impact on adoption. Whereas candidates running in districts with a higher percentage of residents in the district with a college degree were more likely to be adopters, candidates in districts with an older population and more nonwhites were less likely to be adopters. In addition, Democrats were more likely than Republicans to be Facebook adopters. At these early and late majority stages (Rogers 2003), there is more concern and more information about the value of an innovation. Hence, we see more attention to constituency demand factors (Williams and Gulati 2013).

By 2010, 82% of House candidates had a Facebook page, representing nearly a fivefold increase in the percentage of candidates adopting since 2006. At this late adoption stage, constituency demographics and party were no longer significant factors in explaining adoption. The competitiveness of the race, which is an early stage factor, also was no longer significant. Instead, strategic and organizational factors became the key drivers that differentiated adopters from nonadopters. In a reversal from the early adoption stage, challengers and open-seat candidates were found to be the nonadopters, as were poorly funded candidates (Gulati and Williams 2011).

On the basis of how quickly campaign websites reached near-universal adoption and the continuing upward trajectory and expansion of the Facebook user community, we expect adoption of Facebook by congressional candidates to have risen in 2012. We also expect this small, nonadopting subset of candidates to differ from adopters in personal characteristics more strongly than at earlier stages. Either they will represent very weak campaigns, struggling organizationally and financially, hold highly skeptical and resistant attitudes about technology innovation, or have some idiosyncratic reason for remaining on the sidelines. Whatever the case may be, these candidates likely will be the outliers in congressional campaigns and constitute only a small percentage of the total field of candidates. After verifying that adoption is near universal and no longer demonstrates any pattern by which we can identify a profile of nonadopters, we need to turn our attention to the impact social media are having on campaigning. Understanding how candidates who adopt the technology actually use it as a campaign tool and what their objectives for doing so are can offer insight into the ways social media are changing how congressional campaigns are waged today. More specifically, studying usage can help us understand whether and how this communication platform could change the structure of relationships and participation opportunities for voters.

Diffusion of Innovation and Social Media Adoption

The literature on diffusion of innovation conceptualizes adoption and implementation decisions as contingent on the right set of factors or opportunities. In most formulations, these decisions depend not only on the characteristics of the adopter but also on characteristics of the innovation or technology (e.g., ease of use, cost) and of the environment. The characteristics of early adopters and also the timing and extent of the adoptions have been studied for both individuals and organizations (Fichman 1992; Frambach and Schillewaert 2002).[4]

For example, T. H. Kwon and Robert Zmud (1987) identify five categories of contextual factors: characteristics of the adopting organization, the user community, the innovation or technology, the task, and the environment. Alan Meyer and James Goes (1988) argue that an organization's innovativeness is influenced by contextual attributes (environmental and organizational variables), innovation attributes (level of risk and skill required), and their interaction. Two empirical studies serve to illustrate the range of indicators that have been used to predict adoption decisions at the organizational and individual levels of analysis. Sigi Goode and Kenneth Stevens (2000) considered six characteristics to explain which *organizations* adopted or failed to adopt World Wide Web technology:

the size and age of the business, its information technology (IT) support and budget, its technology experience (all characteristics of the adopting organization), and its industry (user community and environment). Se-Joon Hong and Kar Yan Tam (2006) considered five sets of factors influencing *individual* decisions to adopt mobile data-services technologies: general (usefulness and ease of use) and specific (service availability and monetary value) technology attributes, psychographics (enjoyment and need for uniqueness), social influence/approval, and demographics (gender, age). The latter two factors reflect a mix of user community, task, and environmental attributes.

A political campaign is unique in that it is an organization where the candidate both determines whether to adopt new technology *and* is also the "product" being promoted to the audience. Thus, in the context of a political campaign, adopter characteristics should be studied at both the organizational and individual levels, together with attributes of the environment that reference collective aggregates: constituency demographics and electoral circumstances. Such mixed metrics are typical of political science studies of the diffusion of campaign websites, which have examined relatively few categories and a somewhat limited number of contextual factors. Most draw on the same finite set, which is divided into constituency factors (the user community) and political system factors (the environment). Constituencies are described demographically by median income; percentage urban, white, college educated, and young; and sometimes rate of Internet penetration (Foot and Schneider 2006). The political environment is described by characteristics of the electoral contest and candidate or public official: level of office, competitiveness of the race, party identification (of the constituency or candidate), party status (major or minor party), status of the seat (incumbent, challenger, open seat), and amount of campaign funds raised. The most common individual adopter characteristics have been the candidate's age and gender (Gulati and Williams 2011).

Most empirical studies investigate adoption in terms of the first of three sequentially ordered questions, namely, when the decision is made and what factors predict who is an early, late, or nonadopter (Fichman 2004). Research suggests that the factors influencing early adopters differ from those influencing those who adopt at later stages, whether the adopter is an individual or an organization (Cooper and Zmud 1990; Davis, Bagozzi, and Warshaw 1989). One reason is because organizations have better information about a technology's destiny in later adoption stages, lowering the risk (Fichman 2004; Meyer and Goes 1988). Moreover, as a technology diffuses, social norms begin to create pressures to keep up with one's peer group, and a critical mass of users is being reached to increase the utility of the communications medium (Frambach and Schillewaert 2002).

The two postadoption research questions are also important but much less studied: how often does an organization adopt innovations, and how thoroughly is the adoption implemented and integrated into the organization, its business processes and practices? These steps are referred to as adaptation, routinization, and infusion (Fichman 1992; Frambach and Schillewaert 2002). They represent the later, second and third stages in the adoption process, namely, implementation and usage. First there has to be technology acceptance, then sustained use (Venkatesh, Morris, and Ackerman 2000). Some evidence suggests that early adopters also will be more aggressive in their rate of implementing an innovation (Fichman 2004). Other research focuses on the organization's absorptive capacity (Cohen and Levinthal 1990) and on the compatibility of the technology with existing systems and with businesses processes and practices (Fichman 2004). At the individual level, an individual's abilities matter, especially when the technology is complex or has high knowledge barriers. The third stage in the process also speaks to the question about how thoroughly the innovation is adopted, focusing on its quality. Measures of the quality of use often rely on demonstrating performance impacts on business processes, productivity, profitability, and firm market value (Fichman 2004). In a campaign context, it would entail changes in staffing and strategy, generation of volunteers, donations and supporters (Facebook "friends," poll standings), press coverage, and ultimately vote share.

Data and Methods

We began our analysis of how candidates are using Facebook by identifying all the Democratic and Republican nominees for every election for the U.S. Senate and House of Representatives in 2012. We identified 66 Senate and 832 House candidates and further differentiated the candidates by their status as an incumbent, a challenger, or contesting an open seat. To identify the candidates who had their own Facebook page, we entered the candidate's name into each medium's internal search engine beginning in summer 2012 and continued the process until the beginning of November.[5] We followed a similar data-collection process for the 2006, 2008, and 2010 elections and draw from those data sources to point to trends and developments over time.

Our search revealed that nearly every candidate running for the Senate, 64 of 66 (97%), adopted a Facebook page for 2012. The only two Senate candidates who were not on Facebook were challengers Tim Chesnut (D-WY) and Albert Gore (D-MS). Every incumbent senator running for reelection and every Republican candidate had adopted Facebook in 2012. The adoption rate for 2012 represents the third consecutive increase in adoption rates for Senate candidates. As can be seen in figure 2.1, Facebook diffusion at the Senate level has been at the late adoption stage since 2008, when 90% of major-party Senate candidates were Facebook adopters. In 2010, 96% of Republican and Democratic candidates for the Senate were on Facebook.

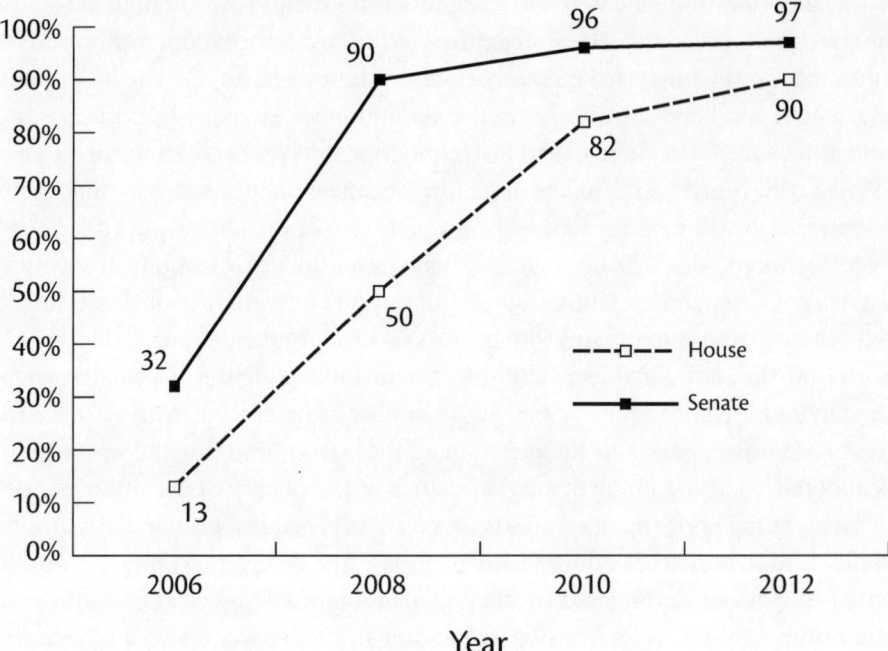

Figure 2.1. Percentage of major-party candidates who adopted Facebook in congressional campaigns, 2006–2012

A record number of 2012 Republican and Democratic candidates for the House of Representatives, 751 out of 832 (90.2%), had a Facebook page by November 1. Another 39 candidates had their own personal Facebook page, bringing the figure to 94.9% of candidates with some sort of Facebook presence. The rate of adoption in 2012 represents a significant increase from 2010, when 82% of the major-party candidates were Facebook page adopters, and sets a record for Facebook adoption. Adoption rates beginning in 2006 are displayed in figure 2.1.

Although the primary focus of this study is how candidates are using Facebook, we also estimated logistic regression models to identify which 2012 House candidates were more likely to adopt Facebook, in order to show how factors predicting usage are different from adoption and to document trends in adoption patterns. Because there were only two nonadopters among major-party Senate candidates, we did not estimate a model of Facebook adoption for Senate races. The dependent variable in the House model—*Facebook Adoption*—was coded "1" if the candidate had a fan page in the Politicians or Government section and coded "0" if he or she did not have a page or only had a personal profile. We coded personal pages as nonadopters because candidates have less control over the layout of the page and have no access to performance metrics, as they do with fan pages. Moreover, Facebook users cannot simply "like" the candidate and become a follower but must instead initiate a request to the candidate to "add friend" and be accepted by the candidate. Thus, we see personal pages as qualitatively different from fan pages and less useful for engaging with supporters and communicating with the larger community of users.

To measure the extent to which the campaigns used Facebook, we counted the number of wall posts that were generated by the candidate between Labor Day (September 3) and Election Day (November 6). The average number of posts to the walls was 29.9, and the median was 27. This amounts to about one wall post every other day. About 4% of the candidates whom we had identified as having adopted Facebook did not post anything to their walls during the nine-week field period. Another 4% posted only one or two times over the course of the fall campaign. Only about 7% of the candidates made 60 or more wall posts, which amount to one or more post a day. All of the five most active Facebook adopters were challengers: Eric Swalwell (D-CA; 122), Joe Garcia (D-FL; 100), Leslie Messenger (D-GA; 97), Sharen Neuhardt (D-OH; 96), and Gary DeLong (R-CA; 89).

Since the number of wall posts is a count and there are a large number of excess zeros (i.e., 31 nonusers), we estimated a zero-inflated Poisson count model to identify who were the most active candidates on Facebook in 2012. There also are a large number of candidates ($n = 30$) with only one or two posts. The content of these posts generally were not substantive in nature but rather conveyed a simple introductory note or seemed to be an experiment to see if the page was working. The rest of the distribution is relatively normal until it gets to the high end of the distribution and tails off with extreme values. For these reasons, we recoded all values of "1" and "2" as "0s."

For independent variables, we constructed dichotomous dummy variables for Democrats (as an indicator for party), challengers, and candidates to open seats. Our second electoral variable is the competitiveness of the race. A race was coded as competitive if it had been designated as a toss-up or leaning toward one party around October 1, 2012, by two of the three leading congressional election forecasters: the Cook Political Report, Larry Sabato's Crystal Ball, and Real Clear Politics.[6] Our indicator for the campaign's financial resources is the natural log of total net receipts collected between January 1, 2011, and the end of the third-quarter reporting period.

Since constituency demographic variables no longer explain adoption of social media (Gulati and Williams 2011; Peterson 2012) but recent studies show that Democrats are more likely to use social media for political engagement than are Republicans (Rainie and Smith 2012), we use the Partisan Voting Index (PVI) to account for constituency demand. Developed by election analyst Charlie Cook, the PVI is an indicator of the partisan distribution in each district. For each candidate's district, the PVI is the difference between the performance of a presidential candidate nationally in the last election subtracted from his performance in the congressional district in the same year.[7] For example, the PVI for Michigan's 12th congressional district, represented by the House's most senior member, John Dingell, would be "+14 Democrat" because Barack Obama won 67% of the vote in that district, compared to 53 percent nationally. Scores have been modified for this study so that the higher scores indicate a district with more Democratic voters, while lower scores indicate a district with more Republican voters.

We included the candidate's gender, race, and age as three salient personal attributes. Race is coded "1" for nonwhite and "0" for white. Gender is coded "1" for female and "0" for male. After searching through multiple sources, we were unable to obtain the birth years for 21 (2.5%) of the candidates. A potential problem was that all of the missing data were for nonincumbents (17 challengers and four open-seat candidates). Thus, we estimated the models with and without age and display the results of both estimations.

To understand how congressional candidates use Facebook and their underlying motives and strategic goals for doing so, we conducted interviews with representatives from 91 different campaigns who had firsthand knowledge of the campaign's Internet strategy and operations between October 15 and December 14, 2012. Using a semistructured interview protocol (see the appendix) developed by the authors, the interviews were conducted by 28 student assistants enrolled in a class on campaigns and elections. Each assistant was randomly assigned approximately 15 races, yielding a list of approximately 29 candidates to interview. Contact information was obtained from the candidates' websites, social media pages, other third-party sources, and in some cases, by browsing the candidate's Facebook page. At least one attempt was made to contact each candidate's campaign either by email or phone, but nearly all of the interviews were conducted over the phone.

All interviewers asked the respondents to explain why their candidates were using social media and which specific applications and features they were using and to describe how they were integrating these into their larger strategy. Candidates who had not adopted social media also were interviewed and asked why they had not done so. In semistructured interviews, every respondent does not answer every question or all of the same questions, nor is the wording and format precisely the same when they do. Thus, the number of responses and the respondents' identities vary by question in our interview data. For this reason, our analysis characterizes the data by central tendencies rather than by exact count or percentages, and we provide excerpts to illustrate the range of responses for each theme.

Although our choice of qualitative methodology is designed to elicit an in-depth understanding of why (and how) some campaigns chose to use (or not use) Facebook, we did strive to obtain a representative sample. In our sample, 51.6% of respondents were from Democratic campaigns, while 50.5% of the candidates in the population were Democrats. Incumbents constituted 44% of our sample and 43.6% of the population. Our interviewees included 40.7%

challengers (versus 42.4% in the population), and 15.4% were candidates running for open seats (versus 14% in the population).

Analysis and Findings

Adoption Models

The results of the logistic regression analysis of Facebook adoption are reported in table 2.1. The first column presents the logistic regression estimates, and the second column presents the standard errors from the model with the candidate's age (Model 1). The third and fourth columns show the estimates for the model with age excluded (Model 2).

Based on recent trends in Facebook adoption (Gulati and Williams 2011), we did not expect Republicans or Democrats to be more or less likely to adopt Facebook. Consistent with this expectation, the first row of data in table 2.1 shows that there is an absence of a relationship between party and Facebook adoption when controlling for all other variables. Although Democrats were the quickest to embrace social media in congressional campaigns, this is the second

Table 2.1. Logistic Regression Analysis of Facebook Adoption in the 2012 U.S. House Elections

	Model 1			Model 2		
	B	S.E.	Sig.	B	S.E.	Sig.
(1) Party (Republican = 1)	.239	.381		.457	.369	
(2) Challengers	−2.250	.584	***	−2.065	.566	***
(3) Open-seat candidates	−2.306	.638	***	−2.008	.623	***
(4) Competitive seat	2.188	1.032	**	2.281	1.029	**
(5) Contributions received (natural log)	.199	.035	***	.203	.033	***
(6) Democratic constituency (PVI)	−.004	.012		−.010	.012	
(7) Gender (female = 1)	.683	.429		.404	.390	
(8) Race (nonwhite = 1)	−.482	.392		−.267	.361	
(9) Age (birth year)	.035	.014	**	—	—	
(10) Intercept	−67.219	27.880	**	.497	.964	
N		807			822	
Percent correctly predicted		92.7			92.0	
Mode		92.1			91.4	
Pseudo R^2		.362			.359	

** $p < .05$, *** $p < .01$; two-sided tests of significance consecutive cycle in which the decision on whether to adopt Facebook is not the result of differences in the political parties' campaign strategies.

The coefficients in the next two rows show that incumbents were significantly more likely to have adopted Facebook than were challengers and candidates for open seats. To overcome the structural and strategic advantages enjoyed by incumbents, it generally has been expected that challengers and candidates for open seats would be more inclined than incumbents to pursue Internet campaigning. But because incumbents can carry over their social media accounts from campaign to campaign, it now is less of an effort for incumbents to have a website, Facebook page, or other social media profile. Challengers are the least able to absorb the various costs of adopting new technologies and significantly more likely to be among the nonadopters than are incumbents or open-seat candidates. This finding is consistent with studies showing that while early adopters are willing to take risks, late adopters, laggards, and nonadopters are more fixated on costs and profitability (Läpple and Van Rensburg 2011). Our findings and past research underscore the importance of taking into account the maturation of the innovation, which by 2012 is in the last phase of the adoption stage.

The third strategic attribute we tested was the effect of the competitiveness of the race on adoption decisions. Whereas competition was a strong predictor of adoption when Facebook was introduced, it no longer differentiated adopters from nonadopters in 2010. This finding is consistent with studies showing that competitive advantage disappears once a technology has fully diffused; only usage is affected (Dholakia and Kshetri 2004). The fourth row of table 2.1 shows, however, that a relationship between the competitiveness of the race and the likelihood of adopting Facebook has reappeared. Another cycle of elections will reveal whether the relationship in 2010 or the relationship observed in 2012 was an aberration.

Because a larger campaign budget provides the needed resources for staff, professional online consultants, and know-how, we expected poorly financed candidates to predominate in the nonadopter group. The coefficients in the fifth row support this hypothesis. The candidates who raised the most money were the most likely to have adopted Facebook, while the candidates who raised less money were the least likely to adopt. The coefficients are statistically significant. Nonadopters of the now mature Facebook medium are apparently more affected by the constraints of a cash-strapped campaign. The lack of campaign funds also may be an indicator of a nonviable campaign and a poor candidate, two factors that are not conducive to social media adoption or adoption of most other campaign tools. Indeed, only 11% of nonadopters won their races, compared with 55% of adopters.

The sixth row of data displays the coefficients for the partisanship of the district. These coefficients show that there is no statistically significant relationship between the Democratic advantage in the district and the likelihood of adopting Facebook. But when we turn to the coefficients in the third and fourth columns, we can see that there is a negative relationship between constituency liberalism and adoption when the candidate's age is omitted from the model. Even though there is a difference between identifiers of the two parties in their use of social media for politics (Rainie and Smith 2012), the evidence is somewhat mixed on whether candidates seem to be influenced by the user community on whether to adopt Facebook.

Personal attributes have been shown to be significant predictors of technology adoption in the late-diffusion stage. In the case of Facebook, the estimations revealed that race and gender had no statistically significant effect. We found, however, that younger candidates were more likely to have adopted Facebook than were older candidates. This finding replicates studies that consistently show age to be a strong differentiator of nonadoption (Uhl, Andrus, and Poulsen 1970; Hall et al. 2003; Laukkanen and Pasanen 2007). Whether the 21 missing cases have any effect on the other coefficients or conclusions can be discerned from the coefficients displayed in the third and fourth columns (Model 2). While the conclusions are the same with and without age in the model, there is an extreme difference in the two intercepts. The source of this difference seems to be that candidates with unpublished birth years or ages are much less likely than the population as a whole to have adopted Facebook (38%). Furthermore, these candidates seem to be weak candidates in general. Of the 21 candidates without age data, 10 did not raise any money for their campaigns, and only one was running in a competitive race.

Activity Models

The results of the two zero-inflated Poisson models of *Facebook Activity* are reported in table 2.2 as Models 3 and 4. Model 3 presents the coefficients from the model with the candidate's age, and Model 4 presents the coefficients from the model with age excluded. What is striking about the results of both models is how different the relationships are from the relationships reported and discussed in table 2.1. Whereas Democrats and Republicans were equally as likely to adopt Facebook, Democrats were significantly more active in using Facebook than were Republicans. In addition, comparing the second and third rows of data in both tables shows that even though incumbents were significantly more likely to adopt Facebook than were nonincumbents, challengers and candidates for open seats were significantly more likely to use Facebook. But while the relationships for party and incumbency status in the two models are strikingly different, the relationships with activity resemble the relationships with adoption at the early and late majority stage (Williams and Gulati 2013).

Table 2.2. Zero-Inflated Poisson Regression Analysis of Facebook Activity in the 2012 U.S. House Elections

	Model 3			Model 4		
	Coef.	S.E.	Sig.	Coef.	S.E.	Sig.
(1) Party (Republican = 1)	−.069	.015	***	−.069	.014	***
(2) Open-seat candidate	.577	.022	***	.579	.021	***
(3) Challenger	.752	.019	***	.752	.018	***
(4) Competitive seat	.080	.018	**	.080	.018	***
(5) Contributions received (natural log)	.041	.004	***	.041	.004	***
(6) Democratic constituency (PVI)	−.0009	.0005		−.0012	.0005	**
(7) Gender (female = 1)	.040	.018	**	.032	.017	
(8) Race (nonwhite = 1)	−.184	.022	**	−.171	.021	***
(9) Age (birth year)	.002	.001	***			
(10) Intercept	−1.097	1.319		2.621	.064	
N	710			718		
Nonzero observations	652			657		
Log likelihood	−4170.2			−4205.9		
LR X^2	2501.68		***	2527.13		***

** $p < .05$, *** $p < .01$; two-sided tests of significance

Similar to what was observed in the adoption model, candidates in more competitive races were more active on Facebook than were candidates running in noncompetitive races. It is likely that in races in which the outcome was not in doubt, both candidates did little in terms of communication and mobilization, whether that be on the air, on the ground, or online. But in races in which either candidate could win, it is likely that both candidates were using every means available, including Facebook, to keep in contact with their supporters and to mobilize them for campaign events and turning out to vote. In addition, the candidates who raised the most money were the most active in posting material to their Facebook walls. Having more money makes it more likely to have the resources to fund a professional campaign, which today includes the adoption of social media. More money also makes more resources available to hire staff dedicated to managing the content on the social media sites on a regular basis.

The results in the sixth row of data displaying the coefficients for the partisanship of the district in Model 3 show that there is no statistically significant relationship at the .05 level between the Democratic advantage in the district and Facebook activity. The coefficients in the model without an estimate for birth year show a negative relationship, however. This finding indicates that the user community influences the candidates' level of activity on Facebook. Furthermore and once again, we see that the findings for how candidates are using Facebook at the late majority stage are similar to what was observed for adoption at a similar point of diffusion (Williams and Gulati 2013). They also show that decisions about adoption and use are subject to different calculations.

The candidate's gender, race, and age all influenced how active the candidates were on Facebook during the final nine weeks of the campaign. Women, whites, and younger candidates were more active than were men, nonwhites, and older candidates. Omitting age from the model continued to show that white candidates were more active, but gender was significant only at the .10 level. On the whole, however, the results indicate that the candidates' personal characteristics are important factors for understanding which candidates are more active on Facebook.

Why and What Campaigns Communicate through Facebook

We now turn to our interviews with candidates to understand the reasons that candidates adopted (or did not adopt) Facebook and other social media and how they intended to use social media in their campaigns. We also asked the representatives of the campaigns how they actually were using it. What will become clear is that few of the intended uses are put into practice once the campaign is under way.

The most frequent reason that the candidates gave for adopting social media in their campaigns was that they felt it was either necessary or important for any congressional campaign. For example, one campaign representative noted, "I have found the power of social media to be increasing with each election season, and it has come to a point where it is an essential part to any campaign."[8] Another campaign pointed out that the simple act of having a presence on social media is a key part of today's elections; when voters cannot find their candidates on social media, it is sometimes off-putting, and they may go as far as to become wary of the legitimacy of the campaign because there is no page for voters to check.[9]

The second-most-common reason for adopting social media cited by our respondents was that it offered a cost-effective means of conducting traditional campaign activities: "Because [my opponent] is able to raise so much money, I need to find alternative ways to sway voters, and Twitter and Facebook are nearly my only opportunity to do so."[10]

Another campaign bemoaned the fact that it was being outspent by a 20-to-1 ratio, and social media provided a low-cost platform capable of reaching dedicated supporters.[11] But the bottom line for most campaigns that mentioned cost was that "social media is the best way to campaign because it is free."[12]

A slight majority of campaigns we interviewed indicated that they were using social media to target a specific group. There was no one group or constituency that stood out as being targeted, however. When a specific group was mentioned, youth and the campaign's supporters and or volunteers were the most common responses. But nearly half of the respondents indicated that they were targeting everyone or no one in particular. Social media are no longer the exclusive province of young voters, although they still are a target of candidates' social media use. In this respect, social media are viewed by campaigns as a vehicle for reaching out to a different demographic group than the audiences that traditional media address.

We turn next to candidates' relationship with voters and the kinds of participatory opportunities social media communications offer. Just over two-thirds of the campaigns said they were using Facebook to reach out and connect with voters by informing them about the candidate's issue positions, educating them about his or her record, or informing them about campaign events. "The things he posts are mainly informational and about himself," one staffer said about a candidate.[13] More specifically, another campaign said that it used social media "just enough and released information that voters wanted to see—for example, pictures of events and speeches, . . . things that are relevant to them and things that they care about."[14] As noted earlier, these communications were not targeted and did not appear to be responding to voters' own concerns or preferences. Nor were they meant to start a dialogue or other two-way interaction. Rather, these self-described efforts were one-directional, that is, pushing content at voters: "The goal was to build brand awareness for the candidate and get [the] name out into the limelight of politics."[15]

Engagement consists of two-way, interactive communication. Some campaigns reported that they made explicit efforts to solicit and respond to voters' feedback. One campaign claimed that its goal "was to make the Facebook page an interactive one"; it "wanted people not just to go on the Facebook page but be active on it."[16] Another campaign realized that social media "allows constituents to express concerns and ask the candidate questions, and that constituent connection was the way to build a strong campaign."[17] According to another, "I like using Facebook because it is easy for me to contact the voters and for the voters to contact me in a public atmosphere. By answering the question of one voter on Facebook, I am actually indirectly speaking to all the voters, which is an amazing opportunity."[18]

These were the exceptions, however, and most of the campaigns we interviewed that claimed that they wanted to be active on Facebook also noted that these efforts were made infrequently. Our interview responses indicate that social media are not being used to create an interactive relationship between campaigns and the voting public. Although social media have the potential and capacity to restructure how candidates and voters communicate, they are not being leveraged to do so. Jennifer Stromer-Galley (2000) points out that interactive communication is resource intensive, and many campaigns avoid it. And indeed, almost all of the congressional campaigns we interviewed reminded us that they did not have large staffs or dedicated social media staff members who could assist in responding to voters in such personalized communications.

Our next related question is whether campaigns are using social media to create different kinds of participatory opportunities for voters. Although enhancing mobilization efforts is another way that campaigns traditionally used the Internet and social media specifically, very few of the campaigns we interviewed used Facebook for this purpose. When mobilizing acts were mentioned, the most commonly referenced were attending events, donating money, and volunteering. Only two campaigns indicated that they conducted research on their Facebook profile pages, despite the availability of statistics about the number of visitors and what they liked or posted. One of these campaigns said it "used the feedback/results from the Facebook page to calculate hits, visits, likes, and what pages/issues people generally were concerned with by seeing who was talking about what and how many people who visited [the candidate's] website were directed from the link on his Facebook page."[19] Another campaign was more informal: "The main thing we looked at closely was how big and how quick of a following [the candidate] got during key points of the election, i.e., after local debates, larger press events."[20] Campaigns' failure to use social media to do much more than promote event attendance is an obvious missed opportunity. Nor are the kinds of participatory activities referenced by campaigns different in ways that leverage the strengths and features of social media. They merely represent a migration of traditional off-line behaviors to the online environment. Although Howard Dean (Kerbel 2009), Barack Obama (Cornfield 2010; Gibson 2012; Karlsen 2013), and Ron Paul (Stirland 2007, 2008) found creative ways to mobilize supporters in online activities, we are not yet seeing this in congressional campaigns.

Conclusions and Implications

Our objectives in this chapter were to identify whether any patterns characterized the few remaining nonadopters of Facebook in the 2012 congressional elections, which types of candidates were more likely to use Facebook, and some of the specific ways that it was being used. We found that nearly all of the candidates for the U.S. Senate and a large majority of the candidates for the House of Representatives had a Facebook page. Among major-party candidates, 97% of the candidates for the Senate were on Facebook, and 90% of the candidates for the House were on Facebook for the 2012 races for Congress. Our logistic regression models of *Facebook Adoption* for House candidates revealed that there were no differences between Republicans and Democrats. Incumbents were significantly more likely to be adopters than were challengers or open-seat candidates. In addition, Facebook adopters were younger, had greater financial resources, and were running in more competitive races. Together these findings indicate that at this late developmental stage, nonadoption persists in situations that characterize weak campaigns.

Our count models of *Facebook Activity* for House candidates revealed some very different patterns than what we observed for acquiring a page. Democrats and nonincumbents were more active on Facebook than were Republicans and incumbents. More active candidates had raised more money and were running in more competitive races. There also was some evidence to suggest that candidates running in more conservative districts were more active on Facebook than were candidates running in more liberal districts. Personal characteristics mattered as well: younger, female, and white candidates were more likely to adopt than were older, male, and nonwhite candidates. This is one of the first studies to show that social media use is a function of candidates' personal characteristics.

Our analysis of Facebook activity confirms expectations from diffusion of innovation theory that the factors influencing early adopters differ from those influencing those who adopt at later stages. At the same time, most of the same factors that predicted early adoption in past election cycles, when the technology was new, also predicted who more aggressively used the innovation in 2012, confirming another expectation from diffusion of innovation theory. Finally, to the extent that Facebook is more in line with the Democratic Party's base and grassroots campaign style, this finding offers evidence that the compatibility of the technology with existing systems, processes, and practices affects use. Money improves the absorptive capacity of an organization, and the importance of personal characteristics confirms that individual capabilities also play a role in use.

Another major contribution of our research is that we uncovered a number of interesting insights into why candidates choose to adopt social media and the ways they use it, insights not previously gleaned from estimates generated with statistical models. Our interviews with representatives of 91 campaigns for the House revealed that campaigns adopt social media in order to communicate their message to the voting public and to engage and mobilize their supporters. Larger strategic goals did not seem to be a major motivator of adoption. Most of the campaigns said that they did not see Facebook or the other social media as necessary or important for winning, and some were either unfavorable or skeptical toward social media's strategic value. Although our statistical models showed that candidates running in competitive races were more likely to adopt Facebook, very few of the candidates who have adopted Facebook see how it can be used to win votes or as necessary for winning.

With Facebook adoption approaching a near universal rate, studies primarily focused on identifying who is more likely to adopt offer little new insight about modern campaign practices. Moreover, many of the candidates who officially are identified as adopters have only acquired a page and are not using it as a means of communication or mobilization. Among those who have adopted Facebook as a campaign tool, there is considerable variation in how actively they use it to communicate and engage with supporters and beyond. Our interviews revealed that although many of the candidates see Facebook as a platform that is conducive for mobilization and engagement and have every intention of using it for those means, for the most part very few candidates do use Facebook and other social media in this way and most have a very limited understanding of social media's capabilities.

Diffusion of innovation theory offers an explanation for how organizational and strategic attributes influence the decision to adopt new technologies and how campaigns use those technologies to further their electoral goals. Our interviews with candidates and staff from the 2012 campaigns provide a richer explanation for the motivation behind candidates' decisions to adopt social media and problems experienced in implementation. We urge others to follow this approach to learn more about how and why candidates adopt social media and how that is changing as the medium matures. At this point in social media's evolutionary path, its transformative potential for elections and democracy is not being realized to any great extent. We are not yet seeing much change in the nature of the relationship between candidates and voters. Campaigns do not seem to be using Facebook in a targeted way to reach out to different or specific groups, nor do they seem to be mobilizing and engaging citizens in different or more kinds of activities through Facebook. That is the next frontier for campaign communications.

Appendix: Semistructured Interview Protocol

A. [Organization] How is the social media team organized?
   a. How much staff is dedicated to the team, backgrounds of staff, resources, etc.?
   b. What is the decision-making process for placing content on the social media sites? How is this physically done? Is this a team effort? How involved is the candidate? How often are the sites updated? How is information from the site used, assuming that it is actually viewed?
B. [Motivations] Why have they adopted social media?
   a. What is it that they hope to accomplish?
   b. Are they targeting certain groups?
   c. Do they feel that social media helps them win votes?
C. [Use] How are they using social media? Are they actually doing anything with the information they obtain from their users or see posted on the sites? How does this process work?
D. For those who are not using social media, why have they not adopted, and how might they be doing some of the same functions in other ways?

Notes

1. Data are provided by the eBizMBA. The most up-to-date rankings and traffic statistics for Facebook and other popular social media sites can be found at http://www.ebizmba.com/articles/most-popular-websites.
2. Ryan Alexander, social media director for Sen. Evan Bayh, telephone interview, October, 18, 2006.
3. Ezra Calahan and Chris Hughes, Facebook executives, telephone interview, October 24, 2006.
4. A parallel, earlier literature exists in political science. See, for example, Hage and Aiken 1967; Mohr 1969; Walker 1969; Gray 1973.
5. Candidates were identified initially by monitoring Politics1.com and several other political websites that maintained candidate lists. We later cross-referenced our list with election-day results reported on *Politico* (http://www.politico.com/2012-election/map/#/House/2012/).
6. See Cook Political Report, "House: 2012 Race Ratings Chart Archive," http://cookpolitical.com/archive/charts/house/race-ratings/2012 (accessed August 12, 2014); Sabato's Crystal Ball, "Recent House Analysis / 2014 House Ratings," December 13, 2012, http://www.centerforpolitics.org/crystalball/articles/category/2012-house/; and Real Clear Politics, "Battle for the House," 2012, http://www.realclearpolitics.com/epolls/2012/house/2012_elections_house_map.html.
7. See David Wasserman, "Introducing the 2014 Cook Political Report Partisan Voter Index," Cook Political Report, April 4, 2013, http://cookpolitical.com/house/pvi.
8. Rep. Colleen Hanabusa (D-HI), telephone interview, October 24, 2012.
9. Staff member for Rep. Morgan Griffith (R-VA), telephone interview, October 29, 2012.
10. Lance Enderle (D-MI), telephone interview, October 15, 2012.
11. Christopher Sheldon (R-MA), telephone interview, October 1, 2012.
12. Ann Kirkpatrick (D-AZ), telephone interview, November 1, 2012.
13. Staff member, Rep. Jose Serrano (D-NY), telephone interview, November 1, 2012.
14. Mike Lukach, campaign manager for Judy Biggert (R-IL), telephone interview, November 30, 2012.
15. Alisia Essig, press secretary for Mia Love (R-UT), telephone interview, December 4, 2012.
16. Staff member for Paul Hirschbiel (D-VA), telephone interview, October 1, 2012.
17. Staff member for Rep. Debbie Wasserman Schultz (D-FL), telephone interview, November 1, 2012.
18. Jonathan Paton (R-AZ), telephone interview, November 1, 2012.
19. Jack Uppal (D-CA), telephone interview, October 24, 2012.
20. Alisia Essig, press secretary for Mia Love (R-UT), telephone interview, December 4, 2012.

References

Cohen, Wesley M., and Daniel A. Levinthal. 1990. "Absorptive Capacity: A New Perspective on Learning and Innovation." *Administrative Science Quarterly* 35:128–152.

Cooper, Randolph B., and Robert W. Zmud. 1990. "Information Technology Implementation Research: A Technological Diffusion Approach." *Management Science* 36:123–139.

Cornfield, Michael. 2010. "Game-Changers: New Technology and the 2008 Presidential Election." In *The Year of Obama: How Barack Obama Won the White House*, edited by Larry J. Sabato, 77–89. Upper Saddle River, NJ: Pearson.

Davis, Fred D., Richard P. Bagozzi, and Paul R. Warshaw. 1989. "User Acceptance of Computer Technology: A Comparison of Two Theoretical Models." *Management Science* 35:982–1003.

Dholakia, Ruby R., and Nir Kshetri. 2004. "Factors Impacting the Adoption of the Internet among SMEs." *Small Business Economics* 23:311–322.

Fichman, Robert G. 1992. "Information Technology Diffusion: A Review of Empirical Research." *Proceedings of the Thirteenth International Conference on Information Systems*, edited by Janice I. DeGross, Jack D. Becker, and Joyce J. Elam, 195–206. Dallas, TX: ACM.

———. 2004. "Going beyond the Dominant Paradigm for Information Technology Innovation Research: Emerging Concepts and Methods." *Journal of the Association for Information Systems* 5:314–355.

Foot, Kirsten A., and Steven M. Schneider. 2006. *Web Campaigning*. Cambridge: MIT Press.

Frambach, Ruud T., and Niels Schillewaert. 2002. "Organizational Innovation Adoption: A Multi-level Framework of Determinants and Opportunities for Future Research." *Journal of Business Research* 55:163–176.

Gibson, Rachel. 2012. "From Brochureware to 'MyBo': An Overview of Online Elections and Campaigning." *Politics* 32:77–84.

Goode, Sigi, and Kenneth Stevens. 2000. "An Analysis of the Business Characteristics of Adopters and Non-adopters of World Wide Web Technology." *Information Technology and Management* 1:129–154.

Gray, Virginia. 1973. "Innovation in the States: A Diffusion Study." *American Political Science Review* 67:1174–1185.

Gulati, Girish J., and Christine B. Williams. 2009. "Closing Gaps, Moving Hurdles: Candidate Web Site Communication in the 2006 Campaigns for Congress." In *Politicking Online: The Transformation of Election Campaign Communications*, edited by Costas Panagopoulos, 48–76. New Brunswick: Rutgers University Press.

———. 2011. "Diffusion of Innovations and Online Campaigns: Social Media Adoption in the 2010 U.S. Congressional Elections." Paper presented at the sixth general conference of the European Consortium for Political Research, Reykjavik, Iceland, August 26.

Hage, Jerald, and Michael Aiken. 1967. "Program Change and Organizational Properties: A Comparative Analysis." *American Journal of Sociology* 72:503–516.

Hall, Laura, John Dunkelberger, Wilder Ferreira, J. Walter Prevatt, and Neil R. Martin. 2003. "Diffusion-Adoption of Personal Computers and the Internet in Farm Business Decisions: Southeastern Beef and Peanut Farmers." *Journal of Extension* 41 (3). http://www.joe.org/joe/2003june/a6.shtml.

Hong, Se-Joon, and Kar Yan Tam. 2006. "Understanding the Adoption of Multipurpose Information Appliances: The Case of Mobile Data Services." *Information Systems Research* 17:162–179.

Karlsen, Rune. 2013. "Obama's Online Success and European Party Organizations: Adoption and Adaptation of U.S. Online Practices in the Norwegian Labor Party." *Journal of Information Technology & Politics* 10:158–170.

Kerbel, Matthew R. 2009. *Netroots: Online Progressives and the Transformation of American Politics*. Boulder, CO: Paradigm.

Kwon, T. H., and Robert W. Zmud. 1987. "Unifying the Fragmented Models of Information Systems Implementation." In *Critical Issues in Information Systems Research*, edited by Richard Boland and Rudy Hirshheim, 227–251. New York: Wiley.

Läpple, Doris, and Tom Van Rensburg. 2011. "Adoption of Organic Farming: Are There Differences between Early and Late Adoption?" *Ecological Economics* 70:1406–1414.

Laukkanen, Tommi, and Mika Pasanen. 2007. "Mobile Banking Innovators and Early Adopters: How They Differ from Other Online Users?" *Journal of Financial Services Marketing* 13:86–94.

Meyer, Alan D., and James B. Goes. 1988. "Organizational Assimilation or Innovations: A Multilevel Contextual Analysis." *Academy of Management Journal* 31:897–923.

Mohr, Lawrence. B. 1969. "Determinants of Innovation in Organizations." *American Political Science Review* 63:111–126.

Peterson, Rolfe Daus. 2012. "To Tweet or Not to Tweet: Exploring the Determinants of Early Adoption of Twitter by House Members in the 111th Congress." *Social Science Journal* 49: 430–438.

Rainie, Lee, and Aaron Smith. 2012. "Politics on Social Networking Sites." Pew Internet and American Life Project, September 4.

Rogers, Everett M. 2003. *Diffusion of Innovations*. 5th ed. New York: Free Press.

Stirland, Sarah Lai. 2007. "Ron Paul Supporters Make History with $6 Million Online Haul—Updated." *Wired*, December 17. http://www.wired.com/threatlevel/2007/12/ron-paul-suppor/.

———. 2008. "Supporters Mull Over Internet Candidate Ron Paul's Fifth Place in Presidential Campaign's Opening Race." *Wired*, January 4. http://www.wired.com/threatlevel/2008/01/supporters-mull/.

Stromer-Galley, Jennifer. 2000. "On-line Interaction and Why Candidates Avoid It." *Journal of Communication* 50:111–132.

Uhl, Kenneth, Roman Andrus, and Lance Poulsen. 1970. "How Are Laggards Different? An Empirical Inquiry." *Journal of Marketing Research* 7:51–54.

Venkatesh, Viswanath, Michael G. Morris, and Phillip L. Ackerman. 2000. "A Longitudinal Field Investigation of Gender in Individual Technology Adoption Decision-Making Processes." *Organizational Behavior and Human Decision Processes* 83:33–60.

Walker, Jack L. 1969. "The Diffusion of Innovations among the American States." *American Political Science Review* 63:880–899.

Williams, Christine B., and Girish J. Gulati. 2013. "Social Networks in Political Campaigns: Facebook and the Congressional Elections of 2006 and 2008." *New Media & Society* 15:52–71.

3

Surrogates or Competitors?
Social Media Use by Independent Political Actors

JULIA R. AZARI AND BENJAMIN A. STEWART

The rise of social media has provided both an opportunity and a challenge for national campaigns.[1] This new medium allows independent groups to reach important constituencies. These groups may act as surrogates for official campaigns, echoing and amplifying the official message of the two presidential campaigns. However, social media can also make it more difficult for campaigns to control the message. Our research question concerns whether these independent political sources used social media in 2012 to act as campaign surrogates or as competitors for control of the campaign message.[2] We focus on the use of Twitter to issue what we call *election narratives*, messages about the meaning and significance of the election.

Campaign Surrogates or Campaign Competitors?

We posit that campaign surrogate behavior can take several forms. Surrogates can play the role of attack dog, going after opponents in ways that would be politically risky for candidates or party organizations. They can also play the role of cheerleader, pointing out the candidate's strengths and victories. In either case, our analysis rests on the assumption that campaign surrogates will tailor their election message to closely follow the election narratives emphasized by the campaign. This also means that organizations acting as campaign surrogates will follow the campaign's issue focus, thus helping the campaign remain "on message."

Alternately, independent groups can act as competitors, challenging the official campaign message. The nature of social media offers independent actors ample opportunity to act as competitors. The new media environment, including social media, allows for what communications scholars have identified as "audience fragmentation," allowing readers to choose content on the basis of topic and point of view (Tewksbury 2005; Baum and Groeling 2008). The implications of audience fragmentation for our research question are twofold. First, to the extent that independent groups might have their own agendas, using social media allows them to make their cases to those who are most likely to agree with them—those who have already chosen to "follow" or "like" them. Second, these groups may target the most ideological factions in their parties; recent scholarship suggests that the growing strength of issue-oriented activist groups is at least partially responsible for the polarization of American party politics since the 1970s (Masket 2009; Layman, Carsey, and Horowitz 2006). Social media present an opportunity for these independent groups not to act as campaign mouthpieces but rather to break from the official narrative and pursue their own ends.

Existing scholarly debates about the impact of social media on American politics have generally been focused on two ways in which social media differ from traditional forms of mass communication. Scholars of political behavior and participation have examined the interactive aspect of sites such as Facebook and Twitter (Carlisle and Patton 2013). More institutionally focused scholars have devoted attention to the ways in which social media allow candidates more control over their own messages in the absence of the "gatekeeping" of traditional media (Gainous and Wagner 2013, 5–6) and have evaluated the use of social media as a campaign tool (Gulati and Williams 2011). Our study speaks primarily to the latter set of debates, evaluating how different types of elite actors use social media during an election campaign and assessing how independent groups affect candidates' ability to control the campaign message.

In order to apply our theory to the case of social media use in 2012, we test three basic hypotheses. Our first hypothesis is that, if acting as surrogates, independent sources would invoke the same issues and ideas as campaign groups when describing the stakes of the election.

Our second hypothesis concerns responses to campaign events. We posit that independent organizations, if acting in the surrogate mold, should respond to campaign events as cheerleaders and attack dogs. When campaign events reflect poorly on their preferred candidates, we expect that independent organizations will come to their defense. When events offer an opportunity to attack an opponent, we expect that independent actors will seize on that opportunity in attack-dog fashion, mentioning the event in their social media use and connecting it to broader election narratives. A corollary to this hypothesis posits that independent groups will not produce social media content that conflicts with the official narrative concerning campaign events.

Finally, we hypothesize that after the election, independent sources on the winning side would need to echo and amplify the messages of the official victors in order to act as campaign surrogates. For the losing side, we would expect surrogates to act as cheerleaders, issuing messages that emphasize the necessity of moving forward or stressing the difficulty of the contest and the formidable nature of the opposing side. At the same time, a version of attack-dog behavior might also surface after the election for surrogate organizations: independent actors might find themselves uniquely poised to challenge the mandate narratives of the winning side.

Research Methods and Design

We draw our inferences from a comparison of campaign and independent groups' use of Twitter to construct election narratives during the 2012 campaign. Such narratives can present the election in a variety of ways: as a retrospective referendum on the incumbent's performance in office, a competition between competing visions of policy, or a contest between the leadership qualities of the two candidates, to name a few possibilities (Azari and Vaughn 2013). Independent groups are defined as those that did not represent a politician running for office or a national party organization. This group included media organizations and personalities, as well as 501(c)3 organizations, such as American Crossroads, which operate independently of official campaigns. Campaign organizations were those affiliated with a candidate or party organization.

In order to make these inferences, we constructed two samples, one for liberal organizations and one for conservative organizations. The composition of this sample is shown in table 3.1. For detailed information about how we constructed our sample, see appendix A. The liberal sample included two campaign sources: the official Barack Obama campaign and the Democratic National Committee (DNC). The independent sources in this sample included mostly media organizations: *Rachel Maddow Show Blog*, run by MSNBC television host Maddow; the *Nation*, a liberal newsmagazine in print since 1865; *Salon*, a progressive online newsmagazine founded in 1995; the *Young Turks*, a phenomenon of the more recent new media movement; and *Daily Kos*, a popular liberal blog founded by Markos Moulitsas in 2002. The liberal sample also included *New York Times* columnist Paul Krugman, the reproductive-rights organization Planned Parenthood, and the Hispanic interest group National Council of La Raza.

The conservative sample consisted of a similar mix. On the campaign side, we looked at tweets from the Romney campaign and from the Republican National

Table 3.1. Summary of Groups by Ideology and Affiliation

Campaign, Liberal Groups/Individuals	Campaign, Conservative Groups/Individuals
Barack Obama	Mitt Romney
Democratic National Committee	Republican National Committee
Independent, Liberal Groups/Individuals	**Independent, Conservative Groups/Individuals**
Salon	Fox Nation
Rachel Maddow Show Blog	Laura Ingraham
Daily Kos	Michelle Malkin
Young Turks	Townhall.com
the *Nation*	National Review
Planned Parenthood	Susan B. Anthony List
National Council of La Raza	Sarah Palin
	American Crossroads
	Americans for Prosperity
	Heritage Foundation

Committee (RNC). The independent sources included *Fox Nation*, the social media mouthpiece of the conservative cable network Fox News; individual commentators Sarah Palin, Michelle Malkin, and Laura Ingraham; the online conservative news page Townhall.com; and conservative newsmagazine *National Review*, founded in 1954. Also included were several interest groups, including the Heritage Foundation and the Susan B. Anthony List, a prolife interest group. Finally, our sample included two independent political action committees, American Crossroads and Americans for Prosperity. This data allowed us to conduct simple quantitative analyses as well as qualitative assessments. We test our first hypothesis by comparing how campaign and independent groups frame the stakes of the election. Our basic unit of analysis is the issue message—on rare occasions, a tweet can contain multiple issue messages (see appendix B). We compare the overall percentage of issue messages that cover a particular topic, such as social issues, foreign policy, or the economy, for campaign and independent groups over the eight weeks leading up to Election Day (see appendix C for detailed presentation of the data).

For the campaign events hypothesis, we examine the social media response to two events that occurred in September 2012. We look at the response to one event that reflected negatively on the Romney campaign, the release of a video that included the candidate's remarks about "47%" of the population that many people perceived to be harsh and unfair. We also include the attacks on the U.S. embassy in Libya and the subsequent questions that arose about the nature of the attacks and the Obama administration's response to them. These events were chosen for two reasons. First, each has relevance for important areas of policy (taxes and social welfare programs in Romney's case, terrorism and national security in Obama's case). Second, these events were relevant to existing narratives about the weaknesses of each candidate. Romney's detractors (including, of course, the Obama campaign) had sought throughout the campaign to depict him as callous and unconcerned with middle-class and poor Americans. In the spring of 2012, for instance, the Obama campaign ran an advertisement in which steel workers described how they lost their jobs after Bain Capital, a company Romney led, took over their employer (Trinko 2012; Mullany 2012). Romney's remarks fit into this existing narrative. For Obama's part, the Libya attacks played into a narrative among opponents that the president was weak and incompetent in foreign affairs (Rove and Gillespie 2012). In order to test our second hypothesis, we also look at the social media response to the three presidential and one vice presidential debate, positing that debates should provide independent organizations with opportunities to act as both attack dogs and cheerleaders. Finally, in order to test our third hypothesis about postelection narratives, we examine and compare social media content produced by independent and campaign sources during the two weeks after the election.

Although this data-collection effort has allowed us to analyze social media use during and after the 2012 campaign, it also highlights some of the challenges of social media research. In particular, our study highlights the difficulty of understanding principal-agent relationships in social media research. In other words, while we explore "who is controlling the message," it is actually very difficult to observe the genesis of social media messages. The Twitter posts assessed in this study were published under the names of campaigns, media outlets, and interest groups. Yet this data-gathering process tells us nothing about the process by which social media messages were crafted within these operations. Are social media messages carefully crafted by highly skilled teams of communications professionals? Or are they treated as an afterthought? Are processes for social media content similar across organizations? In other words, it is difficult to ascertain whose ideas social media messages reflect and transmit.

Differences in Issue Coverage

The use of social media allows politicians, parties, media, and interest groups to send frequent messages about the stakes of the election. In the 2012 campaign, these messages included traditional policy areas, such as economic policy, foreign policy, social issues, trade, energy, health care, and immigration. They also linked the election to other, nonpolicy ideas. One such idea was the future of the nation overall, which we included as its own category. We also included an "other" category, which encompassed much of the social media traffic about the candidates' beliefs, character, and statements. This category also included comments about actions the candidates might take in office that were not related to specific issues, such as Supreme Court appointments. From there, we divided our data into four subsets: liberal-campaign, liberal-independent, conservative-campaign, and conservative-independent. We calculated the total number of issue messages for each subset during the eight weeks leading up to the election. We then calculated the percentage of messages from each category during the eight-week period, again for each subset. Figures 3.1 and 3.2 show the average percentages for each issue over the eight-week period, broken down by campaign and independent groups.

For liberal groups, shown in figure 3.1, only two issues had statistically significant differences in coverage between campaign and independent sources. One was discussions of the election in terms of the country's future ($p < .05$). In this case, independent groups almost never referred to the election in these terms, and campaign groups rarely did (less than 1% of issue messages on average). Perhaps more importantly, there exists a significant difference between the inclusion of social issues in election narratives between campaign and independent groups ($p < .05$). For both campaign and independent social media

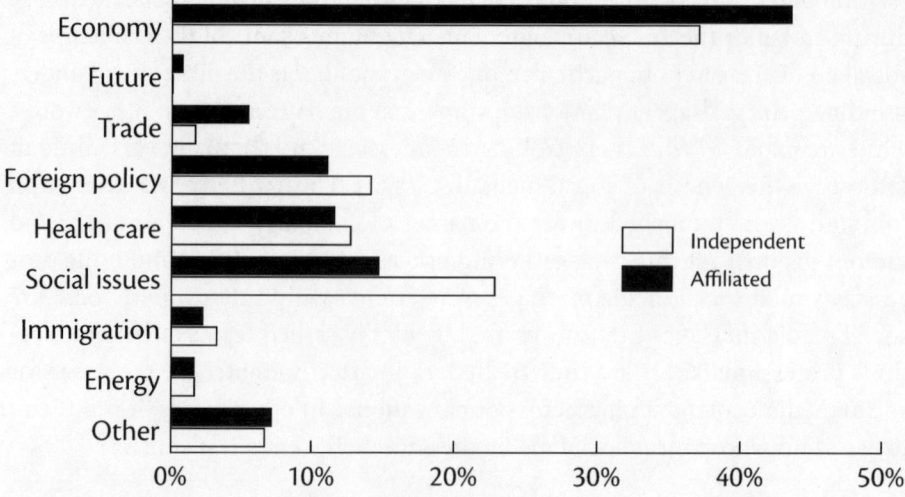

Figure 3.1. Liberal groups and preelection issue coverage

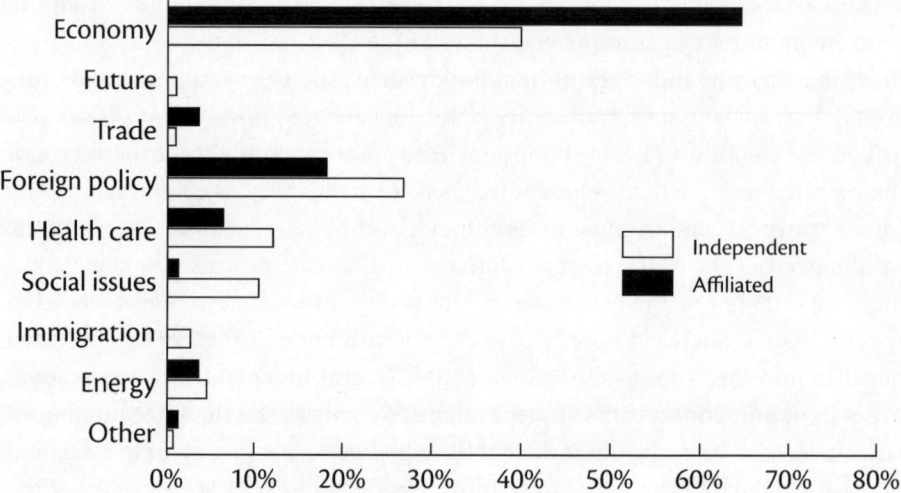

Figure 3.2. Conservative groups and preelection issue coverage

sources, coverage of social issues, such as abortion, LGBT (lesbian, gay, bisexual, and trans) rights, and contraception, came in second only to the economy in terms of percentage of issue messaging. (By contrast, for conservatives, social issues received less coverage than did the economy, foreign policy, health care, and, on the campaign side, energy.) Both campaign and independent sources devoted attention to social issues, often stressing similar themes. For example, after the Senate candidate Richard Mourdock made controversial comments about rape and abortion, the Obama campaign tweeted that Romney's social policies were from the 1950s (Obama 2012b). Earlier in the campaign, the DNC touted the repeal of the so-called Don't Ask, Don't Tell policy concerning gay service members (2012b). The substance of tweets and posts from independent groups resembled an attack-dog posture, pointing out that Romney was losing with women (*Daily Kos* 2012d) and claiming that "Romney's extreme positions insult us" (*Nation* 2012a).

Independent conservative sources appear to have used social media to craft a somewhat different narrative about the stakes of the 2012 election than did campaign sources. The Romney campaign and the RNC overwhelmingly stressed economic issues and pushed for a narrative of the election as a referendum on Obama's economic performance. Over the eight weeks surveyed in the analysis, economic issues constituted an average of 64% of tweets from Romney and the RNC. On the other hand, independent commentators mentioned economic issues only 39% on average ($p < .01$). Also, although the differences were not statistically significant, independent groups offered more commentary about health care and foreign policy. Independent groups also devoted a higher percentage of tweets to social issues. Romney and the RNC devoted hardly any tweets to abortion, gender issues, or the gay-rights question, averaging 1.4% of issue messages over eight weeks. These messages included the Romney campaign touting its support from Catholic leaders (Romney 2012b), as well as efforts by the RNC to link the Obama campaign to rapper Jay-Z (2012b) and to illegal guns used in the botched "Fast and Furious" operation.

In contrast, independent groups mentioned social issues in more than 10% of their issue messages. The Susan B. Anthony List, an independent prolife group, frequently addressed Obama's record on the abortion issue in its Twitter posts, referring to Obama as the "most pro-abortion president ever" (2012a) and citing his position on the issue as a deterrent for independent voters; Michelle Malkin (2012b), *Fox Nation* (2012c), and Townhall.com (2012a) similarly criticized the president for his connections with Planned Parenthood. Other social issue messages were positive, such as Laura Ingraham's tweet quoting New Jersey governor Chris Christie as saying that Romney was "deeply committed to the pro-life agenda" (2012b).

We argue that the disparity in the treatment of social issues between campaign and independent sources has important implications for the surrogate-competitor question. Due to the salience and emotional impact of social issues, they had an especially high likelihood of detracting and distracting from the official election narrative. For example, a *USA Today* / Gallup poll in 2012 found that a plurality of registered female voters in "twelve key swing states" listed abortion as the most important issue in the election (Dugan 2012). Furthermore, the fall of 2012 was a challenging time for Republicans and social issues. The tone was set in August when Missouri Senate candidate Todd Akin made controversial comments about rape and abortion, prompting Romney and the RNC to distance themselves from the candidate and the issue (Costa 2012). In sum, it seems likely that the Romney campaign and the RNC preferred to keep the focus generally trained on Obama's economic performance, while avoiding hot-button issues such as abortion and same-sex marriage.

Reaction to Campaign Events

As the 2012 campaign unfolded, several events occurred that had the potential to change or shape the narrative about the meaning and stakes of the election. The revelation of Mitt Romney's remarks at a Republican fundraiser about the "47%" of Americans who would always be dependent on government, the attacks on the U.S. embassy in Benghazi, and the four debates constitute such events. We find that in each case, independent sources were more responsive than their were campaign counterparts, although the difference was most pronounced in the case of the Benghazi attacks, in which independent sources on both sides embraced the attack-dog role.

Romney's "47%" Remarks

On September 17, 2012, journalists discovered a video from a Republican fundraising dinner the previous May. In the video, Romney, who presumably did not know he was being recorded, stated, "There are 47 percent of the people who will vote for the president no matter what . . . who are dependent upon government, who believe that they are victims. . . . These are people who pay no income tax. . . . And so my job is not to worry about those people. I'll never convince them that they should take personal responsibility and care for their lives" (Capehart 2012). The remarks attracted a great deal of media and public attention and appeared to have an impact on public evaluations of Romney as a candidate (Newport 2012).

In using social media to comment on the remarks, campaign and independent sources made similar choices. On September 17, when the story broke, the Obama campaign mentioned Romney's comments, as did the *Rachel Maddow Show Blog* (2012c) and *Salon* (2012a). The next day, the narrative began to take shape. The Obama campaign issued a comment via Twitter that it was "for all Americans, not just 53%" (2012a). Independent sources adopted a similar line, although their lack of formal affiliation with the campaign allowed them to more directly link the comments to the trajectory of the election. *Daily Kos* referred to the comments as "the day Mitt Romney lost the election" (2012b), and *Salon* maintained that Romney was "self-destructing" in the wake of the comments (2012a). The comments remained a substantial part of the social media conversation for another week; Obama and the DNC tweeted about them during the week of September 25, and left-wing media sources, including *Salon* and *Daily Kos*, made comments such as "this is why Romney is losing" (*Salon* 2012b) and "he still doesn't get it" (*Daily Kos* 2012c).

The social media response to Mitt Romney's "47%" remarks was, in sum, quite similar across campaign and independent actors. Both groups responded quickly to the story and continued to tweet about it for about a week and a half. Obama and the DNC attacked Romney for his remarks and used them to draw contrasts between the two candidates. A subtle difference between campaign and independent sources, however, is the way that independent sources took a slightly harsher tone and made stronger causal arguments about the linkages between the attitudes revealed by the comments and Romney's predicted defeat. Different incentives likely led the two groups to vary in their depiction of the election; while the Obama campaign and other affiliated groups likely wanted to avoid portraying election victory as a foregone conclusion for fear of complacency and lost contributions, independent groups enjoyed more latitude to discuss "why Romney is losing." As a result, independent sources on the left began constructing a narrative of the election that drew on the "47%" incident and used these ideas to craft an explanation for Obama's victory long before the votes were cast or counted.

On the conservative side, the response to Romney's remarks was much more limited. The RNC and the Romney campaign said nothing about the remarks. Independent sources made a few attempts to defend Romney; Michelle Malkin said, "this election is about America's makers vs. America's takers. Romney should NEVER be defensive or apologetic about making that clear" (2012a). Sean Hannity commented on a remark that Obama had made in 1998 expressing a favorable opinion of "redistribution" (2012). Hannity's effort to offer a counterweight to the "47%" story fell short, however, insofar as the incident received little attention among the other independent conservatives in our sample.

Consular Attacks in Benghazi, Libya

The attacks against the United States' diplomatic mission in Benghazi, Libya, which occurred on the eleventh anniversary of the September 11, 2001, terrorist attacks, were initially presented to the American public as the result of a spontaneous response to an anti-Muslim video. It was eventually revealed, however, that the bombings, which resulted in the deaths of four Americans, had been planned rather than spontaneous. The tragic events themselves, combined with accusations that the administration had either blundered or lied about the nature of the attacks (Starr and Levine 2012), presented a challenge for the Obama campaign and its supporters and an opportunity for the Romney camp to question Obama's competence and honesty in foreign-policy matters.

Sources on the left used social media to respond to Republican reactions to the event. Controversy had broken out almost immediately as the attacks unfolded; still under the impression that the attacks were a response to an anti-Islamic video, the American embassy in Cairo issued a statement condemning "any intentional effort to denigrate religious beliefs." Romney attributed the statement to the administration and commented, "It's disgraceful that the Obama administration's first response was not to condemn attacks on our diplomatic missions, but to sympathize with those who waged the attacks" (*New York Times* 2012). With the picture of actual events still unclear, independent actors on the left used social media to respond to Romney's statement. Rachel Maddow, the first in our sample to comment, accused Romney of "digging deeper" instead of correcting his position, as the crisis unfolded (*Rachel Maddow Show Blog* 2012a). Such narratives can present the election in a variety of ways: as a retrospective referendum on the incumbent's performance in office, as a competition between competing visions of policy, or as a contest between the leadership qualities of the two candidates. *Daily Kos* suggested that Romney's remarks revealed that he was "not ready to be president" because of his choice to "play politics" with the events (2012a). On September 14, the DNC picked up this narrative, tweeting that Romney was "unpresidential" (2012a). The Obama campaign refrained from using Twitter to discuss these events.

Predictably, the dynamics on the right were somewhat different following the Libya attacks. Conservative media personalities quickly seized on the Benghazi story in order to criticize Obama's record on foreign policy. For example, Laura Ingraham defended the Romney comments, commenting, "Romney right to expose Obama when he did. Obama has emboldened our enemies and insulted our friends" (2012a).

After the week of September 11, the groups we followed on the left turned their focus to other topics and did not continue to engage with the Romney campaign or the conservative media on the emerging Benghazi story. Conservative groups continued to tweet about the story for several weeks, however. A week after the events, the *National Review* commented on "appeasement" and (American) "weakness" (2012a), while *Fox Nation* referred to the Benghazi attacks as terrorism (2012a). On the campaign side, the RNC tweeted, "State Department: Stop Asking Us about Benghazi" (2012a). These comments followed the development of the story well into October. For example, *Fox Nation* (2012b) and American Crossroads (2012a) both asked on October 9 about what the administration had known, and *National Review* stated that the administration was "in disgrace" over the events (2012b). Further, as we shall see in the next section, the debates offered new opportunities for conservative groups to discuss the administration's reaction to and culpability for the attacks.

The Benghazi attacks constituted a contingent campaign event with both policy implications and potential to shift the narrative of the campaign. Our evidence suggests that independent actors were the leaders in using social media to publicize a narrative criticizing the president's actions, as well as in defending the administration from criticism. Parties and candidates were slower to take to social media to discuss and examine the incident, although the RNC issued a series of tweets (about one per week) criticizing the president for failing to offer a clear and consistent story about what had transpired in Libya. In the weeks following this event, independent sources on both sides behaved like campaign surrogates.

Presidential and Vice Presidential Debates

In October 2012, Obama and Romney participated in three debates, while vice presidential candidates Joe Biden and Paul Ryan debated each other once. There is some evidence that debates constitute important campaign events, with the potential to alter at least some voters' perceptions and preferences (Geer 1988; Benoit, Hansen, and Verser 2003), and although most voters had decided whom to vote for by October, the 2012 debates still appeared to have some significance for the campaign. Jeffrey Jones of Gallup reported that Romney actually experienced an appreciable "bounce" in approval after the first debate, which Romney was generally thought to have won (Jones 2012).

After the first debate on October 3, a clear narrative emerged: Romney had won, and the president had lost. Of debate watchers, 72% reported that Romney had been the winner (Jones 2012). However, the debate appeared to have little impact on the narrative offered via social media on the left or the right. For example, although foreign policy played a negligible role in the first debate, the conservative groups in our sample, campaign and independent, continued to criticize the president's record in ways that were similar to their narrative before the debate. They also continued to repudiate Obama's foreign policy in the week after the debate; foreign policy accounted for about 16% of the issue messages during the week of October 2 (although this number was down from 23% the previous week). On October 9, the RNC tweeted that since the debate, Obama had not mentioned Libya once in his campaign speeches but had referred to *Sesame Street*, in light of Romney's debate comments that he favored cutting funding to PBS, thirteen times (2012c). On the left, we observe little effort among potential campaign surrogates to defend the president's debate performance or to attack Romney's statements.

After the final debate, we observe some additional campaign-surrogate behavior.[3] American Crossroads took on the attack role as it summed up all three presidential debates for its audience by noting that "the debates were proof that Obama has no record to run on" (2012b). On the liberal side, the DNC went on the attack, quoting the *New York Times*'s assertion that Romney had seemed "completely lost" in the foreign-policy debate (2012c). Independent sources were mostly quiet about the debate, although the *Young Turks* said that Obama's victory on foreign policy issues made him look "presidential" (2012).

We conclude that while the use of social media to respond to the debates was sparse overall, independent groups behaved more like campaign surrogates than competitors. They also appear to have followed the lead of the campaigns, issuing few messages about the debates in general. When they used social media, they embraced cheerleader and attack-dog roles. We found that this was also the case on both sides after the consular attacks in Libya; however, we found that independent conservative groups did not defend Romney after the "47%" remarks to the extent that we might have expected had they been acting as campaign surrogates.

Interpreting the Election Results

The final opportunity for independent groups to act as surrogates or competitors came after the election, when they had the chance to interpret the result. In the days and weeks following the 2012 election, campaign sources on the Democratic side made fairly strong statements interpreting the election as a mandate for the president's economic plans. On November 15, Obama used Twitter to claim, "I've got a mandate to help the middle class families, and families that are working to get into the middle class," quoting from a press conference the previous day (2012c). In most respects, the independent groups on the left acted as surrogates, repeating versions of this claim. The *Nation* tweeted on November 9 that "voters did not choose austerity" and that "voters want higher taxes on the wealthy" (2012b). Other liberal media outlets interpreted the victory in terms of the upcoming "fiscal cliff" debates in Congress. *Salon* tweeted that "Obama campaigned on ending Bush tax cuts" and "America didn't vote for a grand bargain" (2012c, 2012d) and echoed the president's comments about class, using even stronger "class warfare" language (2012f).

In a few instances, independent groups used social media to offer alternate ideas about the election's meaning. For example, Planned Parenthood said that the election had sent a message about women's ability to make their own health-care decisions (2012). In a similar issue vein, *Salon* tweeted a link to its own story about a woman in Ireland who was unable to obtain an abortion and subsequently died, quoting a comment from progressive filmmaker and activist Michael Moore: "What America voted against last week" (2012e). However, none of these alternate frames for the election seriously challenged the dominant economic and class-based message.

After Romney's election loss, neither the Romney campaign nor the RNC offered social media commentary on the reasons behind the result. However, on the independent side, several sources began to criticize what they saw as the central economic message of the election. On November 7, *National Review* tweeted "how Romney lost," with a link to a story claiming that "class warfare works" (2012c). The idea that the election result showed that the nation comprised "more takers than makers" appeared on the Twitter feeds of *Fox Nation*. *Fox Nation* also later quoted Rush Limbaugh saying that "it's very difficult to beat

Santa Claus" (2012e). Laura Ingraham quoted Jonah Goldberg of the *National Review* as stating that "the conservative cause is only lost if WE decide to give up" (2012c), and the Heritage Foundation urged its supporters to continue to "stand up and fight big government" (2012). *Fox Nation* also argued, quoting *Washington Post* columnist Charles Krauthammer, that there was "no mandate" because Obama had "gone small" during the election (2012d). With regard to issues other than the economy, the response was mixed. Townhall.com admitted that gay marriage had won at the ballot box (2012b), but the Susan B. Anthony List maintained that the Republicans should "return to fundamentals" of conservatism in foreign and social as well as economic policy (2012b). Similarly, Michelle Malkin urged the party not to abandon conservative ideals in favor of "identity politics" (2012d) and suggested that the GOP should avoid "amnesty" (2012b) and "Kabuki compromises" (2012c) in immigration policy.

Independent political organizations on the left appear to have embraced their role as surrogates in their use of Twitter to interpret the 2012 election result. There is little evidence that these groups veered away from official interpretations in order to promote their own agendas. The picture on the conservative side is more complicated, however. Campaign sources met the election defeat with social media silence, but independent sources had much to say over Twitter about the election result. Several of these messages questioned the choice of the electorate by making references to "takers" and "Santa Claus" and encouraging adherence to issue positions in the face of electoral defeat. These positions fit the competitor model better than the surrogate model. Surrogate behavior might involve interpreting the election in ways that undermine the victor's claim to a policy mandate, by emphasizing the role of incumbency or the modest economic recovery that accompanied Obama's reelection. Instead, commentators such as Malkin and Ingraham issued messages that found fault not with the candidate or the campaign but rather with the voters who had reelected the president.

Conclusion

The evidence presented here suggests that independent organizations act as campaign surrogates in several important ways. For Democrats, their issue coverage was very similar to that of official campaign organizations, and we found little evidence of efforts by liberal media or interest groups to challenge the official election narrative.

On the Republican side, we found a somewhat different pattern. Independent groups stressed different issues than the Romney campaign and the RNC did, devoting a smaller percentage of posts to the economy and a greater percentage to social issues. Independent organizations and outlets served as attack dogs after the Benghazi incident and the presidential debates. However, their fulfillment of the "cheerleader" role after the discovery of Romney's "47%" remarks was much more limited. Furthermore, the postelection narratives proffered by independent sources on the conservative side appear to have been designed to serve the agenda of the media organizations and interest groups in question, rather than the electoral interests of the Republican Party. In sum, conservative groups appear to have used social media to act as competitors more often than did their liberal counterparts.

There are several possible reasons for this disparity. First, our findings may reflect a deeper dynamic within the Republican Party, which has also been evident in recent struggles between economic and social conservatives, as well as competition between Tea Party and establishment factions of the party. However, the disparity may have less to do with general differences between liberal and conservative use of social media and instead may be rooted in the particular facts of the 2012 election. It is possible the explanation lies with the fact that movement conservatives were skeptical of the Romney candidacy or that independent conservatives may have wished to distance themselves from the Romney campaign in anticipation of an election loss. Further research is needed in order to adjudicate among these potential explanations.

Finally, incumbency may have driven the patterns we observe in Twitter use. Because the Republicans were out of power, we should expect that a number of factions would compete to be the main voice of conservative opposition. In contrast, the Obama White House had, by 2012, a great deal of experience developing strategies to stay "on message." Further study of Twitter use in an open contest, as well as in an election with an incumbent Republican president, could yield insights about the role of incumbency. If differences persist between incumbents and nonincumbents, such a finding could point to another implication of this research: the availability of social media may magnify incumbency advantage in national elections.

Social media are powerful tools for the transmission of election narratives. As with previous media developments, the presence of social media has facilitated new practices and influenced the nature of the message. Candidates and parties can use social media to disseminate their own narratives and ideas, without the "gatekeeping" function of traditional media (Gainous and Wagner 2013). In the contemporary party environment, social media allow actors to act as campaign surrogates, underscoring their issue messages and sometimes saying what official candidates cannot. At the same time, platforms such as Twitter allow independent actors to act like campaign competitors, challenging the ability of candidates and parties to control the message.

Appendix A: Sample Construction

The first step in gathering the data was deciding which Twitter accounts to include in our analysis. We ultimately sought to construct two reasonably well-matched samples—one liberal, the other conservative—that would be representative of the groups and individuals on both sides who were actually using social media to disseminate messages about the 2012 presidential campaign. We began with approximately 50 accounts, divided evenly between conservatives and liberals. We then narrowed our focus to those accounts that provided election-relevant messages. Many actors on our original list were subsequently eliminated on the basis that their messages were primarily aimed at their constituents rather than a national audience. We also eliminated Twitter feeds that were updated too infrequently to merit inclusion in our data set. In particular, this led to the elimination from our list of many members of Congress, who used their social media accounts as platforms to engage with constituents. Through these criteria, we excluded the Twitter accounts of many congressional leaders. Our winnowing process also resulted in the exclusion of several independent conservative organizations, including Focus on the Family. The final result was lists of conservative and liberal Twitter accounts that roughly mirrored each other along subgroups and advocacy positions. Both included a mix of official sources, media outlets and personalities, and interest groups.

In order to test the reliability of our coding scheme for issue categories, we had a sample of the data set coded independently by a colleague. She was presented with the text from 368 tweets, without any context, including attached links or the source of the tweets. We chose this approach in order to subject our coding scheme to a difficult test by removing any clues about how we might have coded the data. On the basis of this independent replication, 81% of the tweets were placed in the same category as in our original coding. Many of the discrepancies were predictable based on this replication method; without context, more tweets were coded as "other." In order to further test reliability, we divided the subsample into two categories: economy (1) and other (0). Using this nominal approach, we calculated Krippendorff's Alpha for the two independent coders, yielding a score of .787 (90.5% agreement).

Appendix B: Issue Messages

Our first task in creating a data set of issue messages was to decide which tweets to include. Our objective was to create a comprehensive data set of messages from official and unofficial actors about the meaning and stakes of the 2012 election. These messages could directly engage with a policy issue, such as immigration or health care, or they could frame the election as a choice between the two candidates' visions for the future, personal characteristics, beliefs, and attitudes.

In coding our data for issue messages, we attempted to create a thorough catalogue of the types of issue messages included in tweets from our selected sources. Our categories for policy topics adhered closely to the language used in the actual posts and tweets, which often referred broadly to the economy, health care, and specific foreign conflicts (usually Libya/Benghazi or Iraq). We also included the "nonissue" categories of "future" and "other," which we explain in the main text. Social issues constituted a larger umbrella category; we categorized any messages relating to abortion, women's health, religious freedom, LGBT issues, and race under this heading. As with the other categories, the messages we assigned to the "social issues" category often used the language of the relevant categories, defining the election and the candidates in terms of positions on abortion, LGBT rights, women's health, traditional values, or race. In other words, we contend that our categories constitute a reliable measure of the content of Twitter posts because we constructed them to reflect the language of those posts as closely as possible without sacrificing generality. Some messages were assigned to more than one category. For example, the RNC Twitter page criticized President Obama because he "prioritized Obamacare over jobs" (2012d), which referred both to Obama's economic record and to the Republican goal of repealing Obamacare. When two policy issues were part of one message, we included the message under the two relevant columns in the data set. In each case, these were straightforward and contained language directly relevant to both columns. For example, on September 18, Mitt Romney tweeted, "Candidate @BarackObama promised to not pass our bills on to the next generation, yet he's increased the debt by $5.4T" (Romney 2012a). This message fell under both the "economy" and "future" categories.

Appendix C: Data

Table 3.2. Preelection Messages, Conservatives, I

Source	Economy	Future	Trade	Foreign Policy
Mitt Romney	63	7	9	9
RNC	275	20	10	126
Americans for Prosperity	221	3	0	0
American Crossroads	39	3	1	21
National Review	36	1	0	88
Fox Nation	65	3	2	90
Townhall.com	19	0	0	16
Susan B. Anthony List	10	0	0	15
Heritage Foundation	84	1	4	65
Laura Ingraham	67	2	4	83
Michelle Malkin	58	1	0	120
Sarah Palin	1	1	0	2
Total	938	42	30	635

Table 3.3. Preelection Messages, Conservatives, II

Source	Health care	Social issues	Immigration	Energy	Other	Total
Mitt Romney	4	1	0	10	1	104
RNC	21	7	0	15	1	475
Americans for Prosperity	18	0	1	20	0	263
American Crossroads	6	0	0	4	0	74
National Review	4	4	0	5	0	138
Fox Nation	5	19	0	10	0	194
Townhall.com	0	41	0	1	0	77
Susan B. Anthony List	0	68	0	0	0	93
Heritage Foundation	41	11	0	29	1	236
Laura Ingraham	10	15	5	9	0	195
Michelle Malkin	27	32	1	14	0	253
Sarah Palin	0	1	2	4	0	11
Total	136	199	9	121	3	2,113

Table 3.4. Preelection Messages, Liberals, I

Source	Economy	Future	Trade	Foreign policy
Barack Obama	276	3	29	87
DNC	150	4	17	68
Rachel Maddow Blog	14	0	0	8
Daily Kos	82	0	8	46
Salon	89	0	11	64
National Council of La Raza	51	1	0	0
Planned Parenthood	1	0	0	0
Nation	92	0	7	35
Paul Krugman	67	0	0	4
Young Turks	86	0	0	43
Total	932	9	72	380

Table 3.5. Preelection Messages, Liberals, II

Source	Health care	Social issues	Immigration	Energy	Other	Total
Barack Obama	65	101	17	18	34	630
DNC	53	69	8	6	46	421
Rachel Maddow Blog	1	3	0	0	7	33
Daily Kos	13	35	1	1	26	212
Salon	15	43	0	17	17	256
National Council of La Raza	13	3	40	1	0	109
Planned Parenthood	68	152	2	0	0	223
Nation	21	37	3	2	12	209
Paul Krugman	5	0	0	0	1	77
Young Turks	15	31	0	6	21	202
Total	318	406	75	69	365	2,626

Table 3.6. Conservatives, Postelection Messages, I

Source	Economy	Future	Trade	Foreign policy
Mitt Romney	0	0	0	0
RNC	3	0	0	0
Americans for Prosperity	0	0	0	0
American Crossroads	0	0	0	0
National Review	1	0	0	1
Fox Nation	4	0	0	2
Townhall.com	2	0	0	0
Susan B. Anthony List	1	0	0	1
Heritage Foundation	3	0	0	0
Laura Ingraham	3	0	0	3
Michelle Malkin	5	0	0	2
Sarah Palin	0	0	0	0
Total	22	0	0	9

Table 3.7. Conservatives, Postelection Messages, II

Source	Health care	Social issues	Immigration	Other
Mitt Romney	0	0	0	0
RNC	0	0	0	0
Americans for Prosperity	0	0	0	0
American Crossroads	0	0	0	0
National Review	1	0	0	2
Fox Nation	0	1	1	6
Townhall.com	0	1	0	8
Susan B. Anthony List	0	2	0	0
Heritage Foundation	2	1	1	1
Laura Ingraham	2	0	0	6
Michelle Malkin	0	1	3	3
Sarah Palin	0	0	0	0
Total	5	6	5	26

Table 3.8. Postelection Messages, Liberals, I

Source	Economy	Future	Trade	Foreign policy
Barack Obama	5	0	0	0
DNC	1	0	0	0
Rachel Maddow Blog	1	0	0	0
Daily Kos	4	0	0	1
Salon	6	0	0	0
National Council of La Raza	2	0	0	0
Planned Parenthood	0	0	0	0
Nation	5	0	0	0
Paul Krugman	5	0	0	0
Young Turks	2	0	0	0
Total	31	0	0	1

Table 3.9. Postelection Messages, Liberals, II

Source	Health care	Social issues	Immigration	Energy	Other
Barack Obama	0	0	0	0	3
DNC	0	0	0	0	3
Rachel Maddow Blog	0	0	0	0	2
Daily Kos	1	1	0	0	1
Salon	0	0	1	2	7
National Council of La Raza	0	0	1	0	1
Planned Parenthood	0	11	0	0	2
Nation	2	4	0	0	9
Paul Krugman	0	0	0	0	4
Young Turks	0	0	0	0	2
Total	3	16	2	2	34

Notes

1. The authors would like to thank Bree Roozen for excellent research assistance.
2. All dates are from 2012 unless otherwise specified.
3. We included social media responses to the second presidential debate, as well as the vice presidential debate, in our analysis, but these two events were generally ignored by the actors in our sample.

References

American Crossroads. 2012a. Twitter post, October 9, 7:07 p.m. https://twitter.com/americanXroads.

——. 2012b. Twitter post, October 23, 2012, 2:55 p.m. https://twitter.com/americanXroads.

Azari, Julia R., and Justin S. Vaughn. 2013. "Barack Obama and the Rhetoric of Electoral Logic." *Social Science Quarterly*. http://onlinelibrary.wiley.com/doi/10.1111/ssqu.12056/abstract.

Baum, Matthew A., and Tim Groeling. 2008. "New Media and the Polarization of American Political Discourse." *Political Communication* 25:345–365.

Benoit, William, Glenn J. Hansen, and Rebecca M. Verser. 2003. "A Meta-Analysis of the Effects of Viewing Presidential Debates." *Communication Monographs* 70:335–350.

Capehart, Jonathan. 2012. "Romney Trashes the 47 Percent." *PostPartisan* (blog), *Washington Post*, September 17. http://www.washingtonpost.com/blogs/post-partisan/post/mitt-romney-r-1-percent-trashes-the-47-percent/2012/09/17/f3ef2b6e-0116-11e2-9367-4e1bafb958db_blog.html.

Carlisle, Juliet E., and Robert C. Patton. 2013. "Is Social Media Changing How We Understand Political Engagement?" *Political Research Quarterly* 66:883–895.

Daily Kos. 2012a. Twitter post, September 12, 6:47 a.m. https://twitter.com/dailykos.

——. 2012b. Twitter post, September 18, 6:29 p.m. https://twitter.com/dailykos.

——. 2012c. Twitter post, September 26, 2:22 p.m. https://twitter.com/dailykos.

——. 2012d. Twitter post, October 2, 1:03 p.m. https://twitter.com/dailykos.

Democratic National Committee. 2012a. Twitter post, September 14, 2:18 a.m. https://twitter.com/thedemocrats.

——. 2012b. Twitter post, September 20, 9:30 a.m. https://twitter.com/thedemocrats.

——. 2012c. Twitter post, October 23, 8:06 a.m. https://twitter.com/thedemocrats.

Dugan, Andrew. 2012. "Women in Swing States Have Gender-Specific Priorities." Gallup.com, October 17. http://www.gallup.com/poll/158069/women-swing-states-gender-specific-priorities.aspx.
Fox Nation. 2012a. Twitter post, September 20, 12:34 p.m. https://twitter.com/foxnation.
———. 2012b .Twitter post, October 9, 7:01 a.m. https://twitter.com/foxnation.
———. 2012c. Twitter post, October 19, 6:59 p.m. https://twitter.com/foxnation.
———. 2012d. Twitter post, November 6, 8:46 p.m. https://twitter.com/foxnation.
———. 2012e Twitter post, November 7, 9:25 a.m. http://twitter.com/foxnation.
Gainous, Jason, and Kevin M. Wagner. 2013. *Tweeting to Power: The Social Media Revolution in American Politics.* New York: Oxford University Press.
Geer, John. 1988. "The Effects of Presidential Debates on the Electorate's Preference for Candidates." *American Politics Research* 16:486–501.
Gulati, Jeff, and Christine B. Williams. 2011. "Diffusion of Innovations and Online Campaigns: Social Media Adoption in the 2010 U.S. Congressional Elections." Paper presented at the European Consortium for Political Research, Reykjavik, Iceland, August 25–27.
Hannity, Sean. 2012. Twitter post, September 18, 4:29 p.m. https://twitter.com/seanhannity.
Heritage Foundation. 2012. November 7, 6:32 a.m. https://twitter.com/heritage.
Ingraham, Laura. 2012a. Twitter post, September 13, 6:44 a.m. https://twitter.com/ingrahamangle.
———. 2012b. Twitter post, October 10, 7:11 a.m. https://twitter.com/ingrahamangle.
———. 2012c. Twitter post, November 8, 8:38 a.m. https://twitter.com/ingrahamangle.
Jones, Jeffrey M. 2012. "Romney Narrows Vote Gap after Historic Debate Win." Gallup.com, October 8. http://www.gallup.com/poll/157907/romney-narrows-vote-gap-historic-debate-win.aspx.
Layman, Geoffrey C., Thomas M. Carsey, and Juliana Menasche Horowitz. 2006. "Party Polarization in American Politics: Characteristics, Causes, and Consequences." *Annual Review of Political Science* 9:83–110.
Malkin, Michelle. 2012a. Twitter post, September 17, 8:04 p.m. https://twitter.com/michellemalkin.
———. 2012b. Twitter post, October 16, 6:55 p.m. https://twitter.com/michellemalkin.
———. 2012c. Twitter post, November 12, 7:08 a.m. https://twitter.com/michellemalkin.
———. 2012d. Twitter post, November 13, 11:04 a.m. https://twitter.com/michellemalkin.
Masket, Seth E. 2009. *No Middle Ground: How Informal Party Organizations Control Nominations and Polarize Legislatures.* Ann Arbor: University of Michigan Press.
Mullany, Gerry. 2012. "Pro-Obama Super-PAC Up with New Bain Attack Ad." *The Caucus* (blog), *New York Times,* June 10. http://thecaucus.blogs.nytimes.com/2012/06/10/pro-obama-super-pac-up-with-new-bain-attack/?ref=baincapital.
Nation. 2012a. Twitter post, October 16, 2.05 p.m. https://twitter.com/thenation.
———. 2012b. Twitter post, November 9, 9:42 a.m. https://twitter.com/thenation.
National Review. 2012a. Twitter post, September 21, 4:07 p.m. https://twitter.com/nro.
———. 2012b. Twitter post, October 10, 5:59 a.m. https://twitter.com/nro.
———. 2012c. Twitter post, November 7, 7:30 a.m. https://twitter.com/nro.
Newport, Frank. 2012. "Voters Reaction to '47%' Comments Tilts Negative." Gallup.com, September 19. http://www.gallup.com/poll/157544/voters-reaction-romney-comments-tilts-negative.aspx.
New York Times. 2012. "What They Said, Before and After the Attack in Libya." September 12. http://www.nytimes.com/interactive/2012/09/12/us/politics/libya-statements.html.
Obama, Barack. 2012a. Twitter post, September 17, 8:03 p.m. https://twitter.com/barackobama.
———. 2012b. Twitter post, October 23, 8:05 a.m. https://twitter.com/barackobama.
———. 2012c. Twitter post, November 15, 9:30 a.m. https://twitter.com/barackobama.

Planned Parenthood. 2012. Twitter post, November 13, 11:41 a.m. https://twitter/ppact.
Rachel Maddow Show Blog. 2012a. Twitter post, September 12, 8:35 a.m. https://twitter.com/maddowblog.
———. 2012b. Twitter post, September 12, 2012, 3:43 p.m. https://twitter.com/maddowblog.
———. 2012c. Twitter post, September 17, 7:43 a.m. https://twitter.com/maddowblog.
Republican National Committee. 2012a. Twitter post, September 17, 9:43 a.m. https://twitter.com/gop.
———. 2012b. Twitter post, September 18, 3:46 p.m. https://twitter.com/gop.
———. 2012c. Twitter post, October 9, 7:44 a.m. https://twitter.com/gop.
———. 2012d. Twitter post, October 25, 7:15 a.m., https://twitter.com/gop.
Romney, Mitt. 2012a. Twitter post, September 18, 3:50 p.m. https://twitter.com/MittRomney.
———. 2012b. Twitter post, September 24, 5:13 p.m. https://twitter.com/MittRomney.
Rove, Karl, and Ed Gillespie. 2012. "How to Beat Obama," *Foreign Policy*, March–April. http://www.foreignpolicy.com/articles/2012/02/27/how_to_beat_obama.
Salon. 2012a. Twitter post, September 13, 9:51 a.m. https://twitter.com/salon.
———. 2012b. Twitter post, September 18, 6:27 a.m. https://twitter.com/salon.
———. 2012c. Twitter post, September 26, 5:30 a.m. https://twitter.com/salon.
———. 2012d. Twitter post, November 8, 5:03 a.m. https://twitter.com/salon.
———. 2012e. Twitter post, November 8, 2:44 p.m. https://twitter.com/salon.
———. 2012f. Twitter post, November 15, 8:50 a.m. https://twitter.com/salon.
———. 2012g. Twitter post, November 17, 11:20 a.m. https://twitter.com/salon.
Starr, Barbara, and Adam Levine. 2012. "Panetta: Terrorists 'Clearly' Planned Benghazi Attack." CNN.com, September 27, http://www.cnn.com/2012/09/27/world/africa/libya-consulate-attack.
Susan B. Anthony List. 2012a. Twitter post, October 3, 6:04 p.m. https://twitter.com/sbalist.
———. 2012b. Twitter post, November 8, 1:18 p.m. https://twitter.com/sbalist.
Tewksbury, David. 2005. "The Seeds of Audience Fragmentation: Specialization in the Use of Online News Sites." *Journal of Broadcasting and Electronic Media* 49:332–348.
Townhall.com. 2012a. Twitter post, October 16, 3:18 p.m. https://twitter.com/townhallcom.
———. 2012b. Twitter post, November 9, 9:20 p.m. https://twitter.com/townhallcom.
Trinko, Katrina. 2012. "New Obama Attack Ad Features Steelworkers Blaming Bain for Job Losses." *National Review*, May 14. http://www.nationalreview.com/corner/299838/new-obama-attack-ad-features-steelworkers-blaming-bain-job-losses-katrina-trinko.
Young Turks. 2012. Twitter post, October 22, 7:30 p.m. https://twitter.com/theyoungturks.

4

The Competition to Control Campaign Messages on YouTube

ROBERT J. KLOTZ

On November 6, 2012, President Obama, instead of trying to control his own message, envisioned himself as the remixer. He was prompted by a New Hampshire radio host asking about Psy's "Gangnam Style" dance. President Obama explained, "I think I can do that move, but I'm not sure that the inauguration ball is the appropriate time to break that out" (WZID 2012). It is a sign that politicians are becoming more comfortable with diminished control of their video message when, on Election Day, the president would wonder about how to adapt an Internet meme. Being able to laugh at yourself is one option for dealing with the new video environment.

Politicians do not have a lot of attractive options for confronting the challenges of controlling their message in an online video environment such as YouTube. The best option is probably to win the competition to shape their video presence. If established political participants can produce compelling content, their videos will be watched, and they will maintain a measure of control over their online video presence. Alternatively, ordinary citizens are so numerous and empowered by democratized video technology that they can conceivably drown out the message of established political participants. These two potential outcomes are supported by competing academic theories about whether the political application of new technology will fit a mobilization thesis in which the political establishment is undermined by newly empowered participants or a normalization thesis in which established political participants retain the ability to "package and control" their message (Gainous and Wagner 2011, 138). To understand video message control in the new media, this study systematically analyzes the YouTube presence of congressional and presidential candidates in the 2012 election.

The Competition to Control the Campaign Message

One critical aspect of election campaigns is the competition to control the message that is sent to voters. Candidates, political parties, and interest groups are advocates who fight to have their message heard. The traditional news media add their own frames of campaign coverage. Citizens may be eager to contribute their own messages. The medium through which participants communicate can affect who wins the competition to have their preferred message heard.

Candidates, political parties, interest groups, and the traditional news media have a good thing going in the broadcast world. These established political participants benefit from scarce spectrum that limits most video communication to media owners and those who purchase expensive advertising time. Citizens are largely excluded from video communication in this environment. They generally cannot afford advertising time. The news media tend to favor elite sources (Bennett et al. 2004) and to omit citizens from campaign stories except as part of a public opinion poll.

The big winner in broadcasting is the traditional news media. The journalists employed by television stations choose their own frames for campaign stories. Over time, the exercise of interpretive journalism has reduced candidate speech to sound bites of about eight seconds, and the vast majority of newscast speaking is now done by journalists (Grabe and Bucy 2009). If candidates, groups, and parties want to speak in an unmediated way on television, they must generally buy advertising time from stations that reap large windfalls in political campaigns.

Candidates also do well in the broadcast world. Although they are losing screen time to journalists, news coverage can boost valuable name recognition. Candidates experience some success in priming the news media to cover issues on which they would like to be judged (Iyengar and Kinder 1987). Candidates can also be players in the paid media. Under the law, candidates pay the lowest advertising rate and can often raise the money to buy time.

Political parties and interest groups also benefit from the broadcast environment. They can spend unlimited amounts distributing their own message independent from candidates. Television stations are happy to sell them time since they can charge these entities a higher rate than candidates. In some instances, parties and groups have so much money that they can drown out the message of candidates.

Although established participants enjoy a privileged position in the broadcasting world, there is a theory that the Internet can dramatically alter the competitive balance for video message producers. Specifically, the technical and financial barriers that prevent nontraditional players from an active role in video messages disappear online. At one time, producing and distributing video was prohibitively expensive. Now it is possible with a low-end camera and Internet access. Citizens may have an advantage in a world in which "professional and big budget equals a sales push [while] indie and raw equals honest" (Fernando 2009, 11). Citizens may also benefit from being better able to relate to other citizens. Wael Ghonim (2012, 86) describes the appeal of setting his Egyptian prodemocracy message to music: "I had never edited a video before, but . . . after three or four hours of work, the video was ready. . . . [Viewers] found the fusion of images, lyrics, and music inspiring and moving, . . . [unlike] the regular practice of lawyers and human rights defenders, who used facts and statistics to garner support."

Further, these technological changes theoretically can alter the formats of campaign communication. Although brief ads are encouraged by broadcast-spectrum scarcity, YouTube imposes few constraints. Communicators can experiment with varied formats to convey their message. At minimum, communication can be extended beyond the 30-second increments that are insufficient for developing arguments about leadership and policy goals. Writing in *Wired*, Clive Thompson (2009, 40) explains that YouTube will prompt new ways to communicate: "We're developing a new language of video—forms that let us say different things and maybe even think in different ways."

Overall, the theory suggests that technological change can undermine the control that established political participants have over the video message that they communicate during campaigns. Ordinary citizens can use democratized video production and distribution to convey their own campaign messages in unconventional formats. In the words of Aaron McKain (2012, 4), "Every John and Jane Q. Public [is] a nascent H. L. Mencken or *Daily Show* contributor, armed with a cheap laptop that comes standard with more AV production equipment than the Beatles had to record *Abbey Road*, and with an internet connection that lets them disseminate information as far and wide as any major media corporation."

Indeed, scholars have theorized the *lack* of control as a fundamental feature of YouTube politics. Vassia Gueorguieva (2008, 295), for example, argues that the online video environment "weaken[s] the level of control that campaigns have over the candidate's image and message since anybody, both supporters and opponents, can post a video." For McKain (2012, 44, 63), loss of control in digital media is driven by the combination of interactive and archival capabilities: "What the materiality of digital media really strips away from us is the ability to self-narrate, to perform, to tell our stories in the order that we see fit. . . . Digital media multiplies our 'selves' that are living, forever, in The Archive while simultaneously, thanks to the inherent interactivity of digital media, eradicating our control (political, existential) over them."

A number of hypotheses are easily deduced from this theory. If the theory is supported, citizens would be expected to account for a large percentage of the prominent videos in political campaigns. The citizen category will benefit from the large numbers of citizens and their ability to relate to the citizen audience. On the other hand, established participants would be expected to produce fewer videos that resonate with viewers. This seems especially true for traditional media organizations that lose their gatekeeping role over spectrum space on YouTube. Finally, the 30-second advertisement would be expected to lose its prominent position in defining the video presence of candidates. Without the constraints of broadcasting space and predetermined 30-second intervals, communication is expected to take a variety of formats to appeal to audience members who have diverse interests. In short, established participants are expected to have less control over their campaign video messages on YouTube.

An extreme version of the loss of control would be a kind of Gangnam Style politics. Around Election Day 2012, the Psy video "Gangnam Style" surpassed a Justin Bieber video to become the most viewed YouTube video in history with about 1 billion views. The South Korean district celebrated in the video is described by Psy as remaining "calm" during the day and "going insane" at night ("Interview" 2012). Applying the distinction to the types of campaign videos on YouTube, it could be that candidates lose control of the calm, cautious video messages that they produce during the day as people go insane at night remixing video and fundamentally undermining candidates' messages.

Early scholarship about online video suggested that traditional players did fairly well in keeping control of their video messages on YouTube. Studying the 2008 campaign, Travis Ridout, Erika Fowler, and John Branstetter (2010) found that candidates accounted for 93% of video advertisements. Examining 113 of the most viewed campaign 2008 videos, Ivan Dylko et al. (2012, 844) characterized only 11% as "amateur videos" in an environment dominated by elite videos: "Even in what may be argued to be the most democratic information outlet—a user-generated video-sharing website—elites undeniably dominate in terms of proportion of the sources featured in the popular YouTube videos." On the basis of the finding that citizen videos peaked during the 2008 election and fell off sharply afterward, Albert May (2010, 509) concluded that his research "supports the argument that it is the old content providers, not the new user-generated YouTubers, who are playing the larger role in attracting audiences in the new medium." Jin Kim (2012, 54, 65) invoked the phrase "institutionalization of YouTube" to describe the producers and format of video: "The dominant portion of videos on online video sites comes from mainstream media, and users borrow not only content to consume but also specific formats in order to produce their clips."

The question is whether the balance changed during 2012, which was a breakout year for YouTube in the election campaign. For the first time, online videos were part of how the average American voter experienced the campaign. Pew Internet (2012) found that 55% of registered voters watched a campaign-related video online. Further, a majority (52%) of registered voters reported having been recommended an online video. The numbers were similar for Republicans and Democrats. The importance of YouTube use by the electorate is magnified by data that show YouTube use in the 2012 election was positively related to offline participation (Zhang, Seltzer, and Bichard 2013).

Given the increasing importance of YouTube in campaigns, the competition to control online video messages is intensifying. Candidates and established participants are trying harder to produce videos, knowing that a majority of the electorate is viewing campaign videos. Citizens continue to benefit from technological advances that simplify video production and editing. The YouTube landscape in 2012 may have been very different from earlier elections, in which YouTube political videos were seen by a minority of the electorate. Who controlled the online video message of candidates in the 2012 election?

New Media Methodology and Online Video

Research on the online video environment benefits from having one widely recognized playing field in YouTube. Founded in 2005 by former PayPal employees with the motto "Broadcast Yourself," YouTube is now the third-most-popular destination on the web, behind only its parent company, Google, and Facebook (Alexa 2014). Of course, some video producers would prefer people to watch videos on their own website. Even so, they do not want to neglect a platform as visible as YouTube. Thus, those who want to communicate about political campaigns will compete to distribute their video message on YouTube.

Further, this widely recognized playing field is one on which communicators compete on largely the same terms. Users follow a similar process to upload videos under similar specifications. At the time of the 2012 election, all users could upload videos up to 15 minutes in length. YouTube makes some exceptions for longer videos from preferred video producers, such as major media outlets.

Another tremendous opportunity for YouTube research is that digital technology generates usage metrics. It is never easy to tell how many views a television or print ad receives. Online, however, it is much easier to count views. Scholars in a range of disciplines have coalesced around the "most viewed" metric. Dylko et al. (2012) defend the "most viewed" methodology as consistent with studies that show people seldom get past the first page of search results. In a study of nursing imagery, Jacinta Kelly, Gerard Fealy, and Roger Watson (2012, 1807) analyze the "ten most viewed" YouTube videos on the grounds that they "constituted an ongoing public discourse."

On the other hand, the most serious challenges to new media research are mitigated on YouTube. The ease of anonymity is a regular challenge for Internet content research. Yet the incentives to claim credit for video production by building a YouTube channel brand are strong and limit anonymous videos. The challenge of evanescence is minimized on YouTube since uploaded videos are not constantly edited like a website. Indeed, videos are only occasionally taken down, and controversial videos are often preserved elsewhere. Another major challenge of new media content analysis is that people receive different targeted content, especially ads, on the basis of their previous online behavior. By employing privacy settings, putting objective criteria into the YouTube search engine, and excluding sponsored videos, researchers can minimize the impact of targeting.

Research Design

In order to test theories about the online video environment and to understand how effective candidates were at controlling their video messages in the 2012 election, it is important to avoid the idiosyncrasies of any particular contest. By examining different candidates and different types of campaigns, confidence is increased that any observed phenomena result from the underlying new media technology. Similarly, a combination of high-profile and low-profile races will secure a broader view of the relationship between online video and message control.

Thus, this study examines the online video messages related to candidates in three campaign types in the 2012 election. First, candidates for the 2012 Republican presidential nomination are studied. The presidential nomination contest has proved a fruitful place to examine technological advances in politics (e.g., Gueorguieva 2008), in part because the visibility of the campaign attracts interest from the public and innovative campaign professionals. Second, the two major-party presidential candidates in the general election are included. Scholarship confirms that both the Obama and Romney campaigns used YouTube to convey major themes, and their videos exhibited the "smooth professionalism" of established political participants (Trosky 2013, 144). Third, all U.S. Senate races in the 2012 general election are considered. U.S. Senate campaigns are ideal for study as they provide tremendous diversity of competitiveness and geography in a politically relevant population of a manageable size that allows for systematic analysis.

Presidential nomination videos were selected in a straightforward way. Candidates were identified based on participation in the October 11, 2011, debate that constituted the final field of announced candidates (i.e., Michelle Bachmann, Herman Cain, Newt Gingrich, Jon Huntsman, Ron Paul, Rick Perry, Mitt Romney, and Rick Santorum). Each candidate's name was input into the advanced search function of YouTube to identify the "most viewed" videos. Videos in which either the first or last name of the candidate is referenced in the title were identified as part of the YouTube presence of the candidate. This objective way to distinguish the subject of the video was necessary to eliminate large numbers of search results that have nothing to do with the candidate (since candidate names are used to attract videos unrelated to the candidate). All videos with the candidate name in the title did relate to the candidate, which shows that compliance with YouTube's community guidelines against "misleading" characterization is high with respect to misleading titles that are easy to detect and the target of enforcement efforts. Campaign proximity was ensured by eliminating videos more than a year old. Conducting the study on January 3, 2012, was designed to capture the YouTube environment left by months of intense competition at the precise moment when Republicans started voting in the Iowa caucuses.

Excluding repeats of the same video clip, the ten most viewed videos associated with each of the eight candidates are included in the study ($n = 80$).

The pool of presidential videos in the general election was obtained in a similar manner. The names of the two major-party candidates (Barack Obama and Mitt Romney) were input into the YouTube search engine to identify the "most viewed" videos. Again, videos must have appeared within a year and included the first or last name of the candidate in the title to ensure proximity to the 2012 campaign. The study captured the YouTube environment on the weekend before the November 6, 2012, election, after months of campaigning and with early voting ongoing and regular voting just hours away. Excluding repeats of the same video clip, the 25 most viewed videos associated with both candidates are included in the study ($n = 50$).

The methodological goal for the Senate videos was to identify the single video for each candidate that won the competition for most viewers. Thus, the name of each of the 66 major-party candidates (and that of Maine independent Angus King, who held a large lead in the polls throughout the campaign) was placed in the YouTube search engine to identify the "most viewed" video. To be included, the video must have been uploaded in the past year, and the name of the candidate actually must be mentioned in the video. This procedure eliminated a few videos in which uploaders employed the dubious strategy of using a prominent senator's name as a keyword to attract traffic even if the video had nothing to do with the senator. The study captured the YouTube environment on the weekend before the November 6, 2012, election. The single most viewed video associated with each of the 67 candidates is included in the study ($n = 67$).

Thus, the research design is consistent across all candidate types. The methodological goal was to identify the pool of 50–80 videos that won the competition for being the most viewed videos associated with candidates in that race. The number of videos per candidate varies to produce a similar aggregate population for each campaign type ($10 \times 8 = 80$ primary presidential election videos; $25 \times 2 = 50$ general presidential election videos; $1 \times 67 = 67$ Senate general election videos). Usage metrics objectively identify the pool of videos that won the most viewers.

Videos were first coded for the type of producer. Classification was determined by who produced the video, not who uploaded the video. Thus, a regular citizen who uploaded PBS debate footage is not credited as the producer, since PBS produced the video and what is important is who produced the video, not whose YouTube channel gets credit. If, however, the PBS footage is modified in a meaningful way, the citizen becomes the producer of a new remixed video. In the unusual cases in which the producer's identity is an anonymous handle, an investigation was conducted to determine if the person's identity was available elsewhere online. If contrary evidence was not found, video producers presenting themselves as ordinary citizens were considered to be ordinary citizens.

Classification of producer types was based on the institutional source of the video, not the background of the people involved. Established participants outside the traditional media include the candidates, political officeholders, political parties, and interest groups. Traditional news media sources originate in a traditional communications medium and continue their traditional media product while also generating Internet content. All other sources were classified as nontraditional sources. As operationalized, the term *nontraditional* captures only the source's role in politics and not any personal characteristics. This is important to recognize since Matthew Hindman (2009) has shown that elite backgrounds are common among the independent bloggers and citizens who produce popular online content. Thus, sources such as universities and comedy troupes are considered nontraditional campaign sources even as they may be prestigious elite institutions in other domains.

Videos were also coded for format on the basis of their production values, length, and context. The most important distinction was between brief, television-style ads and other formats. Similar to Ridout, Fowler, and Branstetter (2010), the ad format is broadly interpreted to include edited video that endeavors to persuade the audience to vote for or against a candidate. Brief ads are shorter than one minute (65 seconds with buffer). Since categories are largely self-explanatory, elaboration is deferred to the results section.

Combined, knowing the producer and format of videos gives a good, if imperfect, sense of candidates' ability to control their video messages. If the video presence of candidates is defined by videos that they produced, it signifies high message control. Even if candidates cannot control video production, there are a number of video formats that allow candidates to retain a measure of control, such as debates, speeches, and news interviews. Perhaps no format threatens a candidate's message control more than an investigative news story that can undermine the candidate's message. Candidates also have almost no control over formats such as music videos, ad parodies, and comedy skits, which can be vehicles for trenchant criticism or lighthearted entertainment.

Analysis and Results

Established campaign participants have been able to preserve their leading role in campaign video messages. The winners in the broadcast world have been able to convert that advantage into a successful presence in the "broadcast yourself" world. Nontraditional sources, however, enjoy a greater presence on YouTube than they do on broadcast television. Indeed, as depicted in figure 4.1, YouTube displays a remarkable balance between these three broad categories of communicators. Thus, there is support for the theory that technology is changing the competitive balance of video communication even though the primary role of established participants is not seriously threatened.

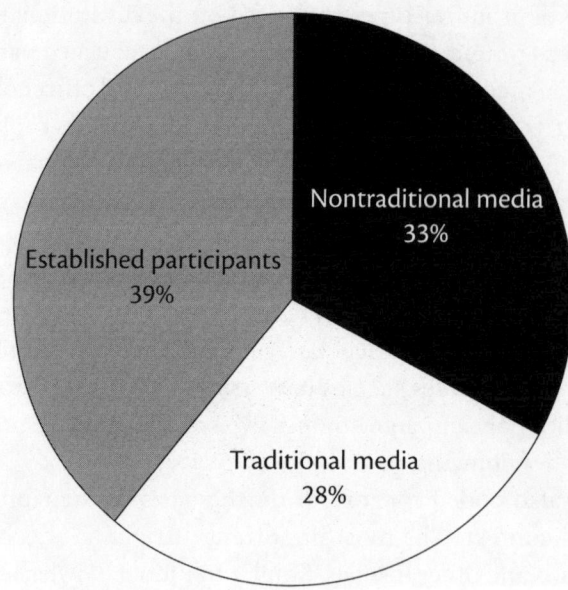

Figure 4.1. Producers of most viewed YouTube videos of campaign 2012

A plurality of the most viewed YouTube videos is obtained by the nonmedia established participants. Candidates dominate this category. They exceed the combined presence of interest groups and political parties. The 2012 election campaign was marked by large independent expenditures that often exceeded candidates' spending on television. Yet candidates were able to maintain an advantage over groups and parties in controlling their video message online. Candidates retained absolute control of one out of every six videos. Only about 5% of videos were produced by the opposing candidate. This represents an impressive ability of candidates to keep control of their YouTube presence away from the immediate opposition.

Traditional media organizations are the communicators most disadvantaged relative to their position in other media environments. Unable to preserve a privileged role as gatekeeper and ad seller, traditional media organizations (radio and television stations, print publications, wire services) are having to compete by providing content that resonates with viewers. They enjoyed some success doing this and accounted for 56 of the 197 most viewed videos during the campaign. This output trailed slightly that of nontraditional sources, including ordinary citizens.

It is also true that ordinary citizens are not all that ordinary. People coming out of nowhere to produce a viral campaign video are rare. The best example is four-year-old Abby's tearful lamentation that she is "tired of Bronco Bamma and Mitt Romney" (Evans 2012). On the other hand, many of the ordinary citizen video producers are celebrities in other fields. This would include videos by the musician Smooth-E and the screenwriter Joss Whedon. More common is the video from the YouTube celebrity. People who work hard to produce regular content that generates a following for their YouTube channel were able to make the list of most viewed campaign videos when they talked about a candidate. The best example is the five videos from Philip DeFranco, who has a popular channel providing earnest commentary about life and politics. Citizen videos were also distinguished by technological savvy. The slick editing of BaracksDubs and Bad Lip Reading won them multiple appearances in the pool of most viewed campaign videos.

As shown in table 4.1, there are some notable differences by campaign type. Candidates were the only producers to secure 10% of the videos across all campaign types. It seems that the frequency of videos from ordinary citizens is partly contingent on the visibility of the race. The percentage of producers who are ordinary citizens declines from about 40% of videos in the high-profile general

Table 4.1. Producers of Top YouTube Videos Associated with 2012 Candidates

Producer	Presidential: Republican primary (#)	Presidential: general (#)	Senate (#)	Total (%)
Ordinary citizen	17	19	2	19.3
Candidate	15	5	13	16.8
National TV station	24	7	2	16.8
Interest group	3	2	18	11.7
Online news program	3	0	8	5.6
Print publication	2	8	1	5.6
Opposing candidate	4	2	4	5.1
Blog	4	1	1	3.0
Comedy troupe	2	4	0	3.0
Local TV station	0	0	5	2.5
Other politician	0	0	4	2.0
C-SPAN	2	0	1	1.5
Opposing party	1	0	2	1.5
Aggregators	2	0	0	1.0
AM/FM radio	0	0	2	1.0
White House	0	0	2	1.0
Wire service	1	1	0	1.0
App provider	0	1	0	.5
Own party	0	0	1	.5
University	0	0	1	.5
Total (*n* = 197)	80	50	67	100.0

presidential race to 20% in the moderate-profile presidential primary to 3% in the Senate races that have a lower profile than the presidential contest. Interest groups reflect the opposite pattern: they account for less than 5% of the videos in high-profile presidential races but make up over one-fourth of the lower-profile Senate races.

Turning to the formats of videos winning the campaign for online viewers in 2012, the big picture is one of diversity. Unlike the dominance of brief ads, debates, and news stories on broadcast television, table 4.2 shows that many formats are resonating with viewers on YouTube. A strong plurality, however, is retained by the television-style brief ad, which accounts for over 20% of the videos. Behind brief ads, seven different formats—debates, news interviews, news commentary, music videos, long ads, speeches, and comedy skits—constitute around 10% of the videos. Numerous other formats have a few examples on the list. Free from the economic constraints of broadcasting, producers seek to utilize many different ways to communicate their message. Viewers proved

Table 4.2. Formats of Top YouTube Videos Associated with 2012 Candidates

Producer	Presidential: Republican primary (#)	Presidential: general (#)	Senate (#)	Total (%)
Brief ad (≤ 65 sec)	6	5	30	20.8
Debate	13	7	4	12.2
Music video	3	12	3	9.1
Long ad (> 65 sec)	9	3	5	8.6
News commentary	6	2	9	8.6
News interview	12	1	3	8.1
Comedy skit	10	5	0	7.6
Speech	5	4	6	7.6
On-street surprise	3	3	1	3.6
Face to camera talk	4	2	0	3.0
Ad parody	2	1	0	1.5
News story	0	0	3	1.5
Town hall meeting	3	0	0	1.5
Animated ed. film	0	2	0	1.0
Clip compilation	1	1	0	1.0
Congress hearing	1	0	1	1.0
Photo slideshow	2	0	0	1.0
Press conference	0	1	1	1.0
Child utterance	0	1	0	.5
Issue documentary	0	0	1	.5
Total (n = 197)	80	50	67	100.0

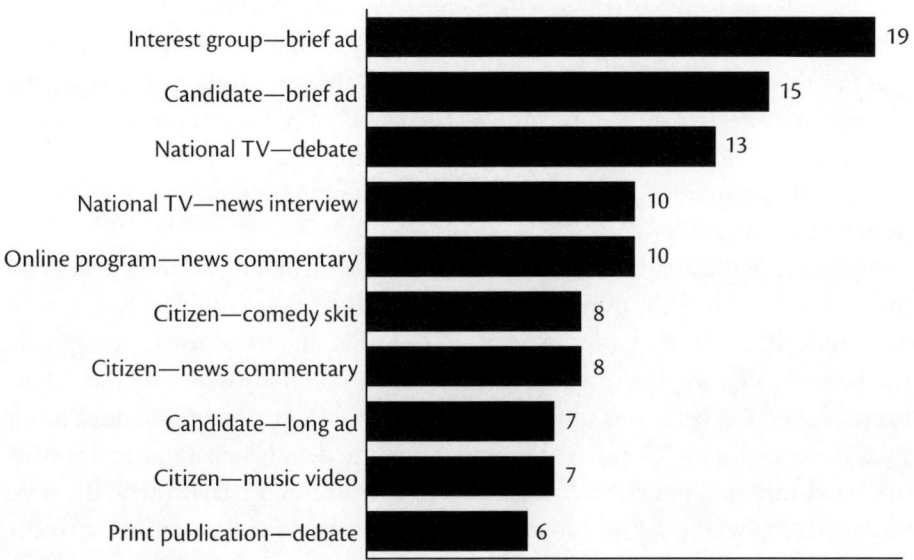

Figure 4.2. Most frequent producer-format types of 2012 campaign videos

receptive to messages in greater than 30-second increments, as the median video length was two minutes 25 seconds.

Combined, the results provide some support for the theory that the Internet is modifying the competitive balance and formats of video communication in campaigns. This is an important development. Yet the overall tenor of the YouTube campaign is not dramatically different from broadcast television. Established participants retain a preeminent position. Nontraditional sources have a presence greater than on broadcast television, but it mostly involves lighthearted entertainment. Traditional campaign television formats still prevail in the midst of greater overall diversity.

This mostly familiar environment might be a comfort to the modern candidate who seeks disciplined message control. The online environment is potentially threatening since it is open to a broader range of participants, and a candidate's video image can be remixed to produce a different message. Yet the reality is that candidates' messages are not being fundamentally undermined on YouTube. Candidates are retaining a surprising amount of control. Some aspects of campaigning that are favorable to candidates' control, such as long ads and campaign speeches, are almost invisible on television but have a meaningful presence online.

Examining the intersection of producers and formats offers a similar story. Figure 4.2 depicts the specific producer-format combinations that accounted for the most videos winning the competition for viewers in 2012. The most common video types are familiar to television viewers. They are well-established formats from established participants. The single most common producer-format type was the interest group brief ad, which came almost entirely from Senate races. The first video type that could not be seen on regular television was the fifth-place online program news commentary, which includes nine videos from the *Young Turks*. Participants in the *Young Turks* generally are not unknowns, and its progressive commentators historically have appeared on cable news shows. Citizens are prominent on the rest of the list but are most associated with entertainment formats.

Symbolic of the ability of candidates to retain a surprising amount of control over their message is the minimal presence of gaffes made visible by YouTube in 2012. Indeed, the major gaffes in 2012 did not originate from YouTube-aspiring trackers videotaping opponents but came from the mainstream media. Their presence on YouTube was almost an afterthought. At the presidential level, Rick Perry's famous "Oops" inability to name the departments cut by his plan occurred in a nationally televised debate. Mitt Romney's claim that the 47% of Americans who paid no income taxes were victims dependent on government was part of a speech leaked to *Mother Jones* magazine that was widely disseminated by the mainstream media and Democratic advertisements. Herman Cain's extended gaffe in which things "twirling" in his head prevented him from articulating a coherent foreign policy occurred in front of a local newspaper's editorial board. The three videos related to comments by Senate candidates about pregnancy resulting from rape all had strong ties to the mainstream media. One was from a national television interview (Akin-MO); one was from a locally televised debate (Mourdock-IN); and another was from a candidate talking to a group of reporters (Smith-PA). One of the 197 videos was *Wall Street Journal* footage of a Tina Fey speech referencing these comments: "If I have to listen to one more gray-faced man with a two-dollar haircut explain to me what rape is, I'm going to lose my mind" (WSJDigitalNetwork 2012). The best case for a tracker-captured gaffe was the video in which West Virginia Senate candidate John Raese told a friendly crowd that forcing businessmen to put up smoke-free signs was the "same thing" as Hitler requiring displays of the Star of David (Raese Flubs 2012). Raese, however, was so far behind that even though it was the most viewed video associated with him, it only had 10,000 views. Symbolic of the minimal impact of candidate gaffes is that two of the most prominent gaffe-like videos were not by candidates but by ordinary citizens who said something in support of their preferred candidate that went viral among nonsupporters. This would include an Obama supporter who asserted that President Obama had given away free telephones and a Romney supporter who told journalist Chris Matthews to "study it out" and learn that President Obama is a "communist" (MSNBC 2012).

Another aspect of candidates maintaining a surprising amount of control is how infrequently candidates' footage is taken completely out of context in a misleading attack. User-friendly editing software means that candidates can be remixed to say just about anything. In practice, however, candidates' words were far more likely to be taken out of context to say nothing rather than anything. Six videos by the anonymous citizen Bad Lip Reading (2012) compiled candidates' words into gibberish, such as Ron Paul's ostensible claim to be "a leprechaun farmer who's a gambler." Five videos from a college student's BaracksDubs channel compiled individual words spoken by President Obama into popular song lyrics. These videos may be amusing and technologically clever, but they communicate nothing about politics and do not undermine the candidate's message.

Finally, the results provide no support for the presence of Gangnam Style politics on YouTube, in which the "calm" and controlled daytime messages of candidates are undermined as people are "going insane" at night remixing them into their own narratives. The videos winning the competition for YouTube viewers in 2012 mostly came from mainstream sources employing time-honored communication formats. Nontraditional sources largely filled a niche of adding levity to the campaign.

In fact, the five most viewed videos of the entire cycle were all music videos from nontraditional sources. These include Obama's words assembled into "Call Me Maybe" (30.3 million views), an Obama versus Romney rap (25.5 million), Obama's words assembled into "Sexy and I Know It" (18.6 million), "Mitt Romney Style" (8.9 million), and Obama's words assembled into "Born This Way" (7.3 million). Three of the videos say nothing about politics as candidates simply mouth lyrics to catchy music. The two other videos were from comedy troupes that offered a modest political message by incorporating well-established perceptions of the two presidential candidates into skillful musical comedy.

Conclusion

On the basis of evidence from the 2012 election, YouTube is changing the competitive balance in video messages. Although elite communicators maintain a preeminent position, they encounter more competition on YouTube than on broadcast television, especially from ordinary citizens. The conventional formats of broadcast television also find competition on YouTube. In short, YouTube is making a contribution to political campaigns by allowing diverse communicators to use varied formats to reach potential voters. Since YouTube had already become part of the way the median voter experienced the campaign in 2012, confidence is increased that these findings represent a competitive dynamic applying to future elections.

It is a competitive dynamic on YouTube that appears to favor candidates in their competition with the news media. Able to bypass the news media on YouTube, candidates are taking the opportunity to produce video communication, and some of their videos are resonating with the electorate. The most prominent clips produced by the traditional news media on YouTube are those in which journalists have less control over the message. These are debates and news interviews in which candidates have significant control, at least after a journalist asks a question. The most viewed media-produced videos on YouTube are ones in which candidates are not reduced to sound bites that support media frames.

Interest groups appear to be a qualified loser on YouTube. Despite spending millions on television, interest groups garnered few of the most viewed YouTube presidential videos. Super PACs communicating about the presidential race clearly were hampered by lacking the social network that other campaign communicators employ to get links to their videos. On the other hand, in lower-profile Senate races, interest groups produced the most viewed video associated with a substantial number of candidates. The visibility of interest group videos in Senate races was probably still less than on television, where they accounted for nearly 30% of advertising in 2012 (Franz 2012). Unlike the television format, in which lack of disclosure typically helps groups to convey negative messages about candidates (Ridout, Franz, and Fowler 2013), the origin of YouTube videos in a social network may provide an enhanced cue about credibility.

Ordinary citizens appear to be winners on YouTube. Although they gravitated toward producing nonpolitical entertainment, citizens did make some substantive contributions to the political message. In a few videos, citizens acted as citizen-journalists who conduct candidate interviews, offer news commentary, or film campaign events. Given the personalized nature of much campaigning, it is surprising how little contribution citizens made through videos that capture one-one-one informal interaction with candidates. It seems that the advantage found in being citizen-journalists for natural-disaster stories (Pew Research Center 2012) is largely mitigated in the campaign-news context.

YouTube offers more diverse video formats than broadcast television does. The broadcast television environment for political messages is dominated by 30-second ads, which do some informing (Patterson and McClure 1976) but preclude in-depth discussion and are often misleading. People, however, have much greater appetites for political communication than what can be filled by a steady diet of 30-second ads. YouTube provides more diverse and extended campaign messages.

The increase in diversity, however, does not represent a fundamental undermining of the candidate's message. Established political participants maintain a sizeable advantage in producing the most viewed videos. Indeed, candidates keep full control of one-sixth of the most viewed videos, and they also have substantial control over the environment that is the basis for other popular formats. Citizens mostly have been content to produce lighthearted entertainment. Investigative journalism that can dramatically change campaign narratives is essentially absent from the most viewed campaign videos. Candidates seeking to control their message have much more to fear from a watchdog press than from the low-paid people following them with handheld video cameras who were nearly ubiquitous on the 2012 campaign trail. After all, opposition trackers capture video of speeches and interactions that are largely controlled by the candidate. The amount of digital video waste from these trackers in 2012 must be astounding.

No doubt some other digital waste from 2012 involves people creating their own Gangnam Style parodies. Of course, for a video depicting the spontaneous energy of a South Korean district, it is remarkably well choreographed. Likewise, the hallmark of the modern political campaign is the desire to control a disciplined message. On Election Day 2012, President Obama publicly joined the list of wannabe Gangnam parodists. President Obama, however, wants to keep control of his remixed Gangnam message. If he were going to "break that out," Obama told his Election Day interviewer, it would be "privately for Michelle." After observing her husband's Gangnam Style dancing, Michelle confessed that she found it a "little embarrassing." Despite the lack of encouragement, President Obama reportedly broke out a few Gangnam Style moves on Inauguration Day. Instead of the camera-filled inauguration ball, Obama saved his moves for a private inauguration after-party that did not allow filming (Boyle and Warren 2013). The struggle for control of the video message continues.

References

Alexa. 2014. "Top Sites." http://www.alexa.com/topsites (accessed July 21, 2014).

Bad Lip Reading. 2011. "Ron Paul—A BLR Soundbite." YouTube, December 5. http://www.youtube.com/watch?v=igQlbesFozA (accessed November 3, 2012).

Bennett, Lance W., Victor W. Pickard, David P. Iozzi, Carl L. Schroeder, Taso Lagos, and C. Evans Caswell. 2004. "Managing the Public Sphere: Journalistic Construction of the Great Globalization Debate." *Journal of Communication* 54:437–455.

Boyle, Louise, and Lydia Warren. 2013. "Inside the White House After-Party." *Daily Mail*, January 21. http://www.dailymail.co.uk/news/article-2266156/Inauguration-2013-party-Obama-Ushers-Gangnam-Style-dance-Michelle-grooves-Beyonce.html.

Dylko, Ivan B., Michael A. Beam, Kristen D. Landreville, and Nicholas Geidner. 2012. "Filtering 2008 US Presidential Election News on YouTube by Elites and Nonelites: An Examination of the Democratizing Potential of the Internet." *New Media & Society* 14:832–849.

Evans, Elizabeth. 2012. "Tired of Bronco Bamma and Mitt Romney." YouTube, October 3. http://www.youtube.com/watch?v=OjrthOPLAKM (accessed November 3, 2012).

Fernando, Angelo. 2009. "Communiqué: Tech Talk." *Communication World*, January–February: 10–12.

Franz, Michael M. 2012. "Interest Groups in Electoral Politics: 2012 in Context." *The Forum: A Journal of Applied Research in Contemporary Politics* 10:62–79.

Gainous, Jason, and Kevin M. Wagner. 2011. *Rebooting American Politics: The Internet Revolution*. Lanham, MD: Rowman and Littlefield.

Ghonim, Wael. 2012. *Revolution 2.0: The Power of the People Is Greater than the Power in People: A Memoir*. Boston: Houghton Mifflin Harcourt.

Grabe, Maria E., and Erik P. Bucy. 2009. *Image Bite Politics: News and the Visual Framing of Elections*. New York: Oxford University Press.

Gueorguieva, Vassia. 2008. "Voters, MySpace, and YouTube: The Impact of Alternative Communication Channels on the 2006 Election Cycle and Beyond." *Social Science Computer Review* 26:288–300.

Hindman, Matthew. 2009. *The Myth of Digital Democracy*. Princeton: Princeton University Press.

"Interview with Singer/Songwriter Psy." 2012. *Talk Asia*. CNN. November 23.

Iyengar, Shanto, and Donald R. Kinder. 1987. *News That Matters*. Chicago: University of Chicago Press.

Kelly, Jacinta, Gerard M. Fealy, and Roger Watson. 2012. "The Image of You: Constructing Nursing Identities in YouTube." *Journal of Advanced Nursing* 68:1804–1813.

Kim, Jin. 2012. "The Institutionalization of YouTube: From User-Generated Content to Professionally Generated Content." *Media, Culture & Society* 34:53–67.

May, Albert L. 2010. "Who Tube? How YouTube's News and Politics Space Is Going Mainstream." *International Journal of Press/Politics* 15:499–511.

McKain, Aaron. 2012. "Fear and Loathing in the New Media Age: How to Realign Our Rhetorical Judgments for the Post-Postmodern, Digital Media Age." PhD diss., Ohio State University.

MSNBC. 2012. "Woman at VP Debate Calls Obama a Communist." YouTube, October 11. http://www.youtube.com/watch?v=2E87gciwebw (accessed November 3, 2012).

Patterson, Thomas E., and Robert D. McClure. 1976. *The Unseeing Eye: The Myth of Television Power in National Politics*. New York: Putnam.

Pew Internet and American Life Project. 2012. *Online Political Videos and Campaign 2012*. Washington, DC: Pew Internet.

Pew Research Center Project for Excellence in Journalism. 2012. *YouTube and News: A New Kind of Visual Journalism*. Washington, DC: Pew Research.

Raese Flubs. 2012. "John Raese Compares Anti-Smoking Laws to Holocaust." YouTube, April 17. http://www.youtube.com/watch?v=tRqld_3AG88 (accessed November 4, 2012).

Ridout, Travis N., Erika F. Fowler, and John Branstetter. 2010. "Political Advertising in the 21st Century: The Rise of the YouTube Ad." Paper presented at the annual meeting of the American Political Science Association, Washington, D.C., September 1–4.

Ridout, Travis N., Michael M. Franz, and Erika F. Fowler. 2013. "Are Interest Group Ads More Effective?" Paper presented at the annual meeting of the American Political Science Association, Washington, DC, August 29–September 1.

Thompson, Clive. 2009. "This Is Your Brain on Video." *Wired*, January: 40.

Trosky, Robert J., Jr. 2013. "Visual Situations: A Social Semiotic Analysis of the 2012 YouTube Channels of Barack Obama and Mitt Romney." PhD diss., Robert Morris University.

WSJDigitalNetwork. 2012. "Tina Fey Blasts Politicians over Rape Controversy." YouTube, October 25. http://www.youtube.com/watch?v=H8yNCMkgk9E (accessed November 3, 2012).

WZID. 2012. *New Hampshire in the Morning*, November 6.

Zhang, Weiwu, Trent Seltzer, and Shannon L. Bichard. 2013. "Two Sides of the Coin: Assessing the Influence of Social Network Site Use during the 2012 U.S. Presidential Campaign." *Social Science Computer Review* 31:542–551.

PART 2

Message Control in the New Media Environment

5

Campaign News in the Time of Twitter

REGINA G. LAWRENCE

As economic and technological upheaval has rocked the news industry, media outlets are adapting unevenly to a new environment of dissolving boundaries and hyperfast speed. These developments are rather perfectly encapsulated in the new prominence of Twitter as a reporting and news-dissemination tool (Enda 2011; Farhi 2009b).[1] Twitter's microblogging capacity has offered journalists new ways to communicate with the public and with each other at warp speed and with some degree of freedom from the constraints of traditional news work.

Twitter is quickly spawning a cottage industry of research by scholars in mass communication and journalism. How Twitter is shaping the realm of campaign reporting—a realm characterized by the hothouse atmosphere of the campaign bus[2] (Crouse 1973) and by the dynamics of "winnowing" (Aldrich 2009; Cohen et al. 2008; Haynes et al. 2004; Matthews 1978; Norrander 2006)—is not yet well understood, however. Particularly in the primary phase of the election season, a large field of candidates can be rather quickly reduced to two contenders, with nothing less than the future of the world's richest nation at stake. Reporters are positioned not just close to the arena but often right in the campaign crossfire. Enormous resources are devoted by the campaigns to managing and manipulating public perceptions, and the press has traditionally been positioned both as the best potential check on those efforts and as a target and conveyor of them.

The purpose of this study is to ascertain how (or how much) social media technologies, particularly Twitter, are changing the nature of campaign news reporting. Put simply, how are the "affordances" of Twitter—those "features of a technology that make certain action possible" (Graves 2007, 332)—being utilized by campaign reporters? I also set out to engage in some bridge building between the established literature in political journalism and the emerging literature on digital journalism. Although that emerging literature has raised intriguing questions about how journalists can engage social media tools while abiding by traditional professional norms, it has not yet leveraged the accumulated knowledge of decades of political communication research demonstrating entrenched patterns of campaign news coverage—particularly reporters' focus on the horse race and strategic "game" of elections. Here, I report on my findings from observation of and numerous interviews with campaign reporters who covered the early 2012 Republican primaries. These interviews and observations lead me to conclude (at least preliminarily) that, at present, new media forms are being adapted to old uses more than vice versa and that Twitter, rather than fundamentally changing campaign reporting, is for the most part simply shifting established reporting routines into overdrive. Thus, the promise of social media seen by many scholars and enthusiasts to improve transparency and broaden the range of voices in the news runs up against deeply entrenched norms and routines of campaign reporting.

In the next two sections, I begin with a review of campaign reporting as we have known it in the decades leading up to this moment of upheaval and potential transformation, followed by a review of the emerging literature on journalists' use of social media.

Campaign News as We Have Known It

Mainstream American campaign news has been shaped by the same norms and routines as other daily news: a norm of objectivity according to which reporters are strongly discouraged from expressing personal opinion (Kovach and Rosenstiel 2007, 2010; Mindich 1998; Schudson 2001); a similar sanction against revealing too much about the mundane, sausage-making aspects of their work (Singer 2005, 179); and a "gatekeeping" concern for protecting journalists' prerogative to define the daily news.

The bedrock concern with objectivity is arguably heightened in campaign reporting, because campaign operatives, pundits, cable news shows, bloggers, and other critics stand ready to pounce at the slightest hint (or perception) of favoritism. And given the stakes of the presidential election, serious news outlets are likely to feel particularly keenly the weight of their assumed responsibility to remain impartial. One result of the objectivity norm at work can be seen in campaign news that resorts to a theater-criticism style to describe—and, in a veiled way, to critique—the efforts of the candidates to sway voters. As thoughtful journalists have observed, the news's obsession with the theater of politics provides a safe perch for a profession whose adherence to the norm of objectivity is constantly contested (Kovach and Rosenstiel 2001; Rosen 2011). Reporters are allowed, within the bounds of nonpartisan objectivity, to point out the man behind the curtain, so to speak—to reveal to their readers the pains campaigns are taking to dupe them. But reporters' own opinions about the candidates are rarely expressed openly (though, as Timothy Crouse [1973] revealed decades ago, those judgments indelibly shape the coverage in more subtle ways).

Ironically, though campaign news is often fixated on candidate stagecraft, the bounds of objectivity usually disallow reporters focusing too much on the conditions in which daily news is made. Candidates' efforts to sway the voters are fair game, but their efforts to manage reporters themselves are usually not considered part of the story. This opacity reflects an overall lack of transparency—or, more accurately, an illusion of transparency—noted by Sparrow: "By presenting themselves as transparent, . . . the media obscure their organizational and institutional existence and minimize the economic, professional, and informational tensions—and, necessarily, compromises—that go into news production" (2006, 150). Jay Rosen (2011) calls this "the production of innocence": "ways of reporting the news that try to advertise or 'prove' to us that the press is neutral in its descriptions, a non-partisan presenter of facts, a non-factor and non-actor in events."

This lack of transparency about campaigns' often meticulous efforts to manage the news explains why a recent *New York Times* story caused a minor firestorm. The *Times* reported that journalists who covered the 2012 presidential race for various media outlets had allowed campaign officials to vet quotations from the candidates and others close to the campaigns before publication—in exchange for reporters' continued access to the candidates (Peters 2012). This so-called quote approval, the *Times* reported, "has become accepted in Washington and on the campaign trail." What had not become accepted, it seems, is public knowledge of the practice. Lack of transparency about even mundane aspects of campaign reporting allows the notion of the objective, distanced reporter to remain intact.

The picture of campaign reporters painted thus far might seem unrealistically constrained and timid. But the reigning norms and routines of traditional journalism also allow reporters considerable leeway to evade campaigns' attempts at manipulation. Just as reporters can pull back the curtain on campaign stagecraft, they can also engage in what John Zaller (1998) calls "product substitution." Presented with the campaign's message of the day, reporters may relegate that message to a lesser place within their story or use that message as the centerpiece of a story about stagecraft—or, occasionally, about the candidate's policy record. Journalists thus retain control over the day's news—thus coming full circle to the gatekeeping function so essential to traditional journalism's claim to professionalism (see Mitchelstein and Boczkowski [2009] for a review). As Jane Singer adroitly explains, the gatekeeping role and the stance of nonpartisan objectivity are intimately related in the professional belief that "proper operation of the gates will yield unbiased news" (2005, 178). In other words, "traditional" journalism—that is, the style that has reigned in the U.S. since roughly the mid-twentieth century (Hallin 1992; Hallin and Mancini 2004; Ladd 2011; Williams and Delli Carpini 2012)—has held that professionalized reporters and editors exercising professional judgment over the daily news product help ensure impartial news.

Journalists also gain some leeway by focusing on the "horse race" among candidates and the strategic aspects of campaigns. As numerous studies have shown, political news tends to be dominated by stories that "emphasiz[e] who's ahead and behind, and the strategies and tactics or campaigning necessary to position a candidate to get ahead or stay ahead" (Cappella and Jamieson 1997, 33; see also Aalberg, Stromback, and de Vreese 2011; Farnsworth and Lichter 2003; Iyengar, Norpoth, and Hahn 2004; Lawrence 2000; Lawrence and Rose 2009, 2011; Patterson 1994; Rosenstiel 2005). As Bartholomew Sparrow notes, horse-race coverage allows reporters "to maintain their independence from partisan politics (and to avoid charges that they are partisan in one way or another)" (2006, 146). Handicapping the race allows them some (limited) distance on their subjects (though, ironically, it also positions them right beside the political insiders they cover [Didion 1988; Rosen 2011]). Focusing on the horse-race and "game" aspects of politics "permits reporters and pundits to play up their detachment" (Rosen 2011), thus reinforcing the prized notion of objectivity.

To recap, decades of research indicates that traditional, mainstream media campaign news is generally bound by strictures against reporters expressing their opinions about the candidates/campaigns or revealing too much about their daily work. At the same time, journalists have maintained their gatekeeping power and upheld notions of objectivity by practicing product substitution and positioning themselves as theater critics and handicappers of the horse race.

Digital Journalism as We Think We Know It

To date, there is something of a disconnect between the established research on campaign news coverage, discussed in the preceding section, and an emerging literature on digital journalism.[3] Much research on social media has focused on their use by nonjournalists and the general public (e.g., Conover et al. 2011; Houston et al. 2013; Huberman, Romero, and Wu 2009; Jansen et al. 2009; McKinney, Houston, and Hawthorne 2013), while other studies have explored how candidates and parties are exploiting social media to woo voters (e.g., Christensen 2013; Conway, Kenski, and Wang 2013). Some observational and ethnographic studies have shed light on how newsrooms are adapting to new technological imperatives and opportunities (e.g., Domingo et al. 2008; Groves and Brown-Smith 2011; Hermida 2010; Hermida et al. 2011; Klinenberg 2005; Singer 2004) and how news outlets are using social media to deliver news to their audiences and increase audience engagement with their sites (e.g., Pew Research Center 2011b).

More directly relevant to the present study, some researchers have explored how reporters are using social media not just to "push out" news to consumers but also to comment on events they cover. Dominic Lasorsa et al. (2011) analyzed the tweets of 500 top journalists on Twitter to determine whether reporters are "normalizing" their Twitter activity to adapt it to established journalistic norms and routines. Similarly, Avery Holton and Seth Lewis (2011) examined a sample of reporter tweets to assess their use of humor, which represents a break from traditional journalistic objectivity. Those studies built on the work of Jane Singer (2005), who analyzed 20 national and local political news blogs when blogging was still relatively new to mainstream news and concluded that political journalist-bloggers were making only partial adaptations of their craft to the new possibilities offered by blogging.[4]

More recently, an in-depth report by CNN's Peter Hamby (2013) explores how journalists and the campaigns interacted with Twitter during the 2012 general election. Hamby concludes that the "filter-free new ecosystem" created by Twitter has encouraged lightning-quick but microfocused news and has soured the relationships between reporters and the campaigns they cover. The younger reporters sent to cover the 2012 campaign—who were also being asked to do more than any generation of campaign reporters before them—were more comfortable using social media not only to report every microdevelopment from the campaign trail but to comment, often sarcastically, on the candidates and their campaigns.

Beyond ratcheting up the speed at which information, even unverified information or personal opinion, can become public, we can surmise other ways social media might challenge, even disrupt, some of the basic routines and norms of campaign reporting. One obvious potential impact of social media on reporting in general—one that has perhaps received the greatest attention so far among scholars of digital journalism—is to open news making to far more contributors. The ability not only to read the views of a vast number of people but to link to and from others' work creates a new challenge to journalists' control over the news agenda, disrupting the gatekeeping role of traditional media. Recognizing this potential, some scholars have argued that "the Internet's participatory potential is bringing about a shift in established modes of journalism and opening up the media to new voices" (Hermida et al. 2011, 130). Lasorsa et al. argue that gatekeeping "undeniably changes in a digital environment where scarcity is no longer a concern, and where audiences may easily share in the filtering process" (2011, 23–24). Jane Singer et al. (2011, 1) describe a "transition to a world in which vast numbers of strangers contribute directly to something that . . . journalists alone once controlled."[5]

Indeed, one recent study indicates that in television newsrooms, nonanchor newsroom employees have, through Twitter, become "gatejumpers" who deliver news without first passing that information through higher-level anchors and editors. Put simply, "with Twitter, . . . each individual employee is just as important a gatekeeper as the next" (Blasingame 2011, 21). More broadly, Alfred Hermida suggests that the linking and retweeting capacities of Twitter can be seen as "a system for creating a shared conversation" (2010, 303). "Traditional journalism defines fact as information and quotes from official sources," he observes, but "social media technologies like Twitter facilitate the immediate dissemination of digital fragments of news and information from official and unofficial sources over a variety of systems and devices" (298).

The degree to which Twitter has indeed become a platform for wide-open, shared conversation among reporters and their audiences is, however, an open question. Although few observers would go so far as to argue that social media have had no impact on gatekeeping, two leading scholars of digital media recently concluded that "various studies suggest that the gate and the gatekeeper role neither remain intact nor are fully replaced but have become a hinge between tradition and change" (Mitchelstein and Boczkowski 2009, 572). According to Hermida et al.'s interviews at two dozen leading national newspapers from North America, Europe, and Israel, "none of the newspapers offered any meaningful opportunities [for citizens] to influence what makes the news" (2011, 139).

Meanwhile, other impacts of Twitter on campaign reporting are possible. The immediacy and networked nature of social media could open the process of campaign reporting to more eyes. If reporters covering the campaign are tweeting even their mundane experiences, the public gets a look inside the sausage factory, increasing transparency. Of course, this effect would depend on reporters using social media in this fashion.

This has been precisely the question of a small body of research, much of which has yielded what Lasorsa et al. (2011, 21) call a "narrative of normalization": rather than immediately refashioning political journalism, they argue, "the real story of political communication during the first decade online was one of normalization," in which reporters fit new media tools to older, established reporting practices. In more recent years, however, "much has changed about digital media and its culture, particularly with the rise of Web 2.0 sites that facilitate user-generated content and user-centered control over information flow" (ibid.; see also Bruns 2008). Though Singer's (2005) study contributed significantly to this normalization narrative, she also concluded that political journalists' blogs in the middle of the first decade of the twenty-first century represented a meaningful if incomplete step toward greater journalistic transparency.

Beyond disrupting gatekeeping and puncturing the opacity of daily campaign reporting, the probable impacts of social media on other routine aspects of traditional campaign news are less clear. Theoretically, we might suppose that if campaign news can now be influenced by an exponentially larger number of people, the traditional media focus on the horse race might be diluted. That would be the case, however, only if social media followers resemble the general public, which is, it is often argued, less interested in the horse race and campaign strategy than it is in candidates' stands on issues (Cappella and Jamieson 1997; Patterson 1994; but see Trussler and Soroka 2013)—and if reporters attend to the preferences of those followers.

Finally, the impact of social media on the bedrock routines of objectivity offers a fascinating question that has generated quite a bit of debate among those who study digital journalism. Some have suggested that the *form* of microblogging lends itself to freer personal expression. Though Twitter did not exist at the time, Matthew Chalmers (2002, 389), for example, has argued that evolving "awareness" systems of computer-aided communication consist primarily of "the ongoing interpretation of representations"—not merely the passing along of facts. A recent Pew Research Center report seems to concur, noting that Twitter's "trim 140-character format . . . readily invites the instantaneous observation," that study of election-related tweets by a wide variety of users found that "tweets contain a smaller percentage of statements about candidates that are simply factual in nature without reflecting positively or negatively on a candidate" (2011b). Twitter, the report concluded, is an even more fluid and opinionated information environment than the blogosphere is.[6]

This opinionated realm might create, if not pressure, then certainly an invitation to reporters to join in. As Paul Farhi (2009b) notes, "With their intimacy and immediacy, social networks can put journalists in murky territory: 'Am I a reporter [when tweeting]? Am I an editor? Am I a critic? Or am I just talking among friends?'" For example, Holton and Lewis found in their study of reporters' use of humor on Twitter that "to the extent journalists immerse themselves in the culture of Twitter, they are more likely to step outside their traditional, serious persona and adopt some of the interpersonal humor and flavor of social media" (2011). Hamby's (2013) interviews reveal the same tension, with some reporters later regretting the snarky tweeting through which they vented their frustrations with the campaigns. On the other hand, to the degree that reporters' social media use is monitored and/or regulated by their employers, we should not expect social media to become a highly opinionated platform for campaign reporters working for established media outlets.

In short, there is some reason to expect that social media may be changing campaign reporting routines yet other reasons to expect less of an impact. According to Lasorsa et al.'s study, "the platform and culture of Twitter presents . . . the possibility for changes to journalistic norms—i.e., for journalists to be more open with opinions, more liberal in sharing their gatekeeping role, and more thorough in being transparent about the news process" (2011, 24). Yet a finding that campaign reporters are not making full use of the "affordances" of social media would be consistent with other previous literature on digital journalism, which suggests that new forms are being adapted to old uses more than vice versa (e.g., Lasorsa et al. 2011; Singer 2005).

The overall question guiding this study, then, is, *To what degree is an evolution occurring in campaign reporting due to social media technologies?* The specific research question examined here is whether campaign reporters use Twitter in ways that deviate from traditional campaign reporting norms and routines.

Methods

The findings presented here derive from interviews with and observations of political reporters and their editors. I traveled to New Hampshire and South Carolina in the days leading up to each state's 2012 Republican primary. From that vantage point,[7] I was able to observe reporters covering candidate events and to conduct impromptu interviews with reporters from a variety of news outlets (though most I happened to speak with work for traditional newspapers). I then conducted semistructured interviews with reporters and editors during visits to the home offices of both the *Washington Post* (a traditional elite outlet working to find its way in the new media environment) and *Politico* (a relatively new, primarily online outlet that has quickly become a leader on political coverage) in late January 2012, overlapping with the Republican primary in Florida. I conducted a total of 23 sit-down or telephone interviews with reporters and editors with the *Post* and *Politico*, plus over 20 additional interviews conducted on my visits to New Hampshire and South Carolina (and a few in other encounters, a few of which preceded or followed my trips to the primaries), ranging from short interviews lasting an average of ten minutes to longer sit-downs lasting an hour or more.

The particulars of each interview varied to some extent with circumstance, but in general, I probed each reporter's thoughts on the following questions (roughly in this order, starting with the questions asked most consistently across interviews):

- To what degree and how are social media integrated into your daily work? How often do you tweet? Post to a blog? Post to Facebook?
- What proportion of your time do you spend on Twitter and other social media versus engaging in more traditional forms of reporting?
- Does your news organization encourage or require you to use Twitter, Facebook, blogging?
- Does your news organization have policies regarding uses of social media (e.g., what kinds of content, expression of opinion, etc.)?
- Do you use Twitter and other social media as a way to gather *new* ideas and sources?
- How do you manage the information flow on Twitter?
- Are social media democratizing the news?
- Are social media helping reporters cover campaigns better, hindering them, or some of both?
- How do social media affect how you write (e.g., length, style, etc.)?
- What kinds of people do you "follow" on Twitter?
- Who do you envision as your social media audience?
- How do reporters and editors measure the play their organizations' stories are

getting on social media? How do they measure story "impact" or "success" in the digital media age?

Although many of these questions concern relatively mundane matters, they provided a relatively neutral starting place for conversation, and I found that many reporters jumped easily off these to larger questions about how social media are affecting the craft of journalism and their ability to make sense of the campaign. The findings presented here do not provide complete answers to the questions raised in the literature review earlier, but they provide a rich, real-world grounding for continuing research that can establish empirically how campaign reporters actually are using social media affordances.

Covering the Campaign in the Time of Twitter

One clear, simple finding emerged in my very first interviews and was reinforced in every subsequent conversation: Twitter has taken a central place in daily campaign reporting. Not long ago, Farhi (2009b) questioned whether "tweeting, if not Twitter, has any staying power," but as of now, Twitter is firmly ensconced as the central informational circuitry of campaign reporting. As one of Hamby's interviewees put it in 2012, Twitter is "the gathering spot, it's the filing center, it's the hotel bar, it's the press conference itself all in one" (2013, 24). Likewise, my interviews suggest that most campaign reporters have gone there willingly— or have been pushed into the Twitterverse by the practical necessity of staying on top of their beats. As Christy Hoppe, the Austin bureau chief for the *Dallas Morning News* and longtime campaign reporter, told me, "I need to know if a candidate just stepped in a cow patty and that's going to be the story of the day."[8] Today, anyone who happens to be at a candidate event can instantly tweet a gaffe or other development to an extended audience of reporters, pundits, bloggers, and hangers-on. That means any reporter who is not constantly following his or her Twitter feed could be caught flat-footed.

But as the "firehose" metaphor suggests, the immediacy and centrality of Twitter can quickly overwhelm its users, and political reporters have devised a variety of strategies to manage the information tide. (After all, most of the reporters I interviewed "follow" hundreds of other users, at least some of whom tweet constantly.) Some reporters simply step out of the Twitter flow from time to time, returning to their pre-social-media routines and crossing their fingers that nothing important happens that they risk missing. A few actively disengage from Twitter while they are trying to file a story or report an event because they find it distracting. A very few check into the Twitterverse only occasionally; these tend to be magazine writers, who have the luxury of taking the larger view of the campaign and therefore do not feel the need to know about every cow patty the moment it drops.

But most adopt a simple strategy of looking for waves of tweets about the same event. This is true of many editors as well as reporters out on the trail. *Politico* editor Isaac Dovere, for example, told me he checks his Twitter feed at least every ten minutes, looking for clusters of tweets that signal a potential story. For Dovere, Twitter serves as something of an "assignment desk." When Newt Gingrich cried while talking about his mother at an Iowa event in December, for example, and the tweets started popping, Dovere says he knew "we need to have something on that right away."[9]

Of course, wave watching can easily lead to a kind of "Twitterthink": a social media version of the "pack" dynamics that Timothy Crouse skewered in *Boys on the Bus* (1973). Bill Hamilton, who spoke with me shortly before he left *Politico* for the *New York Times* earlier this year, described this phenomenon as "incestuous and instantaneous." Some moments immediately "enter the bloodstream" via Twitter, Hamilton said, and come to dominate the conversation. If there is one good story, he told me, it will get retweeted by 30 people, and soon "everyone is feasting off the same carrion." One could say Twitter has opened up the range of participants in the chatter, said Hamilton, but it is "the same group—like sitting around at the bar" in earlier days.[10]

Gatekeeping and the Expanded "Bubble"

Twitter has in one sense extended "the bubble," as many reporters refer to the traveling press corps. The campaign bus has opened up to a theoretically unlimited universe of observers via social media. For reporters who are not assigned to the trail but who need political context for their own reporting, such as Erica Greider, who in 2012 covered the U.S. South for the *Economist*, Twitter "approximates the experience of being on the campaign trail."[11] Even for reporters actually on the trail, Twitter has become an indispensable window on events they cannot personally attend that nevertheless inform their own reporting.

But while Twitter has extended the bubble, for the most part, campaign reporters are still encased in the insider's circle (see Lawrence et al. 2013). As Byron Tau, the White House reporter for *Politico*, put it, Twitter offers an efficient conduit to the insiders, since "the whole Beltway crowd is there."[12] The number of reporters I encountered who could describe using social media to expand the range of their sources for stories can be numbered on one hand.

Politico's Juana Summers told me she uses Facebook to locate sources and do research on constituencies by, for example, looking at the demographics of those who "friend" candidates. Sometimes she messages these people with a link to her profile to gain perspectives for a story, and she estimates about 40% to 50% of those she has contacted in this way respond. Summers also "geolocates" eyewitnesses to an event in order to interview them. For example, she says, when Mitt

Romney made his "I like firing people" remark the day before the New Hampshire vote, she used social media to find people who had been in the room to see how they reacted to it.[13]

A few others described at least occasionally locating sources via social media. Jeff Zeleny of the *New York Times* said that during the 2010 midterm elections, he used Twitter to locate Tea Partiers in Ohio and messaged them asking for interviews.[14] But far more commonly, reporters I talked with said they are wary of using social media to find new sources. Nearly all stated a common reason: social media users are "not disinterested," as Greider put it. Rachel Van Dongen, then the deputy political editor at *Politico*, told me that Twitter gives her a "wider source pool." When I asked in what sense, she specified that through Twitter she can follow the campaign "embeds" who travel on the campaign bus and state-level reporters, who often have good local knowledge and have good on-the-ground information in a campaign state. But, Van Dongen said, she is skeptical if she does not know someone, and she avoids following people who are "partisan." When I asked if she would use Twitter to identify potential sources beyond other reporters, she suggested she rarely would. "At least if they're a reporter, that's their job"—to be informed, to be nonpartisan, she said. Similarly, another *Post* reporter told me she only rarely uses social media to reach out to new sources, when she is looking for particular expertise and has seen a tweet by someone who seems to have it. In fact, she said, if the person is on Twitter, then almost by definition he or she is not a different kind of source: "people I know who are on Twitter are other journalists."[15] These sentiments were echoed by others with whom I spoke.

Thus, the affordances of social media do not appear as advantageous to many political reporters as they might seem to digital media theorists. The "people formerly known as the audience" are not necessarily seen by these reporters as useful potential sources. David Frum of *Newsweek* and *The Daily Beast*, who I happened upon at a Concord Starbucks, gave me a flat "no" when I asked if journalists are using Twitter to identify new sources. Journalists want two things, Frum said: "eyewitness accounts and expertise." People with eyewitness information will most likely contact him via email, not social media; as for expertise, he said, it is possible that a professor of political science could use Twitter to reach out to him, but he thought that unlikely.[16] (Echoing the pattern noted earlier, Frum did not mention using social media to proactively reach out to potential sources.)

As for crowd-sourcing—a practice increasingly common inside newsrooms scrambling to engage a dwindling audience—most campaign reporters are too protective of their own stories to use social media in this way. *Politico*'s Dovere described crowd-sourcing as "very weird": if you are a reporter, you should "do your own reporting," he said, and asking your Twitter followers for information simply tips off other reporters about what you are working on. Others echoed this sentiment. Beth Frerking, assistant managing editor at *Politico*, agreed that there is a contradiction raised by Twitter: it encourages sharing among reporters, but they tend to have a norm of "don't tell *anyone* what you're working on."[17]

Twitter (and the Internet more generally) *has* leveled the playing field among news outlets of various kinds: between national reporters and the local political reporters who know the candidates from their home states; between the elite newspapers and the lowly TV embeds who provide the daily blow-by-blow from the trail; and between what is now quaintly called the mainstream media and their new media competitors, such as David Corn, Washington bureau chief for *Mother Jones*, who has over 62,000 Twitter followers and was described to me more than once by reporters from mainstream outlets as a prolific source of ongoing reporting from the campaign trail.

In some reporters' eyes, therefore, social media have blown up the bubble. Philip Rucker of the *Washington Post* insisted that Twitter has "expanded the universe dramatically" because he is "exposed to so much more reporting" than before, everything from *BuzzFeed* and *The Daily Beast* to the *Des Moines Register*.[18] But the reporters I spoke with rarely, if ever, mentioned think tanks, interest groups, grassroots groups, academic experts, or even "average voters"—all of the voices that research has continually found lacking in political news. Although Twitter has expanded the bounds of the bubble, the bubble has not burst.

Transparency and "Followers"

Just as most of the reporters I talked with do not think of their social media audiences as potential sources, they did not reveal much interest in the greater transparency afforded by Twitter. They did speak of their ability, via Twitter, to convey specifics of live events—the atmosphere in the room, the reactions of the crowd, and so on. But few spoke of revealing more about the sausage making to their audiences. And many discussed how their work is more closely monitored than ever by campaign operatives who scour reporters' Twitter accounts for any evidence of bias or error. As *Politico*'s Summers put it, everyone is on the record all the time now—not just the candidates but reporters, too.

Politico's Beth Frerking noted that many reporters include on their Twitter bio page a note that "RT doesn't equal endorsement" (i.e., retweeting the views of another user does not mean one agrees with that view). But that does not work for tweets that move beyond Twitter and become evidence of "bias," especially when taken out of context or circulated among people who do not know you, she said. Twitter brings "heightened exposure and heightened responsibility," Frerking said, and it was clear from many of my conversations that journalists at elite news outlets are concerned about this heightened visibility—a concern that may dampen transparency and at the same time heighten attention to objectivity.

Objectivity and the Horse Race

My interviews indicated concern among mainstream reporters that Twitter has encouraged journalists to deviate from standards of objectivity. Some expressed ambivalence about the ways other reporters use Twitter to publicize their opinions and engage in "snark." As Byron Tau of *Politico* described it, Twitter is defined by "look at me" and "don't be boring." On Twitter, "you can be snarky, mean, and opinionated, and two of those are okay" (the first two).[19] Summers thinks young reporters need to decide whether they are going to "be kick-ass reporters" or do "commentary and analysis." She wants to be known for her strong reporting, and so she diligently avoids commentary. More senior reporters, including Jeff Zeleny of the *Times* and Dan Balz of the *Post*, also said they avoid engaging in commentary on Twitter. And for some reporters, this commitment to objectivity presents a social media dilemma: as Todd Gilman of the *Dallas Morning News* put it, "How do you build a huge following while being circumspect?"[20]

Finally, a few interviewees were clearly troubled by what they see as a Twitter-driven intensification of horse-race reporting. According to *Politico*'s Juana Summers, the increased competition among reporters set in motion by the lightning-fast speed of Twitter has increased horse-race coverage—in fact, she said she did not think it could get any more intense, but it has. Because everyone can get scooped so quickly, it ups the competition for any scoop, but almost all "scoops" are horse race oriented. The *Post*'s Dan Balz spoke with deep concern about what he called the "ESPN-ization" of news, in which political news becomes more and more like sports coverage, with its emphasis on plays, strategies, and who is ahead or behind.[21]

But more reporters talked about a general concern that Twitter is trivializing campaign news by reducing it to "info bits." Karen Tumulty of the *Washington Post* called it "nano news," in which "everything goes micro" because of the condensed form and breakneck speed of Twitter.[22] Many described feeling pressure to resist this trend: since "everyone" (everyone who is on Twitter, that is) already knows events the moment they occur, good reporters have to work harder to differentiate their stories from others', they told me. But again and again, when reporters were prompted to reflect on how social media are affecting their work, they talked about how the form of Twitter and the 60-second news cycle it has engendered are breaking news into ever-smaller bits. Todd Gilman, following Jill Abramson's terminology (Strupp 2011), called it "scooplets." Wayne Slater called it "atomization"—news bits dribble out all day long "like a salt shaker."[23] The *Post*'s Phil Rucker worried that "context is lost, and sometimes fairness and balance are lost" in the atomized Twitterverse. Karen Tumulty agreed. Reporters, especially less experienced ones, can "catch the gaffe" but miss the bigger story, she said. The *Post*'s senior political correspondent, Dan Balz, worries that the speed of today's news cycle and the microform of Twitter compromise reporters' ability to see the bigger picture. "We get things in smaller bits," he told me, and it is "harder to put things in context," especially since on Twitter "nothing sticks": everything moves quickly, and much is quickly forgotten.

Interestingly, fewer reporters beyond those just quoted offered much reflection on how Twitter might either intensify or dilute standard horse-race reporting. Perhaps because I did not ask the right questions or perhaps because they were reluctant to talk about it—or perhaps, as Rosen (2011) and Sparrow (2006) might suggest, because they are too immersed in the frame to see it critically—stepping outside the horse-race frame was not something most reporters talked about. But implicitly there is a strong connection between their concerns with trivialization and scholars' concerns with game-framed reporting. In the age of Twitter, the info bits *are* the horse race, the game of politics reduced to micromoves. If the 140-character form of Twitter can do little to engage complicated policy debates or issue stands, it lends itself perfectly to theater criticism and ongoing revelations of minigaffes and ever so slight off-message statements.[24]

Indeed, an observation reported by Farhi (2009b) is unintentionally revealing in this regard: Twitter "works best in situations where the story is changing so fast that the mainstream media can't assemble all the facts at once.... The plane crash, the riot, the political event—these are the kinds of stories where time is important and the facts are scattered." Things are rarely so chaotic on the tightly managed presidential campaign trail, but the form and norms of Twitter encourage the same breathless pace—hence what Chris Cillizza and Aaron Blake (2012) describe as the "mountain" election, as in what every campaign molehill now threatens to become.

Moreover, there may be a multiplier effect or a vicious cycle at work, as Twitter atomizes reporters' attention and also the attention of the campaign teams. Many reporters I spoke with talked about the campaigns' new ability to monitor reporters closely via Twitter and to intervene early and assertively to try to influence the unfolding story of the day (or the hour) (see Hamby 2013). And according to the *Post*'s Karen Tumulty, the campaigns' hyperrapid response mode means that "they swing at every ball"—that campaigns do not or cannot discern what is worth responding to. The reporters I spoke with mentioned this microscrutiny of their work far more than any greater transparency that social media afford to citizens.

Conclusion

Various champions have waxed eloquent about the potential of digital media to transform journalism and democracy (Alterman 2008; Gilmor 2004; Russell 2011). Yet, "as with most [new] media technologies, there is a degree of hyperbole about the potential of Twitter" (Hermida 2010, 303; see also Lasorsa et al.

2011). Indeed, research has uncovered a variety of ways in which the participatory and democratizing potential of new media has been tamed and corralled in the hands of traditional media practitioners (Thurman and Hermida 2010; Domingo et al. 2008).

My interviews reveal a variety of responses by journalists to the new possibilities and imperatives of the Twitter-driven news environment. A few have immersed themselves, many more use Twitter and other social media selectively, and a few retain their distance. Attitudes toward the upsides and downsides of social media also vary, but standard journalistic concerns, particularly with objectivity and with being selective about sources, hold fast.

During blogging's adolescence in the first decade of the twenty-first century (a time period perhaps comparable to the current one with regard to Twitter), Singer concluded that, "particularly among national blogs associated with traditional mainstream media, . . . journalists are remaining steadfastly at the gate" with regard to user-generated content, particularly at elite news outlets, and she concluded that blogging was creating "a sort of online echo chamber of mass-mediated political views" (2005, 186, 192). My findings are consistent with Singer's, and with those of Hermida et al.: "while audience participation has become an integral part of professionally edited online publications, it is misleading to suggest that journalists are embracing opportunities to share jurisdiction over the news" (2011, 143). Perhaps these findings are unsurprising, given Mark Deuze's typology of "online journalisms" in which mainstream media remain primarily concerned with "convey[ing] stories to people 'out there'" rather than working "as a facilitator of people telling each other stories" (2003, 207). Journalists' adherence to traditional routines is also unsurprising given Gaye Tuchman's (1978) foundational observation that journalists producing news with limited resources and on a deadline seek ways to "routinize" the news.

To a significant degree, and at least for the time being, it seems likely that new media technologies may simply be shifting established campaign-reporting routines into overdrive. Among the journalists I interviewed, I found little to challenge Mark Liebovich's (2011) contention in the *New York Times* that "the usual suspects of American politics operate in a well-worn feedback loop, trade in the same green room stories, follow the same Twitter feeds" (though many reporters would presumably object to his last charge that they "traffic in the same parochial concerns and conventional wisdom that they in turn inflict on the masses"). At the same time, following Eugenia Mitchelstein and Pablo Boczkowski (2009), nor does it seem that traditional media gatekeeping is entirely intact.

Notes

1. Twitter use is expanding quickly but is much more common among journalists and politicos than among the general public, only a small percentage of whom use it (Pew

Research Center 2012). Industry research has suggested that Twitter early adopters are more likely than the general public to use it to find *news* in particular (Farhi 2009b), and a recent Pew Center survey indicated rapid growth in the number of people who "follow" various news organizations on Twitter (Pew Research Center 2011a).

2. Today, reporters are less likely to ride the bus, or the campaign plane, than in Timothy Crouse's time, in part because of the expense and partly because of new media tools that make it easier to cover the campaign virtually rather than from inside the "bubble," as reporters often refer to it (see Farhi 2009a).

3. It does seem true that in the emerging research on social media and journalism, "most studies continue to apply existing lenses to look at new phenomena," although "the potential for theoretical renewal is becoming increasingly evident" (Mitchelstein and Boczkowski 2009, 575), but the opposite problem seems also to be the case: that too little effective use is being made of research conducted on mainstream or traditional news by scholars taken with the novelty of new media platforms and tools. Indeed, as Mitchelstein and Boczkowski also observe in their review of that literature, "Historical matters have not figured prominently in the scholarship about online news production, [which] runs the risk of overemphasizing novelty and gives a sense of shallowness to the empirical findings and associated theoretical conclusions of many studies" (ibid.).

4. To the best of my knowledge, however, little if any research has been conducted on social media use by *campaign* reporters, particularly in the thick of a presidential primary campaign.

5. Of course, this gatekeeping function has been eroding since the advent of online news. As Singer (2001) noted, "Mr. Gates [a metaphorical shorthand for the gatekeeper/editor] may soon find himself out of a job"—though debates have continued about the degree to which gatekeeping persists even in seemingly noneditorial processes such as citizen bloggers-as-aggregators (Hayes, Singer, and Ceppos 2007).

6. The tension between the professional objectivity norm and how reporters might really use social media is evident in a recent version of the *Washington Post*'s social media policy, which states, "Nothing we do must call into question the impartiality of our news judgment. We never abandon the guidelines that govern the separation of news from opinion, the importance of fact and objectivity, the appropriate use of language and tone, and other hallmarks of our brand of journalism" (Hohmann et al. 2011, 44).

7. I am particularly indebted to Glenn Frankel, director of the School of Journalism at the University of Texas–Austin, whose personal contacts with the Washington press corps were invaluable, and to Dan Balz, senior political correspondent with the *Washington Post*, and Beth Frerking, assistant managing editor at *Politico*, both of whom were tremendously helpful to me in gaining access to reporters at their organizations and in the traveling press corps.

8. Interview with the author, *Dallas Morning News* Austin Bureau, Austin, Texas, December 16, 2011.

9. Interview with the author, *Politico* offices, Washington, D.C., January 31, 2012.

10. Telephone interview with the author, September 15, 2011.

11. Interview with the author, Austin, Texas, May 29, 2012.

12. Interview with the author, *Politico* offices, Washington, D.C., January 31, 2012.

13. Interview with the author, Myrtle Beach, South Carolina, January 16, 2012.

14. Interview with the author, Florence, South Carolina, January 17, 2012.

15. Interview with the author, *Politico* offices, Washington, D.C., January 31, 2012.

16. Interview with the author, Concord, New Hampshire, January 9, 2012.

17. Interview with the author, *Politico* offices, Washington, D.C., January 31, 2012.

18. Telephone interview with the author, January 10, 2012.
19. As these comments suggest, objectivity is every bit as much a concern at the upstart *Politico* as it is at the old-school *Washington Post*—not surprisingly, since its founders were longtime mainstream reporters themselves. That commitment to objectivity was firmly reiterated in my interview with managing editor Bill Nichols: at the time *Politico* was launched, Nichols said, there was "fervent debate" about whether nonpartisan, objective news could survive, whether there was any place for it anymore. According to Nichols, "The old timers won" that debate (interview with the author, *Politico* offices, Washington, D.C., February 1, 2012).
20. Interview with the author, Washington, D.C., January 30, 2012.
21. Interview with the author, Concord, New Hampshire, January 10, 2012.
22. Interview with the author, *Washington Post* offices, Washington, D.C., February 1, 2012.
23. Interview with the author, Austin, Texas, January 13, 2012.
24. For example, during the January 16, 2012, Republican primary debate televised from Myrtle Beach, South Carolina, which I watched along with reporters in the media room, Mitt Romney said he was "not opposed" to releasing his income tax records, which differed from his previous stonewalling on that question. Romney's seemingly improvised answer set off a wave of tweets, and within minutes, *Politico*'s Alexander Burns had posted a story. In contrast, that night's debate also featured a rather lengthy discussion of Social Security and related issues, and the candidates offered fairly detailed and complicated answers. Far fewer tweets appeared during that ten minutes or so of the debate, and nothing that looked like a wave. (The twitterers, at least those I was following, were also strangely quiet when the studio audience reacted raucously to a racially charged exchange between Newt Gingrich and that night's moderator, Juan Williams.)

References

Aalberg, Toril, Jesper Stromback, and Claes H. de Vreese. 2011. The framing of politics as strategy and game: A review of concepts, operationalizations and key findings. *Journalism* 13 (2): 162–178.

Aldrich, John. 2009. The invisible primary and its effects on democratic choice. *PS: Political Science & Politics* 42 (1) (January): 33–38.

Alterman, Eric. 2008. Out of print: The death and life of the American newspaper. *New Yorker*, March 31, 48–60.

Blasingame, Dale. 2011. Gatejumping: Twitter, TV news, and the delivery of breaking news. *International Symposium on Online Journalism* 1 (2): 5–28.

Bruns, Axel. 2008. The active audience: Transforming journalism from gatekeeping to gatewatching. In *Making news online: The ethnography of new media production*, edited by Chris Patterson and David Domingo, 171–184. New York: Peter Lang.

Cappella, Joseph N., and Kathleen H. Jamieson. 1997. *Spiral of cynicism*. New York: Oxford University Press.

Chalmers, Matthew. 2002. Awareness, representation, and interpretation. *Computer Supported Cooperative Work (CSCW)* 11 (3–4): 389–409.

Christensen, Christian. 2013. Wave-riding and hashtag-jumping: Twitter, minority "third parties," and the 2012 U.S. elections. *Information, Communication & Society* 16 (5) (June): 646–666.

Cillizza, Chris, and Aaron Blake. 2012. The mountain campaign. *The Fix* (blog), *Washington Post*, April 20. http://www.washingtonpost.com/blogs/the-fix/post/2012-the-mountain-campaign/2012/04/20/gIQAhvvEVT_blog.html.

Cohen, Marty, David Karol, Hans Noel, and John Zaller. 2008. *The party decides: Presidential nominations before and after reform.* Chicago: University of Chicago Press.

Conover, Michael D., Jacob Ratkiewicz, Matthew Francisco, Bruno Goncalves, Alessandro Flammini, and Filippo Menczer. 2011. Political polarization on Twitter. Association for the Advancement of Artificial Intelligence, Proceedings of the Fifth International Conference on Weblogs and Social Media. http://jrnetsolserver.shorensteincente.netdna-cdn.com/wp-content/uploads/2012/03/conover_icwsm2011_polarization.pdf.

Conway, Bethany A., Kate Kenski, and Di Wang. 2013. Twitter use by presidential primary candidates during the 2012 campaign. *American Behavioral Scientist* 57 (11) 1596–1610.

Crouse, Timothy. 1973. *The boys on the bus.* New York: Random House.

Deuze, Mark. 2003. The web and its journalisms: Considering the consequences of different types of newsmedia Online. *New Media and Society* 5 (2): 203–230.

Didion, Joan. 1988. Insider baseball. *New York Review of Books*, October 28. http://www.nybooks.com/articles/archives/1988/oct/27/insider-baseball/.

Domingo, David, Thorsten Quandt, Ari Heinonen, Steve Paulussen, Jane B. Singer, and Marina Vujnovic. 2008. Participatory journalism practices in the media and beyond: An international comparative study of initiatives in online newspapers. *Journalism Practice* 2 (3): 326–342.

Enda, Jodi. 2011. Campaign coverage in the time of Twitter. *American Journalism Review*, October–November. http://www.ajr.org/article.asp?id=5134.

Farhi, Paul. 2009a. Off the bus. *American Journalism Review*, December–January. http://www.ajr.org/article.asp?id=4644.

———. 2009b. The Twitter explosion. *American Journalism Review*, April–May. http://www.ajr.org/article.asp?id=4756.

Farnsworth, Stephen J., and Robert S. Lichter. 2003. *The nightly news nightmare: Network television's coverage of U.S. presidential elections, 1988–2000.* Lanham, MD: Rowman and Littlefield.

Gillmor, Dan. 2004. *We the media: Grassroots journalism by the people, for the people.* Sebastopol, CA: O'Reilly.

Graves, Lucas. 2007. The affordances of blogging: A case study in culture and technological effects. *Journal of Communication Inquiry* 31:331–346.

Groves, Jonathon, and Carrie Brown-Smith. 2011. Stopping the presses: A longitudinal case study of the *Christian Science Monitor* transition from print daily to web always. *International Symposium on Online Journalism* 1 (2): 86–128.

Hallin, Daniel C. 1992. The passing of the "high modernism" of American journalism. *Journal of Communication* 42 (3): 14–25.

Hallin, Daniel C., and Paolo Mancini. 2004. *Comparing media systems.* New York: Cambridge University Press.

Hamby, Peter. 2013. Did Twitter kill the boys on the bus? Searching for a better way to cover a campaign. Joan Shorenstein Center on the Press, Politics, and Public Policy.

Haynes, Audrey A., Paul-Henri Gurian, Michael H. Crespin, and Christopher Zorn. 2004. The calculus of concession: Media coverage and the dynamics of winnowing in presidential nominations. *American Politics Research* 32:310–337.

Hermida, Alfred. 2010. Twittering the news: The emergence of ambient journalism. *Journalism Practice* 4 (3): 297–308.

Hermida, Alfred, David Domingo, Ari Heinonen, Steve Paulussen, Thorsten Quandt, Zvi Reich, Jane Singer, and Marina Vujnovic. 2011. The additive recipient: Participatory journalism through the lens of the Dewey-Lippmann debate. *International Symposium on Online Journalism* 1 (2): 129–148.

Hohmann, James, and the 2010–2011 ASNE Ethics and Values Committee. 2011. 10 best practices for social media: Helpful guidelines for news organizations. ASNE. http://asne.org/portals/0/publications/public/10_best_practices_for_social_media.pdf.
Holton, Avery E., and Seth C. Lewis. 2011. Journalists, social media, and the use of humor on Twitter. *Electronic Journal of Communication* 21 (1–2). http://www.cios.org/EJCPUBLIC/021/1/021121.html.
Houston, J. Brian, Mitchell S. McKinney, Joshua Hawthorne, and Matthew L. Spialek. 2013. Frequency of Tweeting during presidential debates: Effect on debate attitudes and knowledge. *Communication Studies* 64 (5): 548–560.
Huberman, Bernardo A., David M. Romero, and Fang Wu. 2009. Social networks that matter: Twitter under the microscope. *First Monday* 14 (1). http://firstmonday.org/ojs/index.php/fm/article/view/2317/2063.
Iyengar, Shanto, Helmut Norpoth, and Kyu S. Hahn. 2004. Consumer demand for election news: The horserace sells. *Journal of Politics* 66 (1): 157–175.
Jansen, Bernard J., Mimi Zhang, Kate Sobel, and Abdur Chowdury. 2009. Twitter power: Tweets as electronic word of mouth. *Journal of the American Society for Information Science and Technology* 60 (11): 2169–2188.
Klinenberg, Eric. 2005. Convergence: News production in a digital age. *Annals of the American Academy of Political and Social Science* 597:48–64.
Kovach, Bill, and Tom Rosensiel. 2001. Campaign lite: Why reporters won't tell us what we need to know. *Washington Monthly*, January–February. http://www.washingtonmonthly.com/features/2001/0101.kovach.rosenstiel.html.
———. 2007. *The elements of journalism: What newspeople should know and the public should expect.* New York: Three Rivers.
———. 2010. *Blur: How to know what's true in the age of information overload.* New York: Bloomsbury.
Ladd, Jonathan M. 2011. *Why Americans hate the media and how it matters.* Princeton: Princeton University Press.
Lasorsa, Dominic L., Seth C. Lewis, and Avery E. Holton. 2011. Normalizing Twitter: Journalism practice in an emerging communication space. *Journalism Studies* 13 (1): 19–36.
Lawrence, Regina G. 2000. Game-framing the issues: Tracking the strategy frame in public policy news. *Political Communication* 17:93–114.
Lawrence, Regina G., Logan Molyneux, Mark Coddington, and Avery E. Holton. 2013. Tweeting conventions: Political journalists' use of Twitter to cover the 2012 presidential campaign. *Journalism Studies*, September 2013. http://www.tandfonline.com/doi/abs/10.1080/1461670X.2013.836378#.UlH2bxYRy5d.
Lawrence, Regina G., and Melody Rose. 2009. *Hillary Clinton's race for the White House.* Boulder, CO: Lynne Rienner.
———. 2011. Bringing out the hook: Exit talk in media coverage of Hillary Clinton and past presidential campaigns. *Political Research Quarterly* 64 (4): 870–883.
Liebovich, Mark. 2011. In Des Moines, seeking the pulse of the people and finding a hall of mirrors. *The Caucus* (blog), *New York Times*, December 31. http://thecaucus.blogs.nytimes.com/2011/12/31/in-des-moines-seeking-the-pulse-of-the-people-and-finding-a-hall-of-mirrors/.
Matthews, Donald R. 1978. "Winnowing": The news media and the 1976 presidential nomination. In *Race for the presidency*, ed. James David Barber, 55–78. Englewood Cliffs, NJ: Prentice-Hall.
McKinney, Mitchell S., J. Brian Houston, and Joshua Hawthorne. 2013. Social watching a 2012 presidential election debate. *American Behavioral Scientist*, October 17, 2013. doi:10.1177/0002764213506211.

Mindich, David T. Z. 1998. *Just the facts: How "objectivity" came to define American journalism*. New York: NYU Press.

Mitchelstein, Eugenia, and Pablo J. Boczkowski. 2009. Between tradition and change: A review of recent research on online news production. *Journalism* 10 (5): 562–586.

Norrander, Barbara. 2006. The attrition game: Initial resources, initial contests, and the exit of candidates during the US presidential primary season. *British Journal of Political Science* 36 (3): 487–507.

Patterson, Thomas E. 1994. *Out of order*. New York: Vintage.

Peters, Jeremy W. 2012. Latest word on the trail? I take it back. *New York Times*, July 15. http://www.nytimes.com/2012/07/16/us/politics/latest-word-on-the-campaign-trail-i-take-it-back.html?pagewanted=all&_r=0.

Pew Research Center 2011a. How mainstream media outlets use Twitter. November 14. http://pewresearch.org/pubs/2130/twitter-news-organizations.

———. 2011b. Twitter and the campaign. December 8. http://www.journalism.org/node/27619.

———. 2012. Twitter use 2012. May 31. http://www.pewinternet.org/Reports/2012/Twitter-Use-2012.aspx.

Rosen, Jay. 2011. Why political coverage is broken. *PressThink*, August 26. http://pressthink.org/2011/08/why-political-coverage-is-broken/.

Rosenstiel, Tom. 2005. Political polling and the new media culture: A case of more being less. *Public Opinion Quarterly* 69:698–715.

Russell, Adrienne. 2011. *Networked: A contemporary history of news in transition*. Malden, MA: Polity.

Schudson, Michael. 2001. The objectivity norm in American journalism. *Journalism* 2 (2): 149–70.

Singer, Jane B. 2001. The metro wide web: Changes in newspapers' gatekeeping role online. *Journalism & Mass Communication Quarterly*, Spring, 65–80.

———. 2004. Strange bedfellows? The diffusion of convergence in four news organizations. *Journalism Studies* 5 (1): 3–18.

———. 2005. The political j-blogger: "Normalizing" a new media form to fit old norms and practices. *Journalism* 6 (2): 173–198.

Singer, Jane B., David Domingo, Ari Heinonen, Alfred Hermida, Steve Paulussen, Thorsten Quandt, Zvi Reich, and Marina Vujnovic. 2011. *Participatory journalism: Guarding open gates at online newspapers*. Malden, MA: Wiley-Blackwell.

Sparrow, Bartholomew H. 2006. A research agenda for an institutional media. *Political Communication* 23:145–157.

Strupp, Joe. 2011. *New York Times*' Abramson on 2012 coverage, alleged liberal bias, and roaming the newsroom. *Media Matters* (blog), September 30. http://mediamatters.org/blog/2011/09/30/new-york-times-abramson-on-2012-coverage-allege/181150.

Thurman, Neil, and Alfred Hermida. 2010. Gotcha: How newsroom norms are shaping participatory journalism online. In *Web journalism: A new form of citizenship?*, edited by Sean Tunney and Garrett Monaghan, 46–62. Eastbourne, UK: Sussex Academic.

Trussler, Marc, and Stuart Soroka. 2013. Consumer demand for negative and cynical news frames. Paper presented at the annual conference of the Political Science Association, Victoria, BC, June.

Tuchman, Gaye. 1978. *Making news: A study in the construction of reality*. New York: Free Press.

Williams, Bruce A., and Michael Delli Carpini. 2012. *After broadcast news: Media regimes, democracy, and the new information environment*. New York: Cambridge University Press.

Zaller, John R. 1998. The rule of product substitution in presidential campaign news. *Annals of the American Academy of Political Science* 560 (November): 109–126.

6

New and Traditional Media Reportage on Electoral Campaign Controversies

MIKE GRUSZCZYNSKI

There has been perhaps no other time in the history of the United States press when candidates had less ability to "control the message." With the advent of a newly reinvigorated partisan press, brought about partly as the result of technological change (Sheppard 2007; Sunstein 2007), campaign operations are now faced with getting their message out with not just a small handful of media outlets but a plethora of sources that hew to their own ideological and partisan divides (Stroud 2011). Moreover, at no other time have candidates had less ability to mitigate the negative political ramifications of campaign scandals, given the fragmented state of the media.

Given the amount of ink spilled discussing these effects of new media, it is sometimes difficult to imagine that the 2012 presidential election was only the third such U.S. election to take place in an information environment characterized by a preponderance of social media and blogs (Hong and Nadler 2012; Li 2013). In the aftermath of the supposed massive communication shift that brought these blogs, social media, and "niche" news to the forefront, numerous scholars have warned of these information sources' role in, among other things, increases in ideological extremism (e.g., Sunstein 2007) and disruption of political consensus (e.g., Stroud and Muddiman 2013; Stroud 2011; Bennett and Iyengar 2008), while still others have retained hope that fundamental changes brought on by the democratization of information production will bring with it, at the very least, a more diverse, democratized media environment (Robinson 2013; Dimitrova and Bystrom 2013; Benkler 2007).

On the basis of this lack of consensus on the effects of the new media on political communication, this research asks, Do new and traditional media sources differ in their reportage on campaign controversies, and if so, how do these differences arise? Due to the diversity of sources in the current media environment, are candidates less able to control their message? In reporting on political controversies, do partisan blogs differentially report on emergent campaign issues on the basis of their ideological dispositions? How do the patterns of partisan blog reportage influence the mainstream media, as well as blogs on the "other side"? These questions are of central importance to our understanding of the new media environment, as well as the broader political world, for several reasons.

For one, an oft-repeated warning of new media critics is that the reemergence of a partisan press furthers ideological extremism through lopsided reportage (e.g., Sunstein 2007; Stroud and Muddiman 2013; Stroud 2011). If consumers of ideologically tilted political information selectively expose themselves only to sources comporting with their beliefs, and the reporting patterns of those sources differ greatly from the "average" of the communication environment, then democratic deliberation is weakened as a result (Stroud 2008; Bennett and Iyengar 2008). On the other hand, if citizens are exposed to similar reportage, regardless of the source, these fears are at least partially unwarranted (though the question of the *content* of those messages would remain a potential problem; see Lawrence, Sides, and Farrell 2010).

This research also serves to illuminate how political blogs fit into the broader American media environment. The emergence of the new media at the turn of the twenty-first century brought with it the possibility that information flows—political or not—would become more democratized, with more opportunities for individuals and groups outside traditional spheres of power to exert influence over the transmission of political information and ideas (Benkler 2007). This research will increase our understanding of whether and how the democratization of the press has altered the dynamics of campaign coverage within U.S. elections and in doing so will help us to understand who, if anyone, controls the message within the electoral context.

To that end, this research makes use of the 2012 United States presidential election as a test bed for an investigation into the dynamics of new media campaign coverage in the broader media environment, specifically as it relates to coverage of campaign controversies during the primary and general presidential elections. As controversies are present in most U.S. electoral contests (see Just, Crigler, and Buhr 1999), focusing solely on the dynamics of their coverage among new and traditional media sources allows for tests of differences in reportage, cross-media influence, and the overall dynamics of an expanded information environment. Six controversies related to the major-party candidates, President Barack Obama and former Massachusetts governor Mitt Romney, were selected for analysis, with focus on the reportage of ten popular political blogs and four mainstream media sources.

Political Controversy in the Traditional and New Media

Scholars have long recognized the tendency of the traditional media to fixate on sensationalism and political controversy. This fixation stems from myriad factors, such as increased movement toward soft news formats due to economic pressures and audience desires (Grabe, Zhou, and Barnett 2001; Hamilton 2005; Plasser 2005; Williams and Delli Carpini 2011), journalistic standards of newsworthiness (Cook 1998), journalists' cynicism toward political leaders and institutions (Patterson 1994; Cappella and Jamieson 1996, 1997), and even the mass media's role themselves as purveyors of political power and influence (Herman and Chomsky 2002). With respect to elections specifically, the gaffes and controversies that are bound to emerge over the course of ever-lengthening campaigns fit into journalists' schemas that view politicians as carefully scripted power seekers, with any deviation from the script seen as indicative of their *true* nature and thus especially worthy of coverage (Patterson 1994; Bennett 1981).

Regardless of whether this fixation represents a failure of the journalistic enterprise, the mainstream press does have incentives to retain some modicum of balance in its reporting, incentives that political blogs in most cases lack. For one, practitioners within the traditional media desire to be perceived as neutral participants in reportage of political controversies (e.g., Kaplan 2006; Cook 2005). This may be due to the mass media's need to attract as large an audience as possible to garner advertising revenue (Hamilton 2005), or it simply may stem from journalists' socialization into professional norms and values that emphasize balanced treatment of issues and leaders (Schudson 2001; Vos 2012).

This objectivity standard has often been noted to be almost entirely absent from mainstream practitioners' counterparts in the new media (see Robertson et al. 2013; Baum and Groeling 2008; Lawrence, Sides, and Farrell 2010). Whereas traditional media outlets have numerous incentives to carry an air of objectivity, similar incentives simply do not exist in the realm of political blogs. From the prospect of curating an audience, the incentive to build readership by appealing to the middle of the political spectrum[1] is often absent from online media, which reside within what Chris Anderson (2008) terms a "long tail" economy of information flows. This long tail emphasizes the catering of content toward small(er) cadres of like-minded individuals, as opposed to content aimed at satisfying the largest audience possible (Anderson 2008; Sheppard 2007; Stroud 2011).

Because of this economy of information flows, individuals who seek out political information online have no incentive to frequent news sources that cater to political moderation, especially when any number of sources comporting to their beliefs litter the Internet (see Stroud 2008, 2011; Sunstein 2007; Negroponte 1996). Stated simply, political blogs have only incentives to be nonobjective in their coverage of political issues and events, a point this essay examines within the context of controversies in the 2012 presidential election.

Ideological Bias, Blogs, and Campaigns

The ideological bias that tends to manifest itself as a result of long-tail incentives has been found to occur not only in blogs' slanted textual content but also in links to like-minded blogs (Meraz 2013; Hargittai, Gallo, and Kane 2008) and the selection of story topics that either benefit their side or harm the other (Baum and Groeling 2008). The latter point is of particular relevance to the study of controversy survival among political blogs, given that those controversies that are most likely to harm the performance of the opposing candidate will more than likely be covered more extensively by blogs than are those controversies potentially harming to their "own" candidate.

Though 2012 marked only the third presidential election to take place within the new media environment, political blogs' propensity to emphasize controversy in an unbalanced manner has already provided plenty of cases for analysis. For example, the 2004 presidential contest between incumbent George W. Bush and Senator John Kerry saw much in the way of slanted controversy coverage within the new media, first with coverage of the Swift Boat Veterans for Truth group's claims about Kerry's Vietnam service record and later with coverage of *CBS News* anchor Dan Rather's evidence against Bush's National Guard service record that was soon after found to be fabricated (see Davis 2009). Although the former story was initially reported in the mass media, with blogs later picking it up, in the latter case, conservative bloggers expended a great deal of time reporting on these controversies to the point of the mainstream media following their lead (Williams et al. 2005).

Similar patterns of behavior emerged in the 2008 presidential contest between then-Senator Barack Obama and Senator John McCain, though this election in particular appeared to represent a more mediated flow of information from the mainstream media to political blogs. Jure Leskovec, Lars Backstrom, and Jon Kleinberg (2009) tracked the diffusion of communication memes across the online media, finding that several controversies in particular were especially prevalent, including Obama's "lipstick on a pig" comment directed at vice presidential candidate Sarah Palin and McCain's "fundamentals of the economy are strong" comment in reference to the flagging economy. What is most interesting in the case of controversial issues from the 2008 campaign was that, in contrast to the 2004 election, the mainstream media appeared to be the primary drivers of their diffusion into the broader media environment (Leskovec, Backstrom, and Kleinberg 2009, but see Wallsten 2007 for further mixed evidence of bidirectional influence).

Media Resources and Their Effects on Issue Coverage Patterns

Blogs tend to expend more of their efforts on campaign controversy reportage than do their traditional counterparts for the simple fact that blogs typically have fewer resources at their disposal (Karpf 2008; Scott 2006). Though a handful of new media platforms—most notably Huffington Post—have begun to resemble traditional media operations, for the most part blogs and blog creators are much more hamstrung in their ability to embark on the type of investigatory journalism that mainstream media sources have used for decades (Davis 2009).

However, given blogs' more opinion-driven nature, coupled with ideological proclivities, they *do* have remarkable leeway to fixate on any number of controversies for extended periods of time.

That said, given that the mainstream media have long been recognized as the primary drivers of the news agenda (e.g., McCombs and Shaw 1972; McCombs 2004), the new media are likely to follow their lead in which issues receive the most attention at any given time in a political campaign. This may be due to the fact that blogs, just like the mainstream media, are likely responsive to what their audience demands in terms of news, especially given news consumers' ability to seek out information online (see Tewksbury 2003). If the brunt of attention in the media environment is focused on one issue, blogs would be remiss to ignore this in reporting on other issues. On this point, Gruszczynski and Wagner (2010) found that blogs are responsive to both public and traditional media attention to issues, demonstrating that even given their supposed freedom to cover whatever issues they please, blogs are just as subject to attentional and agenda pressures as any other entity within the political sphere.

This susceptibility to outside influences is shown in other research on blogs' place within the agenda-setting cycle. Kevin Wallsten (2007) found that political blogs very often pick up on the state of the current media agenda in deciding which issues to report, though a blog-to-media relationship sometimes manifested itself as well (see also Lee 2007). Additionally, partisan blogs have been shown to engage issues from counterattitudinal blogs, demonstrating agenda-setting influences *within* the new media environment (Hargittai, Gallo, and Kane 2008). That said, the spread of "viral" political controversy does appear to be driven more by blogs than by the mainstream media, as evidenced by a recent study undertaken by Karine Nahon et al. (2011).

This research furthers our understanding of mainstream and new media sources' coverage patterns within the campaign context by leveraging six issues that emerged during the 2012 presidential campaign. Specifically, I make use of data on these issues, first, to test the hypothesis that political blogs give more attention to campaign controversies than do their mainstream counterparts and, second, to determine whether agenda-setting effects in the case of these 2012 campaign controversies were unidirectional (e.g., mainstream media → political blogs) or bidirectional (e.g., mainstream media ↔ political blogs). The methods employed in these analyses are considered in the following section.

Sampling the New Media Environment

One of the primary difficulties in studying political blogs is garnering a sufficiently representative sample from a population of a size that is, unfortunately, unknown; simply put, a decision has to be made on which blogs to include and which to exclude. Given that this research is primarily concerned with the interaction between political blogs and the mainstream media, however, the onus of which blogs to sample is less on being as representative as possible and more on capturing the dynamics of elite (or at least close to elite) new media sources vis-à-vis traditional media. Thus, I followed the lead of Wallsten (2007, 2008) and Eszter Hargittai et al. (2008) in assembling a set of "A-list" political blogs from the Technorati.com blog-tracking website's "Top 100" political blogs list.[2] Technorati is a long-running blog-tracking service that ranks blogs using a variety of factors, most notably the degree to which a blog's posts are linked to by other blogs, in order to rate them on their level of influence in the broader new media environment. Similar to the method of Wallsten (2007), the top-five liberal and top-five conservative blogs were selected from the Top 100 list in an attempt to capture a representative sample of those sources most likely to have some modicum of influence within the media environment.

The ideological leanings of each blog were surmised by first checking the "About" page for cues as to its slant; most of the blogs sampled made clear on these pages which direction they lean.[3] The five liberal blogs included *ThinkProgress*, *Talking Points Memo*, *Daily Kos*, *Crooks and Liars*, and *America Blog*. The five conservative blogs in the sample include *RedState*, *The Daily Beast*, *Instapundit*, *HotAir*, and *Michelle Malkin*.

In order to get a glimpse of mainstream media reportage on campaign controversies during the 2012 presidential campaign, four traditional sources were selected. The *New York Times*, often cited as the national newspaper of record, was selected for analysis.[4] In addition, CBS News was selected, given that most Americans continue to receive political news primarily from broadcast outlets,[5] as well as Fox News and MSNBC because of their status as the primary cable news networks for many Americans.[6] Given their oft-perceived ideological slants (Turner 2007), including these two cable news networks in the analysis should provide a fuller view of the pattern of reportage within the mainstream media environment.

Selection of Campaign Controversies

Six controversies that emerged in 2012 were selected for analysis. For Obama, the controversies selected included the administration's handling of the attacks on the U.S. embassy in Benghazi, as well as his "you didn't build that" and "private sector is doing fine" comments. Inclusion of coverage on the Benghazi attacks is appropriate because of widespread criticism of the Obama administration's handling of the September 11, 2012, attacks on the U.S. embassy in Libya. The "you didn't build that" comments were made by Obama in a July 13, 2012, interview in which he noted the importance of federal support of private businesses—comments that came under a great deal of scrutiny from the right. The "private sector is doing fine" comments were likewise made by Obama in an interview in

June of that year and received criticism due to the ongoing economic downturn at that time.

For Romney, controversies included his "47%" comments, his gaffe-prone trip to Europe, and reports about the Romney family strapping their dog to the roof of a car during a trip to Canada. The 47% comments, which stated that a large proportion of Americans receive government benefits without paying taxes, drew much ire in the national media and from Democrats in particular. The issue of the trip centers on his tour of England and Continental Europe, where Romney criticized preparations of the upcoming Summer Olympics and made several other gaffes to various leaders. The dog episode, which involved the family canine, Seamus, was politicized early on in the Republican primaries by Newt Gingrich and received quite a lot of attention in the national media throughout the campaign.

In selecting these six controversies, the hope was to get a look at how the time of the controversy, as well as its character, influenced blog and mainstream media dynamics during various points of the election. As such, these six controversies are appropriate, as one originated during the Republican primaries (Romney's dog), three originated in the summer prior to the general election ("didn't build that," "private sector is doing fine" and Romney's European trip), and the two largest controversies took place in the midst of the general election ("47%" and Benghazi). As in any campaign, numerous controversies were undoubtedly left out of this analysis, but I believe selection of these particular six represents a good test of the hypothesis offered previously. It is important to note that due to Obama's status as the incumbent during the 2012 election, in addition to not having to field a challenger in a primary, we might expect for the Obama campaign to have an easier go at controlling the message than the Romney campaign, owing to the entrenched nature of the former vis-à-vis the latter. As is always the case, however, the data may or may not end up speaking to this expectation.

The sampled blogs were scraped using author-designed software that searched each site for terms related to each issue,[7] while mainstream media articles were obtained through the LexisNexis online database. Articles were downloaded from the initial point of the controversy until Election Day, November 6, 2012. As is the case in most article-selection procedures, many of the articles culled for analysis were not actually relevant to the issue in question. With this in mind, each article was topic coded by skimming the full text and using keyword-in-context software designed by the author.[8] Of 11,550 blog articles and 2,286 mainstream media articles initially culled, 2,588 blog and 1,490 media articles were deemed relevant to the issues selected for analysis. Given that articles may mention more than one topic, some are included in analyses across issues; the number of articles repeated across issues was small, making up about 8% of the blog articles and 3% of the mainstream media articles.

Discussion of Results

Figure 6.1 presents the number of articles obtained for each of the six issues selected in this study, broken down by the source of coverage. The issues receiving the most coverage by both traditional and new media sources overall were those covering controversy over the Obama administration's handling of the Benghazi attacks and Romney's "47%" comments. That these controversies received so much coverage is especially surprising given how close they occurred to Election Day—both the Benghazi attacks and "47%" comments emerged onto the public stage in mid-September—and as such, there was less time for media coverage than was the case with the other issues under study. As would be expected, liberal blogs covered the Benghazi controversy much less than did either conservative blogs or the mainstream media, while conservative blogs likewise covered the "47%" comments substantially less than liberal blogs and the mainstream media did.

Obama's "you didn't build that" comment, stated in reference to private businesses receiving financial support from the federal government, also received

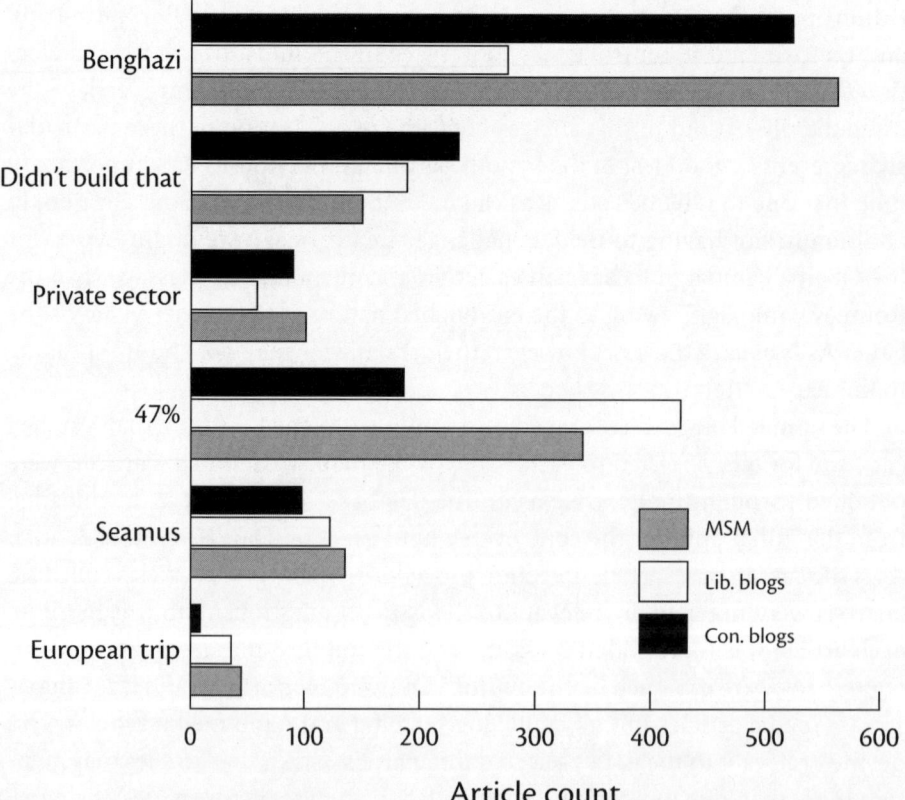

Figure 6.1. Article counts, by issue and media source

quite a lot of coverage from political blogs, though more from conservative blogs, which may owe in part to the fact that Republicans featured the slogan "We Built This" at their national convention. The similar "private sector is doing fine" comment from Obama, made on June 8, 2012, received the least amount of coverage of the Obama-related controversies and, as with the others, received more attention from conservative than liberal blogs, with the mainstream media reporting on the comment at the highest frequency.

The two other Romney-related controversies, centering on the Romney family's dog Seamus's trip on top of their car and Romney's controversy-laden European visit in summer 2012, received comparatively low levels of attention from any of the sources under study. Interestingly, both the Seamus and European-trip controversies received more coverage from the mainstream media than from either liberal or conservative blogs.

Figure 6.2 plots time-series data of blog and mainstream media coverage of controversies related to Obama from their onset until the election. What is most striking from these plots, though not surprising given the issue, is the amount of sustained coverage that was given to the Obama administration's handling of the Benghazi attacks. As would be expected, conservative blogs gave the Benghazi incidents the highest volume of coverage throughout most of its life span, liberal blogs the least, and the mainstream media somewhere between the two. Though coverage levels of the controversy decayed quickly immediately following its occurrence—dropping from an immediate high of about 25 articles from each source in the days after September 11—coverage of Benghazi spiked numerous times as the campaign progressed, with conservative blogs and the mainstream media releasing over 20 stories a day at several points around the time of the first and second presidential debates in early October. Moreover, at only one point in time—late October—did conservative blogs devote substantially more coverage to the Benghazi attacks than did the traditional media. Though the data is not available for testing why this was the case at that particular time, it should be noted that in late October the Republican candidate for the seat of retiring Senator Richard Lugar of Indiana, Richard Mourdock, made a much-maligned comment regarding abortion and religion that garnered a great deal of media coverage. Given what we know about partisan political blogs' patterns of reportage, it is perhaps not surprising that attention would continue to be oriented toward a Democratic controversy, while the rest (mainstream and liberal) media switched away from that same controversy.

Controversy over Obama's "you didn't build that" statement exhibits more of a trend that we might expect from controversies, with a large spike of about 15 stories from conservative blogs at the onset of the controversy, persisting for about half a month and then decaying to the point where it received about three mentions a day, on average. The second large spike in this controversy, which

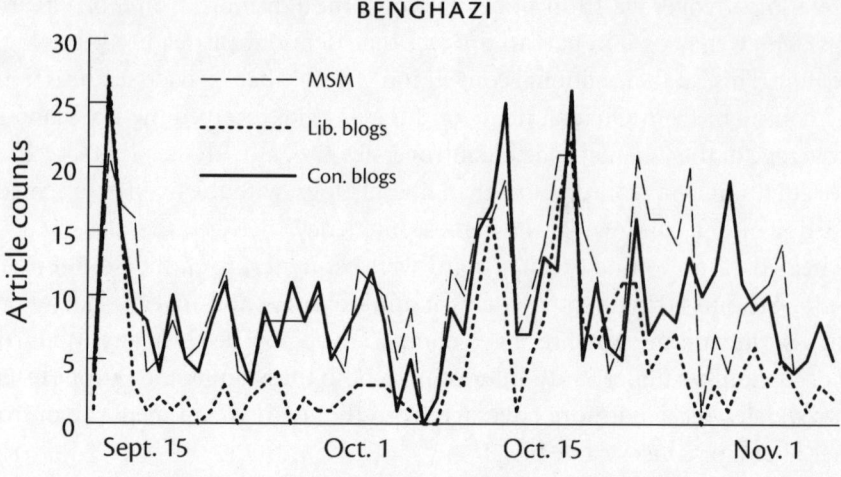
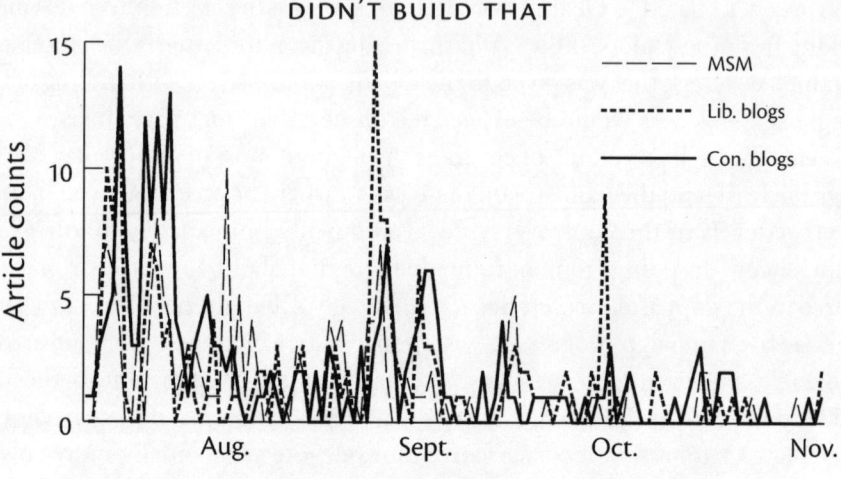
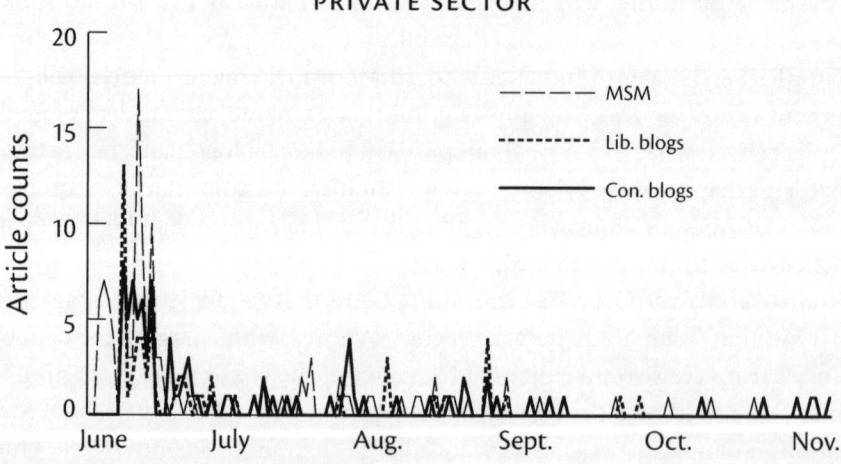

Figure 6.2. Obama controversy coverage over time

was somewhat surprisingly driven mostly by liberal blogs, occurred around the Republican National Convention, where a turn on the phrase was used as a slogan.

Obama's "private sector is doing fine" comments exhibit a similar spike and decay to that of the previous issue, with an early peak of 17 stories at the controversy's onset declining to an average of one mention a day after half a month's time. Interestingly, the brunt of coverage of the "private sector" comment came from liberal blogs, especially early on; however, most subsequent coverage of this controversy was driven by conservative blogs, which reported on the comments periodically from their inception through to the end of the campaign.

Given these results over time, it appears that each of these three cases had a major part in the communication environment of the 2012 campaign, though by far the most covered was the Obama administration's response to the Benghazi attacks. When one keeps in mind that Obama was occupying the Oval Office at the time of the campaign, it is not surprising that the largest controversy involved an actual policy issue, and a tragic one at that, rather than just a gaffe or campaign mistake. This is of course in direct contrast to Mitt Romney's candidacy, which because he had not occupied political office for a decade, featured only non-policy-related controversies, shown in figure 6.3.

Romney's "47%" comments at a private fundraiser in spring 2012, which were revealed on September 17, 2012, by the online edition of *Mother Jones* magazine, stirred up a great deal of controversy because of his admonishment of citizens who did not pay taxes while receiving government benefits. Of the controversies examined in this analysis, this one in particular received the greatest amount of attention from blogs and the mainstream media, though as would be expected, the brunt of it came from liberal blogs, which reported on the video 50 times in one day shortly after its release. This controversy also had a great deal of staying power, with an average of ten reports on the comments a day by liberal blogs and the mainstream media following this initial spike and less (an average of seven reports per day) by conservative blogs after the initial spike.

Romney's European foreign-policy trip, coverage of which is shown in the top-right quadrant of figure 6.3, also had its fair share of controversy to it, including his negative comments to the mayor of London about the city's preparedness for the upcoming Summer Olympics and other numerous gaffes. This controversy received much less coverage, with the spike in coverage (ten articles by liberal blogs) occurring in early August, about a month after the trip. Unlike the "47%" comments, coverage of this controversy decayed very quickly, as by mid-August few stories were published by any of the sources in question. This likely owes to this controversy occurring earlier in the campaign season, as well as its being out of reach of much of the U.S. media.

Finally, the infamous episode of the Romney family strapping their dog, Seamus, to the roof of their suburban while on a trip to Canada came up quite early

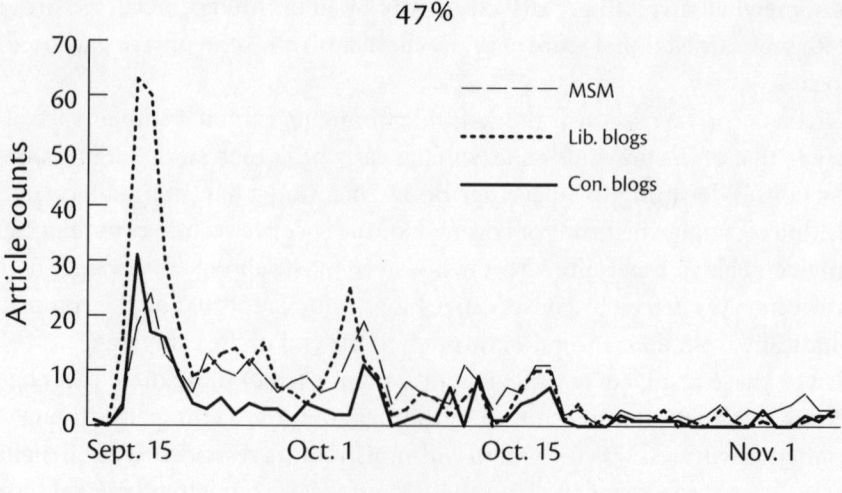
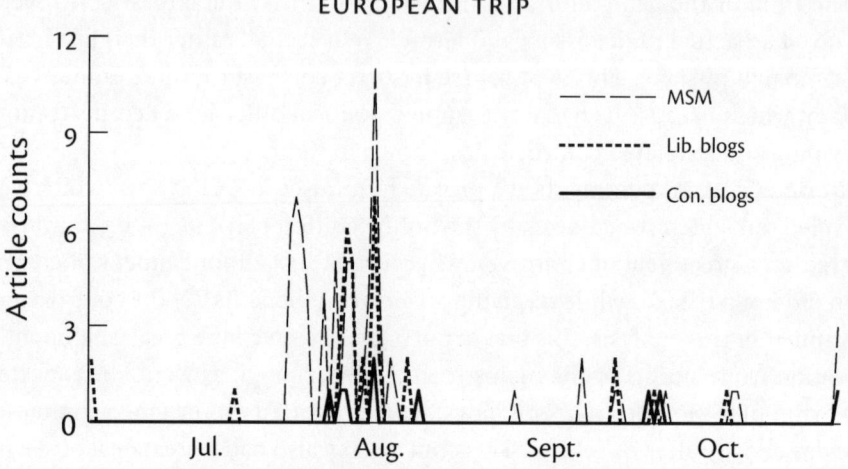
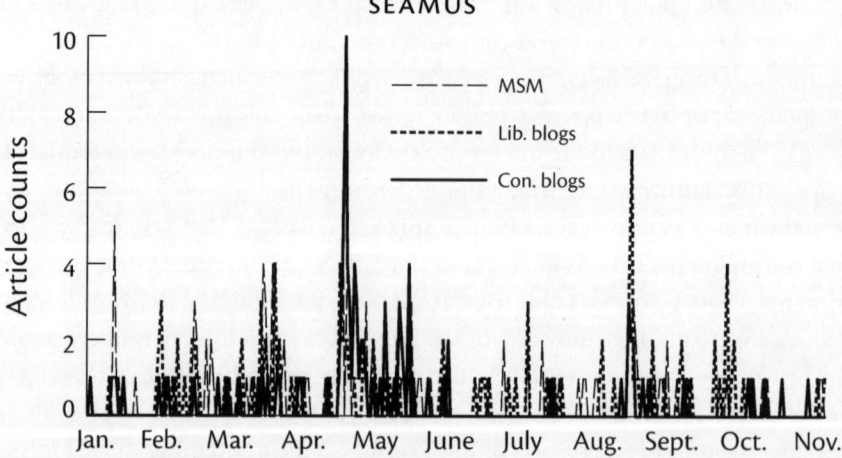

Figure 6.3. Romney controversy coverage over time

in the campaign, during the primary season, and experienced moderate spikes (the highest being in early April, with ten articles by conservative blogs) at various points throughout the campaign. However, the pattern of coverage for this controversy did not resemble the "early peak with quick downturn" pattern seen in the other controversy cases but rather spiked to its highest point in April. Consequently, these spikes are likely due to the fact that Romney had effectively won the Republican nomination, which may have brought with it an uptick in "replays" of his past negative coverage.

Although graphical displays of each controversy's coverage are illuminating, more stringent tests are needed to tell us if differences in coverage patterns manifested themselves for each of the issues. Tables 6.1 and 6.2 present negative binomial regression models for each of the issues.[9] Two models were run for each controversy, the first with standard dummy-coded indicators for liberal blogs and the mainstream media (conservative blogs were the reference group) and the second with Helmert contrasts, which allow for comparisons between the two blog types as well as between all blogs and the mainstream media. Additionally, a variable (*elapse*) was included to predict how quickly coverage decays after the initial spike in each controversy; this variable was interacted against the contrast variables to test for whether different source types caused more persistence or quicker decay in coverage of each controversy.

Table 6.1 presents the models for each of the Obama-related controversies in the 2012 campaign. What is immediately striking about these models is that, save for the Benghazi controversy, the most consistent predictor of the level of coverage given to each issue was simply the amount of time that elapsed since its emergence. As one would expect, each of these significant elapsed time variables were negatively signed, demonstrating that with the onset of time came decreased attention for each issue. The exception to this was the Benghazi issue, which showed significantly lower probabilities of coverage for liberal blogs as compared to conservative blogs, as well as a higher probability of coverage from the mainstream media as compared to combined (liberal and conservative) blog coverage in Model 2.

At least for the Obama-related controversies, these results are indicative that neither the level of coverage nor the rate of its persistence/decline dramatically differed between blogs and the mainstream media. This finding is striking given that blogs have been noted in the past to be independent of the perceived failings of the mainstream media (see Vos, Craft, and Ashley 2012). Even though political bloggers have full license to cover controversies to a different extent than the mainstream media does, in these cases they apparently did not. Taking these results together with those present in the time-series plots in figure 6.2, it appears that for the most part coverage of these controversies by the traditional and new media mirrored each other quite closely, and for the amount of coverage at least, no substantive differences existed on the basis of media type or

Table 6.1. Negative Binomial Models for 2012 Obama Campaign Controversies

	Benghazi attacks		"Didn't build that"		"Private sector"	
	Model 1	Model 2	Model 1	Model 2	Model 1	Model 2
Elapse	.003	.003	−.023**	−.023**	−.024**	−.031**
	(.006)	(.003)	(.004)	(.002)	(.004)	(.003)
Lib:Con	−.848**	−.424**	−.466	−.233	−.321	−.161
	(.279)	(.139)	(.303)	(.152)	(.424)	(.212)
MSM:Con	.089		−.314		.474	
	(.257)		(.304)		(.373)	
MSM:Blogs		.171*		−.027		.211^
		(.071)		(.090)		(.112)
Lib:Con*Elapse	−.0002	.0001	.001	.001	−.013	−.007
	(.009)	(.004)	(.005)	(.003)	(.009)	(.004)
MSM:Con*Elapse	.001		−.003		−.008	
	(.008)		(.006)		(.007)	
MSM:Blogs*Elapse		.0003		−.001		−.001
		(.002)		(.002)		(.002)
Intercept	2.090**	1.837**	1.720**	1.460**	.623**	.674**
	(.183)	(.111)	(.207)	(.125)	(.266)	(.166)
χ^2	46.66**		104.01**		130.75**	
Pseudo R^2	.045		.089		.167	
N	171		351		456	

** p < .01, * p < .05, ^ p < .10, standard errors in parentheses. Model 1 reports standard dummy coding. Model 2 reports Helmert comparison groups.

ideological slant. At least with regard to coverage patterns of campaign controversies, the new media (as represented by the political blogs under study here) may be offering more of the same, rather than coverage above and beyond that of their traditional counterparts.

Table 6.2 presents the same models on each of the Romney-related controversies in the 2012 campaign. As before, the most consistent predictor of coverage counts of each controversy was the time count following its emergence (save for Model 1 of the European-trip controversy), all of which were again negatively signed. Unlike coverage of the Obama controversies, however, there were more statistically different levels of coverage between source types for several of the Romney campaign issues. For example, the "47%" and European-trip controversies each netted significantly higher probabilities of coverage from both liberal blogs and mainstream media sources, as compared to conservative blogs.

Furthermore, the interaction between the liberal blog indicator and elapsed time variable was negative and significant for the "47%" issue, indicating a more rapid decline in coverage of the issue among liberal blogs as compared to conservative blogs as time went on. Given just how contentious this issue was in the late stages of the 2012 presidential campaign, it is surprising that coverage of it would decline so much more quickly for liberal than conservative blogs. Also for "47%," the coefficient for the mainstream media*elapse interaction (Model 2) was positive and significant, indicating that the decay for this issue was actually longer in the traditional media than in blogs overall. A similar pattern of coverage emerged for the issue of the dog Seamus (both Models 1 and 2), with liberal blogs' coverage decreasing on the issue less quickly as time went on as compared to conservative blogs.

That these models showed more substantive differences between blog and mainstream media coverage as compared to what emerged in the Obama controversies begs the question of whether blogs cover the "horse race" (as campaign controversies are apt to be; see Patterson 1994) in a manner not unlike

Table 6.2. Negative Binomial Models for 2012 Romney Campaign Controversies

	47%		European trip		Romney dog	
	Model 1	Model 2	Model 1	Model 2	Model 1	Model 2
Elapse	−.051**	−.056**	−.010	−.017**	−.005**	−.003**
	(.009)	(.005)	(.012)	(.006)	(.002)	(.001)
Lib:Con	1.107**	.554**	1.904^	.952^	−.500	−.250
	(.281)	(.141)	(1.023)	(.512)	(.350)	(.175)
MSM:Con	.558*		2.252*		.311	
	(.277)		(1.007)		(.323)	
MSM:Blogs		.002		.433^		.187
		(.077)		(.260)		(.093)
Lib:Con*Elapse	−.028*	−.014*	−.012	−.006	.004^	.002^
	(.012)	(.006)	(.016)	(.008)	(.002)	(.001)
MSM:Con*Elapse	.014		−.011		.001	
	(.011)		(.015)		(.002)	
MSM:Blogs*Elapse		.009**		−.002		−.0003
		(.003)		(.004)		(.001)
Intercept	2.134**	2.689**	−2.229*	−.844*	−.565*	−.628**
	(.208)	(.112)	(.816)	(.394)	(.241)	(.137)
χ^2	128.86**		18.786**		26.34**	
Pseudo R^2	.151		.053		.019	
N	153		387		903	

** p < .01, * p < .05, ^ p < .10, standard errors in parentheses. Model 1 reports standard dummy coding. Model 2 reports Helmert comparison groups.

their mainstream brethren. For example, Thomas Patterson (1994) notes that the frontrunner in a political contest will often receive more negative coverage than less successful candidates do. It could be that, because Obama was at no point ever behind in opinion polls, controversies related to his candidacy simply demanded more coverage than did Romney, who was consistently behind. Conversely, because of Romney's consistent underdog status, blogs may have been more likely to play to their stereotypical roles as cheerleaders for their side (e.g., Baum and Groeling 2008). Whether this pattern is consistent across elections will of course require more research (and further elections in a new media environment), but it certainly does call into question just how different coverage is across media types. That said, the most reliable and consistent predictor of controversy reportage remained the proximity in time to the emergence of controversy in the first place, as was the case with the Obama controversies.

Regardless, what these models do not give us a good glimpse of is the dynamic relationship between blogs and the mainstream media. The lack of substantial differences in coverage patterns between these sources, as well as high correlation coefficients across issues ($r = .69$ between liberal and conservative blogs; $r = .80$ between conservative and mainstream media; $r = .71$ between liberal and mainstream media), suggests that a high degree of agenda setting occurred between source types during the 2012 campaign. In order to test this, I make use of a more time-dependent approach offered by vector autoregression (VAR) models, with lagged values of each source's coverage regressed on the other sources' coverage in order to examine the dynamics of the news cycle (see Jerit and Simon 2010; Brandt and Williams 2006). Preliminary tests for proper time lags indicated that five-day lags were appropriate for these analyses, which is in line with Wallsten's (2007) findings of a similar lag time in his research. Because individual effects in VAR models are difficult to interpret given multiple lags in simultaneous equations, posttest Granger causality tests were used to illuminate the overall dynamics of influence between sources.

Table 6.3 presents these Granger causality results. Given the complexity of the analyses, discussion of these results proceeds by looking at each source's influence across all issues, with specific departures from the norm noted. First, it is apparent from these models that the traditional media had a great deal of success in influencing the agendas of both liberal and conservative blogs, as 10 of the 12 models including mainstream media coverage as a predictor showed a significant influence over blog agendas. The only exception to this was Benghazi for both liberal and conservative blog coverage as dependent variables. Likewise, liberal blogs influenced either mainstream media or conservative blog coverage in 10 of the models, with the only nonsignificant relationships occurring on coverage of the "private sector" comments when conservative blogs and mainstream media were included as dependent variables.

Table 6.3. Vector Autoregression and Granger Causality Test Results—Media Coverage of 2012 Controversies

	DV: Liberal blog coverage			DV: Conservative blog coverage			DV: Mainstream media coverage		
	Predictor	χ^2	R^2	Predictor	χ^2	R^2	Predictor	χ^2	R^2
47%	Con. blogs	5.084	.611	Lib. blogs	9.980^	.638	Con. blogs	9.802^	.696
	Mainstream media	**12.394***		Mainstream media	**43.034****		Lib. blogs	**29.317****	
Europe	Con. blogs	**28.491****	.437	Lib. blogs	**32.786****	.400	Con. blogs	**19.533****	.659
	Mainstream media	**16.660****		Mainstream media	**31.789****		Lib. blogs	**80.858****	
Seamus	Con. blogs	9.822^	.095	Lib. blogs	**13.557***	.394	Con. blogs	**31.342****	.227
	Mainstream media	10.214^		Mainstream media	**24.736****		Lib. blogs	**14.155***	
Benghazi	Con. blogs	3.585	.582	Lib. blogs	**19.622****	.441	Con. blogs	3.106	.538
	Mainstream media	4.509		Mainstream media	4.018		Lib. blogs	**35.743****	
"Didn't build that"	Con. blogs	9.674^	.436	Lib. blogs	9.633^	.651	Con. blogs	**13.925***	.479
	Mainstream media	**22.729****		Mainstream media	**19.707****		Lib. blogs	**21.171****	
"Private sector"	Con. blogs	4.604	.274	Lib. blogs	5.141	.468	Con. blogs	**13.801***	.626
	Mainstream media	**23.464****		Mainstream media	**32.375****		Lib. blogs	2.788	

** $p < .01$, * $p < .05$, ^ $p < .10$. Bolded coefficients significant below $p < .10$ level. All individual models showed significant model fit at the $p < .001$ level.

Conservative blogs had the least influence of the sources analyzed, though still a great deal, with 8 of 12 models showing a significant relationship. This finding was most prominent with regard to their influence over liberal blog coverage of these controversies and especially those related to Obama's candidacy. For example, these models showed no influence of conservative blogs over liberal coverage on the Benghazi and "private sector" issues, which is not surprising given mixed evidence of interplay between differing ideological views online (see Hargittai et al. 2008). Conservative blogs also had no effect over their liberal counterparts on the "47%" issue. With regard to their influence on the mainstream media, only in the case of the Benghazi attacks did conservative blogs exert coverage influence.

Overall, it appears that there was a great deal of collusion of agendas between blogs and the mainstream media in both directions, as well as quite a lot of blog-to-blog influence, though these latter relationships were decidedly more mixed than the former. These results make sense given past findings of cross talk between the traditional and new media (e.g., Wallsten 2007) along with mixed evidence of liberal-to-conservative (and vice versa) interplay online. This is additionally in line with recent evidence suggesting that news consumers display a not-insubstantial degree of heterogeneity in their media usage (Li 2013). At least in terms of the 2012 election, these results speak to the notion that blog coverage tends to be more of the same, rather than a reinvigoration of the information environment.

Conclusion

Since the emergence of blogs on the political scene in the early to middle of the first decade of the twenty-first century, they have been occasionally heralded as a paradigm shift in coverage of political and policy issues (e.g., Graber 2009; see especially Benkler 2007). The idea goes that, freed from the constraints of corporate ownership and its requisite elite control (Entman 2006), political blogs would be free to report on substantive issues and, at their best, avoid the trappings of a mainstream media so frequently set on covering the sensationalistic at the expense of serious political discussion (Grabe et al. 2001).

Of course, for every individual with hopes for blogs' reinvigoration of the public sphere, there have been at least as many individuals concerned with the ramifications of a set of new media sources that do just the opposite (e.g., Stroud and Muddiman 2013; Sunstein 2007; Stroud 2011; Johnson and Kaye 2013). Because of the relative newness of blogging as a political phenomenon, the jury may still be out on whether it is the naysayers or the optimists who are correct, but the fight appears to be leaning in the direction of the former rather than the latter (Li 2013; Baum and Groeling 2008; Hargittai et al. 2008; Lawrence et al. 2010). And while this research cannot directly speak to these value judgments, the evidence presented here suggests that, at least for the elite blogs under study, the new media *at least* do not appear to be any less likely to fixate on campaign controversies than do their mainstream brethren.

The finding most prevalent in this research is that the new media do not differ substantially from the traditional media in the dynamics of campaign controversy coverage. The overtly partisan blogs under study did not appear to cover politics differently from one side of the political spectrum to the other; though blogs varied most frequently with regard to their coverage of Romney-related controversies, no overwhelmingly consistent difference in the amount of coverage for these controversies was manifest in the results. This brings up an interesting critique of blogs' pattern of coverage overall; whereas much has been noted of bloggers' disdain for the way traditional media sources cover politics, sensationalistic or no (Vos et al. 2012), it does not appear that blogs escape those criticisms when we examine the extent to which they report on presidential campaign politics.

There is a flip side to these null results, however, and it pertains to cross-media influence. Even though, by the 2012 campaign, the new media had only existed long enough to take part in three presidential elections, their influence over the information environment appears to have been immense. Recall that in the time-series results, a consistent, bidirectional relationship was manifest between political blogs and the mainstream media. In all but two instances, conservative and liberal blogs had a significant impact on the mainstream media's reportage on the campaign controversies in question, and the mainstream media had a similar level of influence over blogs' agendas. That such a strong bidirectional relationship has emerged so early in the new media's history as political players serves to turn our understanding of media dynamics on its head.

For example, scholars have most often conceptualized the process of agenda setting to consist of a one-way flow of information, from the mass media to citizens (e.g., McCombs and Shaw 1972; McCombs 2004). To this point, the status of mainstream sources as primary agenda setters has served scholars of political communication well, given that the mainstream media have traditionally held a monopoly on the information environment. However, the sudden increase in the number and type of news sources in the early twenty-first century has brought with it more sources grappling for influence over information flows (Benkler 2007), which was manifest in this research. As I have shown, political blogs have a surprising capacity to shape the mainstream media agenda, just as the mainstream media wields a great degree of influence over the blog agenda. Importantly, though a modicum of bidirectional influence has been shown in research on past presidential campaigns (see Wallsten 2007 for an investigation using the 2004 election), this research has revealed a more consistent pattern of bidirectional influence than has been shown previously. Given this finding, it may be that the ability of the new media to control the message has only increased as its place within the broader political environment becomes more entrenched.

Other than adding to our knowledge of who can set the agenda, there is an especially obvious upside to these findings of bidirectional influence. New media scholars, including Cass Sunstein (2007) and Natalie Stroud (2011; see also Stroud and Muddiman 2013), show grave concern for a public exposed to a media environment that differs greatly depending on the ideology of the media source. For example, if ideologically biased media sources report on substantially different issues, the likelihood that different segments of the public are paying attention to different issues increases, and with this differential attention, a fragmentation of the public agenda may result (see also Bennett and Iyengar 2008). That the mainstream and new media both did not differ consistently in the issues making up their agendas *and* served to influence each other suggests that these fears may be unfounded. For example, criticisms of the Obama administration's handling of the Benghazi embassy attacks were covered to a great extent, regardless of the media source. Coverage of Mitt Romney's "47%" comments was reported on likewise. It simply did not matter a great deal which source was reporting on these controversies, because regardless of the political leanings of the sources under study, the issues received play.

What could be the explanation for these similarities in reporting patterns? For one, the fact that this research centered on campaign controversies may play a large role. In any given campaign, there is undoubtedly going to be only a limited number of activities that reach a sufficient level of controversy to merit coverage by any media source. What many of the new media critics seem to miss is that the new media do not operate in an information vacuum but are rather a part of the same political environment and hence are prone to report on the same issues that may arise during the campaign season (see Wallsten 2007), which is only compounded by their being subject to the same audience demands as mainstream sources (e.g., Tewksbury 2003). In concluding, then, while it is clear that the topics of reportage among blog and mainstream sources is quite similar within the campaign context, who controls that topic, and hence the message, is spread out between the old guard and the new.

Notes

1. Of course, this incentive has decreased in the "postbroadcast" media era, a fact most exemplified by media sources such as Fox News and MSNBC (see Prior 2007).
2. Importantly, research in the past has also utilized sites such as TheTruthLaidBear.com. Unfortunately, most sites other than Technorati are no longer in active service.
3. For example, the *RedState* "About" page indicates a rightward slant by stating, "Today, RedState is the most widely read right of center blog on Capitol Hill, is the most often cited right of center blog in the media, and is widely considered one of the most influential voices of the grassroots on the right." Likewise, the *Daily Kos* "History" page demonstrates the blog's liberal tilt in labeling itself "the largest progressive community blog in the United States."
4. Only articles appearing in the paper copy of the *New York Times* were selected for analysis; *New York Times* blogs were omitted.
5. Importantly, CBS News was selected over either ABC or NBC News because a greater range of news transcripts were available from the LexisNexis online database for that news source.
6. As was the case with the selection of CBS News for analysis, transcripts for CNN were not as widely available within the LexisNexis database as either Fox or MSNBC.
7. For each of the issues, the following search terms in parentheses were used: 47 percent (*47 percent Romney*); European foreign policy trip (*Romney Europe*); Seamus, the Romneys' dog (*Romney dog*); Obama administration's handling of the Benghazi attacks (*Benghazi or Libya Obama*); "you didn't build that" (*Obama build that*); and "private sector is doing fine" (*Obama private sector fine*).
8. Code for both the web-scraping and content analysis software used in this study is available from the author upon request.
9. Another option for count data is to use Poisson regression models; however, Poisson models assume that the variances of the count data are equal to the means, which was not the case

with this study. Negative binomials were chosen given that the data consists of counts and featured a bit of overdispersion that is characteristic of these types of data.

References

Anderson, Chris. 2008. *The Long Tail: Why the Future of Business Is Selling Less of More*. Rev. and updated ed. New York: Hyperion.

Baum, Matthew A., and Tim Groeling. 2008. "New Media and the Polarization of American Political Discourse." *Political Communication* 25:345–365.

Benkler, Yochai. 2007. *The Wealth of Networks: How Social Production Transforms Markets and Freedom*. New Haven: Yale University Press.

Bennett, W. Lance. 1981. "Assessing Presidential Character: Degradation Rituals in Political Campaigns." *Quarterly Journal of Speech* 67 (3): 310–321.

Bennett, W. Lance, and Shanto Iyengar. 2008. "A New Era of Minimal Effects? The Changing Foundations of Political Communication." *Journal of Communication* 58 (4): 707–731.

Brandt, Patrick T., and John Taylor Williams. 2006. *Multiple Time Series Models*. Thousand Oaks, CA: Sage.

Cappella, Joseph N., and Kathleen Hall Jamieson. 1996. "News Frames, Political Cynicism, and Media Cynicism." *Annals of the American Academy of Political and Social Science* 546:71–84.

———. 1997. *Spiral of Cynicism: The Press and the Public Good*. New York: Oxford University Press.

Cook, Timothy E. 1998. *Governing with the News: The News Media as a Political Institution*. Chicago: University of Chicago Press.

———. 2005. *Governing with the News: The News Media as a Political Institution*. 2nd ed. Chicago: University of Chicago Press.

Davis, Richard. 2009. *Typing Politics: The Role of Blogs in American Politics*. New York: Oxford University Press.

Dimitrova, Daniela V., and Dianne Bystrom. 2013. "The Effects of Social Media on Political Participation and Candidate Image Evaluations in the 2012 Iowa Caucuses." *American Behavioral Scientist* 57 (11): 1568–1583.

Entman, Robert M. 2006. "Punctuating the Homogeneity of Institutionalized News: Abusing Prisoners at Abu Ghraib versus Killing Civilians at Fallujah." *Political Communication* 23:215–224.

Grabe, Maria Elizabeth, Shuhua Zhou, and Brooke Barnett. 2001. "Explicating Sensationalism in Television News: Content and the Bells and Whistles of Form." *Journal of Broadcasting & Electronic Media* 45 (4): 635–655.

Graber, Doris A. 2009. *Mass Media and American Politics*. 8th ed. Washington, DC: CQ.

Gruszczynski, Michael W., and Michael W. Wagner. 2010. "Google It: A New Way to Measure the Agenda-Setting Effect." Unpublished manuscript.

Hamilton, James T. 2005. "The Market and the Media." In *Institutions of American Democracy: The Press*, edited by Geneva Overholser and Kathleen Hall Jamieson, 351–371. Oxford: Oxford University Press.

Hargittai, Eszter, Jason Gallo, and Matthew Kane. 2008. "Cross-Ideological Discussions among Conservative and Liberal Bloggers." *Public Choice* 134 (1): 67–86.

Herman, Edward S., and Noam Chomsky. 2002. *Manufacturing Consent: The Political Economy of the Mass Media*. London: Pantheon.

Hong, Sounman, and Daniel Nadler. 2012. "Which Candidates Do the Public Discuss Online in an Election Campaign? The Use of Social Media by 2012 Presidential Candidates and Its Impact on Candidate Salience." *Government Information Quarterly* 29 (4): 455–461.

Jerit, Jennifer, and Adam F. Simon. 2010. "Time Series Analysis and the Study of Political Communication." In *Sourcebook for Political Communication Research: Methods, Measures, and Analytical Techniques*, edited by Erik P. Bucy and R. Lance Holbert, 466–482. New York: Routledge.

Johnson, Thomas J., and Barbara K. Kaye. 2013. "The Dark Side of the Boon? Credibility, Selective Exposure and the Proliferation of Online Sources of Political Information." *Computers in Human Behavior* 29 (4): 1862–1871.

Just, Marion, Ann Crigler, and Tami Buhr. 1999. "Voice, Substance, and Cynicism in Presidential Campaign Media." *Political Communication* 16 (1): 25–44.

Kaplan, Richard L. 2006. "The News about New Institutionalism: Journalism's Ethic of Objectivity and Its Political Origins." *Political Communication* 23 (2): 173–185.

Karpf, David. 2008. "Understanding Blogspace." *Journal of Information Technology & Politics* 5 (4): 369–385.

Lawrence, Eric, John Sides, and Henry Farrell. 2010. "Self-Segregation or Deliberation? Blog Readership, Participation, and Polarization in American Politics." *Perspectives on Politics* 8 (1): 141–157.

Lee, Jae Kook. 2007. "The Effect of the Internet on Homogeneity of the Media Agenda: A Test of the Fragmentation Thesis." *Journalism & Mass Communication Quarterly* 84 (4): 745–760.

Leskovec, Jure, Lars Backstrom, and Jon Kleinberg. 2009. "Meme-tracking and the Dynamics of the News Cycle." In *Proceedings of the 15th ACM SIGKDD International Conference on Knowledge Discovery and Data Mining*. Paris.

Leskovec, Jure, Mary McGlohon, Christos Faloutsos, Natalie Glance, and Matthew Hurst. 2009. "Cascading Behavior in Large Blog Graphs: Patterns and a Model." Unpublished manuscript.

Li, Jo-Yun. 2013. "Re-examining the Two-Step Flow of Information in the Age of Digital Media: The Case of the 2012 Presidential Election in the United States." Master's thesis, Iowa State University.

McCombs, Maxwell. 2004. *Setting the Agenda: The Mass Media and Public Opinion*. Cambridge, UK: Polity.

McCombs, Maxwell E., and Donald L. Shaw. 1972. "The Agenda-Setting Function of the Mass Media." *Public Opinion Quarterly* 36 (2): 176–187.

Meraz, Sharon. 2013. "The Democratic Contribution of Weakly Tied Political Networks: Moderate Political Blogs as Bridges to Heterogeneous Information Pools." *Social Science Computer Review* 31 (2): 191–207.

Nahon, Karine, Jeff Hemsley, Shawn Walker, and Muzammil Hussain. 2011. "Fifteen Minutes of Fame: The Power of Blogs in the Lifecycle of Viral Political Information." *Policy & Internet* 3 (1): 6–33.

Negroponte, Nicholas. 1996. *Being Digital*. New York: Vintage.

Patterson, Thomas E. 1994. *Out of Order*. New York: Vintage.

Plasser, Fritz. 2005. "From Hard to Soft News Standards? How Political Journalists in Different Media Systems Evaluate the Shifting Quality of News." *Harvard International Journal of Press/Politics* 10 (2): 47–68.

Prior, Markus. 2007. *Post-broadcast Democracy: How Media Choice Increases Inequality in Political Involvement and Polarizes Elections*. Cambridge: Cambridge University Press.

Robertson, Scott P., Bryan Semaan, Sara Douglas, and Misa Maruyama. 2013. "Mixed Media: Interactions of Social and Traditional Media in Political Decision Making." *Proceedings of the 46th Annual Hawaii International Conference on System Sciences* 2013:2013–2022. doi:10.1109/HICSS.2013.408.

Robinson, Cara. 2013. "The Empowered Citizen? Online Political Discussion in the United States." *St Antony's International Review* 8 (2): 47–69.

Schudson, Michael. 2001. "The Objectivity Norm in American Journalism." *Journalism* 2 (2): 149–170.

Scott, D. Travers. 2006. "Pundits in Muckrakers' Clothing: Political Blogs and the 2004 U.S. Presidential Election." In *Blogging, Citizenship, and the Future of Media*, edited by Mark Tremayne, 39–57. New York: Routledge.

Sheppard, Si. 2007. *The Partisan Press: A History of Media Bias in the United States*. Jefferson, NC: McFarland.

Stroud, Natalie Jomini. 2008. "Media Use and Political Predispositions: Revisiting the Concept of Selective Exposure." *Political Behavior* 30 (3): 341–366.

———. 2011. *Niche News: The Politics of News Choice*. Oxford: Oxford University Press.

Stroud, Natalie Jomini, and Ashley Muddiman. 2013. "The American Media System Today." In *New Directions in Media and Politics*, edited by Travis N. Ridout, 6–23. New York: Routledge.

Sunstein, Cass R. 2007. *Republic.com 2.0*. Princeton: Princeton University Press.

Tewksbury, David. 2003. "What Do Americans Really Want to Know? Tracking the Behavior of News Readers on the Internet." *Journal of Communication* 53 (4): 694–710.

Turner, Joel. 2007. "The Messenger Overwhelming the Message: Ideological Cues and Perceptions of Bias in Television News." *Political Behavior* 29 (4): 441–464.

Vos, Tim P. 2012. "'Homo Journalisticus': Journalism Education's Role in Articulating the Objectivity Norm." *Journalism* 13 (4): 435–449.

Vos, Tim P., Stephanie Craft, and Seth Ashley. 2012. "New Media, Old Criticism: Bloggers' Press Criticism and the Journalistic Field." *Journalism* 13 (7): 850–868.

Wallsten, Kevin. 2007. "Agenda Setting and the Blogosphere: An Analysis of the Relationship between Mainstream Media and Political Blogs." *Review of Policy Research* 24 (6): 567–587.

———. 2008. "Political Blogs: Transmission Belts, Soapboxes, Mobilizers, or Conversation Starters?" *Journal of Information Technology & Politics* 4 (3): 19–40.

Williams, Andrew Paul, Kaye D. Trammell, Monica Postelnicu, Kristen D. Landreville, and Justin D. Martin. 2005. "Blogging and Hyperlinking: Use of the Web to Enhance Viability during the 2004 US Campaign." *Journalism Studies* 6 (2): 177–186.

Williams, Bruce A., and Michael X. Delli Carpini. 2011. *After Broadcast News: Media Regimes, Democracy, and the New Information Environment*. Cambridge: Cambridge University Press.

7

Traditional Media, Social Media, and Different Presidential Campaign Messages

MATTHEW ESHBAUGH-SOHA

There is a common perception among pundits, politicians, and scholars of presidential campaigns and American politics that new media have changed the nature of electoral politics.[1] Like the advent of television before it, new media—but especially Internet blogs, online news websites, and social media—appear to have altered the essence of the presidential campaign. Whereas previous advances in media ushered in an era of candidate-centered politics and greater reliance on independent fundraising to advertise on television, more online media have increased the range of voters' sources of information and have shaped campaigns in distinct ways. The omnipresence of Twitter on postdebate news coverage reinforces the perception. Indeed, if we were to summarize the 2012 presidential election, it would likely reference Big Bird, binders, horses, bayonets, and other debate comments that were accentuated through social media.

Social media traffic in the 2012 presidential election campaign appears to have driven campaign messages and, in turn, predicted its outcome easily. Just as Obama won reelection handily in the Electoral College (332 to 206), a snapshot of the social media campaign reveals that Obama also trounced Romney in social media attention. The president enjoyed more Facebook "likes" than Romney (27.5 million to 2.9 million), Twitter followers (18 million to 787,080), and YouTube subscribers (207,434 to 12,570) (Pew Research Center Project for Excellence in Journalism [PEJ] 2012b). Even when the Republican primary debates dominated traditional news coverage, the president exceeded Romney's Twitter presence by nearly 15 times: over 15 million assertions on Twitter for Barack Obama to just over 1.5 million for Mitt Romney (PEJ 2011c). Given that social endorsement is more important than partisanship in news story selection on social media (Messing and Westwood, forthcoming), the impact of Obama's presence on social media may have also influenced Romney supporters.

That changes in media communications technology have affected presidential elections is not unique to 2012. Media advances have often signaled changes to presidential campaigns, with perhaps the most famous of these being the first televised presidential debate between John F. Kennedy and Richard Nixon, held on September 26, 1960. Public perception of this debate differed starkly by one's exposure to television or radio. Viewers of television, which emphasizes style over substance and image over experience, proclaimed a young and inexperienced (but television-friendly) Kennedy the debate winner (Druckman 2003). Although radio listeners heard Nixon's command of foreign and domestic policy and proclaimed him the winner, television viewers saw a sweaty, pasty, and shifty-eyed sitting vice president and determined that he had lost (Vancil and Pendell 1987). Therefore, television may have affected the outcome of one of the closest presidential elections in U.S. history (Hellweg, Pfau, and Brydon 1992).

Although we have yet to witness as defining an event with the Internet or social media, there is sufficient anecdotal evidence that their advent has ushered in a new era of campaign messages and politics, one that might rely more on user-driven messages and that may therefore be more democratic. Independently created political videos, whether depicting a fan (Obama Girl) or a candidate himself (George Allen, 2008 Senate campaign), have shaped traditional news conversations (see Hendricks and Denton 2010). Twitter feeds and Facebook posts were part of traditional news analysis and fueled much of the campaign conversation in 2012. Today, political candidates avoid outreach through the Internet and social networking sites at their peril (Haynes and Pitts 2009). Social media have changed the distribution of campaign information, there is no doubt. Whether they have substantially altered who controls the campaign message—and the campaign itself—is less clear.

This chapter focuses on answering the following question: how did traditional and social media cover the 2012 presidential election campaign? To answer this question, I compare both traditional and social media across several dimensions, including volume and tone, using data provided by the Pew Center's Project for Excellence in Journalism (PEJ). I report that while there are important differences in how these media affect campaign messaging, much of the tone and volume of social media coverage matches traditional news coverage. If anything, social media tend to be more negative than traditional news sources. But their impact on the 2012 presidential campaign may not have been significantly different in comparison with new media featured in previous elections. Instead, their importance may lie in how they facilitate the dissemination of messages deemed interesting to the wired electorate (such as Big Bird), not necessarily the journalists who traditionally report on campaign events.

Internet-Based Media in American Campaigns

What do we know about the content and effect of Internet-based media in presidential election campaigns? To be blunt, we know very little, especially in comparison with the much-larger literature on traditional media effects (see Patterson 1993) and the impact of alternative sources of televised politics, such as late-night television (Baum 2005; Parkin 2010) or soft news programs (Baum 2003) on public opinion. Because there are significant data limitations and other difficulties associated with collecting social media data, research has not yet examined social media at length but has rather investigated other forms of Internet-based political communication, such as online news sites. Beyond revealing important connections between these media and American politics, much of this literature reflects on whether new media developments have been good for American democracy and why.

The literature paints a mixed picture of the Internet's effects on learning and participation, despite its ubiquity and increasing prevalence among consumers of news (PEJ 2012c). On the one hand, exposure to online news increases knowledge in both a campaign (Kenski and Stroud 2006) and a noncampaign context (Kwak, Poor, and Skoric 2006). More so, exposure to online news has had a positive impact on political interest (Boulianne 2011) and voter turnout, especially among people with low levels of political interest (Kruikemeier et al., forthcoming). It also increased participation and political efficacy among college students during the 2008 presidential election (Kushin and Yamamoto 2010). Research is clear, furthermore, that citizens are more likely to seek out online news during a high-profile political event such as a presidential primary (Tewksbury 2006; see Boczkowski, Mitchelstein, and Walter 2012). On the other hand, Shelley Boulianne's (2009) meta-analysis reveals that Internet use has had a marginal impact on political involvement, such as voting, even though the two are positively correlated.[2] Indeed, exposure to online news leads to less recall of political information than does reading a print newspaper (Eveland, Seo, and Marton 2002; Tewksbury and Althaus 2000), although this may be a function of the substantive content provided by different media (D'Haenens, Jankowski, and Heulvelman 2004).

Indeed, the content of information may have the most pronounced impact on voters' political engagement. Conservative media, including Fox News Channel (and presumably its online counterpart), help conservative viewers make sense of complex issues by offering a coherent, ideological presentation of political news. This, in turn, increases those viewers' likelihood of voting (Jamieson and Cappella 2008).[3] On the other hand, however, conservative media's preference for ridicule over reason contributes to the polarization of the electorate (see Morris 2005), which appears to undermine sensible deliberation on issues of national concern. That Internet users select one-sided information sources (Gainous and Wagner 2011, chap. 6) that advocate one perspective at the exclusion of another further segments the American electorate as the Internet grows as the primary source of news for Americans.

A burgeoning literature is only beginning to explore the impact of social media on political learning and engagement (see Edgerly et al. 2013 for some of this research). The conventional wisdom about social media, much as it was speculated about cable television and online news before them, is that they are good for democracy by engaging voters and providing them an efficient vehicle through which to express their political preferences (Haynes and Pitts 2009, 53). Audrey Haynes and Brian Pitts (2009) examined websites that track Internet usage and found the following. First, website traffic appears to fluctuate with news coverage of a candidates' position in the horse race. Second, blog entries on candidate websites mirror volume of traditional news stories (Haynes and Pitts 2009, 56). As a representative example, Hillary Clinton enjoyed roughly 38% of all candidates' blog entries and 35% of all traditional news stories between November 26 and December 26, 2007. Third, a candidates' number of MySpace friends and YouTube views approximated the candidates' placement in the polls and, likely therefore, their traditional news coverage.

Other studies examine the impact of social media on voting or political learning, with mixed results. Matthew Kushin and Masahiro Yamamoto (2010) found that although access to Internet news sites and government webpages produced higher levels of participation and political efficacy among college students during the 2008 presidential election, these benefits did not result from increased exposure to Facebook. Nevertheless, Brian Houston et al. (2013) tracked Twitter usage during the first 2012 presidential debate and found that those who tweeted most frequently during the debate also learned more about the debate.

Beyond these investigations are questions about the impact of new media on informational equality and democracy. Whereas the Internet and social media allow individuals the opportunity to express what their political campaign messages would be, these virtual conversations appear to appeal mostly to those who are already interested in politics. Although Markus Prior (2007) stops short of analyzing social media, he notes that advances in television and print media technologies have reduced the chances that one might learn accidentally about politics. Newer media, by themselves, do not motivate otherwise-uninterested voters to participate in elections. Rather, the byproduct of postbroadcast media is informational inequality or greater information disparities between those who consume news and those who are not interested in doing so.

All in all, the literature on Internet and social media produces a range of preliminary findings, with the largest effects occurring for those media formats that most closely resemble traditional media technology. Just as the Internet has mixed effects on voter involvement and learning, its impact on voters is greatest for online news sites, many of which parallel the content of their print or televised versions. Even though candidates undoubtedly use social media to reach voters who interact on these platforms, our initial understanding of social media and politics reveals that social media have had only a limited or at least mixed substantive impact on presidential elections and politics.

Toward a Theory of New Media Content

Scholars of traditional media often explain the content of traditional news sources with a profit-seeker model (Dunaway 2008; Hamilton 2004). This is so because news organizations base what they can charge advertisers on the size of their audience. Traditional media need consumers and will decide what is newsworthy in part on the basis of what their audience wants to see or read. One might speculate that social media are run independent of a profit incentive, but Facebook increasingly targets users' preferences with advertisements, perhaps more so since it became a publicly traded company. Twitter is also likely to follow suit (Chace 2013).

The potential distinction between the profit incentive of traditional and social media may be even less apparent when we consider what users of social media post online and where they receive their information. Certainly, a user of social media could post pictures of herself with a presidential candidate, report on what she heard at a political rally, or reflect on a personal conversation that she had with her family about the election. Yet much of what a user may post may be driven by traditional media and the events that she is tuned in to. Twitter posts during the 2012 presidential debates provide a vivid example of this, as viewers used Twitter to reflect on these highly predictable and traditional campaign events. The content of Twitter feeds may be driven by individuals' opinions, but those opinions are just as likely to have been spurred by traditional broadcast or news coverage of those events.

Thus, I contend that traditional news media drive news coverage across all forms of media. If this assumption holds, then theories of traditional media should transcend traditional news and apply to all media in the postbroadcast age. Admittedly, there is very little empirical evidence of the causal relationships between traditional and Internet-based media to justify this assumption without controversy. Still, three recent studies begin to support it. First, Matthew Eshbaugh-Soha and Evan Lowe (2013) show a number of similarities between traditional and Internet-based news media, including that Associated Press wire reports make up a substantial percentage of news reports on both the Huffington Post and FoxNews.com. Second, Ben Sayre et al. (2010) illustrate that before the 2008 election during which Californians voted on Proposition 8, newspaper coverage led Internet blogs' attention to same-sex marriage. Third, variation in Haynes and Pitts's (2009) data shows that social media campaign coverage mirrors traditional news media coverage and does not provide independent or truly alternative coverage. Candidates with the most social media attention in 2008 were also those candidates who led in the polls or were actively campaigning at the time of the authors' data collection.

In addition to the causal direction of news flow is the idea of complementarity. Traditional and nontraditional media are not competing news sources, according to this argument, but rather work together and reinforce each other (Dutta-Bergman 2004). This argument leads to two suggestions. First, the content of traditional and postbroadcast news should be more similar than different. Second, we are not likely to see viewers leave traditional for new media en masse, which preserves traditional media's dominance in news coverage of presidential election campaigns (PEJ 2012c). Scott Althaus and David Tewksbury (2000) support the idea that online news does not replace traditional news consumption, at least among college students, especially because college students' primary means of using the Internet is for entertainment, not information.[4]

Given evidence that traditional news media drive Internet-based media, that the two media complement rather than compete with each other, and that social media have strong leanings toward making a profit, the profit incentive that dictates the tone and volume of traditional news stories will also affect the tone and volume of social media postings. Because I expect similarities between types of media, I hypothesize that both the volume and tone of all media coverage of the 2012 presidential election campaign should be comparable, such that both traditional and social media will offer voluminous and mostly negative campaign news coverage.

Audience interest also matters to the profit theory of news coverage. Simply, news outlets will report on those stories that their audiences want to read or view. Thus, users of different outlets should reflect these differences in their views about both candidates. That is, if one type of media is consumed primarily by supporters of one candidate, then that candidate will receive more coverage on it. This is most obviously true for the rise of partisan media on both Fox (which should favor Romney) and MSNBC (which should favor Obama). Moreover, users' preference for one candidate means that they are also likely to be more critical of the other.

Our understanding of users of social media is less clear. Although the number of Facebook "likes" and Twitter followers mentioned in the introduction insinuates that Obama should have had a decided social media advantage in the 2012 election, there is little difference between liberal Democrats and conservative Republicans in their usage of social media. Liberal Democrats are more inclined to "like" something on Facebook, but more Republicans post political content than Democrats do, 39% to 34%. Research also produces mixed results concerning partisanship and the use of Twitter (Houston et al. 2013; McKinney, Houston, and Hawthorne 2014). All in all, party differences on social media usage for the 2012 presidential election cycle are negligible, with only 39% of Americans using social media during the election, besides (Pew Internet and American Life Project 2012).[5] Therefore, it is not obvious that Obama benefited from a more favorable social media audience with more, and more positive, social media coverage.

Finally, news events should matter to both traditional and Internet-based news coverage. The presence and importance of events dictate traditional news coverage, as news organizations will cover and report on typical developments, such as conventions, debates, and traditional media interviews. It is possible that social media, which is purportedly more independent and decentralized than traditional news sources are, could drive subsequent social media activity irrespective of events surrounding the contest. But consistent with my theory of continuity between traditional and postbroadcast media, both forms of media should similarly follow regular campaign events.[6]

Data

Our understanding of social media and their impact on American political campaigns is limited. One reason for this is the relative novelty of social media. Twitter, for example, became popular during the 2008 presidential election,[7] limiting a thorough treatment of Twitter's impact on presidential election campaigns to 2012. Another reason for our limited understanding of social media in American politics is the difficulty of data collection. Whereas studies of traditional news media involve collecting and coding data from a regularly scheduled television broadcast or daily newspaper, new media are highly decentralized and user driven, making collecting and comparing such information highly variable.

Recent advances in machine coding of text have enhanced the possibilities to analyze social media data systematically. Fortunately, the premier data-driven website that studies American politics and media—the Pew Research Center's Project for Excellence in Journalism—used such an advance to collect data on traditional and social media during the 2012 nomination and general election campaigns. Created by Gary King (Hopkins and King 2010), Crimson Hexagon collects data from a variety of sources to create the universe of data on some issue and by media type. For example, it pulls its universe of tweets from the "Twitter Firehose Data Feed," a proprietary database of Twitter feeds not currently available to the public. It also samples thousands of blogs and stories from the traditional press, some of which are analyzed by human coders.[8]

Because the PEJ released its data at various time points throughout the campaign, it was not usually possible to compare media across the entire campaign. Instead, I describe the nature of campaign news coverage at specific time frames as identified by PEJ in its online reports. Although I also rely on some earlier data—including data from the Republican nomination season and other, more refined time points—the bulk of the data come from three primary time frames, selected by PEJ to capture most of the major campaign events of the 2012 presidential election: May 29–August 5, 2012; August 27–October 21, 2012; and October 29–November 5, 2012.[9]

Findings

The data support each of the foregoing expectations that concern the tone of coverage, volume of coverage, and social media usage by candidate supporters. There are several expected differences but also many similarities between traditional and social media coverage of the 2012 presidential election campaign.

Volume of Coverage

The volume of coverage was similar across media and candidates during the 2012 presidential election campaign. Overall, President Obama enjoyed more coverage than did Governor Romney throughout much of the campaign, including a 69%–61% advantage in significant traditional news coverage between August 27 and October 21, 2012 (PEJ 2012f). Even during much of the 2011 Republican primary campaign season, President Obama received nine times more news coverage than any Republican did (PEJ 2011b). Still, the amount of mainstream news coverage fluctuated, as one would expect, with each candidate's party convention. Just as Obama enjoyed more coverage during his party's convention and Romney more during his,[10] the volume of total campaign coverage trended upward after the first presidential debate (PEJ 2012f).

Obama outpaced not only Romney's traditional news coverage but also his volume of attention on three social media outlets: Twitter, Facebook, and Internet blogs (PEJ 2012b). What is more, the ratio of coverage volume for mainstream media outlets roughly mirrored that on social media but still advantaged the president. Whereas Obama enjoyed approximately 1.36 times more coverage than Romney did on mainstream media sites, his advantage grew to 1.44 (on Twitter), 1.54 (on blogs), and 1.77 (on Facebook).

The last two weeks of the presidential election campaign further solidified Obama's advantage in volume of coverage in comparison with Governor Romney. Yet there was little variation in Obama's lead when comparing traditional and social media. Obama's volume of coverage on mainstream media exceeded Romney's at a ratio of 1.34 on Twitter and 1.29 on traditional news broadcasts. In absolute terms, Obama enjoyed 3.9 million to Romney's 2.9 million tweets, just as he was a significant presence on 80% (to Romney's 62%) of traditional news broadcasts[11] (PEJ 2012f).

Tone of Coverage

The 2012 campaign was negative, as both candidates suffered nearly identical 2.5 times more negative than positive coverage of their character and career records. Compared with recent elections, 2012 was most similar to 2004, in which candidates John Kerry and George W. Bush received roughly the same proportion of negative news coverage. In 2008 or 2000, conversely, one candidate (the Democrat Obama in 2008 and the Republican Bush in 2000) received noticeably more positive coverage than his opponent (PEJ 2012d). As with most prior elections, the pattern of negativity was a function of the schedule of particular campaign events and developments unique to the 2012 election.

From the end of the conventions until the last two weeks of the campaign, Romney's traditional news coverage was more negative, at 38% to Obama's 30% negative coverage (PEJ 2012f). The month of September was a particularly poor month for Romney. In the wake of the Democratic Party's successful national convention, Romney sought to "reboot" his campaign and limit the damage of the "47%" video, both of which garnered a significant amount of negative coverage throughout the month of September: 54% negative for Romney to 24% negative traditional news coverage for Obama (PEJ 2012f). Romney recovered after a strong first debate performance, however, and the tone of his traditional news coverage improved to only 23% negative to Obama's 37% negative between October 4 and 16, 2012 (PEJ 2012f). Nevertheless, horse-race coverage, which amounted to over 46% of all traditional news coverage during the last two weeks of the campaign, benefited Obama greatly, with only 16% negative horse-race coverage to Romney's 29% negative horse-race coverage.[12] The emphasis on horse-race coverage in the last weeks of the campaign is reflected in more positive coverage for Obama during that time.

Table 7.1 presents more specific tonal data by candidate and according to a variety of media. Aside from partisan cable news and talk radio, which predictably support one candidate over the other, both candidates experienced more negative than positive coverage across all media. Time 2 presents the best comparative data, and it shows that although Romney suffered more negative coverage than Obama did, almost all media covered both candidates more negatively than positively, a typical description of most presidential campaigns (Farnsworth and Lichter 2008).[13]

One additional similarity between the tone of traditional and social media is variation by events. Simply, the occurrence of political events drove both traditional news and social media tone in similar ways, albeit more dramatically on traditional news sources. During the candidates' respective political conventions, for example, each received much less negative news coverage than his opponent, with the opposite being true when his party was not on the national stage (PEJ 2012f). This is typical of what we have come to expect concerning traditional news coverage of unified conventions, which also lead to a small bump to candidates' position in the horse race (Holbrook 1994). Fluctuation in social media also tracked traditional coverage of the debates, most obviously on Twitter and the blogs. Surprisingly, Facebook posts trended less negative after the conventions and fluctuated less in response to the October debates (PEJ 2012a).

Table 7.1. Tone of Campaign Coverage by Medium

	Time 1				Time 2				Time 3			
	Obama		Romney		Obama		Romney		Obama		Romney	
Media	Pos.	Neg.	Pos.	Neg.	Pos.	Neg.	Pos.	Neg.	Pos.	Neg.	Pos.	Neg.
Online news	24	76	31	69	25	33	14	44				
Newspapers	35	65	34	66	12	18	19	16				
Networks*	42	58	29	71	25	23	16	33	23	25	17	32
Fox	14	86	44	56	6	46	28	12	5	56	42	11
MSNBC	54	46	12	88	39	15	3	71	51	0	0	68
Conservative radio	7	93	62	38								
Liberal radio	64	36	11	89								
Twitter					25	45	16	58	27	41	32	45
Facebook					24	53	23	62	33	47	23	54
Blogs					19	44	18	27	28	42	24	40
Overall traditional					19	30	15	38	29	19	16	33

Source: Time 1, May 29–August 5, 2012; PEJ Report for August 23, 2012. Time 2, August 27–October 21, 2012, PEJ Report for November 2, 2012; Time 3, October 29–November 5, 2012, PEJ Report for November 19, 2012.
* Time 1 network estimates include morning and evening newscasts. Time 2 and 3 reflect only evening network coverage, with Time 3 being an approximation of PEJ's numbers that it reports separately for the penultimate and last weeks of the campaign.

The primary difference between traditional and social media tone is that social media tended to be more negative than traditional news. For example, whereas traditional news peaked at 44% and 33% negative for Romney and Obama, respectively, each experienced considerably more negative coverage on social media during the same time frame, at 62% and 53% negative Facebook comments, for Romney and Obama, respectively. This implies that social media is not necessarily a boon to a candidate's message, as some pundits, politicians, and scholars might speculate, and might insinuate that a candidate's control of his or her campaign message is not enhanced but rather undermined through social media technology.

Although future research is needed to explore whether social media is generalizably more negative than traditional news is, social media's greater negativity could be a function of the vitriol that users of social media use to express their opinions (but see Thorson, Vraga, and Kligler-Vilenchik 2014) in comparison with traditional news and traditional news media's standards of journalism, which may temper more negative opinionating. Indeed, most social media posts are personal, which may be driven more heavily by predispositions than what is on the news.[14] Just as these numbers suggest a lack of candidate control over social media conversations, they also show that social media conversations are not simply a reflection of traditional news coverage. This independence of social media is evidence of greater voter control of the campaign conversation, which perhaps signals the dawn of a more democratic (or at least more decentralized) campaign dialogue.

Variation in Social Media Coverage by Candidate

Although President Obama appears to have enjoyed a greater following on social media, social media activity is evenly distributed by party identification (Pew Internet and American Life Project 2012). At least for the 2012 campaign, social media usage may not have played a dominant role in voter acquisition of campaign information online. The PEJ, for example, analyzed links provided on posts for each candidate (whether on Twitter, YouTube, or Facebook), and, for both, the candidate's website was the primary information source provided (PEJ 2012b). In other words, social media appear to be but a vehicle to direct voters to an older variety of new technology—the campaign website—that candidates use to communicate additional information to voters. Specifically, 71% and 76% of posts link the campaign's website, versus 5% and 10% that link a candidate's social media profile, for Obama and Romney, respectively. This happens because campaigns exert greater control over the messages they convey on their own webpage, which can also be more substantive or detailed than a single tweet.

Even social media coverage of important campaign events tended to reflect traditional news events and broadcasts. Romney won the first presidential debate handily, by a 72%–20% margin, according to Gallup (Jones 2012). Romney's victory was reflected accurately and consistent with traditional news in the blogosphere. Here, Romney enjoyed a 45% to 12% advantage in favorable coverage (PEJ 2012e), which compares with 23% and 37% negative traditional news coverage for Romney and Obama, respectively (PEJ 2012f). At first, it would appear that the president's presence on Twitter (35%–22% favorable advantage) and Facebook (at a slightly less but still favorable 40% to 36% margin) was more favorable and did not follow traditional news coverage of the Romney victory. Yet PEJ (2012e) disaggregates these numbers to illustrate that much of the pro-Obama tally was critical of Romney (only 9% of the 35% praised Obama on Twitter) and that even the favorable Romney commentary was more critical of Obama than lauding Romney. If social media posts were more favorable to Obama, they certainly were not more positive.

All in all, these data suggest substantial variation by social media and some advantage to President Obama. Some social media, especially Internet blogs, were more likely to follow traditional news in its coverage of the first presidential debate. Other social media, such as Twitter and Facebook, reflected a slight Obama advantage, likely given his superior number of Facebook friends and

Twitter followers. Still, the advantage was not so substantial that we could discount outright evidence that illustrates how social media users are fairly balanced ideologically (Pew Internet and American Life Project 2012). Moreover, it would not be fair to say that the disparities in social media between candidates was a determining or, perhaps, even a consequential factor in the 2012 presidential election campaign, despite their correlation with the eventual outcome.

Conclusion

This chapter examines the content of both traditional and social media coverage of the 2012 presidential election campaign. In doing so, it makes an important contribution to a burgeoning literature on how newer media cover presidential elections and the extent to which this coverage differs from traditional news coverage. Using the best readily available data provided by the Pew Research Center's Project for Excellence in Journalism, this chapter reveals that although social and other forms of Internet media provide citizens with new and different ways to express their political opinions and learn about politics, this technology has produced only marginal differences in the substance of campaign news coverage. Whereas social media were more negative, they still tend to follow traditional news coverage, which, as expected, follows regular events—both scheduled or not—throughout the election campaign.

As this study is limited to the 2012 presidential election campaign, the generalizability of the conclusions is limited. We cannot say whether users of new media would have participated in recent elections absent this technology or whether voters' control of the campaign message is dependent on the existence of social media. Yet reflecting on other changes to media in recent elections suggests that most people, particularly younger voters who have been quick to adopt newer media, will participate with whatever media are cutting-edge, but only if they are already interested in participating in politics. Candidates in the 1992 presidential election campaign, which witnessed a sizeable turnout among young voters—and, in fact, a higher turnout rate among 18- to 29-year-olds than in 2008 (United States Election Project 2010)—relied on toll-free phone numbers to raise money and MTV to reach the younger audience. In 2008, turnout was also high, although it was text messages and phone apps used to raise money and Facebook and YouTube (not to mention candidate webpages) to communicate.

It is unlikely that if social media were unavailable in 2012, these voters would be oblivious to and disinterested in the presidential campaign. After all, the increase in voter participation, even among the young, was greater between 2000 and 2004 than between 2004 and 2008 (United States Elections Project 2010), when social media rose to prominence in American electoral politics. Thus, being able to claim that new media were *the* reason for higher participation among users of social media, in general, and young voters, in particular, is dubious, especially given the strong and complementary link between traditional and new media as well as the lack of unambiguous scholarly evidence that the Internet or social media do well to engage voters.

Regardless, we know that candidates will use new media because some voters also use it. But, like 1992, this may reflect a smart politician using all available technology to expand his or her reach and maximize control of his or her campaign message. It is not that these new media somehow invigorated a generation that would have ignored presidential politics without a technological advance. Rather, new media provide, by definition, an innovative vehicle through which candidates can express their messages and voters can learn about those messages if they are predisposed to use that technology. Social media provide voters more opportunity to speak with an independent campaign voice, nevertheless, that, while it currently tracks traditional news, may provide more message variation and decentralized control of that message in future elections.

The question may yet be asked whether a new medium matters to the outcome of an election. Although the nature of the relationship—the technological means to communicate—is qualitatively different, new media do not necessarily enhance a presidential candidate's ability to win an election. Rather, our theories of political communication and campaigning should hold regardless of changes in technology. That being said, future research is still needed to examine with greater sophistication the causal relationships between traditional and nontraditional media to substantiate the claims of this essay and to determine who really influences whom in the postbroadcast era of presidential campaigns and who will control the message in future campaigns.

In point of fact, social media have increased the capacity of participating Americans to communicate their views about politics and the campaign. Social media are opinion-driven, decentralized forms of communication. Still, this study maintains that even these individualized comments are driven by the overarching and typical events of a presidential campaign and the traditional means through which most have watched presidential campaign events, such as debates, since 1960. Yes, people can watch campaign events on their computer or phones; but it is traditional content that drives the campaign message, even if there now may be many more perspectives on these events and additional information sources for traditional media to tap in their reporting of campaign events. Nevertheless, this development alone now requires candidates to be alert to any new messages that may help or hurt their chances for victory, adding yet another wrinkle to effective campaign communications and strategies to control the campaign messages now and into the future.

Notes

1. Whereas new media is defined as electronic interactive media, such as the Internet and other postindustrial forms of telecommunication (New media 2012), old media is considered to be media in existence before the arrival of the Internet, such as newspapers, books, television, and cinema. I operationalize traditional media the same way as the Pew Center's Project for Excellence in Journalism, so that traditional media include virtually all media except social media, whereas new media include Facebook, Twitter, blogs, and when coded, YouTube.
2. Others interpret Boulianne's article much more positively. Nisbet, Stoycheff, and Pearce (2012, 253), for example, emphasize the positive relationships between Internet use and political engagement but do not consider the qualifications to these findings raised by Boulianne in the discussion section of her article. She concludes that research is not conclusive as to the causality of the relationship between Internet use and political engagement. Moreover, most positive effects wash out if a study controls for a user's prior political interest.
3. Although Jamieson and Capella's (2008) book focuses on traditional media, one can reasonably extrapolate their findings to the web version of Fox News Channel: Foxnews.com.
4. As both Dutta-Bergman (2004) and Althaus and Tewksbury (2000) studied only the early years of postbroadcast media, it remains to be seen if their conclusions persist into the age of Facebook and Twitter. Moreover, how people use the Internet may change during a highly salient national event such as a presidential election campaign (see Tewksbury 2006). Interestingly, the PEJ shows only a marginal increase in social media usage during the height of the 2012 presidential election campaign. It reports only slight increases in the percentage of regular Twitter (2% to 4%), YouTube (3% to 7%), and Facebook (6% to 12%) users for news (PEJ 2012c).
5. The overall conclusion of this study reinforces this idea. Lee Rainie, director of the Pew Research Center, told ABC News, "There is a mixed picture along party lines. One party doesn't have an obvious social media edge. The biggest driver here is whether you are interested in politics in the first place. If you talk about it with friends, you are going to use the social tools to talk politics" (Stern 2012).
6. Although this hypothesis should also extend to the topic of news coverage—just as traditional media focus primarily on the horse race, so, too, should social media—PEJ does not report horse-race-related posts on social media.
7. There are studies of social media in the 2010 midterm elections, nevertheless (Bode et al. 2011).
8. The PEJ documents and describes each of its coding decisions at the end of every study (see PEJ 2012f, for one example). It also reports intercoder reliability statistics for human coders, indicating agreement in the range of 78% to 91%.
9. PEJ does not specify why it selected these range of dates or why it missed one week in October, for example.
10. The importance of events on fluctuation is not limited to either the general election contest or comparisons between Obama and Romney. Traditional media followed its events-driven approach with Herman Cain coverage, as he became more newsworthy after his Florida straw poll victory in September 2011. The volume of his traditional news coverage continued to increase and then explode after he struggled to answer questions related to Libya and allegations (and later admission) of an extramarital affair (PEJ 2011b).

11. PEJ (2012f) was careful to tally only campaign coverage in these percentages, not coverage of Hurricane Sandy. Only 4% of campaign coverage concerned the storm.
12. Positive coverage tracks negative, at 37% and 20% positive horse-race coverage for Obama and Romney, respectively.
13. Romney enjoyed more positive newspaper coverage, whereas Obama enjoyed more positive network television news coverage.
14. The PEJ (2012f) reports that at least on Election Day, for example, posts were not used for substantive discussions but rather for users to express their personal views on the election (28% of mentions on Twitter and blogs; 50% on Facebook).

References

Althaus, Scott L., and David Tewksbury. 2000. "Patterns of Internet and Traditional News Media Use in a Networked Community." *Political Communication* 17: 21–45.

Baum, Matthew A. 2003. *Soft News Goes to War: Public Opinion and American Foreign Policy in the New Media Age*. Princeton: Princeton University Press.

———. 2005. "Talking the Vote: Why Presidential Candidate Hit the Talk Show Circuit." *American Journal of Political Science* 49:213–234.

Boczkowski, Pablo J., Eugena Mitchelstein, and Martin Walter. 2012. "When Burglar Alarms Sound, Do Monitorial Citizens Pay Attention to Them? The Online News Choices of Journalists and Consumers during and after the 2008 U.S. Election Cycle." *Political Communication* 29:347–366.

Bode, Leticia, David Lassen, Young Mie Kim, Ben Sayre, Dhavan Shah, Michael M. Franz, Erika Franklin Fowler and Travis N. Ridout. 2011. "Putting New Media in Old Strategies: Candidate Use of Twitter during the 2010 Midterm Elections." Paper presented at the annual meeting of the American Political Science Association, Seattle, September 1–4.

Boulianne, Shelley. 2009. "Does Internet Use Affect Engagement? A Meta-Analysis of Research." *Political Communication* 26:193–211.

———. 2011. "Stimulating or Reinforcing Political Interest: Using Panel Data to Examine Reciprocal Effects between News Media and Political Interest." *Political Communication* 28:147–162.

Chace, Zoe. 2013. "Chips, Beer, Tweets: Why TV Is Key to Twitter's Prospects." *Planet Money* (blog), NPR Online, November 13. http://www.npr.org/blogs/money/2013/11/06/243521425/chips-beer-tweets-why-tv-is-key-to-twitters-prospects.

D'Haenens, Leen, Nicholas Jankowski, and Ard Heulvelman. 2004. "News in Online and Print Newspapers: Differences in Reader Consumption and Recall." *New Media & Society* 6: 319–339.

Druckman, James N. 2003. "The Power of Television Images: The First Kennedy-Nixon Debate Revisited." *Journal of Politics* 65:559–571.

Dunaway, Johanna. 2008. "Markets, Ownership, and the Quality of Campaign News Coverage." *Journal of Politics* 70:1193–1202.

Dutta-Bergman, Mohan J. 2004. "Complementarity in Consumption of News Types across Traditional and New Media." *Journal of Broadcasting & Electronic Media* 48:41–60.

Edgerly, Stephanie, Leticia Bode, Young Mie Kim, and Dhavan V. Shah. 2013. "Campaigns Go Social: Are Facebook, YouTube, and Twitter Changing Elections?" In *New Directions in Media and Politics*, edited by Travis N. Ridout, 82–99. New York: Routledge.

Eshbaugh-Soha, Matthew, and Evan M. Lowe. 2013. "The More Things Change, the More They Stay the Same." Presented at the Annual Meeting of the Western Political Science Association, Hollywood, CA.

Eveland, William P., Mihye Seo, and Krisztina Marton 2002. "Learning from the News in Campaign 2000: An Experimental Comparison of TV News, Newspapers, and Online News." *Media Psychology* 4:352–378.

Farnsworth, Stephen J., and Robert Lichter. 2008. *The Nightly News Nightmare: Television's Coverage of U.S. Presidential Elections, 1988–2004*. 2nd ed. Lanham, MD: Rowman and Littlefield.

Gainous, Jason, and Kevin M. Wagner. 2011. *Rebooting American Politics: The Internet Revolution*. Lanham, MD: Rowman and Littlefield.

Hamilton, James T. 2004. *All the News That's Fit to Sell*. Princeton: Princeton University Press.

Haynes, Audrey A., and Brian Pitts. 2009. "Making an Impression: New Media in the 2008 Presidential Nomination Campaigns." *PS: Political Science & Politics* 42:53–58.

Hellweg, Susan A., Michael Pfau, and Steven R Brydon. 1992. *Televised Presidential Debates: Advocacy in Contemporary America*. New York: Praeger.

Hendricks, John Allen, and Robert E. Denton, Jr., eds. 2010. *Communicator-in-Chief: How Barack Obama Used New Media Technology to Win the White House*. Lanham, MD: Lexington Books.

Holbrook, Thomas M. 1994. "Campaigns, National Conditions, and U.S. Presidential Elections." *American Journal of Political Science* 38:973–998.

Hopkins, Daniel, and Gary King. 2010. "A Method of Automated Nonparametric Content Analysis for Social Science." *American Journal of Political Science* 54:229–247.

Houston, J. Brian, Mitchell S. McKinney, Joshua Hawthorne, and Matthew L. Spialek. 2013. "Frequency of Tweeting during Presidential Debates: Effect on Debate Attitudes and Knowledge." *Communication Studies* 64:548–560.

Jones, Jeffrey M. 2012. "Romney Narrows Vote Gap after Historic Debate Win." Gallup.com, October 8. http://www.gallup.com/poll/157907/romney-narrows-vote-gap-historic-debate-win.aspx.

Kenski, Kate, and Natalie Jomini Stroud. 2006. "Connections between Internet Use and Political Efficacy, Knowledge, and Participation." *Journal of Broadcasting & Electronic Media* 46:54–71.

Kruikemeier, Sanne, Guda van Noort, Rens Vliegenthart, and Claes H. de Vreese. Forthcoming. "Unraveling the Effects of Active and Passive Forms of Political Internet use: Does it Affect Citizens' Political Involvement?" *New Media and Society*.

Kushin, Matthew James, and Masahiro Yamamoto. 2010. "Did Social Media Really Matter? College Students' Use of Online Media and Political Decision Making in the 2008 Election." *Mass Communication and Society* 13:608–630.

Kwak, Nojin, Nathaniel Poor, and Marko M. Skoric. 2006. "Honey, I Shrunk the World! The Relations between Internet Use and International Engagement." *Mass Communication & Society* 9: 189–213.

Jamieson, Kathleen Hall, and Joseph N. Cappella. *Echo Chamber: Rush Limbaugh and the Conservative Media Establishment*. Oxford: Oxford University Press.

Messing, Solomon, and Sean J. Westwood. Forthcoming. "Selective Exposure in the Age of Social Media: Endorsements Trump Partisan Source Affiliation When Selecting News Online." *Communication Research*.

McKinney, Mitchell S., J. Brian Houston, and Joshua Hawthorne. 2014. "Social Watching a 2012 Republican Presidential Primary Debate." *American Behavioral Scientist* 58:556–573.

Morris, Jonathan S. 2005. "The Fox News Factor." *Harvard International Journal of Press/Politics* 10:56–79.

New media. 2012. *Cambridge Dictionary*. http://www.dictionary.cambridge.org/.

Nisbet, Erik C., Elizabeth Stoycheff, and Katy E. Pearce. 2012. "A Multinational, Multilevel Model of Internet Use and Citizen Attitudes about Democracy." *Journal of Communication* 62:249–265.

Parkin, Michael. 2010. "Taking Late Night Comedy Seriously: How Candidate Appearances on Late Night Television Can Engage Viewers." *Political Research Quarterly* 63:3–15.

Patterson, Thomas E. 1993. *Out of Order*. New York: Knopf.

Pew Internet and American Life Project. 2012. "Social Media and Political Engagement Survey." October 19. http://pewinternet.org/Reports/2012/Political-Engagement.aspx.

Pew Research Center Project for Excellence in Journalism. 2011a. "Cain's Bad Stretch." November 9. http://www.journalism.org/analysis_report/cains_difficult_week.

———. 2011b. "The Media Primary." October 17. http://www.journalism.org/analysis_report/cr.

———. 2011c. "Twitter and the Campaign." December 8. http://www.pewresearch.org/2011/12/08/twitter-and-the-campaign/.

———. 2012a. "The Final Days of the Media Campaign 2012." November 19. http://www.journalism.org/analysis_report/final_days_media_campaign_2012.

———. 2012b. "How the Presidential Candidates Use the Web and Social Media." August 15. http://www.journalism.org/analysis_report/how_presidential_candidates_use_web_and_social_media.

———. 2012c. "Internet Gains Most as Campaign News Source but Cable TV Still Leads." October 25. http://www.journalism.org/commentary_backgrounder/social_media_doubles_remains_limited.

———. 2012d. "The Master Character Narratives in Campaign 2012." August 23. http://www.journalism.org/analysis_report/2012_campaign_character_narratives.

———. 2012e. "Social Media Debate Sentiment Less Critical of Obama than Polls and Press Are." October 25. http://www.journalism.org/commentary_backgrounder/social_media_debate_sentiment_less_critical_obama_polls_and_press_are.

———. 2012f. "Winning the Media Campaign 2012." November 2. http://www.journalism.org/analysis_report/winning_media_campaign_2012.

Prior, Markus. 2007. *Post-broadcast Democracy: How Media Choice Increase Inequality in Political Involvement and Polarizes Elections*. Cambridge: Cambridge University Press.

Sayre, Ben, Leticia Bode, Dhavan Shah, Dave Wilcox, and Chirag Shah. 2010. "Tracking Attention to California Proposition 8 in Social Media, Online News, and Conventional News." *Policy & Internet* 2:7–31.

Stern, Joanna. 2012. "Liberal Democrats More Likely to Hit 'Like' than Conservative Republicans, Says Pew Report." *Technology Review* (blog), ABC News Online, October 19. http://abcnews.go.com/blogs/technology/2012/10/liberal-democrats-more-likely-to-hit-like-than-conservative-republicans-says-pew-report/.

Tewksbury, David. 2006. "Exposure to the Newer Media in a Presidential Primary Campaign." *Political Communication* 23:313–332.

Tewksbury, David, and Scott L. Althaus. 2000. "Differences in Knowledge Acquisition among Readers of the Paper and Online Versions of a National Newspaper." *Journalism and Mass Communications Quarterly* 77:457–479.

Thorson, Kjerstin, Emily Vraga, and Neta Kligler-Vilenchik. 2014. "Don't Push Your Opinions on Me: Young Citizens and Political Etiquette on Facebook." In *Presidential Campaigning and Social Media: An Analysis of the 2012 Campaign*, edited by John Allen Hendricks and Daniel Schill. New York: Oxford University Press.

United States Election Project. 2010. "2008 Current Population Survey Voting and Registration Supplement." http://elections.gmu.edu/CPS_2008.html.

Vancil, David L., and Sue D. Pendell. 1987. "The Myth of Viewer-Listener Disagreement in the First Kennedy-Nixon Debate." *Central States Speech Journal* 38:16–27.

PART 3

Social Media's Impact on Campaign Politics

8

The Influence of User-Controlled Messages on Candidate Evaluations

JOSHUA HAWTHORNE AND BENJAMIN R. WARNER

The rise of social media as a potent political force in campaign politics played a major role in journalistic analyses of the 2012 presidential election. Traditional media lavished attention on the content of political discussions on social media platforms (Fouhy 2011; Sloan 2012), the influence of social media on electoral outcomes (Parker 2012), and the predictive power of social media trends on election results ("Did Social Media Predict the 2012 Presidential Election Results?" 2012). Driving this coverage was the fact that social media were more widely used during the 2012 election than at any previous time. For example, a picture of President Barack Obama hugging his wife, Michelle Obama, which was posted to commemorate his victory, became the most "liked" Facebook post ever (Willis 2012) and the most retweeted photo of all time (Parker 2012). Election night was the most live-tweeted event in U.S. history when considering the number of tweets posted ("Election Night 2012" 2012), closely followed by the first presidential debate ("Dispatch from the Denver Debate" 2012). Researchers at the Pew Internet and American Life Project determined that 39% of American adults used social media for political purposes during the 2012 election (Ranie et al. 2012). Given the wide use of social media in the 2012 election, no analysis of campaign messaging would be complete without examining the implications of these new communication platforms.

The wide use of social media in the 2012 campaign is significant because, perhaps more than any other technological innovation in electoral politics, Facebook and Twitter allow the user to control the message. Facebook users are not only authors of their own political content when they post status updates and comment on the updates of their friends; they are also gatekeepers of information when they manage their friend lists, hide posts from their feed, and distribute links to articles and videos to their own friends. Similarly, Twitter allows users to be the authors of their own brief messages, to distribute links to other campaign messages, and to select the sources they would like to receive information from in their own Twitter stream. Relative to other (especially traditional) modes of campaign communication, these social media platforms provide the greatest amount of control to individual users.

Though individual users in social media environments dominate message control, research has yet to demonstrate what effect, if any, social media communication has on attitudes toward candidates. More specifically, does social media communication influence how candidates are perceived? This is the central question addressed by the research presented here. In this chapter, we evaluate the relationship between social media communication about specific political events and perception of candidates by conducting two case studies from the 2012 election: one examining social media communication about the first presidential debate and one examining Governor Mitt Romney's leaked comments about the 47% of Americans whom he identified as not paying income tax.

Social Media and Politics

Although social media are among the most widely used communication media, social media use for political purposes is a relatively new phenomenon (Sloan 2012) that campaigns use inconsistently at best (Conway, Kenski, and Wang 2013). Social media can be defined as any Internet-based application that allows users to create, post, and share content with other users while having access to the content posted by others. This includes social networking sites such as Facebook and MySpace, as well as traditional blogging platforms such as Blogger and Wordpress, microblogs such as Twitter and Tumblr, and digital-content-sharing platforms, such as YouTube, Instagram, and Flickr. The main purpose of social media is to provide users the ability to communicate with others in the same digital space. Relative to traditional media of campaign communication (e.g., traditional news media, campaign-generated paid media, and campaign events such as conventions and debates), social media offer users an unprecedented amount of control over the message environment, within which users choose which messages to spread (Dylko et al. 2012) as well as whose messages to receive. The ease of communication through these platforms has facilitated broad-ranging political discussion and activity. Of the roughly 60% of American adults who use social media sites, two-thirds use social media for purposes related to political or civic engagement (Ranie et al. 2012).

Given the rise of social media as a tool for political engagement, researchers have begun to explore the political habits of social media users in a variety of contexts. In research on American participation in politics via social media, Rainie and colleagues (2012) asked users if they promoted material related to political or social issues, encouraged people to vote, posted their own thoughts or comments on political or social issues, reposted content related to political or social issues written by someone else, encouraged other people to take action on political or social issues, posted links to political stories, belong to a group on a social media site that is related to political issues, and used social media tools to follow elected officials. Participation in politics through social media was defined as engagement in one of those activities. The least popular activity, following an elected official or candidate for office, was done by 20% of those who use social media. Other researchers have explored engagement in politics on social media in relationship to live-tweeting political events (Anstead and O'Loughlin 2011; Hawthorne, Houston, and McKinney 2013; Houston et al. 2013; McKinney, Houston, and Hawthorne 2014; Shamma, Kennedy, and Churchill 2009), engaging in acts of political consumerism (Warner, Turner-McGowen, and Hawthorne 2012), communicating about political protests (Lotan et al. 2011; Rahimi 2011; Tufekci and Wilson 2012), and regarding elections (Tumasjan et al. 2011). Researchers have also begun to explore how engagement in politics using social media affects people, with preliminary findings suggesting that those who use social media for political purposes are more likely to engage offline (Kushin and Yamamoto 2010; Tufekci and Wilson 2012; Valenzuela, Arriagada, and Scherman 2012; Vitak et al. 2011).

Despite these initial findings, however, little research has explored the potential influence of social media on electoral outcomes. While Dimitrova and Bystrom (2013) found that candidate trait evaluations in primary elections are influenced by exposure to social media, and McKinney, Houston, and Hawthorne (2014) found that the frequency of candidate mentions on social media during the debate corresponded to gains or losses in electability and viability ratings of the candidates, the role of social media communication on candidate evaluation is still underresearched and largely unknown. To begin the investigation of social media influence, we turn to literature regarding the effects of other forms of political communication.

The Effects of Political Communication on Candidate Evaluations

Since there has been little academic exploration of any potential effect of social media communication on vote choice, literature regarding three different political media sources may provide guidance regarding any potential effect. The three most researched media of political communication effects are political advertising, presidential campaign debates, and political news. Since we are testing the effect of exposure to social media discussions about the first presidential debate and a prominent news story from the campaign that was featured in candidate ads, we expect these traditional media to provide some insight about the potential effects of social media in the context of our study.

Political advertisements, or sponsored messages that appear on a medium to promote a stance on a political issue (including political candidates), are the most common and dominant form of political communication (Kaid 2004). Also, according to Kaid (2004, 169), "The finding that exposure to political spots can affect candidate image evaluation has been confirmed in both experimental and survey research settings." Generally speaking, the more money a candidate spends on advertising in a given media market, the more votes he or she gets from that market (Shaw 1999), but the amount of influence is dependent on individual differences and the nature of the ads (Bowen 1994; Faber, Tims, and Schmitt 1993; Franz and Ridout 2010; Kaid, Fernandes, and Painter 2011; Krupnikov 2012; Painter 2013; Rothschild and Ray 1974). Advertising is distinct from social media communication in that it is paid media controlled by candidates and political action committees. Social media communication, by contrast, is free, and individual users control the content of messaging. Nevertheless, early research suggests that much of the content on social media is still generated by traditional elites (Dylko et al. 2012; Hawthorne, Houston, and McKinney 2013; Auer 2011). That is, while individual users of social media can control the messages they are exposed to by managing their social networks and selecting which (if any) traditional sources to follow, the messages that people generate and spread through social media have tended to reflect narratives that are dominant in traditional campaign communication media.

While candidate advertisements reach voters through paid media channels and are tightly controlled messages carefully designed by candidates, campaign debates offer candidates the ability to communicate directly to the electorate in spontaneous and competitive settings, a feature that has made campaign debates one of the most important pieces of political communication. Indeed, debates reach the largest audience of any single campaign event (McKinney and Carlin 2004). Debates also serve as focal points in campaigns, as candidates use the opportunity to present the best argument for their election (Carlin 1992). However, despite being an excellent outlet for candidate messaging, debates do little to change predebate voting intentions (McKinney and Carlin 2004). The best predictor of voting intention following debate viewing is predebate vote choice (Holbrook 1996). This does not mean that there is no effect but just that the effect on vote change is limited. Debates can influence the voting intention of citizens if those citizens are undecided, conflicted, or weak partisans (Chaffee and Choe 1980; McKinney 1994; Benoit and Hansen 2004) and can influence the criteria that voting decisions are made on (Benoit, McKinney, and Holbert 2001). Scholars estimate that debates may have had a decisive influence in elections that were especially close or featured many undecided voters (McKinney and Carlin 2004). However, research suggests that as important as the debate itself is, the debate after the debate to frame who won may be more important (McKinney and Carlin 2004; Hwang et al. 2007). It is here that social media could be most influential, as Twitter and Facebook allow this narrative to form in real time as the debate is happening (Hawthorne, Houston, and McKinney 2013) and permit individual users to participate in the formation of the debate narrative. In short, while candidates and media control the messages in the debate itself, social media allow users greater control over the postdebate narrative as they filter the messages they receive about the debate, distribute messages they find favorable to their social networks, and craft messages of their own. Early research regarding social media use during political debates shows that the amount of discussion about candidates corresponds to changes in electability and viability of that candidate, such that the more a candidate is mentioned, the more he or she is perceived to be an electable and viable candidate (McKinney, Houston, and Hawthorne 2013), and the number of times an individual tweets corresponds to the amount of factual information he or she recalled from the debate (Houston et al. 2013), indicating that those who discuss candidates over social media in debate contexts both may experience changes in their evaluations of candidates and may remember more of that information.

News media also have an effect on candidate evaluations. As an important communication hub within the political system, the media offer interpretations of political events, exploring candidate motivations and placing events in a larger campaign context (Gulati, Just, and Crigler 2004). Further, news coverage of political events can influence candidate evaluations (Chaffee and Dennis 1979; Fridkin et al. 2008; Gulati, Just, and Crigler 2004; Hellweg, Pfau, and Brydon 1992; Page and Shapiro 1982; Steeper 1978). Coverage of political news is often evaluated differently (on levels of perceived partisan bias, informativeness, and interestingness) depending on the partisanship of the viewer (Coe et al. 2008). News coverage is often characterized by the use of a specific frame or emphasis on parts of a story, making those parts more salient at the expense of other elements of the story (Entman 2003). Entman (2003, 2004) describes a process, called cascading activation, through which a frame is passed down from the media to the public. Within the cascading activation process, there is a path that allows the public to contribute to the frame that is adopted by the media, but this is usually only accomplished through news coverage of political polls or protests (Entman 2004). Social media alter this equation by allowing citizens to engage in cascading activation framing more easily, thereby providing a pulpit for normal citizens to communicate on a mass communication scale (Hawthorne, Houston, and McKinney 2013). Communication about politics on social media therefore shares more in common with news coverage of politics because it allows users to offer interpretations of a political event on a mass scale.

Each of these forms of political communication influences candidate evaluations in either a positive or negative manner depending on the context. Furthermore, each form of political communication is similar to the process of viewing information about politics using social media. However, social media offer several different ways to communicate; so comparing social media to these passive media forms provides guidance regarding this effect, but we cannot draw definitive conclusions solely on the basis of past research.

Media Effects in the Social Media Landscape

Any assessment of campaign media effects, whether digital or broadcast, is foregrounded by a long history of media effects theory. It was initially believed that there was a strong media effect likened to a hypodermic needle that injected attitudes directly into the audience as if they were empty receptacles waiting to be filled with whatever content was presented to them by the media. Early research in propaganda, however, found no evidence of a strong direct effect of media on opinion formation, and hence a limited effects model of the media dominated for a period (Katz and Lazarsfeld 1955; Klapper 1960). This limited effects model gave way to various nuanced perspectives on media effects, such as agenda setting (McCombs and Shaw 1993), priming (Iyengar and Kinder 1986), and framing (Iyengar 1994). The emergence of digital media has complicated this understanding because users are less beholden to traditional media outlets for news and are thus less subject to the dominant media agenda. This change has caused some observers to speculate that a new era of minimal effects may be upon us, as people tend exist in individualized media environments and are thus isolated from dominant narratives (Bennett and Iyengar 2008, 2010). Others have argued that, because digital media afford more control over messages to the individual, media effects will not be limited but rather more prone to attitude reinforcement as people self-select into attitude-consistent media networks (Holbert, Garrett, and Gleason 2010).

The debate over media effects in a digital environment is, at its core, a debate about the control afforded to users over what messages they receive and which they choose to share. In terms of social media, this suggests that users may experience less of an agenda-setting and framing effect from traditional media and campaign elites and, conversely, may be more engaged in the process of constructing a campaign narrative. Entman's (2003, 2004) cascading activation of frames theory best describes this process. This theory posits that much interpretation of the news occurs from the top down as frames emerge from traditional sources (political elites and the news media) and cascade down to the broader public. However, some frames and ideas emerge from the ground up as the public asserts itself on traditional elites, a process that typically happens through public-opinion polling or political demonstrations.

The cascading activation of frames that occurs through social media will follow a similar process to the extent that messages from candidates, campaigns, and news media have the greatest audiences and tend to dominate the social media conversation (Auer 2011; Hawthorne, Houston, and McKinney 2013). The frames established by traditional opinion leaders are thus the most likely to influence the interpretation of the campaign. However, because individuals have greater control over which messages they receive and have more potential sources via the high-choice digital environment (Prior 2007), attitude reinforcement may be a more dominant effect as individual users select frames consistent with their own attitudes. Furthermore, because individuals can participate in campaign communication in real time, there is greater ability for user-driven frames to gain mainstream traction (through the retweets, trending topics, shares on Facebook, etc.). For example, in the first presidential debate, when Mitt Romney mentioned Big Bird while threatening to cut funding for PBS, users on Twitter reacted strongly and quickly, establishing this as one of the key debate moments before the news media and campaigns had even begun their traditional debate spin (Sakwa and Steers 2012). This moment was picked up by the Obama campaign and the news media immediately after the fact (Chaggaris 2012), demonstrating how social media provide the public more direct access to the activation of cascading frames. Nevertheless, we expect that the dominant narratives spread through traditional elite sources will dictate the direction of any effect of social media communication on candidate favorability such that events generally considered positive for one candidate will translate into improvements in that candidate's favorability.

To summarize, social media alter the nature of media effects by fragmenting messages and undermining the ability of traditional communication sources to present a single media narrative. Social media also increase message control for users by providing greater choice over source selection and by giving users the ability to participate in narrative formation. Social media also allow for communication both between anonymous entities and between people with existing social ties (Grabowicz et al. 2012). Further, it is more likely that social media will be used to engage in discussions with those whom people already have existing relationships with rather than new individuals (Haythornthwaite 2005). These existing social networks, when studied in offline settings, have been more ideologically segregated than traditional media environments (Mutz and Martin 2001). Furthermore, political communication with family, friends, and acquaintances in unmediated contexts is known to affect candidate evaluations (MacKuen and Brown 1987). It is therefore likely that the influence of known communication partners differentiates social media use from other forms of mediated political communication and possibly increases the influence of messages, as messages received from familiar and trusted sources are less likely to be ignored or rejected.

Politicians such as Barack Obama have started to capitalize on the possibility that familiar networks will have greater social influence through social media. For example, Facebook was used to leverage supporters to contact their friends and motivate them to vote (Cornfield 2010; Issenberg 2012a, 2012b; Madrigal 2012). While direct efforts by campaigns to leverage social media for their benefit are still in the early stages, a great deal of political communication occurred organically through social media during the 2012 election (Ranie et al. 2012). Given past findings that political communication can influence candidate perceptions in contexts of ads, news media, and debates, we expect social media political communication to have some effect on candidate evaluations. Furthermore, given the nature of choice in social media environments and the ideological segregation typical of offline social networks, we expect any effect to be moderated by preexisting attitudes and to primarily be one of reinforcement. Since campaign communication is inherently context dependent, any effect of social media communication should also be tied to a specific context. For example, discussion of Missouri Senate candidate Todd Akin's controversial remarks about "legitimate rape" (e.g., Lieb 2012) should have a negative effect on his standing because the context of the conversation is not positive for him. While not all contexts for discussion would favor one candidate over the other as clearly, this study seeks to test the effect of social media communication in two separate political contexts: one that should favor Romney (the first presidential debate) and one that should favor Obama (Romney's 47% comments).

The first set of hypotheses focus on the context of the first presidential debate. Prior to the first debate, even though the race between Obama and Romney was tightening (Silver 2012a), many members of the media speculated that Romney needed a strong performance to keep his campaign alive (Marlantes 2012; Silver 2012d). Immediately following the debate, news media converged on the narrative of a decisive Romney win; his performance was praised, and Obama's was roundly criticized (Dickerson 2012; Dutton et al. 2013; Schoen 2012). Romney also enjoyed a significant bounce in the polls following the first debate (Silver 2012b). As a result, to the extent that people were communicating about the first debate in their social media networks, the messages would likely favor Romney. Thus, our first hypothesis proposes that social media communication about the first presidential debate will predict higher evaluations of Romney than Obama.

Because social media can allow people to self-select reinforcing messages, because motivated skepticism is common when dealing with political beliefs (Taber and Lodge 2006), and because interpretations of debate performances tend to be subject to partisan filtering (McKinney and Carlin 2004), any effect of social media conversation about the debate should be moderated by party affiliation. We therefore hypothesize that the effect of social media communication on evaluations of Romney will depend on political party affiliation such that Republicans will demonstrate higher evaluations of Romney in proportion to their social media communication about the debate, relative to those who are not affiliated with the Republican Party.

Because debates are direct competitions between the two candidates for president, and because Obama was widely criticized in the media for his performance, we expect that greater discussion of the debate through social media will reduce evaluations of Obama. If this effect is present, it should be subject to the same partisan processing just discussed. We thus hypothesize that social media communication about the first presidential debate will predict lower evaluations of Obama than Romney. We also hypothesize that the effect of social media communication on evaluations of Obama will depend on political party affiliation such that Democrats will demonstrate less reduction in their evaluation of Obama as their social media communication about the debate increases, relative to those who are not affiliated with the Democratic Party.

Our second set of hypotheses focus on Romney's 47% comments. In a leaked recording of Romney speaking to a small group of campaign donors, he criticized 47% of the electorate, who he stated were reliant on government aid and refused to take responsibility for their own lives (Corn 2012). Romney said that it was not his job to worry about these individuals and reiterated that he could never convince them to vote for him (Corn 2012). Upon release of the recording, Romney initially downplayed the comments and eventually called them completely wrong (Hunt 2012). While it is important not to overstate the effect of a single gaffe (Sides 2012), polling suggests that these comments had some influence on the election (Silver 2012c; RAND 2012; RickinStLouis 2012). As a result, we could infer that if an individual communicated more about these comments over social media, he or she would view Romney less favorably. We therefore propose a fifth hypothesis: social media communication about Romney's 47% remarks will predict lower evaluations of Romney.

Because social media allow people to follow those whom they tend to agree with and spread messages friendly to their own identity, any effect of social media communication about Romney's comments should be subject to the same motivated skepticism as we predict with messages about the presidential debate (e.g., Taber and Lodge 2006). Thus, any negative effect should be especially present among those who do not identify with the Republican Party, and to the extent that Republicans do discuss Romney's comments through social media, the negative effect should be minimized. Hence, our sixth hypothesis predicts that the effect of social media communication on evaluations of Romney will depend on the political party affiliation of the respondent such that Republicans will experience less reduction in their evaluations of Romney as social media communication about the 47% comments increases, relative to those who are not affiliated with the Republican Party.

While the media coverage and polling over Romney's 47% comments suggest that they would hurt evaluations of him, they do not directly implicate Obama in any way. We would not expect discussion of Romney's comments to have any direct influence on Obama's favorability. We thus hypothesize that social media communication about Romney's 47% comment will not significantly predict evaluations of Obama.

Analyzing the Influence of Social Media on Candidate Evaluations

To test the preceding hypotheses, we surveyed two independent convenience samples at colleges and universities across the United States. While the use of convenience samples will limit the generalizability of our findings, the advantages justify convenience sampling in this instance. Meta-analysis of debate and advertising effects show that convenience samples of college students show no statistically significant difference relative to random samples of adults (Benoit, Hansen, and Verser 2003; Lau et al. 1999). We hypothesize that advertising and debate effects will be similar to the effect of social media communication, and therefore the results of these meta-analyses provide some justification for the use of a convenience sample in this context. However, social media is different from both debates and political advertising in some important ways. Specifically, young college students are the most likely to actively use social media (Ranie et al. 2012) and thus will have somewhat different use habits than an older, more representative sample. Therefore, we view the use of a convenience sample as a limitation to this project and our findings. Nevertheless, the sampling procedure adopted here allowed for an expansive survey that included a large number of questions without making the cost of the survey prohibitive. Furthermore, because research in the effects of social media communication is still in preliminary stages, findings from convenience samples can build initial theory and be used as the basis for funding larger investigations into the effects of social media use in political contexts; thus, the use of a convenience sample is appropriate for this project. Participants were asked to indicate how likely they were to engage in social media discussion about the first presidential debate in the first sample and Mitt Romney's comments regarding the 47% of Americans who pay no income tax in the second. The participants were also asked to evaluate Barack Obama and Mitt Romney.

Samples

Surveys were distributed to two independent samples in relation to two of the more significant events in the 2012 presidential election. The first data collection dealt with the first presidential debate and was conducted immediately before participants watched the live broadcast of the vice presidential debate as part of an unrelated project. This sample contained 436 participants from universities in Alabama, Georgia, Massachusetts, Missouri, Oregon, Tennessee, Texas, Virginia, and Wisconsin. They ranged in age from 18 to 58, with an average age of 20.87 ($SD = 3.67$). Of the participants, 143 (32.8%) were male and 280 (64.2%) were female; 181 (41.5%) indicated that they were Republican, 138 (31.7%) indicated that they were Democrat, and 109 (25%) were either independent or affiliated with a third party.

We selected the first presidential debate because it marked one of the most significant events in a relatively stable election. Romney was thought to have made significant gains as a result of his performance, and Obama was widely criticized (Dickerson 2012; Dutton et al. 2013; Schoen 2012). Romney received a bounce in nearly all postdebate polling (on average, 2.9 percentage points) and in *FiveThirtyEight*'s election forecast (Silver 2012b). Because of these factors, the first debate represents arguably the most significant moment of the campaign, as it was a potential turning point for the Romney campaign and provided him the momentum he attempted to ride to electoral victory.

The questions about social media use in the second sample focused on discussion of Romney's 47% remarks. Respondents in the second independent sample were given a link to an online survey in the ten days leading up to the election. The survey included a variety of items pertaining to their political attitudes, behaviors, and feelings about the election. Among these were questions about their likelihood to engage in social media communication about Romney's comments. The sample contained 585 participants from universities in Iowa, Kansas, Massachusetts, Missouri, Ohio, Tennessee, Texas, and Virginia. The participants ranged in age from 18 to 39, with an average age of 20.2 ($SD = 2.85$). Of the respondents, 210 (35.9%) were male and 375 (64.1%) were female; 213 (36.4%) reported being Republican, 199 (34%) reported being Democrat, and 173 (26.9%) were either independent or affiliated with another party.

Romney's remarks were selected for the second case study because they are a different type of political event (a gaffe as opposed to a scheduled debate), they provide contrast to Romney's positive debate experiences, and there is some credible polling evidence that these comments may have influenced voter attitudes.

Romney's comments were deemed a significant political gaffe by the *Wall Street Journal* ("Notable Political Gaffes" 2012), and Romney, after originally stating that the remarks were not elegant, later called them completely wrong (Hunt 2012). Further, it is at least somewhat likely that these comments affected the polls to the detriment of Romney (Silver 2012c). As Silver (2012c) points out, it is difficult to disentangle a single event from the larger electoral context, but the leak of Romney's remarks coincided with Obama's largest lead of the campaign. The clearest evidence that the 47% comments hurt Romney is seen in RAND's national tracking panel, which showed the president's lead jump from about three percentage points prior to the leak to nearly eight points after (RAND 2012). While it is important not to overestimate the influence of any single gaffe (Sides 2012), the RAND data suggests that these leaked comments were among the more significant events in the campaign (RickinStLouis 2012). Because the RAND tracker was a panel survey (and not multiple independent samples, like other tracking polls), it may be a better indication of actual movement in voter intentions. Furthermore, RAND's estimates were among the most accurate in the 2012 election cycle (Silver 2012e). Although it is unclear what role the 47%

remarks played in Obama's eventual victory, they appear to have been one of the more influential story lines of the election.

To test for a direct media effect of social media communication on candidate evaluating, respondents in each sample were asked to complete an online questionnaire with items designed to measure overall social media communication over the first presidential debate for the first sample and Romney's 47% comments for the second sample, as well as a measure of candidate evaluation. Respondents were also asked to indicate their political party affiliation so that it could be determined whether the effect of social media use on candidate evaluation was moderated by the respondent's preexisting disposition toward the candidates. Specific operationalization of these variables—social media communication, candidate evaluation, and party affiliation—are discussed in the following section.

Variables

Social media communication was measured with a 14-item social media engagement scale adapted from Warner, Turner-McGowen, and Hawthorne (2012). Items in the social media communication scale are presented in table 8.1 and were reported on a seven-point likelihood scale ranging from "extremely unlikely" to "extremely likely," unless otherwise specified. The social media engagement scale achieved high reliability both for the first presidential debate ($\alpha = .906$, $M = 4.24$, $SD = 1.4$) and Romney's 47% remarks ($\alpha = .918$, $M = 3.14$, $SD = 1.24$). Social media communication is operationalized in reference to distinct media, Facebook and Twitter. At the time of data collection, Facebook and Twitter were the two most popular social media sites in the United States in terms of minutes spent on those sites (Nielsen 2012). Based on their popularity, we isolated those sites as a proxy for social media communication.

Candidate favorability was measured using feeling thermometer scores adapted from the American National Election Studies (ANES) survey. Respondents were asked to rate both candidates on a scale from 0 to 100, where 0 represented very cold or unfavorable, 100 represented very warm or favorable, and 50 indicated no feeling at all. Respondents slightly favored Obama in the first sample regarding the debate (Obama $M = 50.48$, $SD = 32.5$; Romney $M = 49.2$, $SD = 31.2$) and more so in the second regarding Romney's comments (Obama $M = 52.86$, $SD = 32$; Romney $M = 45.15$, $SD = 31.8$). Party affiliation was measured by asking respondents whether, in general, they considered themselves Democrats, Republicans, or affiliated with neither major party. To evaluate whether in-group bias moderated the effect of social media communication on candidate evaluation, party identification was dummy coded for models predicting evaluation of Romney such that 1 = Republican and 0 = Democrat/other and in models predicting evaluation of Obama such that 1 = Democrat and 0 = Republican/other.

Table 8.1. Items in Measure of Social Media Use

Facebook
1. Information about [subject] popped up on my Facebook timeline.
2. I read a link or watched a video about [subject] that I saw on Facebook.
3. I saw friends discussing [subject] on Facebook.
4. I posted a comment in a discussion about [subject] on Facebook.
5. I "liked" a status or comment about [subject] that I saw on Facebook.
6. I posted a status update or shared a link about [subject].
7. How much attention would you pay to information about the subject if it appeared on your Facebook feed?*

Twitter
1. Information about [subject] showed up in my Twitter stream.
2. I followed a link about [subject] that I saw on Twitter.
3. My friends or acquaintances were tweeting about [subject].
4. I retweeted something about [subject].
5. I "favorited" a tweet that I saw about [subject].
6. I personally tweeted something about [subject].
7. How much attention would you pay to information about the subject if it appeared on your Facebook feed?*

* Response options: None, I would completely ignore it; Very little, I am not interested; Somewhat little, I would be unlikely to glance at it; I don't know whether I would pay attention to it or not; Some attention, I might glance at it; I would pay attention, I'd at least look it over; Quite a bit of attention, I'm very interested in these things.

Results

This project sought to determine whether social media communication in two different cases, one about the first presidential debate and the other about Romney's 47% remarks, would affect respondents' evaluations of the candidates and whether the effect would be dependent on the political party identification of the respondent. To test the hypotheses, four simple moderation models were specified using PROCESS (Hayes 2013). Among other things, PROCESS computes interaction terms to test moderation and provides regression coefficients for all terms in the model as well as estimates of significance, data for visualizing the conditional effect of the independent variable on the dependent variable, and an estimate of the effect size of the interaction term. The four specified models were the conditional effect of social media communication about the first debate on evaluations of Romney moderated by political party (H1–H2); the conditional effect of social media communication about the first debate on evaluations of Obama moderated by political party (H3–H4); the conditional effect of social media communication about the 47% comments on evaluations of Romney moderated by political party (H5–H6); and the conditional effect of the 47% comments on evaluations of Obama as moderated by political party (H7). While no moderation was hypothesized for the effect of social media communication about the 47% comments on evaluations of Obama (because the hypothesis was that there would be no relationship), moderation was tested to ensure that inverse partisan effects did not mask an overall conditional effect.

Table 8.2. Regression Coefficients for Predictors of Candidate Favorability

Type of event	Romney		Obama	
	Debate 1	47%	Debate 1	47%
Social media communication	−3.109**	−.369	−1.982	.132
	(.975)	(.953)	(1.104)	(1.064)
Party	15.973*	34.704***	29.708***	40.467***
	(7.041)	(5.462)	(8.439)	(5.974)
Social media communication × party	6.837***	3.409*	3.668*	.422
	(1.557)	(1.625)	(1.835)	(1.75)

* $p < .05$, ** $p < .01$, *** $p < .001$

The first hypothesis predicted that social media communication about the first presidential debate would improve evaluations of Romney, and the second specified that this effect would be strongest among Republicans. As can be seen in table 8.2, social media communication about the first debate had a significant effect on evaluations of Romney. However, contrary to the hypothesis, those who communicated about the debate more tended to favor him less. Table 8.2 also shows a significant interaction between social media communication and political parity affiliation such that the effect of social media communication on evaluations of Romney was moderated by political party affiliation. Figure 8.1 shows evaluations of Romney at high, medium, and low levels of social media communication (high/low levels represent one standard deviation above and below the mean; the medium amount is represented by the mean). As depicted in the figure, high amounts of social media communication about the debate caused Republicans to evaluate Romney higher relative to Republicans who did not discuss the debate on social media. However, Democrats and people not affiliated with either party evaluated Romney less favorably the more they discussed the debate on social media. This supports the second hypothesis that the effect of social media communication about the first debate would be moderated by partisan identification. The overall regression model testing the first and second hypotheses was significant, $R = .737$, $F(3, 402) = 158.949$, $p < .001$; $R^2 = .543$. The amount of variance explained by the moderation was also significant, $\Delta R^2 = .022$, $F(1, 402) = 19.293$, $p < .001$.

The third hypothesis predicted that social media communication about the first presidential debate would diminish perceptions of Obama. The fourth hypothesis specified that this effect would be moderated by party identification such that Democrats would not reduce their evaluations of Obama to the same extent as Republicans and unaffiliated voters did. As can be seen in table 8.2, there was no direct effect of social media communication about the first presidential debate on evaluations of Obama. However, there was a significant interaction effect between social media communication and party. As can be seen in figure 8.2, the conditional effect was such that the more Republicans and unaffiliated respondents discussed the debate on social media, the less favorable they were to Obama, while evaluations of Obama were stable among Democrats regardless of how frequently they engaged in social media communication about the debate. The overall regression model testing the third and fourth hypotheses was significant: $R = .662$, $F (3, 402) = 104.318$, $p < .001$; $R^2 = .438$. The amount

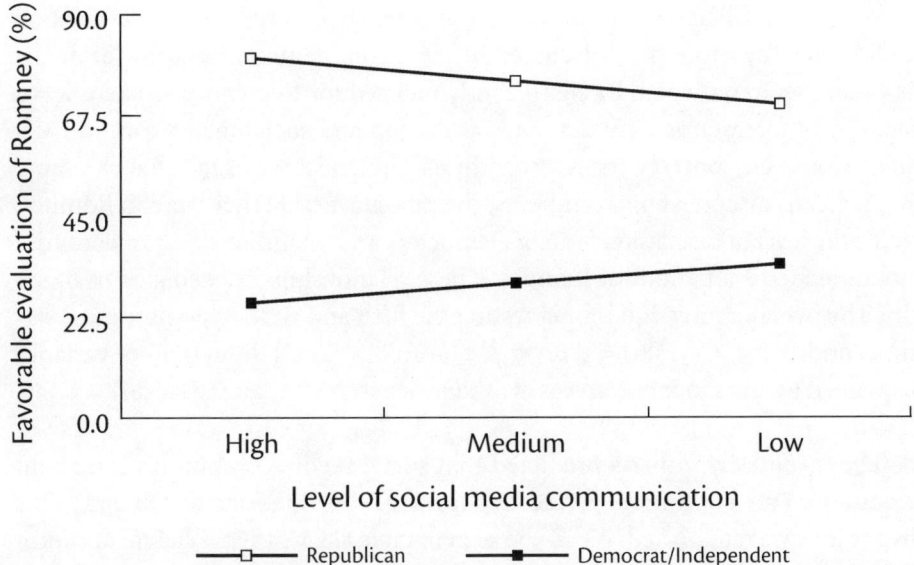

Figure 8.1. Evaluations of Romney at high, medium, and low levels of social media communication about the first presidential debate

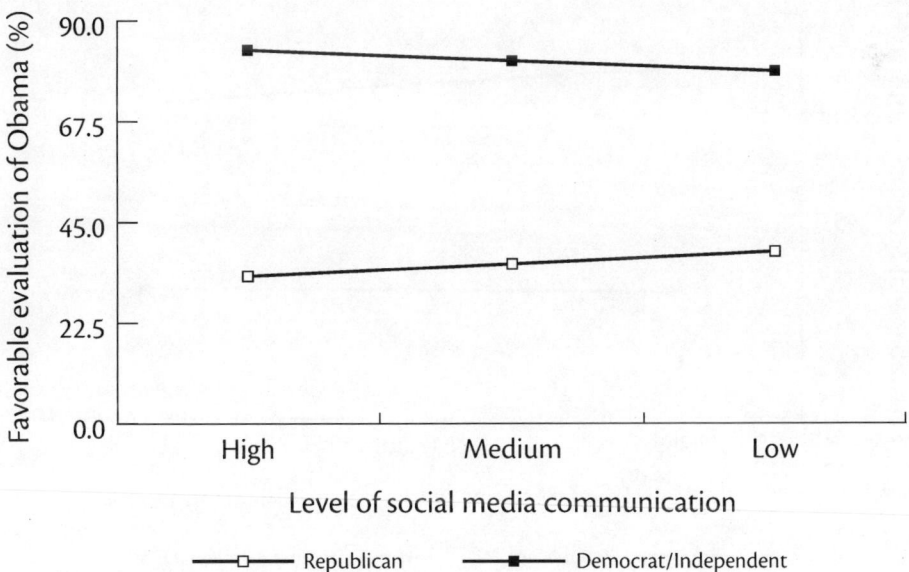

Figure 8.2. Evaluations of Obama at high, medium, and low levels of social media communication about the first presidential debate

of variance explained by the moderation was also significant: $\Delta R^2 = .006$, $F(1, 402) = 3.993$, $p < .05$.

The fifth hypothesis predicted that social media communication about Romney's 47% comments would reduce evaluations of him. As can be seen in table 8.2, there was no direct effect of social media communication about Romney's comments. The sixth hypothesis predicted a conditional effect such that those who are not affiliated with the Republican Party would reduce their evaluation of Romney the more they discussed his 47% comments through social media but that this trend would be significantly reduced for Republicans. There was a significant interaction between party affiliation and social media communication. However, contrary to the hypothesis, the effect was such that the more Republicans discussed his comments, the more favorable they were to Romney, while the level of discussion among Democrats and unaffiliated respondents did not influence evaluations of Romney. These relationships are depicted in figure 8.3. The overall regression model testing the fifth and sixth hypotheses was significant: $R = .69$, $F(3, 581) = 176.377$, $p < .001$; $R^2 = .477$. The amount of variance explained by the moderation was also significant: $\Delta R^2 = .004$, $F(1, 581) = 4.399$, $p < .05$.

The seventh hypothesis predicted that social media communication about Romney's 47% comments would not influence evaluations of Obama. This hypothesis was supported. As can be seen in table 8.2, neither social media communication nor the interaction between social media communication and party was significant. Social media communication about Romney's comments did

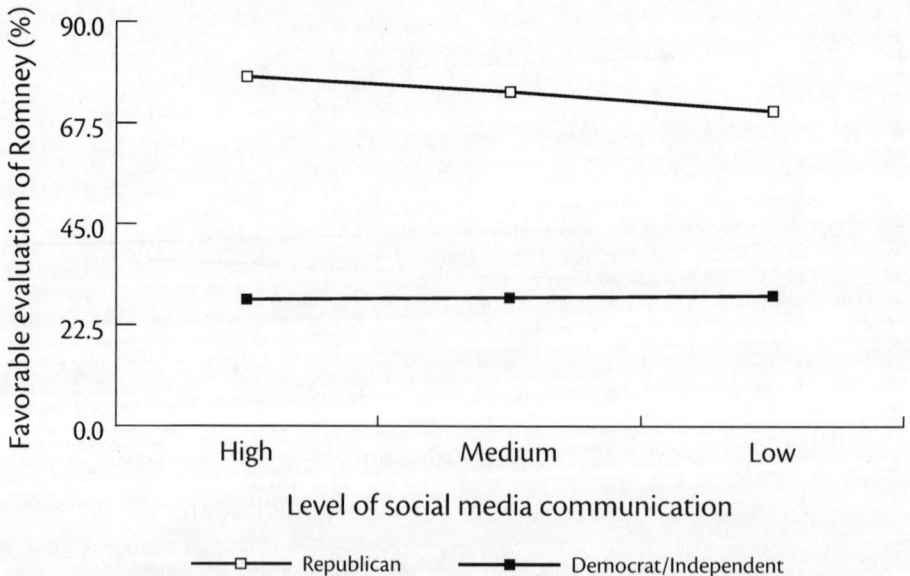

Figure 8.3. Evaluations of Romney at high, medium, and low levels of social media communication about Romney's 47% comments

not influence evaluations of Obama regardless of whether the discussion was by Democrats or by Republican and unaffiliated participants.

Discussion

In this project, we sought to explore the effects of communicating about politics over social media on candidate evaluations. We asked participants how likely they were to participate in various social media communication behaviors regarding two important political events from the 2012 presidential election, the first presidential debate and Romney's 47% comments, and how they evaluated the two presidential candidates. We found that there were significant relationships between how much a person communicated on social media and candidate evaluations and that these effects varied depending on the context (e.g., the debate or the gaffe) and the political party affiliation of the respondent.

The results of this study suggest two major findings: first, social media communication about major events in a campaign is related to candidate evaluations, and second, this relationship is dictated by party identification. While our data do not indicate that social media conversation caused the candidate evaluations, the results suggest the possibility of a causal relationship. The case for a reversal of causality, that candidate evaluations influence the likelihood of participating in social media conversations about these events, is undermined by the lack of relationship between Romney's 47% comments and favorability ratings of Obama. Since Obama's favorability was equal across all levels of social media communication about the 47% comments, we can infer that the communication was the driving force for the other effects. Specifically, people who liked Obama more were no more likely to communicate about Romney's comments than were people who did not like him. If causality were reversed and greater levels of favorability caused respondents to engage in more frequent social media communication, we would have expected to see a strong association between Obama's favorability and frequency of communication about Romney's 47% comments. Also, the first finding is consistent with research that has demonstrated effects of political ads (Kaid 2004; Bowen 1994; Faber, Tims, and Schmitt 1993; Kaid, Fernandes, and Painter 2011; Rothschild and Ray 1974), campaign debates (McKinney 1994; McKinney and Carlin 2004; Chaffee and Choe 1980), and news coverage (Chaffee and Dennis 1979; Fridkin et al. 2008; Gulati, Just, and Crigler 2004; Hellweg, Pfau, and Brydon 1992; Page and Shapiro 1982; Steeper 1978). Therefore, we conclude that messages on social media, like traditional forms of campaign communication, can influence perceptions of candidates.

Our second finding illustrates that the influence of social media communication is a function of context. As with traditional media, we expected the effect of messages shared on social media to be context dependent such that messages about the debate would favor Romney and hurt Obama while messages about the 47% comments would hurt Romney. However, because digital media (and especially social media) give users much more control over which messages they receive, share, and create, we also expected more partisan processing (e.g., Coe et al. 2008; Taber and Lodge 2006). As a result, we expected messages to reinforce existing beliefs (Holbert, Garrett, and Gleason 2010) such that when the context was perspective affirming (when Republicans were reacting to Romney's debate performance and non-Republicans were reacting to Romney's 47% comments), the effect would be stronger than when the context was perspective challenging (when Democrats were reacting to Obama's debate performance and Republicans were reacting to Romney's comments). Our findings demonstrated that partisan filtering was strong enough to dictate the nature of every effect we observed. In what follows, we will discuss the specific conditional effects of social media communication as moderated by party identification and explore possible theoretical and contextual explanations for these effects. We will then consider what these findings mean for the larger discussion of political messages in the highly user-controlled environments provided by social media. We will conclude by discussing limitations of this study and proposing directions for future research.

We hypothesized that, because Romney was widely believed to have won the first presidential debate, the general trend would be for discussion of the debate to improve evaluations of Romney. However, our findings suggest that the effect of social media communication about the debate was entirely conditional on the respondent's political party affiliation. As expected, Republican evaluations of Romney improved the more they discussed the debate. However, contrary to expectations, people not identified with the Republican Party actually evaluated Romney less favorably the more they discussed the debate. This conditional effect is consistent with past findings about partisan interpretations of debates (McKinney and Carlin 2004) and motivated processing (Taber and Lodge 2006). Nevertheless, the finding that partisanship trumps context such that only Republican discussion of the debate benefited Romney was unexpected.

There are several possible explanations for why Republicans who discussed the debate more through social media reported more positive evaluations of Romney. The Republicans who discussed the debate over social media could have been reliving the positive moments of the debate, they could have been exposed more to the media narrative regarding his win, or the conversation could have extended their memory of the win. On the basis of our data, we cannot determine which, if any, of these processes are responsible for Romney's in-group gains. Future research should attempt to isolate the various social media communication processes to determine if this effect is mediated by increased exposure to the event (e.g., a direct exposure effect), the media narrative (e.g., an agenda-setting effect), or enhanced salience of the event outcome (e.g., a framing effect).

The divergence of evaluations of Romney between Republicans and non-Republicans may also be caused by a variety of processes. First, those who did not support Romney could have been fact-checking many of Romney's debate claims and finding that his statements were less than accurate (as was observed in the media, e.g., ABC News 2012). If so, this might suggest selective exposure in social media networks such that people are opting to expose themselves to attitude-congruent messages—perhaps because the people who make up their social network contacts are generally like-minded. While Garrett (2009) has found little evidence of partisan selective exposure in online news consumption, perhaps social media are unique because they are heavily composed of friend networks that may be more homogeneous. Offline social networks tend to be more ideologically segregated than individual media diets are (Goldman and Mutz 2011; Mutz and Martin 2001); perhaps the same is true for Facebook and Twitter. Himelboim, McCreery, and Smith (2013) found that Twitter conversations about politically controversial topics largely occur among ideologically similar groups and for the most part do not occur between individuals who were ideologically dissimilar, indicating that social media communication is ideologically segregated much like offline social networks. The partisan processing observed here might therefore be a function of the homogeneity in online networks.

Conversely, the moderation effect could be attributed to bias processing of the debate (e.g., McKinney and Carlin 2004) or partisan processing due to some variation of a hostile media effect (e.g., Coe et al. 2008; Taber and Lodge 2006). In other words, it is unclear whether the effect was moderated because Democrats and independents were sharing different information than Republicans were or whether the same information was framed by prior political attitudes such that in-group members interpreted the same information more favorably than did out-group discussants. Future research should explore the content of conversation to determine if Republicans, Democrats, and independents are processing the same information differently (partisan processing) or if partisans are influenced differently because they are discussing different information (selective exposure).

As we expected Romney to benefit from discussion of the first debate, we expected greater discussion of a debate that Obama was thought to have lost decisively (e.g., Dickerson 2012; Dutton et al. 2013; Schoen 2012) to generate lower evaluations of Obama (H3). This was the case for out-group members—the more non-Democrats discussed the debate, the less favorably they evaluated Obama— but no effect was observed for Democrats, confirming our fourth hypothesis that any social media effect would be moderated by party identification. Again, this could be the result of selective exposure such that Democrats were not exposed to as much criticism of Obama, or it could be a feature of partisan processing of the mediated messages (Taber and Lodge 2006) or the debate itself (McKinney and Carlin 2004). Future research should account for the type of messages people are exposed to in their social media networks to determine if this effect is a product of different content or different interpretation of the same content.

While we expected discussion of the first debate to favor Romney on the basis of the media coverage (e.g., Hunt 2012; RickinStLouis 2012) and the ability of media to frame audience reactions to major political events (Entman 2003, 2004), we hypothesized that Romney would lose standing from more social media communication about his 47% remarks. However, among Republicans, Romney actually gained ground the more his comments were discussed. This could be because the Republicans discussing the comments actually agreed with him (undermining any media framing effect), because they were placing his comments in a more favorable context (enacting some form of vicarious apologia), or because they were simply not exposed to the critical media (partisan selective exposure). Further analysis of the content of the communication itself could clarify the process by which this partisan effect is manifested.

We hypothesized that non-Republicans would rate Romney less favorably the more his comments were discussed on social media. What we actually found was that his favorability did not vary with the level of conversation. Those Democrats and independents who communicated about his comments on social media with the most frequency found him just as favorable as those who did not discuss the gaffe. This is contrary to the expected reinforcement effect of friendly media. Our research design may drive this finding because data were collected in the ten days prior to the election, well after the initial report on Romney's comments. Any change in Romney's favorability may have already occurred based on initial exposure to his comments, such that further conversation would have no additive consequence. Any effect of communicating about this event over social media may have leveled by the time our data collection occurred. It could have also been the case that this group of people already viewed Romney as a callous capitalist, which was consistent with Obama's campaign narrative, so the video only echoed their position. While we would expect attitude reinforcement to be associated with further reductions in Romney's favorability, perhaps the penalty for his image was already priced in to his evaluation scores. Finally, it may be that political gaffes do not hurt candidates as much as is often suggested by the media (e.g., Sides 2012).

Limitations and Directions for Future Research

Although our findings provide evidence of an effect of social media communication on candidate evaluations, these results are limited in several ways. First, the overall effect observed was small and is not likely to have a large influence on vote choice. It could be the case that social media communication influences vote choice over the long term (e.g., an entire election cycle) and that small effects compound into a larger effect that culminates into significant attitude change by the end of the campaign. However, the modest changes in favorability observed here are unlikely to sway an election such as the 2012 presidential contest. Any election-altering effect would likely require both a very close election and a political event of major significance. Future longitudinal research should evaluate the development of this effect over time.

The findings are further limited because our data is cross-sectional. It is therefore impossible for us to demonstrate causality. We cannot determine whether social media communication about these events caused the relationship we observed or whether those who supported the candidates were just more likely to communicate about these events using social media. We interpret our data to indicate that social media influenced candidate evaluations because the case for reverse causality is undermined by a lack of relationship between Romney's 47% comments and evaluations of Obama (see earlier). Nevertheless, future research should confirm the direction of causality through experimental or longitudinal studies that isolate the direction of the relationships found in these samples.

Finally, the sample was composed of undergraduate college students. While young people are more likely to use social media to talk about politics (Ranie et al. 2012), the effect in this high-use group may be unique compared to an older population. Furthermore, not all young people are similar to those enrolled at research universities. Although we had a wide sample of university students, they are perhaps more likely to find political information in their social media environments than are young people not at a university. This type of research should therefore be replicated in representative samples. In spite of these limitations, this study helps establish the foundation of social media effects research in political communication. While social media are a relatively new phenomenon in political communication, the 2012 election provides scholars an opportunity to understand the influences of this emerging technology. This study demonstrates a moderate but significant conditional influence of social media communication on candidate evaluations depending on the partisanship of the communicator. As future researchers explore the mechanisms of this conditional effect, the effects of social media on politics will become increasingly clear. We hope that this study helps advance just such a project.

References

ABC News. 2012. "Fact Checking the Presidential Debate in Denver." *Otus* (blog), ABC News Online, October 3. http://abcnews.go.com/blogs/politics/2012/10/fact-checking-the-presidential-debate-in-denver/.

Anstead, N., and B. O'Loughlin. 2011. "The Emerging Viewertariat and BBC Question Time." *International Journal of Press/Politics* 16:440–462. doi:10.1177/1940161211415519.

Auer, M. R. 2011. "The Policy Sciences of Social Media." *Policy Studies Journal* 39 (4) (November): 709–736. doi:10.1111/j.1541-0072.2011.00428.x.

Bennett, W. L., and S. Iyengar. 2008. "A New Era of Minimal Effects? The Changing Foundations of Political Communication." *Journal of Communication* 58:707–731. doi:10.1111/j.1460-2466.2008.00410.x.

———. 2010. "The Shifting Foundations of Political Communication." *Journal of Communication* 60:35–39.

Benoit, W. L., and G. J. Hansen. 2004. "Presidential Debate Watching, Issue Knowledge, Character Evaluation, and Vote Choice." *Human Communication Research* 30:121–144. doi:10.1111/j.1468-2958.2004.tb00727.x.

Benoit, W. L., G. J. Hansen, and R. M. Verser. 2003. "A Meta-analysis of the Effects of Viewing U.S. Presidential Debates." *Communication Monographs* 70:335–350. doi:10.1080/0363775032000179133.

Benoit, W. L., M. S. McKinney, and R. L. Holbert. 2001. "Beyond Learning and Persona: Extending the Scope of Presidential Debate Effects." *Communication Monographs* 68:259–273. doi:10.1080/03637750128060.

Bowen, L. 1994. "Time of Voting Decision and Use of Political Advertising: The Slade Gorton–Brock Adams Senatorial Campaign." *Journalism Quarterly* 71:665–675.

Carlin, D. P. 1992. "Presidential Debates as Focal Points for Campaign Arguments." *Political Communication* 9:251–265.

Chaffee, S. H., and S. Y. Choe. 1980. "Time of Decision and Media Use during the Ford-Carter Campaign." *Public Opinion Quarterly* 44:53–69.

Chaffee, S. H., and J. Dennis. 1979. "Presidential Debates: An Empirical Assessment." In *The Past and Future of Presidential Debates*, edited by Austin Ranney, 75–106. Washington, DC: American Enterprise Institute for Public Policy Research.

Chaggaris, S. 2012. "Big Bird Stars in New Obama TV Ad." CBS News Online, October 9. http://www.cbsnews.com/8301-250_162-57528383/big-bird-stars-in-new-obama-tv-ad/.

Coe, K., D. Tewksbury, B. J. Bond, K. L. Drogos, R. W. Porter, A. Yahn, and Y. Zhang. 2008. "Hostile News: Partisan Use and Perceptions of Cable News Programming." *Journal of Communication* 58:201–219. doi:10.1111/j.1460-2466.2008.00381.x.

Conway, B. A., K. Kenski, and D. Wang. 2013. "Twitter Use by Presidential Primary Candidates during the 2012 Campaign." *American Behavioral Scientist* 57:1596–1610. doi:10.1177/0002764213489014.

Corn, D. 2012. "SECRET VIDEO: Romney Tells Millionaire Donors What He REALLY Thinks of Obama Voters." *Mother Jones*, September 17. http://www.motherjones.com/politics/2012/09/secret-video-romney-private-fundraiser.

Cornfield, M. 2010. "Game-Changers: New Technology and the 2008 Presidential Election." In *The Year of Obama: How Barack Obama Won the White House*, edited by Larry J. Sabato, 205–231. Upper Saddle River, NJ: Pearson.

Dickerson, J. 2012. "Romney's Big Night." *Slate*, October 4. http://www.slate.com/articles/news_and_politics/politics/2012/10/mitt_romney_wins_the_presidential_debate_did_the_republican_nominee_have_one_good_night_or_has_he_changed_the_race_against_barack_obama_.html.

"Did Social Media Predict the 2012 Presidential Election Results?" 2012. *SFGate*, November 9. http://www.sfgate.com/business/prweb/article/Did-Social-Media-Predict-the-2012-Presidential-4022746.php#src=fb.

Dimitrova, D. V., and D. Bystrom. 2013. "The Effects of Social Media on Political Participation and Candidate Image Evaluations in the 2012 Iowa Caucuses." *American Behavioral Scientist* 57:1568–1583. doi:10.1177/0002764213489011.

"Dispatch from the Denver Debate." 2012. *Twitter Blog*, October 4. http://blog.twitter.com/2012/10/dispatch-from-denver-debate.html.

Dutton, S., J. De Pinto, A. Salvanto, F. Backus, and L. Boerma. 2013. "Poll: Uncommitted Voters Say Romney Wins Debate." CBS News Online, December 14. http://www.cbsnews.com/8301-250_162-57525698/poll-uncommitted-voters-say-romney-wins-debate/.

Dylko, I. B., M. A. Beam, K. D. Landreville, and N. Geidner. 2012. "Filtering 2008 US Presidential Election News on YouTube by Elites and Nonelites: An Examination of the Democratizing Potential of the Internet." *New Media & Society* 14:832–849. doi:10.1177/1461444811428899.

"Election Night 2012." 2012. *Twitter Blog*, November 7. http://blog.twitter.com/2012/11/election-night-2012.html.

Entman, R. M. 2003. "Cascading Activation: Contesting the White House's Frame after 9/11." *Political Communication* 20:415–432. doi:10.1080/10584600390244176.

———. 2004. *Projections of Power Framing News, Public Opinion, and U.S. Foreign Policy*. Chicago: University of Chicago Press.

Faber, R. J., A. R. Tims, and K. G. Schmitt. 1993. "Negative Political Advertising and Voting Intent: The Role of Involvement and Alternative Information Sources." *Journal of Advertising* 22:67–76.

Fouhy, B. 2011. "Elections 2012: The Social Network, Presidential Campaign Edition." Huffington Post, April 17. http://www.huffingtonpost.com/2011/04/17/elections-2012-social-media_n_850172.html.

Franz, M. M., and T. N. Ridout. 2010. "Political Advertising and Persuasion in the 2004 and 2008 Presidential Elections." *American Politics Research* 38:303–329. doi:10.1177/1532673X09353507.

Fridkin, K. L, P. J. Kenney, S. A. Gershon, and G. S. Woodall. 2008. "Spinning Debates: The Impact of the News Media's Coverage of the Final 2004 Presidential Debate." *International Journal of Press/Politics* 13:29–51. doi:10.1177/1940161207312677.

Garrett, R. K. 2009. "Politically Motivated Reinforcement Seeking: Reframing the Selective Exposure Debate." *Journal of Communication* 59:676–699. doi:10.1111/j.1460-2466.2009.01452.x.

Goldman, S., and D. C. Mutz. 2011. "The Friendly Media Phenomenon: A Cross-National Analysis of Cross-Cutting Exposure." *Political Communication* 28:42–66. doi:10.1080/10584609.2010.544280.

Grabowicz, P. A., J. J. Ramasco, E. Moro, J. M. Pujol, and V. M. Eguiluz. 2012. "Social Features of Online Networks: The Strength of Intermediary Ties in Online Social Media." *PLoS ONE* 7:1–9. doi:10.1371/journal.pone.0029358.

Gulati, G. J., M. R. Just, and A. N. Crigler. 2004. "News Coverage of Political Campaigns." In *Handbook of Political Communication Research*, edited by L. L. Kaid, 155–202. Mahwah, NJ: Lawrence Erlbaum.

Hawthorne, J., J. B. Houston, and M. S. McKinney. 2013. "Live Tweeting a Presidential Primary Debate: Exploring New Political Conversations." *Social Science Computer Review* 31:552–562. doi:10.1177/0894439313490643.

Hayes, A. F. 2013. *Introduction to Mediation, Moderation, and Conditional Process Analysis: A Regression-Based Approach*. New York: Guilford.

Haythornthwaite, C. 2005. "Social Networks and Internet Connectivity Effects." *Information, Communication & Society* 8:125–147.

Hellweg, S. A., M. Pfau, and S. R. Brydon. 1992. *Televised Presidential Debates: Advocacy in Contemporary America*. New York: Praeger.

Himelboim, I., S. McCreery, and M. Smith. 2013. "Birds of a Feather Tweet Together: Integrating Network and Content Analyses to Examine Cross-Ideology Exposure on Twitter." *Journal of Computer-Mediated Communication* 18:154–174.

Holbert, R. L., R. K. Garrett, and L. S. Gleason. 2010. "A New Era of Minimal Effects? A Response to Bennett and Iyengar." *Journal of Communication* 60:15–34. doi:10.1111/j.1460-2466.2009.01470.x.

Holbrook, T. M. 1996. *Do Campaigns Matter?* Thousand Oaks, CA: Sage.

Houston, J. B., M. S. McKinney, J. Hawthorne, and M. L. Spialek. 2013. "Frequency of Tweeting during Presidential Debates: Effect on Debate Attitudes and Knowledge." *Communication Studies*, 64:548–560. doi:10.1080/10510974.2013.832693.

Hunt, K. 2012. "Mitt Romney: '47 Percent' Comments Were 'Just Completely Wrong.'" Huffington Post, October 4. http://www.huffingtonpost.com/2012/10/04/mitt-romney-47-percent_n_1941423.html.

Hwang, H., M. R. Gotlieb, S. Nah, and D. M. McLeod. 2007. "Applying a Cognitive-Processing Model to Presidential Debate Effects: Postdebate News Analysis and Primed Reflection." *Journal of Communication* 57:40–59. doi:10.1111/j.0021–9916.2007.00328.x

Issenberg, S. 2012a. "Obama Does It Better." *Slate*, October 29. http://www.slate.com/articles/news_and_politics/victory_lab/2012/10/obama_s_secret_weapon_democrats_have_a_massive_advantage_in_targeting_and.html.

———. 2012b. *The Victory Lab: The Secret Science of Winning Campaigns*. New York: Crown.

Iyengar, S. 1994. *Is Anyone Responsible? How Television Frames Political Issues*. Chicago: University of Chicago Press.

Iyengar, S., and D. R. Kinder. 1986. "More than Meets the Eye: TV News, Priming, and Public Evaluations of the President." *Public Communication and Behavior* 1:136–171.

Kaid, L. L. 2004. "Political Advertising." In *Handbook of Political Communication Research*, edited by L. L. Kaid, 155–202. Mahwah, NJ: Lawrence Erlbaum.

Kaid, L. L, J. Fernandes, and D. Painter. 2011. "Effects of Political Advertising in the 2008 Presidential Campaign." *American Behavioral Scientist* 55:437–456. doi:10.1177/0002764211398071.

Katz, E., and P. F. Lazarsfeld. 1955. *Personal Influence: The Part Played by People in the Flow of Communication*. New York: Free Press.

Klapper, J. T. 1960. *The Effects of Mass Communication*. New York: Free Press.

Krupnikov, Y. 2012. "Negative Advertising and Voter Choice: The Role of Ads in Candidate Selection." *Political Communication* 29:387–413. doi:10.1080/10584609.2012.721868.

Kushin, M. J., and M. Yamamoto. 2010. "Did Social Media Really Matter? College Students' Use of Online Media and Political Decision Making in the 2008 Election." *Mass Communication & Society* 13:608–630. doi:10.1080/15205436.2010.516863.

Lau, Richard R., L. Sigelman, C. Heldman, and P. Babbitt. 1999. "The Effects of Negative Political Advertisements: A Meta-analytic Assessment." *American Political Science Review* 93:851–875.

Lieb, D. A. 2012. "Todd Akin 'Legitimate Rape' Comments Remain Focus of Missouri Senate Race." Huffington Post, October 25. http://www.huffingtonpost.com/2012/10/25/todd-akin-senate_n_2015666.html.

Lotan, G., E. Graeff, M. Ananny, D. Gaffney, I. Pearce, and d. boyd. 2011. "The Revolutions Were Tweeted: Information Flows during the 2011 Tunisian and Egyptian Revolutions." *International Journal of Communication* 5:1375–1405. doi:1932–8036/2011FEA1375.

MacKuen, M., and C. Brown. 1987. "Political Context and Attitude Change." *American Political Science Review* 81:471–490. doi:10.2307/1961962.

Madrigal, A. 2012. "When the Nerds Go Marching In." *Atlantic*, November 16. http://www.theatlantic.com/technology/archive/2012/11/when-the-nerds-go-marching-in/265325/.

Marlantes, L. 2012. "What Does Mitt Romney Need to Do in the Presidential Debates? (+video)."

Christian Science Monitor, September 26. http://www.csmonitor.com/USA/DC-Decoder/Decoder-Wire/2012/0926/What-does-Mitt-Romney-need-to-do-in-the-presidential-debates-video.

McCombs, M. E., and D. L. Shaw. 1993. "The Evolution of Agenda-Setting Research: Twenty-Five Years in the Marketplace of Ideas." *Journal of Communication* 43:58–67.

McKinney, M. S. 1994. "Design and Implementation of the Focus Group Study." In *The 1992 Presidential Debates in Focus*, edited by D. B. Carlin and M. S. McKinney, 21–35. New York: Praeger.

McKinney, M. S., and D. B. Carlin. 2004. "Political Campaign Debates." In *Handbook of Political Communication Research*, edited by L. L. Kaid, 203–234. Mahwah, NJ: Lawrence Erlbaum.

McKinney, M. S., J. B. Houston, and J. Hawthorne. 2014. "Social Watching a 2012 Republican Presidential Primary Debate." *American Behavioral Scientist* 58:556–573. doi:10.1177/0002764213506211.

Mutz, D. C., and P. S. Martin. 2001. "Facilitating Communication across Lines of Political Difference: The Role of Mass Media." *American Political Science Review* 95:97–114.

Nielsen. 2012. *State of the Media: The Social Media Report 2012*. New York: Nielson. http://www.nielsen.com/content/dam/corporate/us/en/reports-downloads/2012-Reports/The-Social-Media-Report-2012.pdf.

"Notable Political Gaffes: Mitt Romney." 2012. *Wall Street Journal*. http://online.wsj.com/article/SB10000872396390443847404577628040656673750.html (accessed December 27, 2012).

Page, B. I., and R. Y. Shapiro. 1982. "Changes in Americans' Policy Preferences, 1935–1979." *Public Opinion Quarterly* 46:24–42.

Painter, D. L. 2013. "Collateral Damage: Involvement and the Effects of Negative Super PAC Advertising." *American Behavioral Scientist*. Advance online publication. doi:10.1177/0002764213506210.

Parker, R. 2012. "Social and Anti-Social Media." *Campaign Stops* (blog), *New York Times*, November 15. http://campaignstops.blogs.nytimes.com/2012/11/15/social-and-anti-social-media/.

Prior, M. 2007. *Post-broadcast Democracy: How Media Choice Increases Inequality in Political Involvement and Polarizes Elections*. New York: Cambridge University Press.

Rahimi, B. 2011. "The Agonistic Social Media: Cyberspace in the Formation of Dissent and Consolidation of State Power in Postelection Iran." *Communication Review* 14:158–178. doi:10.1080/10714421.2011.597240.

RAND. 2012. "The RAND Continuous 2012 Presidential Election Poll." RAND American Life Panel. September 28. https://mmicdata.rand.org/alp/index.php?page=election.

Rainie, L., A. Smith, K. L. Schlozman, H. Brady, and S. Verba. 2012. *Social Media and Political Engagement*. Pew Internet and American Life Project. Washington, DC: Pew Research Center.

RickinStLouis. 2012. "RAND Tracker: The 47% Are Deciding the Election." *Daily Kos*, October 26. http://www.dailykos.com/story/2012/10/26/1150540/-RAND-Tracker-The-47-are-Deciding-the-Election.

Rothschild, M. L., and M. L. Ray. 1974. "Involvement and Political Advertising Effect: An Exploratory Experiment." *Communication Research* 1:264–285.

Sakwa, J., and J. Steers. 2012. "Debate Wrap-Up: Big Bird and Big Trends in Social Media." CBS News Online, October 4. http://www.cbsnews.com/8301-505263_162-57526216/debate-wrap-up-big-bird-and-big-trends-in-social-media/.

Schoen, D. E. 2012. "A Win for Romney in the First Round of Debates." Fox News Online, October 4. http://www.foxnews.com/opinion/2012/10/04/win-for-romney-in-first-round-debates/.

Shamma, D. A., L. Kennedy, and E. F. Churchill. 2009. "Tweet the Debates: Understanding Community Annotation of Uncollected Sources." In *Proceedings of the First SIGMM Workshop on Social Media*, 3–10. WSM '09. New York: ACM. doi:10.1145/1631144.1631148.

Shaw, D. 1999. "The Effect of TV Ads and Candidate Appearance on Statewide Presidential Votes, 1988–96." *American Political Science Review* 93:345–362.

Sides, J. 2012. "Mitt Romney and That 47%." *The Monkey Cage* (blog), September 17. http://themonkeycage.org/blog/2012/09/17/mitt-romney-and-that-47/.

Silver, N. 2012a. "Oct. 1: Is the Presidential Race Tightening Heading Into the Debates?" *FiveThirtyEight* (blog), *New York Times*, October 1. http://fivethirtyeight.blogs.nytimes.com/2012/10/02/oct-1-is-the-presidential-race-tightening-heading-into-the-debates/.

———. 2012b. "Oct. 7: National Polls Show Signs of Settling." *FiveThirtyEight* (blog), *New York Times*, October 7. http://fivethirtyeight.blogs.nytimes.com/2012/10/07/oct-7-national-polls-show-signs-of-settling/.

———. 2012c. "Sept. 27: The Impact of the '47 Percent.'" *FiveThirtyEight* (blog), *New York Times*, September 28. http://fivethirtyeight.blogs.nytimes.com/2012/09/28/sept-27-the-impact-of-the-47-percent/.

———. 2012d. "Sept. 30: Romney Down a Touchdown?" *FiveThirtyEight* (blog), *New York Times*, October 1. http://fivethirtyeight.blogs.nytimes.com/2012/10/01/sept-30-romney-down-a-touchdown/.

———. 2012e. "Which Polls Fared Best (and Worst) in the 2012 Presidential Race." *FiveThirtyEight* (blog), *New York Times*, November 10. http://fivethirtyeight.blogs.nytimes.com/2012/11/10/which-polls-fared-best-and-worst-in-the-2012-presidential-race/.

Sloan, P. 2012. "Mark 2012 as History's Last 'Social Media' Election." CNET, November 6. http://news.cnet.com/8301-1023_3-57545544-93/mark-2012-as-historys-last-social-media-election/.

Steeper, F. T. 1978. "Public Response to Gerald Ford's Statements on Eastern Europe in the Second Debate." In *The Presidential Debates: Media, Electoral, and Policy Perspectives*, edited by G. F. Bishop, R. G. Meadow, and M. Jackson-Beeck, 81–101. New York: Praeger.

Taber, C. S., and M. Lodge. 2006. "Motivated Skepticism in the Evaluation of Political Beliefs." *American Journal of Political Science* 50:755–769. doi:10.1111/j.1540-5907.2006.00214.x.

Tufekci, Z., and C. Wilson. 2012. "Social Media and the Decision to Participate in Political Protest: Observations from Tahrir Square." *Journal of Communication* 62:363–379. doi:10.1111/j.1460-2466.2012.01629.x.

Tumasjan, A., T. O. Sprenger, P. G. Sandner, and I. M. Welpe. 2011. "Election Forecasts with Twitter: How 140 Characters Reflect the Political Landscape." *Social Science Computer Review* 29:402–418. doi:10.1177/0894439310386557.

Valenzuela, S., A. Arriagada, and A. Scherman. 2012. "The Social Media Basis of Youth Protest Behavior: The Case of Chile." *Journal of Communication* 62:299–314. doi:10.1111/j.1460-2466.2012.01635.x.

Vitak, J., P. Zube, A. Smock, C. T. Carr, N. Ellison, and C. Lampe. 2011. "It's Complicated: Facebook Users' Political Participation in the 2008 Election." *CyberPsychology, Behavior & Social Networking* 14:107–114. doi:10.1089/cyber.2009.0226.

Warner, B. R., S. Turner-McGowen, and J. Hawthorne. 2012. "Limbaugh's Social Media Nightmare: Facebook and Twitter as a Space for Political Action." *Journal of Radio & Audio Media* 19:257–275. doi:10.1080/19376529.2012.722479.

Willis, A. 2012. "Infographic: Biggest Social Media Moments of 2012." Mashable, December 23. http://mashable.com/2012/12/23/social-media-2012/.

9

Terms of Engagement
Online Political Participation and the Impact on Offline Political Participation

MEREDITH CONROY, JESSICA T. FEEZELL, AND MARIO GUERRERO

Less than ten years ago, in 2004, Howard Dean revolutionized the way in which politicians campaign and fundraise in elections. Using the online web tool meetup.com, Dean and his supporters mobilized citizens to raise $15 million in small donations in one fundraising quarter. Similarly, Barack Obama's 2008 campaign efforts included a strategic social networking element at MyBarackObama.com. Obama went on to easily surpass Dean's fundraising efforts and set a new record by raising half a billion dollars online in just a 21-month span (Vargas 2008).

Beyond fundraising, political campaigns are incorporating more interactive online strategies to win elections. For example, during the 2012 election, the Obama campaign successfully utilized the online social networking site Twitter to reach out to potential supporters. Obama used Twitter eight times as often as Mitt Romney to reach over 21 million followers, compared to Romney's 1.7 million followers (Moore 2012). President Obama also reminded people to vote when he participated in the first presidential "ask me anything" (AMA) on the content-sharing site Reddit. Obama directly responded to participants' questions on the website by typing his answers himself for 30 minutes. The Obama AMA was Reddit's top post of 2012, with over 5 million page views (Smith 2013). Clearly, the Internet is enabling political candidates to interact with potential supporters in new and innovative ways that are proving to be inclusive of large numbers of people. The interactive nature of efforts such as Twitter and Reddit are changing the way in which political messages are disseminated and received, likely having an impact beyond election outcomes.

We are only beginning to understand the effects of online mobilization efforts and personal online political activities. We seek to add to this scholarship theoretically, through a refining of measurement, by making a clear distinction between online political venues that are noninteractive, such as a candidate's personal website, and those that are interactive, such as Facebook and Twitter, to better understand their unique influence. Twitter and Facebook allow politicians to reach out directly to followers and subscribers; in return, followers and subscribers can easily respond and share those interactions with their networks. These characteristics distinguish Facebook and similar social networking sites (SNS) from traditional Internet websites, in that activities on SNS are largely communal, interactive, and directed by users (Tedesco 2007). We also add to this scholarship with empirical analysis using an exploratory study in which we survey university-age students about their Internet activity and offline behaviors. Our intention is that this exploratory study will guide subsequent theoretical and empirical analysis on a more thoughtful course than current scholarship directs.

In this chapter, we build on previous research that examines the effects of online interactive and individually directed venues. In particular, we examine how the interactive social networking site Facebook affects political participation. In this analysis, we develop a theory of Facebook's impact on perceptions of citizenship norms and how these perceptions are altering the landscape of political participation in the United States. We argue that as online political activity on SNS increases, certain norms of citizenship will emerge as others simultaneously fade. Specifically, due to the nature of SNS and their interactive characteristics, we expect that those individuals more politically active on SNS will be more likely to revere notions of institutionally challenging activities. Meanwhile, those individuals who are less politically active on SNS will maintain adherence to traditional notions of political activity, through institutionalized channels. Overall, we expect that increases in political activity on SNS will influence norms of citizenship, which in turn decreases institutional forms of offline political participation. Although numerous studies have examined the effects of different forms of Internet use on political participation, there has yet to be an examination of how this new medium may be shifting perceptions of citizenship and corresponding notions of effective forms of offline political activity. By understanding the impact of online political activity on norms of citizenship, we can more comprehensively understand the impact of online political activities on the democratic process as a whole.

Political Participation and Citizenship Norms

Citizenship norms refer to a "shared set of expectations about the citizen's role in politics" (Dalton 2008, 78; see also Almond and Verba 1963). According to Russell Dalton (2008), there are two broad notions of citizenship among individuals in industrialized nations. The first is duty-based citizenship, which is allied with an adherence to social order. Dalton finds "duty-based citizenship [to have] a restrictive definition of participation—it dissuades people from participating in direct, [institutionally] challenging activities" (91). For duty-based citizenship, good citizens are expected to report crimes, obey laws, and serve in the military. Engaged citizenship, on the other hand, is related to self-expressive, individualized, and direct political action. Engaged citizens should support those who are

Table 9.1. Dimensions of Democratic Citizenship (from Dalton 2008)

Variable	Citizenship dimension	
	Duty-based citizenship	Engaged citizenship
Report a crime	.84	.12
Obey the law	.77	.09
Serve in the military	.64	.15
Serve on a jury	.63	.32
Vote in elections	.56	.43
Form own opinions	.29	.47
Support those worse off	.16	.65
Be active in politics	.15	.80
Volunteer	.10	.84
Eigenvalue	2.56	2.37
Percent variance	28.5	25.8

worse off, do volunteer work, and form their own opinions (see also Bennett 2007; Bennett, Wells, and Freelon 2011). More specifically, engaged citizenship embraces a larger definition of participation that includes protesting, consumerism, and awareness of minority rights, as well as distrust in formal institutions and increased faith in loose networks of community organizations.

Dalton (2008) establishes distinct citizenship norms for engaged and duty-based citizenship by using factor analysis based on nine questions in the 2005 U.S. "Citizenship, Involvement, Democracy" (CID) Survey (table 9.1).[1]

These contrasting views of what it means to be a good citizen have separate and independent effects on offline political participation and the political process generally. For example, those who revere duty-based citizenship norms are more supportive of traditional forms of political action, through long-standing institutional routes, such as electoral participation. The literature suggests that duty-based citizenship should "stimulate political engagement, especially turnout in elections" (Dalton 2008, 86). Furthermore, those who subscribe to duty-based citizenship norms often reject alternative forms of political action that do not take place through electoral channels, such as protests and demonstrations. Alternatively, those who revere engaged citizenship norms are supportive of self-expressive values, political autonomy, and participating directly in the political process. Dalton suggests that social forces, in addition to rising levels of education and changing generational experiences, decrease support for authority (81). Thus, this norm is more predictive of participation that does not necessarily rely on electoral channels, such as boycotting, buycotting, and illegal protesting (Dalton 2008).

Highlighting the difference that citizenship norms play in predicting modes of offline political participation may help to shine light on the causes of declines in certain forms of political participation in the United States (Hibbing and Theiss-Morse 2002; Putnam 2000; Wattenberg 2002). Indeed, our political values and norms correspond with the way we participate in the political process. As Dalton (2008, 84) aptly points out, "The norms of citizenship should shape the political behavior of Americans—norms indicate what the individual feels is expected of the good citizen. Citizenship norms may shape expectations of our role as participants in the political process, and our images of the role of government and specific policy priorities." Certainly, marginalized groups and individuals use alternative routes to participate in politics out of necessity. Yet as these groups take to the Internet to organize, and do so successfully, there should be more widespread familiarity and acceptance of unconventional forms. This attitude shift among nonmarginalized groups may account for what has been conceptualized as a decline in political participation in the United States.

We expect that shifts in values regarding what is appropriate political activity will be captured by perceptions of citizenship norms. Previous research has implicated a number of factors that correspond with the decline in political participation, such as generational changes and age (Dalton 2008; Putnam 2000). For example, Nicole Goodman et al. (2011) found that younger voters tend to be more accepting of nonvoting than are older cohorts. While we do not disagree with previous accounts of the decline, we expect that online social networking activity is shifting values regarding what is appropriate political behavior and thus may also explain some of this theoretical puzzle.

In addition to broadening our understanding of the behavioral components of participatory decline, we also need to broaden our conceptualization of political participation. In response to increased concern around declining levels of political participation among youth in particular, researchers draw attention to the need to reconceptualize our understanding of political participation, in order to represent a more accurate picture of participation in the United States. Scholarship in this vein examines unconventional forms beyond party politics and institutionalized routes, such as community-based activities and political protests, in order to better grapple with the state of affairs (Brady, Verba and Schlozman 1995; de Vreese 2007; Inglehart 1997; Norris 2002).

Recent scholarship has attempted to assess the effects of Internet activity on different forms of offline political participation; the majority of this work finds politically oriented Internet activities to have a positive effect on political participation such as voting in elections (Tolbert and McNeal 2003; Park, Kee, and Valenzuela 2009, Xenos and Moy 2007) and campaigning (de Zuniga, Puig-i-Abril, and Rojas 2009; Kittilson and Dalton 2011). However, while this scholarship finds that certain forms of online activities predict positive effects on political participation, the effects of recreational Internet use are less straightforward. Negative effects on political and civic engagement have been found to result form recreational uses, such as demobilization and lower levels of trust

Online Political Activity → Citizenship Norms → Offline Political Activity

Figure 9.1. Theoretical path model of predicting offline participation

among users (Pasek, More, and Romer 2009; Shah, Kwak, and Holbert 2001). However, positive influences resulting from interest-based online engagement have also been observed (Kahne, Lee, and Feezell 2012).

Although different conclusions regarding the impact of SNS on political participation have been drawn, there has been a paucity of scholarship assessing the potential impact of Internet use on values pertaining to citizenship and norms of political participation in the United States. We suggest that forms of offline participation derive from what citizens perceive as valid routes of activity and that increases in online political activity are altering these perceptions. Our study makes a distinction between the valuing of engaged citizenship norms and duty-based citizenship norms, which we expect is facilitated, in part, by differential forms and amount of online political activity by individuals.

Analyzing Online Political Activity

We propose that Internet use and activities are key to understanding citizenship norms and their connection to offline political activity. The Internet is connecting individuals and groups to each other in ways that were previously impossible. For instance, the Internet facilitates communication in a less hierarchical and more horizontal fashion that allows for easier engagement and involvement among users (Bimber 2003, 2012). Internet use is also of low cost to users (once a user is set up), lacks geographical boundaries, is largely free from regulation and intrusion by government officials, and provides a level of anonymity not available in face-to-face interactions (Barber, Mattson, and Peterson 1997; Dahlgren 2005; Sparks 2001). In particular, of the many new uses of the Internet that exist and seem to emerge, SNS allow citizens to engage with one another and help them to overcome collective-action problems by providing information, coordinating political action, and providing common bonds (Postmes and Brunsting 2002; Shirky 2008).

Social networking sites are particularly interesting because they combine the capacity of Internet use with social interactions. Social interactions provide the ability to discuss content, which Matthew Nisbet and Dietram Scheufele (2004) find imperative for increases in political efficacy. Similarly, John Tedesco (2007), using an experimental design, found interactive web activities, such as sending messages, to predict increases in efficacy; this outcome was not observed for participants who did not engage in interactive web activities.[2] Similarly, interactive uses of the Internet, such as chat-room participation and email correspondence, predict higher voting rates (Mossberger, Tolbert, and McNeal 2008). The more "personalized" information that is exchanged in and on SNS is enhancing "the relevance of political information, as well as motivating people to act on the basis of the information" (Enjolras, Steen-Johnsen, and Wollebœk 2012, 4). In many ways, the functions of online social networks mimic those of offline social networks, while being more accessible than offline social networks. Thus, in addition to providing opportunities for interaction, SNS give individuals a sense of belonging and hold individuals accountable through obligations. For example, examining online group membership on Facebook, Meredith Conroy, Jessica Feezell, and Mario Guerrero (2012) find that those who are more active in political online groups are more politically active offline, with online group membership mimicking some of the positive effects of offline group membership.

We expect that the social nature of political activity on SNS is changing the notions of appropriate offline forms of political participation among users. In particular, we expect that those who are more politically active online through SNS will be more likely to participate in certain forms of offline participation and less likely to participate in others, namely, an increase in more direct and social forms of offline participation, such as political protesting, and a decrease in more indirect, nonsocial forms of offline participation, such as donating money to a campaign,

This study tests four primary hypotheses surrounding our expectations. Two hypotheses regard correlations between online political activity and citizenship norms, and two regard online political activity and offline political participation. First, due to the interactive and social nature of SNS, we expect that those who are more politically active on Facebook will revere notions of engaged citizenship, which includes activities that are more social in nature, such as volunteering and helping those who are worse off. Accordingly, we hypothesize that a higher level of online political activity on SNS is positively correlated with engaged citizenship norms.

We also expect that those who are more politically active on Facebook will reject notions of duty-based citizenship, which include activities that uphold the social order, such as serving in the military and always obeying laws and regulations. As a result, our second hypothesis predicts that a higher level of online political activity on SNS is negatively correlated with duty-based citizenship norms.

Given previous work assessing the effects of citizenship norms on offline political participation, and our theory about the impact of online activity on citizenship norms, we expect that levels of online political activity on Facebook will have consequences for offline participation; this leads us to our third and fourth hypotheses. Our third hypothesis expects that a higher level of online political activity on SNS is positively related to increased offline engaged forms of political participation.

As online participation on SNS is inherently social in nature, it is naturally expected to increase engaged forms of participation because they involve political participation through interactions with other people. Conversely, moving to the final hypothesis, we expect that with higher levels of political activity on Facebook, we will see a negative correlation with duty-based participation. Thus, our final hypothesis is that a higher level of online political activity on SNS is negatively related to offline duty-based forms of political participation.

Duty-based participation is identified as political activity that uses traditional channels of electoral participation. The social nature of online political activity does not intuitively seem to reinforce institutionalized norms of the electoral system. That is, a direct connection between the social connections one establishes online and duty-based participation seems weak, at best.

We sampled undergraduate students at four-year universities to test our hypotheses. Although an undergraduate sample is not ideal for generalizability, our sample is optimal for two important reasons. First, at the time of the study, users aged 14 to 24 constituted 39% of Facebook's users. Those aged 25 to 34 made up 29% of users, compared to 16% aged 35 to 44 (Socialbakers 2012). Thus, the majority of Facebook's users were younger, when this survey was administered. While younger people are leaving Facebook for newer social networking sites (Neal 2014), analyzing Facebook is important to understanding social networks, in general. Second, as previously mentioned, most research has suggested that age accounts for a difference in citizenship norms (Goodman et al. 2011; Dalton 2008). While we accept these findings, we also expect there to be some variation among younger people and for some of that variation to be explained by SNS activity. Thus, we reject the assumption that all young people revere engaged citizenship norms and reject duty-based norms. Our sample will allow us to more precisely assess citizenship norms among youth.

We expect to find that youth who use SNS in political ways are more likely to participate offline in engaged and inherently social formats because of the engaged and social nature of the online medium. Conversely, we expect that using SNS in political ways will do little to foster duty-based forms of participation because the stimulus does little to promote the associated characteristics. Homing in on the causal mechanism will give us better understanding of how the Internet is altering perceptions of citizenship and notions of appropriate forms of political participation.

Facebook Use

Facebook is an online social networking website that lets users interact with each other by sharing information about themselves via personal profiles. As of 2014, Facebook is currently considered the largest online social network with over

1 billion monthly active users, far surpassing any other online social network sites (Pew Internet and American Life Project 2011). Originally created by several Harvard students in February 2004, Facebook was modeled after paper pages that Harvard circulated profiling staff, faculty, and students. Facebook originally began as a service only offered to universities but continually expanded its availability until eventually allowing global registration in September 2006. Since then, Facebook has grown rapidly, becoming especially popular among younger generations and college students.

Although the premise of Facebook rests with sharing information via an online profile that contains basic information about the user, there have been important additions to the site that have fundamentally changed how users interact with others on the site. Currently, Facebook organizes profile information in a chronological fashion, allowing other users to share statuses, links, and photos on a time line. Yet Facebook has a number of other spaces that users can go to, to share information and interact with others. For example, "pages" are time lines made available to the general public to interact under a common interest. The popular television show *The Simpsons*, for instance, is the seventh-most-popular page on Facebook (Darwell 2013). *The Simpsons* page posts updates about the show. Anyone who visits the page can comment on the updates and interact with other users of the page. Similarly, groups provide a common space where users can create organizations and invite others to join. The group administrator can disseminate information about that topic and start public discussions relevant to that topic for other group members to contribute to. These particular forums enable users not necessarily directly connected to one another as "friends" to interact with one another. These new additions to Facebook elevate the public interactions on Facebook from mere friend-to-friend contact to the potential for contact with all its users.

Methodology

This study relies on data gathered from a survey conducted in November 2012 using a convenience sample collected at California universities. The study sampled six undergraduate political science courses ($n = 232$). These undergraduate courses are diverse in terms of the students' individual majors, as each course was selected because it also fulfilled general education requirements at the universities. When compared to the national population, the external validity and representativeness of the sample is limited, a common problem when surveying undergraduates (Sears 1986). However, when compared to the population of undergraduates at other California universities, this sample closely matches the reported demographics of California college students.

Our key independent variable, *online political activity on SNS*, is measured through seven forms of political participation on Facebook. These measures include frequency of visiting political "pages"; use of political groups to access political information; membership in an organized political group on Facebook; posting political content to one's own Facebook feed; paying attention to others' political content posts; commenting on political content; and attending political events organized on Facebook. These measures constitute an aggregate measure of political use of Facebook, which is measured on a scale from 0 to 1 (Cronbach's α = .86, M = .50, SD = .16). We use an index to design a comprehensive variable that captures a user's general online political behavior tendencies. While each behavior is unique, our intention is to measure general political activity on Facebook that is social in nature, with the understanding that individuals need not engage in each type of social interaction that Facebook provides to be considered politically active on the website.

For the first two hypotheses, we focus on an individual's commitment to good citizenship norms as the dependent variable. This concept is broken down into two norms of citizenship: duty-based citizenship and engaged citizenship norms. *Duty-based citizenship* is operationalized using the answers to five questions, each measured on a ten-point scale, measuring the importance of duty-based aspects of citizenship (see the appendix for question wording). *Engaged citizenship* is operationalized using the answers to four questions, also measured on a ten-point scale, asking about the importance of four engaged aspects of citizenship. Adding together individuals' responses on these measures and then reducing the total by dividing individuals' totals by the highest possible score, 40, we created a duty-based citizenship score and engaged citizenship score between 0 and 1 for each respondent. Thus, if individuals indicated that they completely agreed with each aspect of each citizenship norm, they would score a 1. Similarly, if they completely disagreed with each notion of each citizenship norm, they would score a 0. For our sample, the mean for duty-based citizenship is .74 (SD = .14) and the mean for engaged citizenship is .76 (SD = .13).

For the second two hypotheses, we focus on individuals' offline political activities as the dependent variable. *Offline engaged participation* includes measures for direct forms of participation that branch outside the bounds of electoral action: attending a rally, participating in a boycott, and signing a petition. *Offline duty-based participation* includes activities tied to a strong sense of civic responsibility that have a direct effect on or through traditional institutions. Offline duty-based participation includes measures for voting in the 2012 election, volunteering for a political campaign, and donating to a political campaign. The main distinction between these two categories is whether electoral channels are necessary for these activities.

We include a number of measures to control for political, socioeconomic, and demographic factors that are shown to influence political participation (Rosenstone and Hansen 1993; Verba, Schlozman, and Brady 1995). To control for the possible impact of sex on political participation, we include a dummy variable for sex, coded 0 for male and 1 for female. We asked subjects to report their family income because this is likely a better indicator of their socioeconomic status than the income of a student is. Family income is reported on an ordinal scale ranging from "under $50,000" to "over $250,000" in $50,000 increments, with 6 representing over $250,000. Party identification is measured using a seven-point scale moving from strong Democrat to strong Republican, with a score of 4 coded for identification as an independent. Political interest is controlled for using a seven-point scale measuring the respondent's overall interest in politics. Lastly, we also control for respondents' racial identity.[3]

Results

Before we assess the impact of online political participation on SNS on citizenship norms, we assess the extent to which our population values the nine indicators of duty-based or engaged citizenship. As is displayed in figure 9.2, all measures of citizenship score well above .5, with the exception of serving in the military. Thus, while most of the young people sampled for our survey accept both forms of citizenship, we expect that different individuals weigh the importance of facets of each form of citizenship in systematically different ways. That supposition leads us to assess our first two hypotheses.

To test the first hypothesis, we compute a Pearson product-moment correlation coefficient, which describes the relationship between two variables. The Pearson product-moment correlation can be anywhere from 1 to −1, where a

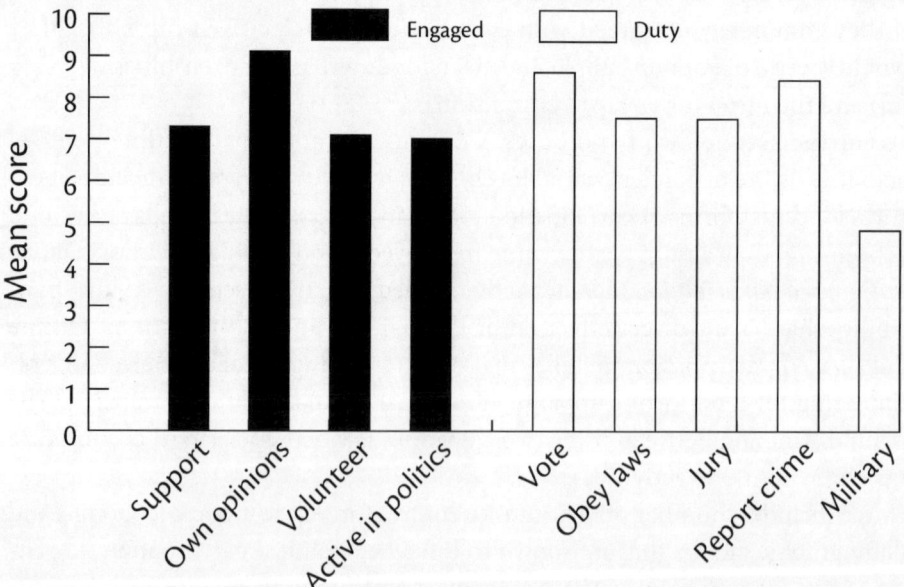

Figure 9.2. The importance of citizenship norms.

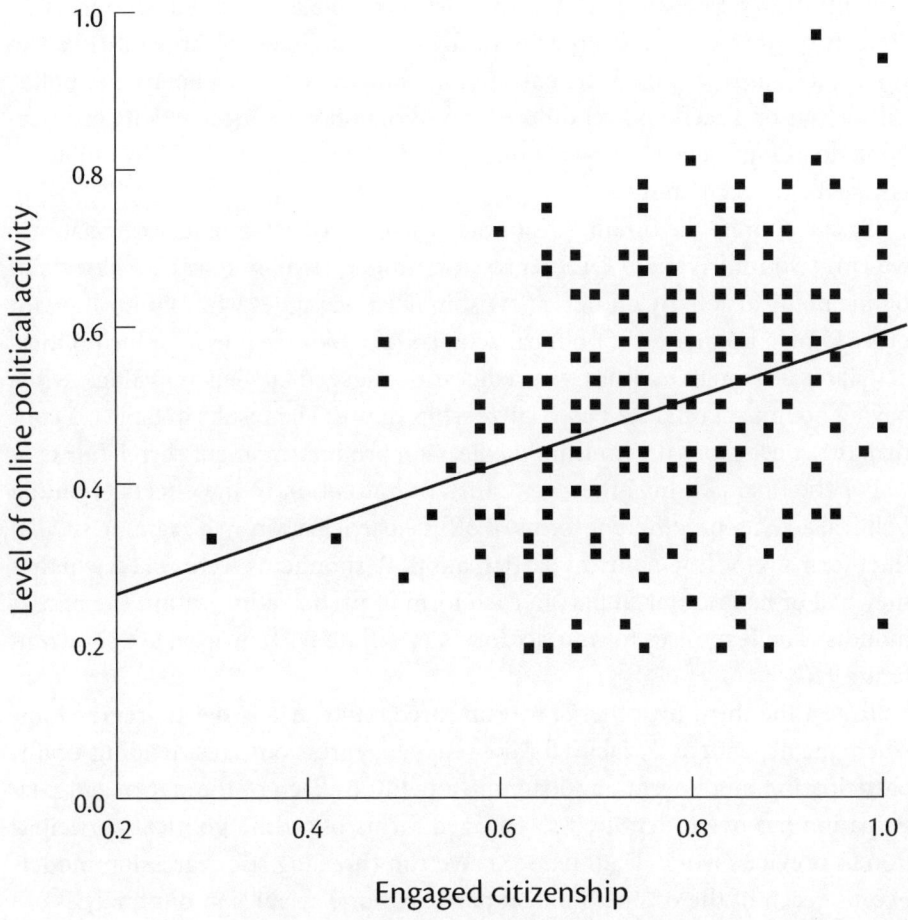

Figure 9.3. Scatterplot of engaged citizenship and online political activity

score of 1 indicates perfect positive correlation and –1 indicates perfect negative correlation. For online political activity and engaged citizenship norms, we find there to be a positive and significant correlation, $r(206) = .362, p < .001$. In figure 9.3, we observe a positive relationship between online political activity on SNS and engaged citizenship norms. This leads us to conclude that individuals who are more politically active on Facebook are more likely to support notions of engaged citizenship norms than are individuals who are less politically active on Facebook. Thus, we confirm this hypothesis.

To test our second hypothesis, we run the same test, only we replace engaged citizenship norms with duty-based citizenship norms. The Pearson product-moment correlation is close to zero, which leads us to conclude that there is not a relationship between online political use of Facebook and duty-based citizenship norms, $r(207) = .095, p < .174$. Additionally, the significance level suggests that online political Facebook activity has no effect on notions of duty-based citizenship norms. Thus, we reject the second hypothesis, which posited a significant and negative relationship between SNS use and dutiful norms. In conclusion, those who are more politically active on Facebook are more likely to revere notions of engaged citizenship norms than are those who are not politically active on Facebook. Yet different levels of online political activity on Facebook do not influence notions of duty-based citizenship; the effect is unique to engaged citizenship norms.

To corroborate the findings from the Pearson product-moment correlations, we run two multivariate OLS regression models, which assess the effects of online political activity on our citizenship norm variables while controlling for other known predictors of political activity. As table 9.2 shows, online political activity is a strong and positive predictor of engaged citizenship values, while having no impact on duty-based citizenship values. The results in table 9.2 confirm the conclusions drawn from the Pearson product-moment correlations.

For the final two hypotheses, we turn our attention to the effects of online political activity on different forms of offline participation. We examine six distinct forms of offline political participation. Respondents were asked whether they had or had not taken part in each form of participation within the past 12 months. The responses for our six forms of offline participation are shown in figure 9.4.

To test the third hypothesis, we run three multivariate logistic regressions, where the dependent variables for the separate regressions are attending a rally, participating in a boycott, and signing a petition. Each of these forms of participation has been identified as engaged forms of offline political participation in previous work (Dalton 2008). We run three logistic regression models because each of the offline political participation variables in our analysis are

Table 9.2. OLS Regression of Online Political Participation and Citizenship Norms

Variables	Engaged citizenship norms		Duty-based citizenship norms	
	b (se)	p value	b (se)	p value
Constant	.566 (.048)	.000	.694 (.053)	.000
Sex	**−.055 (.017)**	**.001**	**−.042 (.019)**	**.030**
Race	−.001 (.006)	.860	.005 (.006)	.400
Family's income	.006 (004)	.163	.006 (.005)	.160
Political interest	.007 (.007)	.323	**.019 (.008)**	**.020**
Party ID	**.016 (.005)**	**.002**	**−.018 (.006)**	**.002**
Online political activity	**.190 (.057)**	**.001**	.031 (.063)	.623
Model Summary				
R^2 (adjusted R^2)	.22 (.19)		.12 (.09)	
F	8.505		3.501	
N	189		190	

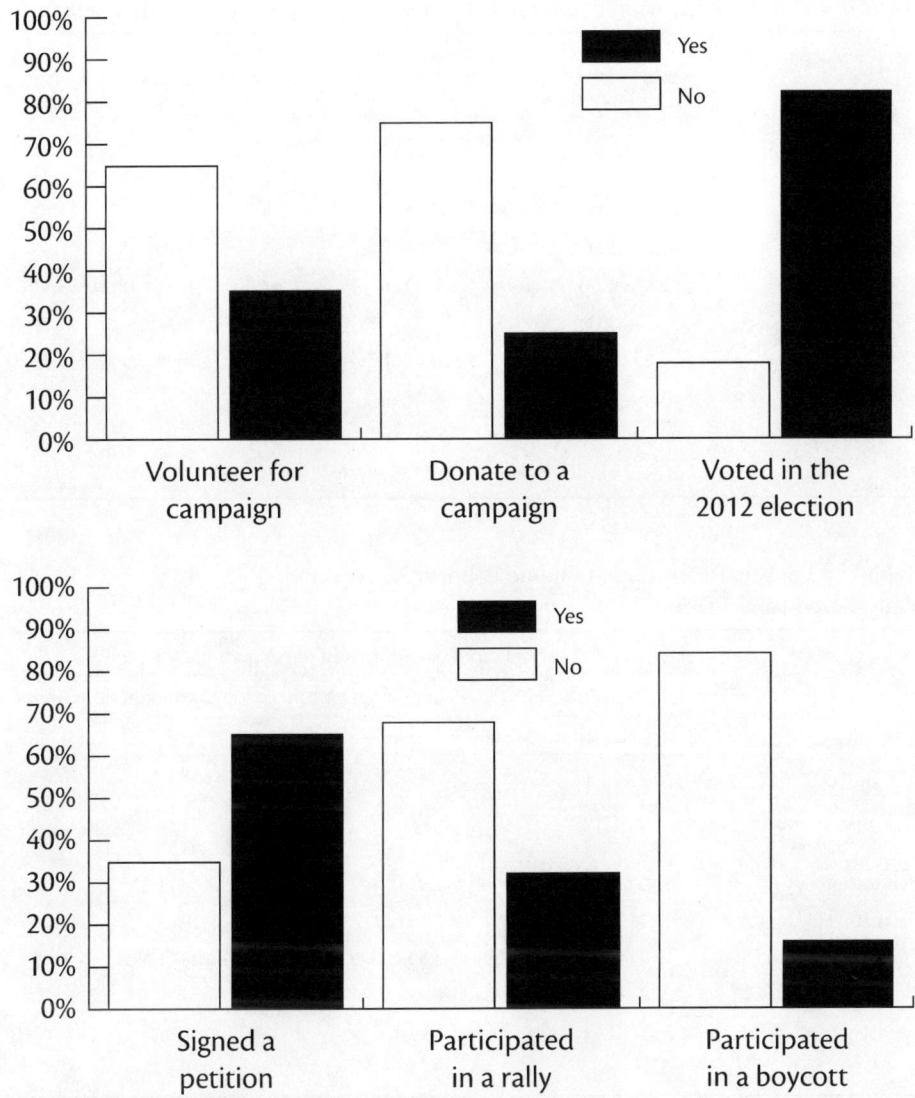

Figure 9.4. Offline political participation

dichotomous, where 1 indicates an individual engaged in the form of participation and a 0 means an individual did not engage in that form of participation in the past 12 months. Table 9.3 presents the results from three separate logistic regressions for attending a rally, participating in a boycott, and signing a petition.

As table 9.3 shows, online political participation on Facebook has a statistically significant effect on attending a rally, participating in a boycott, and signing a petition. In addition, the effect of online political use of Facebook and the three significant forms of engaged participation are positive. Thus, as online political activity on SNS increases, so too does the likelihood of these specific forms

Table 9.3. Logistic Regression of Online Political Activity and Engaged Participation

	Engaged forms of participation					
	Attend rally		Boycott		Sign petition	
Variables	b (se)	Odds ratio	b (se)	Odds ratio	b (se)	Odds ratio
Sex	.13 (.37)	1.14	−.66 (.49)	.52	−.63 (.35)	.53
Race	−.13 (.13)	.88	−.02 (.17)	.98	.03 (.12)	1.03
Family's income	**.23 (.09)**	**1.26**	.16 (.11)	1.18	−.05 (.08)	.95
Political interest	**2.82 (1.28)**	**16.77**	−.49 (1.60)	.61	.41 (1.03)	1.50
Party ID	**.31 (.13)**	**1.37**	**.53 (.21)**	**1.70**	**.27 (.10)**	**1.30**
Online political activity	**5.05 (1.41)**	**156.48**	**4.05 (1.79)**	**57.48**	**4.98 (1.32)**	**145.19**
Constant			−6.84		−2.96	
R^2	.35		.23		.25	
N	190		190		190	

Table 9.4. Logistic Regression of Online Political Activity and Duty-Based Participation

	Duty-based forms of participation					
	Vote		Campaign volunteer		Campaign donation	
Variables	b (se)	Odds ratio	b (se)	Odds ratio	b (se)	Odds ratio
Sex	−.05 (.44)	.96	−.47 (.35)	.63	**−.99 (.42)**	**.37**
Race	**.31 (.13)**	**1.37**	−.01 (.12)	.99	.01 (.15)	1.01
Family's income	.11 (.12)	1.12	.12 (.08)	1.13	.05 (.10)	1.06
Political interest	**3.42 (1.25)**	**30.54**	**2.99 (1.19)**	**19.91**	**2.84 (1.42)**	**17.04**
Party ID	.184 (.13)	1.20	.19 (.11)	1.21	.19 (.13)	1.21
Online political activity	−.63 (1.61)	.533	**3.84 (1.27)**	**46.56**	**6.28 (1.57)**	**534.25**
Constant	−3.12 (1.20)		−6.05		−7.54	
R^2	.19		.27		.34	
N	180		190		190	

of offline participation. We accept the third hypothesis because online political activity on SNS affects each form of engaged political activity and is statistically significant in the expected direction.

Next, we test the final hypothesis, which states that online political activity on Facebook predicts negative levels of duty-based forms of participation. Again, we run three different logistic regressions, which are displayed in table 9.4. The logistic regressions use three discrete dependent variables, identified as duty-based forms of offline participation—planning to vote in 2012, volunteering for a political campaign, and donating to a political campaign.

The results in table 9.4 show that there is a statistically significant relationship between online political activity and volunteering for a political campaign and donating to a political campaign. Thus, according to our results, online political activity on SNS is shown to positively affect volunteering for a political campaign and donating to a political campaign. However, the results also show that there is a negative relationship between online political participation on SNS and voting in the 2012 election, though this relationship is not statistically significant. Although we anticipated that a negative relationship would exist between Facebook participation and voting, we do not accept the fourth hypothesis because it is a statistically insignificant predictor. In addition, we accept the null hypothesis because of the existing and positive relationship between online political participation and two forms of offline duty-based political participation: volunteering for a political campaign and donating money to a campaign.

The results of our logistic regressions do not conform completely to our expectations. In particular, political activity on Facebook does not seem to directly translate into the two norms of citizenship as outlined by the factor analysis conducted by Dalton. Nevertheless, several important conclusions can be drawn, and we address these in the following section.

Conclusion

For today's youth, social networking sites are an unquestioned part of their daily lives. Although older Americans also use social networking websites, younger generations cannot remember a time when websites such as Facebook did not exist. For this reason, younger generations are especially susceptible to the changes engendered by these websites. The effects of online social networking sites on the political process are only recently beginning to be understood, and this analysis illustrates how increases in online political activity are having an affect on notions of citizenship.

Scholars argue that as we become more engaged online, there are likely to be corresponding effects on offline participation (Bimber 2003; Conroy, Feezell, and Guerrero 2012; de Zuniga, Jung, and Valenzuela 2012; Mossberger, Tolbert, and McNeal 2008). Thus, as the arenas for political activity change, we should see corresponding differences in political expression. From our analysis of the data, we find Facebook to be affecting notions of what it means to be a good citizen and differences in offline behavior to possibly be moderated by these notions. We find that those who are more politically active on Facebook are more likely to revere engaged citizenship norms than are those who are less politically active on Facebook.

Our findings add to previous scholarship on the topic of changing citizenship norms and online political activity. For instance, we conclude that differences in notions of citizenship are not based solely on differences in age. Thus, it is not that the youth automatically revere engaged norms of citizenship. Instead, youth tend to be more active politically on SNSs, which encourages the adoption of engaged norms of citizenship. This finding should direct future scholarship to assess the specific characteristics of engaged citizenship that are fostered online, such as feelings of efficacy and individual empowerment.

Our findings regarding corresponding effects on offline participation forms did not strictly conform to our hypotheses. Online political activity on Facebook was a positive and statistically significant predictor of all forms of engaged participation; it was surprisingly a significant predictor of two out of the three forms of duty-based participation as well. The negative coefficient for voting suggests that there may be a diverging trend for this specific activity, but without longitudinal data, we cannot say with confidence that online political activity on Facebook dissuades participation from duty-based forms generally. Yet, given our results, we are confident in suggesting that as people continue to gravitate toward online political activity on SNS, we should see certain forms of participation such as boycotting or petitioning flourish as a result.

At the very least, this exploratory study suggests that particular forms of offline participation are more affected by online political activity than others are and that shifts in citizenship norms may be responsible. The intention of this exploratory research was to draw a theoretical distinction between different forms of online and offline behavior and also to consider how norms of citizenship are relevant. It is our expectation that future analyses will by mindful of the distinction unmasked here and will consider more refinement in their variables tapping online activities and behaviors, given the complexity and capacity of Internet spaces.

Appendix A: Question Wording for Citizenship Variables

To be a good citizen, how important would you say it is for a person to:

a. support people who are worse off:

1 2 3 4 5 6 7 8 9 10
Extremely Unimportant   Extremely Important

b. vote in elections:

1 2 3 4 5 6 7 8 9 10
Extremely Unimportant   Extremely Important

c. always obey laws and regulations:

1 2 3 4 5 6 7 8 9 10
Extremely Unimportant   Extremely Important

d. form his or her own opinion:

1	2	3	4	5	6	7	8	9	10
Extremely Unimportant						Extremely Important			

e. be active in voluntary organizations:

1	2	3	4	5	6	7	8	9	10
Extremely Unimportant						Extremely Important			

f. be active in politics:

1	2	3	4	5	6	7	8	9	10
Extremely Unimportant						Extremely Important			

g. serve on a jury if called:

1	2	3	4	5	6	7	8	9	10
Extremely Unimportant						Extremely Important			

h. report a crime that he or she may have witnessed:

1	2	3	4	5	6	7	8	9	10
Extremely Unimportant						Extremely Important			

i. for men to serve in the military when at war:

1	2	3	4	5	6	7	8	9	10
Extremely Unimportant						Extremely Important			

a, b, d, e, and f measure engaged citizenship norms.

Notes

1. Factor analysis captures the interrelationships between selected items. Dalton (2008) included nine items in his factor analysis; the nine items sorted effectively into two broad categories, which Dalton designates as Citizen Duty and Engaged Citizenship.
2. Political efficacy, which is the feeling that individual political actions can influence government, is an important predictor of political participation (Campbell, Gurin, and Miller 1954).
3. For a copy of the full survey instrument, please contact Meredith Conroy at mconroy@csusb.edu.

References

Almond, Gabriel A., and Sidney Verba. 1963. *The civic culture: Political attitudes and democracy in five nations*. Princeton: Princeton University Press.

Barber, Benjamin R., Kevin Mattson, and John Peterson. 1997. *The state of "electronically enhanced democracy": A survey of the Internet*. New Brunswick, NJ: Walt Whitman Center for the Culture and Politics of Democracy.

Bennett, W. Lance. 2007. Civic learning in changing democracies: Challenges for citizenship and civic education. In *Young citizens and new media: Learning for democratic participation*, edited by Peter Dahlgren, 59–77. New York: Routledge.

Bennett, W. Lance, Chris Wells, and Deen Freelon. 2011. Communicating civic engagement: Contrasting models of citizenship in the youth web sphere. *Journal of Communication* 61 (5): 835–856. doi:10.1111/j.1460-2466.2011.01588.

Bimber, Bruce. 2003. *Information and American democracy: Technology in the evolution of political power*. New York: Cambridge University Press.

———. 2012. Digital media and citizenship. In *The SAGE handbook of political communication*, edited by Holli A. Semetko and Margaret Scammell, 115–126. Thousand Oaks, CA: Sage.

Brady, Henry E., Sidney Verba, and Kay L. Schlozman. 1995. Beyond SES: A resource model of political participation. *American Political Science Review* 89 (2): 271–294.

Campbell, Angus, Gerald Gurin, and Warren E. Miller. 1954. *The voter decides*. Evanston, IL: Row, Peterson.

Conroy, Meredith, Jessica T. Feezell, and Mario Guerrero. 2012. Facebook and political engagement: A study of online political group membership and offline political engagement. *Computers in Human Behavior* 28 (5): 1535–1546.

Dahlgren, Peter. 2005. The Internet, public spheres, and political communication: Dispersion and deliberation, political communication. *Political Communication* 22 (2): 147–163.

Dalton, Russell J. 2008. Citizenship norms and the expansion of political participation. *Political Studies* 56:76–98.

Darwell, Brittany. 2013. Top 25 Facebook pages January 2013. Inside Facebook, January 1. http://www.insidefacebook.com/2013/01/01/top-25-facebook-pages-january-2013/.

de Vreese, Claes H. 2007. Digital renaissance: Young consumer and citizen? *Annals of the American Academy of Political and Social Science* 611:207–217.

de Zuniga, Homero G., Nakwon J. Jung, and Sebastian Valenzuela. 2012. Social media use for news and individuals' social capital, civic engagement and political participation. *Journal of Computer-Mediated Communication* 17 (3): 319–336.

de Zuniga, Homero G., Eulaia Puig-i-Abril, and Hernando Rojas. 2009. Weblogs, traditional sources online and political participation: An assessment of how the Internet is changing the political environment. *New Media & Society* 11 (4): 553–574.

Enjolras, Bernard, Kari Steen-Johnsen, and Dag Wollebœk. 2012. Social media and mobilization to offline demonstrations: Transcending participatory divides? *New Media & Society*. doi:1177/1461444812462844.

Goodman, Nicole, Heather Bastedo, Lawrence LeDuc, and Jon H. Pammett. 2011. Young Canadians in the 2008 federal election campaign: Using Facebook to probe perceptions of citizenship and participation. *Canadian Journal of Political Science* 44 (4): 859–881.

Hibbing, John, and Elizabeth Theiss-Morse. 2002. *Stealth democracy: Americans' beliefs about how government should work*. New York: Cambridge University Press.

Inglehart, Ronald. 1997. *Modernization and postmodernization*. Princeton: Princeton University Press.

Kahne, Joseph, Nam-Jin Lee, and Jessica T. Feezell. 2012. The civic and political significance of online participatory cultures among youth transitioning to adulthood. *Journal of Information Technology & Politics* 10 (1): 1–20. doi:10.1080/19331681.2012.701109.

Kittilson, MikiCaul, and Russell J. Dalton. 2011. Virtual civil society: The new frontier of social capital? *Political Behavior* 33 (4): 625–644. doi:10.1007/s11109-010-9143-8.

Moore, Martha T. 2012. Twitter index tracks sentiment on Obama, Romney. *USA Today*, August 1.

Mossberger, Karen, Caroline J. Tolbert, and Ramona S. McNeal. 2008. *Digital citizenship: The Internet, society, and participation*. Cambridge: MIT Press.

Neal, Ryan W. 2014. Facebook gets older: Demographic report shows 3 million teens left social network in 3 years. *International Business Times*, July 14. http://www.ibtimes.com/facebook-gets-older-demographic-report-shows-3-million-teens-left-social-network-3-years-1543092

Nisbet, Matthew C., and Dietram A. Scheufele. 2004. Internet use and participation: Political talk as a catalyst for online citizenship. *Journalism and Mass Communication Quarterly* 81 (4): 877–896.

Norris, Pippa. 2002. The bridging and bonding role of online communities. *Harvard International Journal of Press/Politics* 7 (3): 3–13.

Park, Namsu, Kerk F. Kee, and Sebastian Valenzuela. 2009. Being immersed in social networking environment: Facebook groups, uses and gratifications and social outcomes. *CyberPsychology and Behavior* 12:729–734.

Pasek, Josh, Eian More, and Daniel Romer. 2009. Realizing the social Internet? Online social networking meets offline civic engagement. *Journal of Information Technology & Politics* 6 (3–4): 197–215.

Pew Internet and American Life Project. 2011. *Social networking sites and our lives*. http://www.pewinternet.org/Reports/2011/Technology-and-social-networks/Summary.aspx.

Postmes, Tom, and Suzanne Brunsting. 2002. Collective action in the age of the Internet: Mass communication and online mobilization. *Social Science Computer Review* 20 (3): 290–301.

Putnam, Robert. 2000. *Bowling alone*. New York: Simon and Schuster.

Rosenstone, Steven J., and John M. Hansen. 1993. *Mobilization, participation, and democracy in America*. New York: Macmillan.

Sears, David O. 1986. College sophomores in the laboratory: Influence of a narrow data base on psychology's view of human nature. *Journal of Personality and Social Psychology* 51:515–530.

Shah, Dhavan V., Nolin Kwak, and R. Lance Holbert. 2001. "Connecting" and "disconnecting" with civic life: Patterns of Internet use and the production of social capital. *Political Communication* 18:141–162.

Shirky, Clay. 2008. *Here comes everybody*. New York: Penguin.

Smith, Andrea. 2013. Barack Obama's AMA is Reddit's top post of 2012. Mashable, January 1. http://mashable.com/2013/01/01/reddits-top-posts-of-2012/.

Socialbakers. 2012. *Facebook statistics* [data file]. http://www.socialbakers.com/facebook-statistics/.

Sparks, Glenn G. 2001. *Media effects research: A basic overview*. 2nd ed. Boston: Wadsworth.

Tedesco, John C. 2007. Examining Internet interactivity effects on young adult political information efficacy. *American Behavioral Scientists* 50 (9): 1183–1194.

Tolbert, Caroline J., and Ramona S. McNeal. 2003. Unraveling the effects of the Internet on political participation? *Political Research Quarterly* 56:175–185.

Vargas, Jose Antonio. 2008. Obama raises half a billion online. *Washington Post*, November 20.

Verba, Sidney, Kay L. Schlozman, and Henry Brady. 1995. *Voice and equality: Civic voluntarism in American politics*. Cambridge: Harvard University Press.

Wattenberg, Martin. 2002. *Where have all the voters gone?* Cambridge: Harvard University Press.

Xenos, Michael, and Patricia Moy. 2007. Direct and differential effects of the Internet on political and civic engagement. *Journal of Communication* 57:704–718.

10

Is Laughter the Best Medicine for Politics?
Commercial versus Noncommercial YouTube Videos

TODD L. BELT

The Internet has a number of campaign uses, from organizing volunteers to fundraising to message force multiplication. But campaigns are not the only sources of political information on the Internet, and not all information is sober. In fact, much of the political information on the Internet is not created by campaigns or even news organizations, and the purpose may be more to entertain rather than to persuade. But entertainment and persuasion are not mutually exclusive, and motivations may differ by content creator.

In this chapter, I examine two different types of Internet content creators: commercial and noncommercial. The content of the political messages created by each is distinguished by a number of factors, including characterizations of candidates, the use of emotional appeals, commentary on political issues, and encouragement to vote. But the real power to control these messages lies in the hands of individual Internet users. It is these users who disseminate Internet campaign messages through social media, email, and other means (e.g., cause the content to "go viral"). Internet content will remain ignored if it does not pique the interest of a broad cross-section of users. I demonstrate the characteristics of the types of content that are more or less likely to gain the interest and accolades of users and evaluate what ramifications these have for democratic discourse.

Building an Internet Audience

Activists groups and lone individuals sought to use the Internet for political gain even before it became a tool of political campaigns (Groper 1996; Kerbel 2009). Individuals are free from the dictates of political campaigns, and interest groups are legally bound to be uncoordinated with campaigns. As the Internet footprint of activist groups and individuals grows larger, there has been a decline in the power of traditional political institutions (Bimber 1998) commensurate with the rise in power of the individual (Mele 2013).

One key to stimulating an audience on the Internet is creating media messages with emotional appeals. A study by Ann Crigler et al. (2012) found that between 80% and 100% of YouTube ads aired by presidential candidates in 2008 contained emotional appeals. Positive emotional appeals include content that evokes enthusiasm, pride, and hopefulness, whereas negative appeals spark emotions such as fear, worry, and anger. Both positive and negative emotions have been shown to stimulate information-seeking behavior (such as continued use of the Internet for political information) and to influence vote choice (Just, Crigler, and Belt 2007; Marcus and MacKuen 1993; Marcus, Neuman, and MacKuen 2000; Crigler, Just, and Belt 2006). One important difference is that negative emotions cause individuals to seek out specific, detailed information (such as information about a candidate's policy positions), whereas positive emotions cause individuals to seek more "abstract, global information" (Isbell, Ottati, and Burns 2006, 81–82) such as "change." Positive emotional content in advertising has also been found to stimulate participation by activating partisan loyalties, and negative emotions stimulate behavior by increasing vigilance (Brader 2005). Taken as a whole, emotional content in media, be it positive or negative, clearly affects how regular citizens engage with politics and political information.

So how can emotional content be most effectively communicated through social media? The answer is audiovisually, and the largest source of audiovisual material on the Internet is YouTube. This website allows anyone to produce and disseminate a range of audiovisual content and commentary, including advertising. In fact, YouTube often posts advertising at the beginning of requested videos. By 2006, YouTube became the top website for streaming video, and its sixth-most-popular page was one that satirized President George W. Bush (Winograd and Hais 2008, 169). In addition to being a top Internet destination, YouTube has introduced features (such as advertising other relevant videos on the right side of the screen) that make a user's average time visiting the site longer than on any other social network (Winograd and Hais 2008), creating a unique online public sphere (Milliken, Gibson, and O'Donnell 2008). The YouTube phenomenon has grown so quickly that it was used by CNN to select and broadcast questions from the public for Democratic and Republican presidential primary debates in 2008.

But just posting a politically oriented video on YouTube does not guarantee an audience. As always, viewers need a reason to "tune in" to content, which generally means high entertainment value. When entertaining videos emerge, links to the content are shared among Internet users through social media and email. This process grows exponentially for particularly popular content, a phenomenon commonly known as "going viral" (see Gosselin and Poitras 2008; Boynton 2009; Gurevitch, Coleman, and Blumler 2009; Wilson 2012).

A main reason people forward links to these videos, but certainly not the only one, is because the videos are often humorous. Although some critics point to humor's effects in boosting cynicism about public officials and trivializing political issues (Baumgartner 2007; West and Orman 2003), political humor has been shown to have many positive effects on audiences. These include grabbing and holding viewers' attention, increasing online engagement, defining political concepts and issues, increasing political knowledge, and casting light on the plight of the oppressed (see Baumgartner and Morris 2006; Compton 2008; Hariman 2008; Lim and Golan 2011; Nilsen 1990). The use of humor and emotionally stimulating content, alongside other standard production techniques, can greatly influence the reach of a political message disseminated through YouTube. The next section discusses how.

Concepts and Hypotheses

In this study, I analyze the content of videos produced by entertainment media (commercial videos) and individual citizens and interest groups (noncommercial videos). Particularly, I focus on those videos that have been distributed through the website YouTube. I look at how well the messages produced by each are disseminated by Internet users in terms of the numbers of views, as well as like and dislike ratings given to the videos.

The motives of commercial and noncommercial content creators differ. Commercial media, such as *Saturday Night Live* and *Jimmy Kimmel Live*, use YouTube to create a buzz that drives viewers to their commercial programming. By contrast, the noncommercial independent groups and citizens seek to affect electoral outcomes. Due to these differing motivations, there are certain expectations we can make regarding the content and appeals made by the YouTube videos produced by each source. First, commercially produced videos should draw a larger audience than noncommercial videos due to higher-quality production values, writing, acting, and brand recognition. Accordingly, I hypothesize that videos produced by commercial media corporations will register more views than will noncommercial videos.

Because noncommercial videos are produced by activist organizations and citizens, the underlying message is usually partisan in nature. Although there should be partisan appeal to these videos, there should also be a degree of backlash in terms of dislikes by opponents of the political bent of the video. This leads to the second hypothesis: commercial videos will register a higher proportion of "likes" than will noncommercial videos.

Continuing with the presumption of partisan advocacy and the desire to impact the election, videos produced by the noncommercial activist organizations and individuals should show other trends in content. Specifically, they should contain more emotional appeals: positive appeals to influence candidate evaluations and negative appeals to stimulate information-seeking behavior and engagement. Since these are not the goals of commercial media, their videos should not manifest these characteristics. Similarly, the noncommercial videos should include more discussion of the consequences of the election and contain more encouragement to vote for a candidate (both in terms of express and latent encouragement) than the commercial videos do. These observations yield the next three hypotheses: that noncommercial videos will contain more positive emotional appeals and more negative emotional appeals than will commercial videos; that noncommercial videos will contain more discussion of the consequences of the election than will commercial videos; and that noncommercial videos will contain more express and latent encouragement to vote than will commercial videos.

There should be further differentiation in content between the videos produced by the two groups in terms of the issues presented and portrayals of the traits of the candidates. Because the noncommercial videos are more interested in advocacy rather than entertainment, their videos should contain more issue-oriented content, giving viewers a reason to vote for the preferred candidate. By contrast, the main goal of the commercial videos is to entertain, often by spoofing the candidates' personal characteristics (satire is "heightened reality," according to *Saturday Night Live* executive producer Lorne Michaels). This leads to my sixth and seventh hypotheses: that noncommercial videos will contain more content dealing with issues than will commercial videos, and that commercial videos will contain more content that reflects the personality traits of the candidates than will noncommercial videos.

Lastly, it is expected that all the aforementioned factors will be significant in predicting the audience appeal of these videos. The likability of a video should generate more views, and vice versa, more views should drive greater likability (people are less likely to share with others a link to a video if they do not like it). Emotional content, both positive and negative, creates drama and should drive a greater number of views. But emotional content should result in a lower proportion of likes due to partisan backlash, as emotionally evocative content is associated with one or another candidate. For the same reasons of drama and partisan backlash, it is expected that discussion of the consequences of the election, express and latent encouragement to vote, discussion of issues and the personality traits of the candidates, and a distinct ideological bent to the message in the videos should drive the number of views up and likability down. As noted in my first hypothesis, the more slickly produced media-company videos should generate more hits and greater likability. Finally, the use of music and humor provide entertainment value that should increase the appeal of the videos to the Internet audience, resulting in a greater number of views and higher likability.

Data and Analysis

Finding and collecting YouTube videos that qualify as "viral" campaign videos presents two unique methodological challenges. The first involves where and how to begin collecting the videos. To do this, I used two starting points: the YouTube "Charts" page, which ranks the most popular videos by genre, and *Politico*'s "Top 10 Best Political Videos" webpage (see Gavin 2012).[1] Beginning with these top videos, I then snowballed the sample by accessing the right-side menu of suggested videos. I did this repeatedly for each video until no new videos appeared on the right-side menu. This technique had the advantage of organically mimicking what any user might do. The collection was undertaken during October, November, and December 2012. Videos were all revisited on December 14, 2012, in order to simultaneously collect information on views, likes, and dislikes.

The second problem involved selecting which videos to include for analysis. Since this study is interested in who "controls the message" with respect to viral videos on the Internet, some winnowing of the videos was necessary. Considering this, videos produced by political campaigns are generally extended campaign TV advertisements and offer no riddle as to who controls the messages therein. Moreover, presidential campaigns *wish* they had as much resonance with the public in terms of recirculating their videos—campaign ads usually average a few hundred thousand views, compared to the millions of views for more entertaining videos. For these reasons, campaign videos were excluded from the analysis. A second concern was determining a threshold of the number of views for inclusion into the study. When analyzing the sample collected, there seemed to be a natural cut point at about 4,000 views.[2] Videos with less than 4,000 views tended to have only a couple of hundred views, very few "likes" or "dislikes," and very few user comments, so these videos were dropped from the analysis.[3]

Two coders were trained and used to code the videos. Concepts analyzed included date uploaded, duration, views, likes, dislikes, genre (humor, music, mashup), candidates portrayed, emotional content associated with the candidates, trait portrayals of the candidates, and issues addressed. Intercoder reliability analysis indicated a high degree of conformity (95.8% agreement, Kappa = .894, $p < .001$).

Most measures were dummy variables indicating the presence or absence of a content characteristic, such as whether a political issue was addressed by the video. Measures for the emotional content of the videos were drawn from the American National Election Study (ANES) and included the emotions of hope, pride, enthusiasm, fear, and/or worry evoked with respect to either presidential candidate (Barack Obama or Mitt Romney). Content that portrayed the personal characteristics of each candidate was measured using three standard ANES "trait" variables: cares about people like me, provides good leadership, and shares my values. Additionally, I included a variable measuring whether the candidate is portrayed as having a vision for the future of the country. Each of these traits was measured for each candidate, and a value of +1 was given for a positive portrayal of the candidate, 0 for no content related to the trait, and −1 for a negative portrayal of the trait. Lastly, content related to issues was measured first as to whether the issue was addressed in the video without association to a candidate.

Next, issues associated with the candidates were noted with a value of +1 if they were associated with a positive tone and −1 if associated with a negative tone. For analyses merely involving presence or absence of traits and issues, the negative values were squared in order to create an overall content score independent of tone.

A total of 71 YouTube videos made the final cut for inclusion into the sample. While this sample may appear small, inclusion of less popular videos in order to increase the sample size would dilute the sample with nonviral videos. A summary of the views and audience reaction in terms of likes and dislikes is presented in table 10.1. The most watched video, which totaled 37,078,086 views, was titled "Barack Obama vs Mitt Romney. Epic Rap Battles of History Season 2," featuring actors portraying the presidential candidates rapping as to why one was superior to the other. The least popular in the sample registered 4,378 views for a video titled "Obama's Fake Romney Attack Ad," focusing on the relationship each candidate had with his dog and satirically implying that Romney's relationship was better because he allowed his dog outside (on top of the car) during trips, whereas Obama's dog was beset with a life of government handouts and dependency. There was a tremendous amount of variance in the number of hits attained by the videos, and a few videos with views in the tens of millions pulled the mean up to 3,280,334. The median view, however, was just under half a million views, at 497,747 (see table 10.1). A few of the videos were rebroadcast on multiple pages, so data for these were summed.

Table 10.1 reports similar scores for the number of likes and dislikes registered by the YouTube users (you must register as a user to like or dislike a video). In order to measure the overall balance of how well a video was liked by viewers, a "percentage liked" statistic was calculated (three videos in the sample did not have a like/dislike feedback option on the page). In order to keep the statistic symmetrical across videos, it was calculated as a percentage of the total likes plus dislikes, instead of as a percentage of views, which would not be symmetrical.

Table 10.1. Descriptives of Videos

	All videos	Audience reaction to individual videos		
		Likes	Dislikes	% liked
Views				
Median	497,747	2,783	201	93.9
Mean	3,280,334	30,700	1,318	89.1
St. dev.	7,432,605	70,754	3,384	13.7
Max.	37,078,086	338,831	25,359	98.7
Min.	4,378	14	1	36.8

$n = 71$

Overall, the videos received very positive feedback from the audience, with a mean of 89.1% liked. The most liked video, at 98.7%, was "Barack Obama and Mitt Romney Singing Hot and Cold by Katy Perry," which registered 22,373 likes to only 291 dislikes. The least liked video was "Chuck Norris Warning to America," in which the actor and his wife warned against reelecting President Obama. This video tallied 3,210 likes to 5,509 dislikes, for 36.8% liked.

Discussion of Results

The first two hypotheses dealt with the number of views and the audience appeal of the commercial versus noncommercial videos. The pattern of views was in the reverse of the hypothesized direction, with a higher mean number of views for noncommercial videos (4,132,181) than for the commercial videos (1,383,040). However, given the tremendous variance in views received, this difference was not statistically significant ($F = 2.110$, n.s.). As hypothesized, the commercially produced videos received a higher percentage of likes (92.7%) than did the noncommercial videos (87.5%), but again the difference was small and statistically insignificant ($F = 2.167$, n.s.; see table 10.2).

Turning to the content of the videos, it was expected that the noncommercial videos would contain more emotional content than the commercial videos would. This was only the case for negative emotional content. In terms of positive emotional content associated with the candidates, the means were nearly identical: .204 positive emotions expressed toward each candidate in the noncommercial videos and .227 for the commercial videos ($F = .019$, n.s.). However, the negative emotional content in the videos tells a different story. In line with the hypothesis, the noncommercial videos were more likely than the commercial videos to invoke negative emotions about the candidates (.898 to .409, $F = 3.392$, $p < .10$). The amount of negative emotional content in the noncommercial videos

Table 10.2. Comparison of Videos by Source

	Noncommercial	Commercial	F
Views			
Median	1,034,331	226,260	
Mean	4,132,181	1,383,040	2.110
St. dev.	8,632,388	2,890,312	
Max.	37,078,086	9,584,312	
Min.	4,378	14,795	
Audience reaction: % liked (mean)	87.5%	92.7%	2.167
n	49	22	

Table 10.3. Comparison of Content of Videos by Source (Means)

	Noncommercial	Commercial	F
Emotions			
Positive	0.204	0.227	0.019
Negative	0.898	0.409	3.392†
Electoral consequences	0.286	0.045	5.520*
Encouragement to vote			
Express	0.245	0.045	4.161*
Latent	0.327	0.091	4.618*
Issues	2.327	2.182	0.038
Candidate traits	1.100	1.273	0.237
n	49	22	

† $p < .10$, * $p < .05$

was almost one emotion evoked per video, more than twice the rate for the commercial videos. The noncommercial videos, produced by individuals and interest groups, were more likely to try to scare viewers with negative emotional content about the candidates, rather than just to entertain (see table 10.3).

Similarly, the noncommercial videos were much more likely to warn about the consequences of the election if the preferred candidate was not victorious. The commercial videos almost never warned about electoral consequences, but over one in four of the noncommercial videos did (.286 versus .045, $F = 5.520$, $p < .05$). And as predicted, the noncommercial videos were much more likely to include both express and latent content encouraging viewers to vote. About one in four noncommercial videos expressly encouraged viewers to vote, whereas nearly none of the commercial videos did (.245 to .045, $F = 4.161$, $p < .05$). And even more of the noncommercial videos, about one in three, made latent appeals to encourage viewers to vote, and again nearly none of the commercial videos did (.327 to .091, $F = 4.618$, $p < .05$). Obviously, the noncommercial videos produced by citizens and interest groups were much more focused on impacting the election rather than merely entertaining an audience.

The last two hypotheses dealt with portrayals of the candidates' personality traits and the issue content of the videos. It was expected that the noncommercial videos would be more issue based than would the commercial videos—giving viewers a reason to vote for the preferred candidate. But this was not the case, as noncommercial and commercial videos addressed roughly the same number of issues, a little over two per video (2.327 to 2.182, respectively, $F = .038$, n.s.). Lastly, it was expected that the commercial videos would be more likely to spoof the personality traits of the candidates than would the noncommercial videos. However, this was not the case either, with each type of video registering just over one portrayal of a candidates' personality traits (1.100 for noncommercial versus

1.273 for commercial, $F = 0.237$, n.s.). The line of reasoning that the "heightened reality" of satire would mean more of a focus on personality (which is safer politically) among the commercial videos was not supported, as it seemed to be a technique mimicked by noncommercial videos.

Before developing a model to predict the success of videos in terms of audience size and appeal, another variable was explored: ideology. Given the public's disdain for the current partisan polarization in Washington, DC, did the ideological nature of the videos have any effect on the number of views and the percentage a video was liked? The answer was yes. When the videos were classified as having a liberal, moderate, or conservative bent, the moderate videos fared better than did their ideological counterparts. The average views for politically moderate videos was 4.8 million, whereas it was 1.5 million for liberal videos and a bit over a quarter of a million for conservative videos (see table 10.4). However, given the tremendously high variances in views, the difference was not statistically significant. As far as popularity by percentage liked, the same pattern occurred. The moderate videos were the most popular, at 93.3% liked, followed by the liberal videos at 86.8%; the conservative videos were the least liked, at 74.6% ($F = 7.936$, $p < .001$). The ideology variable was then collapsed into a dummy variable to indicate whether the video was ideological or not, as moderate videos would be thought to have greater audience appeal.

Predictive models were created by combining the aforementioned variables and including dummy variables for source (commercial or noncommercial), as well as the presence or absence of humor and music. As stated earlier, humorous videos are expected to be more likely to be circulated, as are music videos, which draw on common associations among viewers. Because videos spread "virally" at an exponential rate, natural log transformations of the dependent variables (views and percentage liked) were performed (curvilinear viral patterns on YouTube were also discovered by Boynton 2009 and Turkheimer 2007). Figures 10.1 and 10.2 illustrate how the natural log transformation ameliorates the skew of the distribution of views and creates a distribution that more closely mirrors normal. It was necessary to perform the natural log transformation on the percentage liked variable for the same reason—the video, if popular within a certain segment of the population, would be spread through members of that population, creating a skew due to selection bias (something akin to stuffing the ballot box).

Table 10.4. Comparison of Videos by Ideological Bent (Means)

	Liberal	Moderate	Conservative	F
Views	1,531,203	4,802,955	287,016	2.190
% liked	86.8%	93.3%	74.6%	7.936***
n	22	41	8	

*** $p < .001$

IS LAUGHTER THE BEST MEDICINE FOR POLITICS? | 209

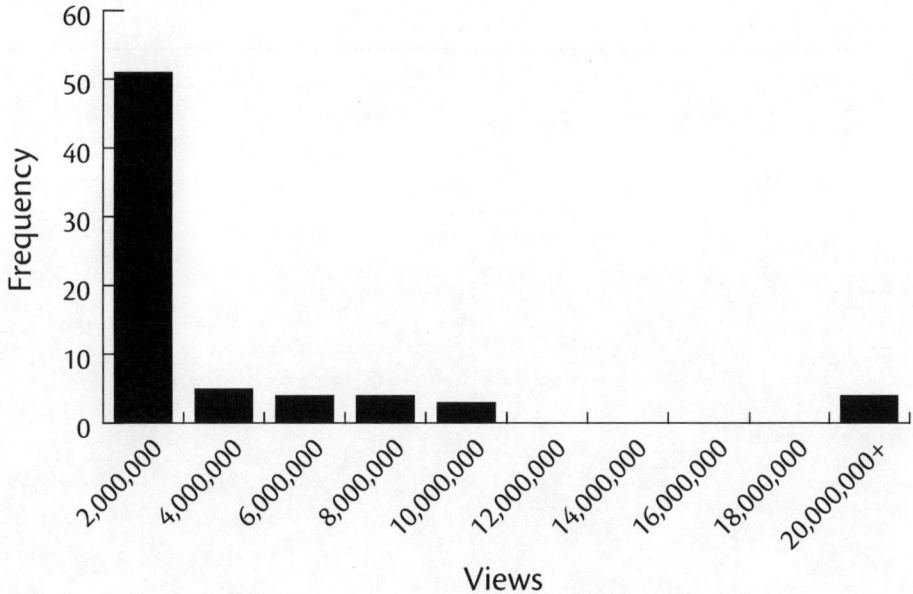

Figure 10.1. Histogram of views

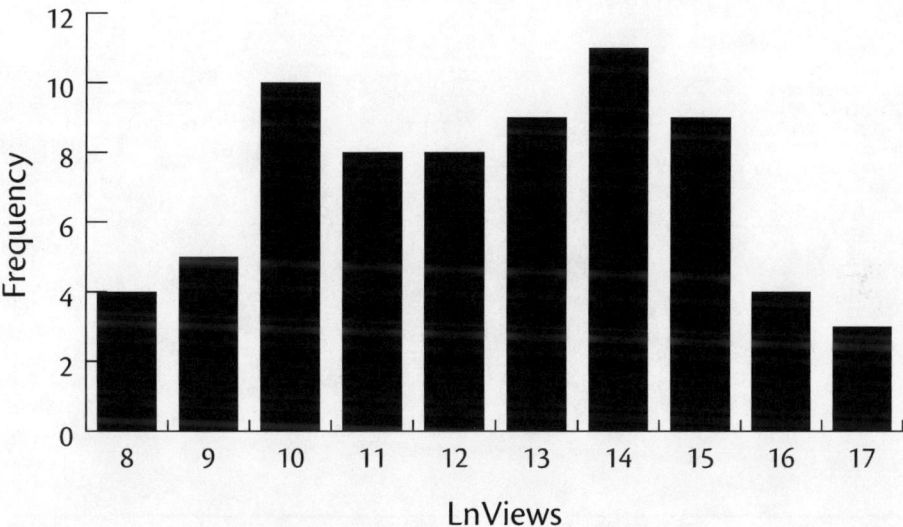

Figure 10.2. Histogram of natural log of views

Table 10.5 reports the results for the regression models predicting the audience appeal of the videos, including number of views and percentage liked. The first column predicts the reach of the videos—how many people viewed them. Not surprisingly, the better liked the video was (in terms of percentage liked), the more views the video obtained. Positive emotional content rather than negative emotional content stimulated views. Although content that discussed the

Table 10.5. Predicting Audience Size and Appeal

	Ln(Views)	Ln(Percentage liked)
Ln(Views)		.021†
		(.011)
Ln(Percentage liked)	2.845†	
	(1.508)	
Emotions		
Positive	1.209*	.041
	(.496)	(.044)
Negative	.230	.047
	(.338)	(.028)
Electoral consequences	−1.428†	.046
	(.855)	(.075)
Encouragement to vote		
Express	2.101†	−.246*
	(1.107)	(.092)
Latent	−.127	.018
	(1.034)	(.089)
Issues	−.056	−.004
	(.093)	(.008)
Candidate traits	−.351	−.024
	(.246)	(.021)
Ideological	−1.707†	.018
	(.743)	(.067)
Source	1.128	−.090
	(.707)	(.061)
Humor	.078	.300***
	(1.073)	(.083)
Music	.802	.037
	(.707)	(.061)
R^2	.449	.438
n	68	68

Note: Multiple regression analysis, natural log transformation of dependent variables; SE in parentheses

† $p < .10$, * $p < .05$, ** $p < .01$, *** $p < .001$

consequences of the election dampened the number of views, express encouragement to vote increased views. Apparently, for individuals to circulate a video, being told the importance of voting is helpful, but discussing the consequences of not doing so suppresses sharing—perhaps such videos become too preachy for many viewers' tastes. Lastly, the videos that were most widely circulated (generating the most views) were politically moderate (nonideological). Either people prefer balance in their entertainment, or the existence of an ideological bent suppresses the reach of the video by appealing only to one side.

The second measure of audience appeal, percentage liked, is predicted by different factors. The more views the video received, the more liked it was, which makes "viral" sense. In contrast to the results obtained for predicting number of views, express encouragement to vote actually made a video less well liked, perhaps because it was seen as too zealous. But far and away, humor was the most important factor in predicting how well liked a video was. Although humor is not a significant characteristic in boosting the number of views, it is what viewers appreciate when registering their opinions of the video.

Conclusion

Many people use the Internet to express their political views comedically and have done so for some time. These actions may take the form of sharing jokes at the expense of political figures, forwarding funny pictures, or linking to videos on social networking spaces. Although "netroots" groups and other exogenous actors may help to drive audience size (see Boynton 2009; Karpf 2009), access to these messages becomes largely based on popularity as Internet users share their finds (one has to know where to look, usually by receiving a link). But what are the political ramifications of this phenomenon? Can new media draw people into the political fray in substantive and meaningful ways, or is it just another form of background noise for a spectator culture?

When individual citizens, by themselves or organized as a group, use the Internet for political expression, the result is much different from what is normally seen in more staid commercial venues such as late-night television. Individuals attempt to empower others, sometimes one viewer at a time, often with a call to collective action.[4] The result is that the noncommercial videos produced by individuals and organizations have much more intense political appeal—expressing the importance of the election and the consequences of inaction, specifically nonvoting. These videos also create negative emotional imagery of opposing candidates in an effort to activate the electorate. And for the most part, they reach a larger number of people than do videos produced by commercial media, such as *Saturday Night Live* and *Jimmy Kimmel Live*.

The data analyzed here provide a sort of recipe for the successful distribution of political videos online. The videos that were most successful in garnering views on YouTube were ones that were less ideological and steered clear of the consequences of the election but simultaneously encouraged individuals to vote. Three videos stood head and shoulders above the rest in terms of the audience they drew. The most widely circulated video garnered 37.1 million views and was titled "Barack Obama vs Mitt Romney. Epic Rap Battles of History Season 2." The video with the second most drew 35.2 million views and was titled "Mitt

Romney Style (Gangnam Style Parody)." The third most popular drew 32.4 million views and was titled "Barack Obama Singing Call Me Maybe by Carly Rae Jepsen." All three of these videos juxtaposed caricatures of the presidential candidates with popular music, feeding off the currently existing appeal of the songs. Even though music alone does not guarantee a large audience, tapping into a contemporarily popular Internet sensation, such as the "Gangnam Style" video (which, as of this writing, is the most watched video in the history of YouTube, with over 1.2 billion views), can guarantee a big audience. Video producers with their fingers on the nation's musical pulse have a distinct advantage in creating content that goes viral.

But just getting a video circulated is no guarantee that the audience will like it (even though this study finds that very large audiences are associated with more liked videos). The two components that really drive whether the audience will "like" a video is the absence of express encouragement to vote and the existence of humor. In the sample, the three most well liked videos gained nearly unanimous approval from YouTube users. The most liked was titled "Barack Obama and Mitt Romney Singing Hot and Cold by Katy Perry," which garnered a 98.7% approval rating. The next most popular was a very similar video, titled "Barack Obama Singing Sexy and I Know It by LMFAO," with 98.5% approval. Both of these videos, again, juxtaposed the candidates with a pop song. In this case, the video producers used the candidates' sound bites to make it appear as though the candidates were themselves singing the song.

The third-most-popular video was titled "Mitt Romney—A BLR Soundbite" and was rated 98.4% positively. This video was produced by a group called BLR—Bad Lip Reading. Essentially, the video portrayed Romney in a number of campaign situations, his real words replaced with silly remarks that seemed to match his lips as he spoke. The remarks were often non sequiturs and nonsensical one-liners that made the candidate appear detached, if not deranged. The video had little to no political merit and was merely entertaining. The BLR crew created several other videos spoofing other candidates as well as the Obama-Romney presidential debates. These videos were also well liked but not to the extent of the Romney video.

So what does all this say about the future of democratic discourse online? As noted earlier, when it comes to online videos, campaigns do not control the entire political message. Commercial and noncommercial content creators are reaching larger online audiences than are the campaigns. These audiences appear responsive to videos that appeal to political action, but there seems to be a line that can be crossed. People want to learn and be entertained when they go to video sites such as YouTube, but entertainment seems to be the higher priority. Worse, the type of videos that gather the most attention regress to a "lowest common denominator" of humor and pop music. In many cases, this leads to a coarsening of political dialogue, reflecting outdated and hurtful stereotypes (see Belt 2012). Although the vast Internet audience largely wants to be entertained, and as content creators push the limits of propriety, there is a glimmer of hope—humor can be used as a vehicle for messages that advocate political involvement. But again, one can be too ideological in creating such content and risk alienating the audience. It is definitely a fine line that must be walked to reach that goal.

Appendix: Videos Analyzed

"Don't Vote for Mitt Romney—DIRECTV Parody (Part 1—Tranny)," http://youtu.be/SZ3IgwnlC7Y

"Don't Vote for Mitt Romney DIRECTV Parody (Part 2—Mormon)," http://www.youtube.com/watch?v=1HOs3Ei3gdw

"Don't Vote for Mitt Romney DIRECTV Parody (Part 3—War on Women)," http://www.youtube.com/watch?v=ZycQslP_5Yw

"Obama's Complete Victory Speech: Obama Wins the 2012 Election—SPOOF," http://www.youtube.com/watch?v=z1yh8JfEbgA

"99 Problems but Mitt Ain't One (Obama Rally)," http://www.youtube.com/watch?v=qKXZ6quhps0

"Chris Rock—Message for White Voters," http://www.youtube.com/watch?v=EDxOSjgl5Z4

"You're So Bain," http://www.youtube.com/watch?v=1fPQ3AuQ1kY

"Barack Obama vs Mitt Romney. Epic Rap Battles of History Season 2," http://www.youtube.com/watch?v=dX_1Bow7Hzc

"I'm Mormon and I Know It," http://youtu.be/ivObAZ3Vzgw

"Saturday Night Live—Cold Opening: Debate," http://www.youtube.com/watch?v=tO2JVacQdMY

"Will the Real Mitt Romney Please Stand Up (feat. Eminem)," http://www.youtube.com/watch?v=bxch-yi14BE

"Barack Obama Singing Sexy and I Know It by LMFAO," http://www.youtube.com/watch?v=OWgO9-AIROI

"U Didn't Build That by MC 'Bama," http://www.youtube.com/watch?v=bQu2SVFF-cU

"Barack Obama Singing Boyfriend by Justin Bieber," http://www.youtube.com/watch?v=spS5CoT3JYU

"Barack Obama Singing Call Me Maybe by Carly Rae Jepsen," http://www.youtube.com/watch?v=hX1YVzdnpEc

"Barack Obama Singing Born This Way by Lady Gaga," http://www.youtube.com/watch?v=AijEQN6AuRs

"Barack Obama and Mitt Romney Singing Hot and Cold by Katy Perry," http://www.youtube.com/watch?v=mwov-7CfLvc

"Barack Obama Singing What Makes You Beautiful by One Direction," http://www.youtube.com/watch?v=8G2ZUWxCkrI

"Saturday Night Live—Weekend Update: Big Bird," http://www.youtube.com/watch?v=gJjn_2fFPx8

"Romney & Obama's Post-Debate Hang Session (Jimmy Fallon)," http://www.youtube.com/watch?v=XsQhVRExObY

"Romney & Obama Watch the VP Debate Together (Jimmy Fallon)," http://www.youtube.com/watch?v=rb0ByPlU4IM

"Mitt Romney Responds to the '47%' Controversy—Jimmy Fallon," http://www.youtube.com/watch?v=5_DuRGHdoVU

"SNL Spoofs Chris Matthews and MSNBC Crew Reaction to First Obama-Romney Debate—MASHUP—10/6/2012," http://www.youtube.com/watch?v=2qbWqMSTZ00

"Saturday Night Live—Cold Opening: Vice Presidential Debate," http://www.youtube.com/watch?v=3-eKugrkYOc

"Saturday Night Live—Cold Opening: Town Hall Debate," http://www.youtube.com/watch?v=ZAyAeaUwBPY

"Jimmy Fallon—Slow Jam the News with Barack Obama: Late Night with Jimmy Fallon," http://www.youtube.com/watch?v=vAFQIciWsF4

"Mitt Romney 4 President," http://youtu.be/qy3S_uQOuCY

"Chuck Norris Anti-Obama Ad (Spoof)," http://youtu.be/VJcbKj5GiZ0

"Excellent Anti Obama Ad (Against Political Correctness): Superb Production Values," http://youtu.be/iys1BWUf-Nc

"Fox News Attacks Obama in an Anti Obama Video May 2012," http://youtu.be/M65MYsfNBD8

"A Song to Obama—Don't Be President (Funny Anti-B.O. Song)," http://youtu.be/QsEL961FiXc

"Obama That I Used to Know—Gotye Parody," http://youtu.be/yJnAp3YxCCw

"Sarah Silverman Let My People Vote 2012—Get Nana a Gun," http://youtu.be/ypRW5q0raTw

"6-Year-Old Bashing President Obama—10 Reasons Not to Vote For," http://youtu.be/aCw3cLwPrgk

"President Obama Acceptance Speech at 2012 [Parody]," http://youtu.be/BkXv2xT2dRI

"He's Barack Obama," http://youtu.be/kVFdAJRVm94

"Best Campaign Ad of 2012 Humorous but True www.RightFace.us," http://www.youtube.com/watch?v=Z1mI_jO8sos

"2012 Presidential Debate Parody," http://youtu.be/B5Xl-WhNdqA

"Obama's Fake Romney Attack Ad," http://youtu.be/C85vCO3JEU4

"Mr. Burns Endorses Romney | The Simpsons | Animation on FOX," https://www.youtube.com/watch?v=ltCIEbLMaQg

"A Message from the Greatest Generation (NSFW)," http://www.youtube.com/watch?v=2ub-c0QRlEU

"Big Bird Responds to Mitt Romney NSFW from MadBigBird," http://youtu.be/OgVJ5k0PCkY

"Barack Obama Singing Can't Touch This by MC Hammer," https://www.youtube.com/watch?v=PLIJc7YE_jw

"Mitt Romney and Barack Obama Presidential Debate," http://www.youtube.com/watch?feature=endscreen&v=aEz2Ejw-VOs&NR=1

"Mitt Romney and Barack Obama Presidential Debate," http://www.youtube.com/watch?v=wAkdHzpXXoo

"Mitt Romney Style (Gangnam Style Parody)," http://www.youtube.com/watch?v=yTCRwi71_ns

"Why I'm Voting for Obama *PARODY*," http://www.youtube.com/watch?v=5QGDJhXznrU

"An Urgent Message from Congressman John Lewis," http://www.youtube.com/watch?v=YcDPtM25S6g

"Chuck Norris Warning to America," http://www.youtube.com/watch?v=9Rw1ioJ99vk

"Samuel L Jackson 'WAKE THE FUCK UP' Barack Obama Ad," http://www.youtube.com/watch?v=og35Uod6WKY

"An Indecent Proposal from Sarah Silverman (explicit)," http://www.youtube.com/watch?v=2B5o6-qNk6Q

"Don't Let Mitt Turn Back Time on Women," http://www.youtube.com/watch?v=c_Es82leIkE

"Call Your Zeyde—Vote Obama," http://www.youtube.com/watch?v=ZWzCmeURevo

"Corporations Are People," http://www.youtube.com/watch?v=fYfJWybKCyo

"Mitt Romney—A BLR Soundbite," http://www.youtube.com/watch?v=e9L9A1IMTQo

"More Mitt—A BLR Soundbite," http://www.youtube.com/watch?v=d5i3FoYnkPo

"Eye of the Sparrow—A Bad Lip Reading of the First 2012 Presidential Debate," http://www.youtube.com/watch?v=QlwilbVYvUg

"2012 Debates Highlights—A Bad Lip Reading of the 2012 US Presidential Debates," http://www.youtube.com/watch?v=SgmARwtptoo

"Joe Biden—A BLR Soundbite," http://www.youtube.com/watch?v=mcjet2MwURo

"Paul Ryan's Video Diary—A Bad Lip Reading of Paul Ryan," http://www.youtube.com/watch?v=ewPo1X5x9Nw

"Trick the Bridesmaid—a Bad Lip Reading of Barack Obama," http://www.youtube.com/watch?v=ehYoIKTsiVo

"Mitt Romney: "Please Don't Watch the Debates" (Jimmy Fallon)," http://www.youtube.com/watch?v=ygq_LuJeWa8

"Bill Clinton: 'Here Comes Honey Bubba'—Jimmy Fallon," http://www.youtube.com/watch?v=mc2aXCV6myo

"Jimmy Fallon Spoofs Julian Castro's DNC Speech," http://www.youtube.com/watch?v=rPZbQ8Gew9k

"Romney & Obama Tell Jim Lehrer: "Shut The F*** Up" (Jimmy Fallon)," http://www.youtube.com/watch?v=64QHFF6l17g

"Horny Mitt Romney," http://www.youtube.com/watch?v=vk6kc8ExgHE

"Mitt Romney's Video Blog—Jimmy Fallon," http://www.youtube.com/watch?v=FUnlFaYczwc

"Jimmy Kimmel Asks a Brooklyn Barbershop about Mitt Romney," http://www.youtube.com/watch?v=iATk-p7fVtQ

"Jimmy Outsources Mitt Romney Zingers to Indian Call Center," http://www.youtube.com/watch?v=kOErbblq_Qk

"'Mister Romney's Neighborhood'—(Jimmy Fallon)," http://www.youtube.com/watch?v=PfSqJ9cYIFE

"SNL on Mitt Romney's SECRET VIDEO footage canceling out 47% of Americans," http://www.youtube.com/watch?v=C3-U0XHBIeI

Notes

1. These websites can be found online at https://www.youtube.com/charts and http://www.politico.com/story/2012/12/10-best-viral-political-videos-of-2012-85487.html?hp=f2.
2. One video that went viral but was not included for analysis was a 22-second video of a toddler crying and telling her mother that she was tired of "Bronco Bama and Mitt Romney." This video registered 17 million hits but had no real content to analyze, nor was it specifically designed to have political or entertainment impact.
3. A popular Internet meme is to congratulate video producers once their video has exceeded 9,000 views. This meme is based on a video taken from the Japanese anime series *Dragon Ball Z*, in which a character notes that the other's power level is "over 9,000!" Only 4 of the 61 videos included in this sample have less than 9,000 views.
4. In 2004, the progressive activist organization MoveOn.org engaged in "crowd-sourcing" its anti-Bush advertisements, selecting a few winners from hundreds of videos. One of the entrants apparently went too far, comparing President Bush to Adolf Hitler. The guidelines for content for individual citizens do not exist in the same way that television writers must conform to FCC regulations and specific guidelines from their own company's Standards and Practices department.

References

Baumgartner, Jody C. 2007. "Humor on the Next Frontier: Youth, Online Political Humor, and the JibJab Effect." *Social Science Computer Review* 25 (3): 319–338.

Baumgartner, Jody C., and Jonathan S. Morris. 2006. "The *Daily Show* Effect: Candidate Evaluations, Efficacy, and American Youth." *American Politics Research* 34 (3): 341–367.

Belt, Todd L. 2012. "Viral Videos: Reinforcing Stereotypes of Female Candidates for President." In *Women and the White House: Gender, Popular Culture, and Presidential Politics*, edited by Justin Vaughn and Lilly Goren, 205–226. Lexington: University Press of Kentucky.

Bimber, Bruce. 1998. "The Internet and Political Transformation: Populism, Community, and Accelerated Pluralism." *Polity* 31 (1): 133–1160.

Boynton, Robert. 2009. "Gong Viral: The Dynamics of Attention." Paper presented at the YouTube and the 2008 Election Conference, Amherst, Massachusetts.

Brader, Ted. 2005. "Striking a Responsive Chord: How Political Ads Motivate and Persuade Voters by Appealing to Emotions." *American Journal of Political Science* 49 (2): 388–405.

Compton, Josh. 2008. "More than Laughing? Survey of Political Humor Effects Research." In *Laughing Matters: Humor and American Politics in the Media Age*, edited by Jody C. Baumgartner and Jonathan S. Morris, 39–63. New York: Routledge.

Crigler, Ann, Marion Just, and Todd Belt. 2006. "The Three Faces of Negative Campaigning: The Democratic Implications of Attack Ads, Cynical News and Fear Arousing Messages." In *Feeling Politics: Affect and Emotion in Political Information Processing*, edited by David P. Redlawsk, 135–163. New York: Palgrave Macmillan.

Crigler, Ann, Marion Just, Lauren Hume, Jesse Mills and Parker Hevron. 2012. "YouTube and TV Advertising Campaigns: Obama vs. McCain in 2008." In *iPolitics: Campaigns, Elections, and Governing in the New Media Era*, edited by Richard L. Fox and Jennifer M. Ramos, 103–124. Cambridge: Cambridge University Press.

Gavin, Patrick. 2012. "10 Best Viral Political Videos of 2012." *Politico*, December 26. http://www.politico.com/story/2012/12/10-best-viral-political-videos-of-2012-85487.html?hp=f2.

Gosselin, Pierre, and Philippe Poitras. 2008. "Use of an Internet 'Viral' Marketing Software Platform in Health Promotion." *Journal of Internet Medical Research* 10 (4): e47.

Groper, Richard. 1996. "Political Participation and the Internet: A Review Essay." *Political Communication* 13 (2): 247–249.

Gurevitch, Michael, Stephen Coleman, and Jay G. Blumler. 2009. "The End of Television? Its Impact on the World (So Far)." *Annals of the American Academy of Political and Social Science* 625 (1): 164–181.

Hariman, Robert. 2008. "Political Parody and Public Culture." *Quarterly Journal of Speech* 94 (3): 247–272.

Isbell, Linda M., Victor C. Ottati, and Kathleen C. Burns. 2006. "Affect and Politics: Effects on Judgment, Processing and Information Seeking." In *Feeling Politics: Affect and Emotion in Political Information Processing*, edited by David P. Redlawsk, 57–86. New York: Palgrave Macmillan.

Just, Marion R., Ann N. Crigler, and Todd L. Belt. 2007. "Don't Give Up Hope: Emotions, Candidate Appraisals and Votes." In *The Affect Effect: Dynamics of Emotion in Political Thinking and Behavior*, edited by W. Russell Neuman, George E. Marcus, Ann N. Crigler, and Michael B. MacKuen, 231–259. Chicago: University of Chicago Press.

Karpf, David. 2009. "Macaca Moments Reconsidered . . . YouTube Effects or Netroots Effects?" Paper presented at the YouTube and the 2008 Election Conference, Amherst, Massachusetts.

Kerbel, Matthew R. 2009. *Netroots: Online Progressives and the Transformation of American Politics*. Boulder, CO: Paradigm.

Lim, Joon Soo, and Guy J. Golan. 2011. "Social Media Activism in Response to the Influence of Political Parody Videos on YouTube." *Communication Research* 38 (5): 710–727.

Marcus, George E., and Michael MacKuen. 1993. "Anxiety, Enthusiasm, and the Vote: The Emotional Underpinnings of Learning and Involvement during Presidential Campaigns." *American Political Science Review* 87 (3): 672–685.

Marcus, George E., Russell W. Neuman, and Michael B. MacKuen. 2000. *Affective Intelligence and Political Judgment*. Chicago: University of Chicago Press.

Mele, Nicco. 2013. *The End of Big: How the Internet Makes David the New Goliath*. New York: St. Martin's.

Milliken, Mary, Kerri Gibson, and Susan O'Donnell. 2008. "User-Generated Video and the Online Public Sphere: Will YouTube Facilitate Digital Freedom of Expression in Atlantic Canada?" *American Communication Journal* 10 (3): 1–14.

Nilsen, Don L. F. 1990. "The Social Functions of Political Humor." *Journal of Popular Culture* 24 (3): 35–47.

Turkheimer, Margot. 2007. "A YouTube Moment in Politics: An Analysis of the First Three Months of the 2008 Presidential Election." Unpublished manuscript, Urban and Environmental Policy Institute, Occidental College.

West, Darrell M., and John Orman. 2003. *Celebrity Politics*. Upper Saddle River, NJ: Prentice Hall.

Wilson, Ralph F. 2012. "The Six Simple Principles of Viral Marketing." *Web Marketing Today*, May 10. http://webmarketingtoday.com/articles/viral-principles/.

Winograd, Morley, and Michael D. Hais. 2008. *Millennial Makeover: MySpace, YouTube, and the Future of American Politics*. New Brunswick: Rutgers University Press.

PART 4

Social Media and Civic Relations

11

Comment Forum Speech as a Mirror of Mainstream Discourse

KAREN S. HOFFMAN

Advances in technology have historically expanded citizens' participation in politics.[1] From Gutenberg's printing press to television, progress in communications technology has given an increasing number of citizens a voice in political debate, creating an information environment that increasingly includes citizens' perspectives and opinions. The Internet continues this trend, as the growth of cable news sites, blogs, and social media has lowered the barriers to participation. One online space that has attracted a growing number of participants is the comment forum commonly attached to news sites and blogs. Indeed, the Pew Research Center reports that 21% of American adults who use the Internet have commented on an online news story or blog post to express an opinion specifically about a political or social issue (Smith 2013, 19). Given that Internet usage rates are increasing rapidly, with 85% of Americans reporting they use the Internet, online contributors represent a significant segment of society (Zickuhr 2013).

In a real sense, speech found in comment forums represents one of the most democratic public spaces in our society, one that is not filtered by the media or pollsters and where there is broad and relatively uncensored access both for consuming and disseminating political information. While critics dismiss these forums as uncivil and negative, an examination of this discourse demonstrates that, in fact, comment forum speech is similar to that found in mainstream political speech. Differences between the two discourses tend to be primarily those of form, not substance, suggesting that online citizen discussion should be viewed as a valuable opportunity for ordinary citizens to add their voice to political discussion.

As a relatively new phenomenon, this type of speech deserves scrutiny, and a presidential election offers an ideal lens through which comment forum speech can be analyzed. If any issue can be expected to attract widespread national attention, it is a presidential election. As media of national discussion, the comment forums attached to news sites provide an ideal opportunity to examine public views about the presidential candidates, the issues, and the election without the filter of opinion polls and the media. In other words, citizen-generated comment forum speech allows a direct glimpse at the manner in which citizens processed information about the presidential election of 2012.

The political commentary found in online comment forums is often viewed negatively. Many readers and/or participants have encountered comment forum posts similar to the following:

> Who's watching the muzzie terrorist in the White House??? . . . you can tax me extra for that campaign[2]
>
> Of course these sickos in Kansas will vote for this purvy Sicktorum. Kansas is known for underage (legal sex and marriage) of minors. Sicktorum for me has already revealed that he likes to fondle and play with underage kids, his god told him it was ok in doing so.[3]

Both comments address political issues insofar as they are responses to articles on political issues. They represent both sides of the political spectrum, and both fall woefully short of most accepted standards for political discourse. Rather than address the political issues raised by the articles, both resort primarily to name-calling. The first respondent claims that President Obama is a Muslim terrorist. The second suggests that presidential candidate Rick Santorum is a pedophile. Neither author engages Obama's or Santorum's positions on any political issue, nor do they provide any support for their negative views. Most people would not be surprised that this language came from online comments, although it is also true that many online comments are of a higher quality.

To take the debate on online comment forums beyond anecdotal examples, this chapter examines more broadly citizens' views about the election as expressed in these forums. I begin with a brief discussion that situates comment forum speech in the realm of political discourse and then address some of the problems and criticisms raised by comment forums. Next, the content of comment forums during the 2012 presidential election is examined, focusing on support for Obama and Romney and the type of speech used to talk about the election. Finally, there is a discussion of mainstream media coverage of the election and its similarities to the speech found in comment forums.

Comment Forums and Democratic Speech

Online comment forums represent a comparatively new digital media phenomenon. The *Washington Post* was one of the first major newspaper websites to provide the opportunity for readers to post comments on articles, posts that numbered approximately 4,600 a day in 2007 (Howell 2007). Many other media sources followed suit, so that most news websites and many blogs today offer the opportunity for readers to post comments. Even a state-level newspaper, such as the *Milwaukee Journal Sentinel*, can draw over 500 comments for any one political article (Gilbert 2012). In one sense, these forums are simply an adaptation of the traditional "letter to the editor" for the digital age. Newspapers have always welcomed readers' feedback, and the Internet has made this process much easier. Partly because of the ease of use, however, feedback is no longer confined to a column or two of the editorial page. It is often the case that readers' comments far exceed the space consumed by journalist-produced articles. Instead of letters that are read by subscribers to a print edition of a newspaper, comments posted online are accessible to an international audience whether the media source is a local online newspaper or a national cable site. Given the importance attached to citizens' feedback, the enlargement of this function is meaningful. As Jaime Loke (2012, 240) notes, "Letters to the editor sections in a newspaper are considered one of the few important spaces for public discussion by ordinary citizens and seen as a key institution in the public sphere." Comment forums thus dramatically increase the space for public discussion.

It is not just quantity, however, that distinguishes print from digital "letters to the editor." Letters written to editors are usually screened and edited before being included in print editions. Most newspapers also require the author's name to be printed with the letters. By contrast, many news websites allow readers to post anonymous comments that are not screened (though some outlets depend on citizen readers for the screening function). This leads to a substantively different type of discourse that many people find objectionable.[4]

In fact, most analyses of comment forums are critical. Loke said that those who post comments "hold extreme political views, and they have been demonstrated to derive exhibitionistic pleasure from venting publicly" (Loke 2012, 240). A report from the National Institute of Civil Discourse at the University of Arizona reported that over one in five comments appearing in the *Arizona Daily Star* during late 2011 were uncivil (Kenski, Coe, and Rains 2012). One blogger said that comment threads can be characterized "by a constant flow of illiterate and often mindlessly provocative brain farts, many of them TYPED IN CAPITAL LETTERS and punctuated with childish and ad hominem attacks" (Seitz 2010).[5] Supporting these anecdotal indictments, a 2011 study found that 64.8% of reporters did not think that online comments promoted "civil, thoughtful discussion." They were "troubled by their content and express[ed] dismay over their newspaper's endorsement of a forum for anonymous discussion, where emotions can run high and mudslinging is the norm" (Santana 2011, 75). Another study found that journalists find comments on online forums to be overly negative (Rosenberry 2011, 11). In addition, a field experiment suggested that, at least sometimes, angry rhetoric is used online in an attempt to attract attention (Ryan 2012, 1149). In sum, this type of speech is often viewed as lacking in substance and too negative to be included in the universe of political debate.

To say that comment forum speech is not legitimate or important implies a very specific standard of political discussion, however. Often, critics of this speech (and other citizen speech) invoke a traditional ideal of deliberation as the standard of evaluation. According to Kim Strandberg (2008, 85), "The nature of online discussion boards themselves, perhaps most importantly the user anonymity, is not a perfect venue for truly deliberative discussion. Creating a true deliberative public forum online would require institutional arrangements and rules of conduct enforced through moderation [that] would enhance the quality of on-line debates." Another critic stated, "uncivil commentary in anonymous forums is antithetical to genuinely deliberative discourse" (Rosenberry 2011, 8). This statement reflects a limited understanding of political debate as "a process of rational and reasonable deliberation that is itself based upon a reciprocal and mutual discussion or conversation open and equally accessible to all" (Fantana, Nederman, and Remer 2004, 11). According to these standards, all talk does not qualify as deliberation. Deliberative speech relies on reason, not passion or emotion. There are certain rules associated with substantive deliberation, and typically the only type of deliberation that qualifies is found in formal governmental settings. "There is a difference, in other words, between the deliberative or thoughtful public opinion one can find in representative institutions, at least at their best, and the uninformed and unreflective preferences commonly found in the mass public" (Fishkin 2002, 226). This understanding of deliberation excludes most of the talk of average citizens, including that found on comment forums.

Some scholars have questioned the utility and normative value of this traditional understanding of deliberation as the standard for political speech. A number of scholars have pointed out that the traditional standards of deliberation are essentially antidemocratic because they insist on standards that most citizens cannot satisfy. Lynn Sanders argues, "appeals to deliberation . . . have often been fraught with connotations of rationality, reserve, cautiousness, quietude, community, selflessness, and universalism, connotations which in fact probably undermine deliberation's democratic claims" (1997, 348). In other words, it is the elites of society who are familiar with the rules of acceptable deliberation, and elite-driven discourse is exclusionary. Simone Chambers (2009, 339) says much the same. "That the poor and marginalized do not have the same access to communicative power as the rich and established is a huge problem for deliberative democratic legitimacy." The access of the poor and marginalized is limited not only by a lack of training in the rules of deliberation but also exclusion from the formal settings where such deliberation takes place. Critics of formal deliberation also argue that the passion, anger, and divisiveness of nonelite speech have value in political discourse. Timothy Ryan finds that anger-evoking speech prompted online readers to seek information, which is generally considered a good thing (2012, 1149). And from a different perspective, W. Lance Bennett (2011) argues that, in the current polarized political environment, "incivility may be a more honest response to some challenges than remaining polite in the face of assaults upon one's values."

For critics of traditional deliberation theory, comment forums have much to recommend them. There are virtually no barriers to access beyond an Internet connection, and because most comment boards are anonymous, everyone is equal in such spaces. There are no hierarchies based on education, position, or any other characteristics. There are very few rules and no qualifications necessary to participate. Comment forums essentially level the playing field and provide a space for more open discourse than the United States has typically seen, potentially increasing citizens' participation and empowering previously unheard voices. And there is evidence that, while elite media opinion disapproves of comment speech, average citizens are more positive. One study that analyzed six high-profile journalistic essays about anonymous online comments and more than 900 citizen responses to the essays found that the responders (who posted their comments online) were very supportive of anonymous comment forums (Reader 2012). More than 70% thought that online forums should be anonymous, and one of the justifications given had to do with the way such speech "encouraged people to speak their minds freely and in many different ways" (Reader 2012, 503–504).

Defenders of comment forums point out that, beyond freedom of access, online forums provide a unique opportunity for a public dialogue because participants can post unpopular views with no fear of retribution. It is also a way for a public conversation to occur on issues and topics not covered by the mainstream media, thereby bypassing the gatekeeping role of the media. In fact, "some journalists describe online engagement as necessary for generating a broader discussion about the news" (Stroud et al. 2013, 3). The nonelite character of the discourse is also significant for some people. Karen Tracy (2010, 5) coined the phrase "ordinary democracy" to describe "the communicative conduct" of citizens in local-level government. Although comment forums do not involve face-to-face "talk," they do involve citizens engaging one another through a written form of "talking," and "the manner in which citizens and officials go about their talking is a powerful emblem of democracy" (Tracy 2010, 6). A blogger, Matt Zoller Seitz (2010), argues that anonymous online comments perform a useful function: "They show us what the species is really like: the full spectrum of human behavior, not just the part that we find reassuring and enlightening. . . . It's impossible for anyone who reads unmoderated comments threads on large websites to argue that racism, sexism or anti-Semitism are no longer problems in America, or that the educational system is not as bad as people say or that deep down most people are good at heart." In other words, he claims that comment speech offers an accurate picture of public opinion.

The fact of the matter is that because this speech is often vilified and dismissed as nonsubstantive ranting, we do not yet know very much about it. Most of our conclusions are drawn from anecdotal evidence, which relies heavily on data provided by journalists (Santana 2011; Kaste 2012: Seitz 2010; Zhuo 2010; Bailey 2009; Howell 2007). Other academic studies typically rely on samples of speech that are relatively small, focus on narrow sources, or involve experimental models that generate their own speech samples (Nekmat and Gonzenbach 2013; Grabill and Pigg 2013; Stroud et al. 2013; Thorson, Vraga, and Ekdale 2010; Papacharissi 2004; Coffey and Woolworth 2004; Light and Rogers 2006; Rosenberry 2011; Loke 2012; Reader 2012). For all the controversy surrounding online comment sites, enough that some new sites have disabled the comment option (Fox News, for instance, during the 2012 presidential campaign season), it is more difficult to find examinations that step back and view the broader universe of this speech.

What we do know is that, while the media pundits and political elites provided running facts and commentary throughout the presidential election, there existed on comment forums a parallel discourse driven entirely by regular citizens. Whatever the final verdict on the deliberative value of comment forums, it is worthwhile to examine ordinary citizens' view of the 2012 election.

Methodology

This chapter examines the contribution of comment forum speech in the context of the 2012 presidential election. The aim is to identify basic characteristics of this speech through a content analysis of the comments attached to articles from a variety of mainstream media sources. Language between sources is be compared to see if any notable differences or similarities exist. Finally, the comment forum speech as a whole is compared to campaign coverage in elite discourse to see whether the conversation occurring among elites differed from that which took place among citizens on comment forums. On the basis of the typically negative views of this discourse, it is expected that the comments will have featured insults, petty language unrelated to political issues, and personal attacks on the presidential candidates. In light of these goals, it was very disappointing to find that Fox News disabled its comment option from spring of 2012 until after the election. As Fox News is the most watched cable news source, those comments would have been valuable data.

To examine whether news comment forum speech lives up to its bad reputation, comments were collected and examined from four mainstream news websites: two national and two state level. The goal was to include the broadest audience possible, so the largest national cable outlet (CNN),[6] the largest broadcast network outlet (NBC), and the two largest Wisconsin newspaper websites (the *Milwaukee Journal Sentinel* [JSonline.com] and the *Wisconsin State Journal* [host.madison.com/wsj]) were selected.[7] On each Monday—beginning August 27, 2012, in conjunction with the Republican National Convention and ending on Election Day (November 6, 2012)—one article covering the presidential election was chosen from each site.[8] The article and comments attached to that article were copied into a Word document. Since some of the comment threads were prohibitively long, only the first 25 pages of comments of each article were analyzed. In all, 44 articles with comments were collected, totaling 2,139 comments. Every comment was counted, regardless of whether it related specifically to the presidential election. Further, each comment was counted separately, whether or not a contributor posted multiple comments on any particular thread. The number of comments collected for each article varied, from a low of zero posts for one *Wisconsin State Journal* article to more than 100 for others.

Since this is a fairly new discourse, the goal was primarily descriptive—to identify the main elements of this speech. Scholars studying this speech, however, highlight some variables of interest. First, many scholars point to the incivility of this discourse. Civility is a complex concept, but scholars have used name-calling as one variable that reflects incivility (Papacharissi 2004; Herbst 2010; Sobieraj and Berry 2011; Kenski et al. 2012). The absence of substance is also viewed as a problem for comment forum speech. Since deliberation scholars typically focus on the discussion of issues as substantive political speech, this study identifies language referring to issues, as well as to character traits.[9] In addition, most mainstream political discourse is considered to be very polarized (Jacobson 2013; Bennett 2011; Garner and Palmer 2011; Iyengar and Hahn 2009; Baum and Groeling 2008), so the distribution between Obama supporters, Romney supporters, and independents is examined to see if the same was true on comment forums. Some studies suggest that citizens are increasingly cynical about politics and the media (Bennett 2011; Kenski et al. 2012; Pew 2012b), so language expressing cynicism about the political system is identified.

Findings

After an initial reading all the comments prior to any coding, several observations were immediately evident.[10] First, the commenters were extremely polarized. In the comments from all four sources, there were few posts that were genuinely neutral; most were clearly in the Romney or Obama camp. More importantly, each side treated the other with contempt. Anything posted by an Obama supporter was typically opposed by a Romney supporter, and vice versa, even if the statement did not reference Obama or Romney or the election itself. This oppositional nature of the comments occasionally reached the level of absurdity in some comment threads when a commenter would assume that any comment that made sense to him or her was authored by an individual with a similar ideology, only to find out that was not the case. For example, a participant with the screen name Chloe3 posted a comment about the decision of the *Milwaukee Journal Sentinel* to stop making endorsements (Walker 2012). Another participant, akaBarrySoetero, found her remarks persuasive and posted,

"Chloe, you make too much sense for the liberal readers to understand" (Walker 2012). It turns out that Chloe3 was a liberal, but akaBarrySoetero could not imagine that anything a liberal said could make sense. This exchange epitomized the binary viewpoint of most contributors. Posts were interpreted as being liberal or conservative; there was no middle ground, even when the subject was difficult to categorize ideologically, such as newspaper endorsements.

Another characteristic immediately evident was the conversational element, which is consistent with other studies of this speech (Santana 2011). Unlike traditional letters to the editor, the comments often included speech that directly responded to other comments. Although isolated posts were sprinkled through the texts, some participants posted many comments, creating an online conversation. In fact, some contributors were present throughout the period of this analysis, suggesting that some people participate regularly. This demonstrates one of the ways in which comment forums potentially enlarge democratic discourse. Their interactive nature allows for conversation, a give-and-take between participants that is very different from the opinions collected by polling.[11] One other characteristic of the discourse was the relatively low level of racially charged language. Although insults and criticism were plentiful, there were very few "birther" references or other obvious statements implicating race.[12]

Initially, the comments were coded in terms of support for Obama or Romney.[13] It is important to note that support for Obama or Romney was often expressed without explicit reference to either candidate but was fairly easy to determine based the context of the thread. For instance, a comment that complained about the liberal polling organizations skewing the results toward Obama was identified as Republican. Or a post that complained that restrictive voting laws were going to hurt the Democratic vote was coded as Democratic. As a first pass, this strategy deliberately ignored all other substantive characteristics of the comments in order to get an overall measure of support for Romney and Obama in the discourse. As shown in table 11.1, the forums contained more Obama than Romney supporters for the national news forums, while the comments were more evenly split in the state newspapers. NBC comments were far more likely to support Obama, which is predictable given NBC's liberal

Table 11.1. Democratic and Republican Comment Summary

	Democratic	Republican
NBC	384	207
CNN	408	286
Wisconsin State Journal	166	152
Milwaukee Journal Sentinel	193	187
Total	1,151	832

reputation.[14] Possibly more interesting is the fact that all four sources contained significant participation on both sides. Anyone reading these forums heard from both sides of the debate.

There were also 156 posts that were deemed neutral in terms of the presidential race. These comments could not be associated with one side or the other for a variety of reasons. Some of these comments did not address politics at all but referenced personal matters, such as several that addressed the death of a police officer on duty when the president's motorcade was in Florida. These posts simply offered prayers or sympathy to the officer's family. Another thread addressed one commenter's story about a family member's death from cancer. Others tried to stay away from the polarization. As one such comment stated, "Chris Christie does speak almost exactly like Joe Biden, for better or worse. I guess when it's 'your guy' you love it, when it's 'their guy' you hate it" (O'Brien 2012). It is also inevitable that some of these comments were posted by people in either the Democratic or the Republican camp but could not be identified as such because there was not enough substance or context in the data we collected to be able to identify their position.

Once the posts were divided according to Obama/Democrat or Romney/Republican support, the text was coded for the following elements: reference to issues, reference to character attributes, name-calling, and reference to cynicism about the media and the government. See appendix B for a discussion of the variables. The unit of analysis for coding was a complete post. That means that a post with one reference to an issue was coded the same as a post with two references to an issue. It was also possible for a single post to contain multiple variables, so that a single post might be coded for both a reference to issues and name-calling, as in, for instance, the following example: "I am disgusted with Romney as a person. Just as his company Bain Capital announced closing down its Sensata Technologies plant in IL and ship all their jobs to China, he stooped so low as to make up a lie about Jeep shipping jobs to China when that company itself had no plans to do so. Romney is a snake oil salesman, it is scary that he even has people believing his b.s." (Wallace, Bohn, and Liptak 2012). This post attacks Romney's character, but it also brings up a plant closing that the commenter attributes to Romney's former company, Bain Capital, and also mentions Romney's campaign ad that claimed that Chrysler was moving jobs to China. Finally, some posts were left uncoded because they did not contain language that specifically mentioned any of the variables being coded for, such as the following: "Just remember, friends, opinions don't win elections, votes do. Please everyone, in the six weeks we have left, do your part on the ground to get out the vote. President Obama has the best grassroots campaign this country has ever seen. Become part of it if you're not already" (Todd et al. 2012). This is clearly an Obama supporter but does not discuss an issue or character, use name-calling, or express cynicism about the media or the government.

Table 11.2. References to Issues

	Democratic issue references	% of total Democratic comments	Republican issue references	% of total Republican comments
NBC	192	50	114	55
CNN	167	41	122	43
Wisconsin State Journal	83	50	61	40
Milwaukee Journal Sentinel	141	73	129	69
Total	583	50	426	51

Given the conventional wisdom about the nonsubstantive nature of comment forums, it is somewhat surprising that there were many references to issues, as outlined in table 11.2. In fact, most sources, with the exception of CNN, contained more references to issues than to character. And even for CNN, it is evenly split, as table 11.2 demonstrates. Of the more than 1,900 comments posted by identifiable Obama and Romney supporters, nearly half made reference to a policy. The *Journal Sentinel* stands out in terms of issues, with the Democratic and Republican issue mentions at 73% and 69%, respectively. At the very least, the speech on these forums is not composed entirely of empty insults, although there are plenty of those. Many of posters expressed anger at Obama or Romney but explicitly linked their anger to issues, such as unemployment, tax policy, and health care. They did not necessarily provide an intellectual discussion but clearly identified that issue as important to them. And some of the posts were quite thoughtful, such as the following:

> I usually side with the incumbent president when it comes to foreign policy. There are things that are happening behind the scenes and I believe that some things should be kept from the public as long as it does not affect national security. For Romney to state that he will get hard on China, that Russia is not an ally, and threaten to get tough on Iran and protect our allies at all costs is dangerous and not good politics.... There are things President Obama should have done differently, but calling out countries before you have the chance to get into the office is not good for Governor Romney (Rothkopf 2012).

Character references, which are represented in table 11.3, were not as prevalent as issue references; however, approximately one-third of comments did make reference to character, with the exception of Democrats on CNN's website, where character references rose to 45%, and both Democrats and Republicans in the *Milwaukee Journal Sentinel*, who referenced character far less than commenters at the other outlets, at 16% and 20%, respectively.[15] There were few differences between Republicans and Democrats on this measure within sources, with the notable exception of Democrats commenting at CNN's website (who tended to mention character more often than Republicans on that site). The fact that most of the media sources were fairly even *within* a source makes sense. Participants on comment forums contributed posts on the basis of the speech found on the site. If the discourse was more serious in a particular forum, such as the *Milwaukee Journal Sentinel*, posters were not provoked as much into exchanging character attacks or name-calling.

There was also surprisingly not a great deal of name-calling, as shown in table 11.4. The most liberal source, NBC, contained the most name-calling. Many of the names were based on derogatory versions of Obama's and Romney's names, such as Odummy, Odumbo, Bammy, Obummer, Obamadus, Obutthead, Obots, OWEbama, Bamster, Myth Romney, RobMe, Mittens, Romnutz, Mitt the Twitt, Rich Romney, RMoney, Flip Flipperton, Twit Bombny, and Nitt and Ruin (for Mitt and Ryan). Other names directed at the political parties included Demon-Rats, Republicons, Repuglicans, Republitards, Teabaggers, Teatards, Repobot, teapyublikkklans, Teapublican, Teanaggers, Teatroll. Then there was the garden-variety name-calling, such as idiot, stupid, echo chamber robot, nut job, anti-Christ, pot-head, clueless narcissist, and buffoon, to name a few examples. Although the character variable captured many of the personal attacks found in the forum discourse, name-calling was simply not as prevalent as issue references were.

Table 11.3. References to Character Traits

	Democratic character references	% of total Democratic comments	Republican character references	% of total Republican comments
NBC	104	27	47	23
CNN	182	45	103	36
Wisconsin State Journal	58	35	47	31
Milwaukee Journal Sentinel	31	16	37	20
Total	375	33	234	28

Table 11.4. Name-Calling

	Democratic name-calling	Republican name-calling
NBC	65	22
CNN	46	26
Wisconsin State Journal	20	31
Milwaukee Journal Sentinel	17	18
Total	148	97

Table 11.5. Media and Government Cynicism

	Democratic media cynicism	Republican media cynicism	Democratic government cynicism	Republican government cynicism
NBC	9	7	14	17
CNN	11	34	2	1
Wisconsin State Journal	3	6	2	7
Milwaukee Journal Sentinel	4	3	0	0
Total	27	50	18	25

The variables about media and government cynicism yielded surprisingly few results, which can be viewed in table 11.5. Most of the cynical statements about the media were bias related from both sides. Republicans complained about the liberal bias of the media, and some Democrats accused CNN of not holding Romney accountable for his campaign statements. There was virtually no expression of cynicism about the U.S. government in general, with the exception of the unemployment figures that were released just before the election; some Republicans thought the drop in the unemployment rate was manufactured to help Obama win the election. Otherwise, most of the cynicism found in the posts was not directed at the government as a whole but at the elected officials who were seen to be subverting the proper function of government.

Discussion

Examining descriptive characteristics of this speech provides a corrective to some of the criticisms directed at comment forums. As critics charge, the speech is, indeed, polarized and negative, but there were a few surprises. It was fairly easy to place participants on one side or the other in terms of the presidential election, and those on one side rarely agreed with someone on the other. If one supported Obama or Romney, it was believed that the victory of the other would be calamitous for the United States, so there were many attacks on the opposition. That said, there were significant references to issues, which was not expected, and there was also less name-calling than anticipated. Almost half of the speech (and more than half in some cases) addressed issues, while character traits of the candidates and parties were also important. Significantly, name-calling was less prevalent than either issue or character references were. It was also interesting that within comment forums, there was similarity between Democrats and Republicans, suggesting that each comment forum discussion has its own norms governing participation—an issue that should receive further study.

Overall, one of the most striking elements of this discourse is its similarity to mainstream political speech. The mainstream media characterized the 2012 presidential as extremely negative. An opinion piece in the *New York Times* asked, "Is This the Nastiest Election Ever?" (Manseau 2012). Adjectives such as "meanest," "most poisonous," "dirtiest," and "most negative" were common in journalist and pundit language describing the election. CNN referred to the "hostile rhetoric" of the presidential campaign (Cohen 2012), while Fox stated that the "'politics of insult' have not faded" in the 2012 election ("Politics of Insult" 2012). *The Stanford Report* noted that "words like *liar* and *felon* have crossed airways and candidates have issued demands for apologies for statements described as beneath the office of the president" (Donald 2012). Even taking into account the media's penchant for sensationalism, there was much talk of the ugly tone of the election, both at the national and the state level.

Ultimately, it is fair to say that there are more similarities than differences between the 2012 election speech on comment forums and that found in mainstream or even elite-driven discourse. Speech in both discourses was extremely polarized, and people were willing to think the worst of those who disagreed with them. Both made claims that seemed wildly exaggerated to people on the other side. Both raised character issues that seemed offensive to some people. Both justified positions with evidence that was often used out of context. One can legitimately object to these tactics in principle, but it is difficult to justify the branding of online comment forum speech as nonsubstantive and unimportant on that basis. Overall, the substance of the language on comment forums seems to be fairly similar to what is found elsewhere. There are many elements of this speech that are not yet well understood, but the substantive similarities are striking. Note the following two statements, one found on a comment forum and the other on a respected television news program:

> Because regardless of the lies, pandering, and fearmongering perpetuated by Obama and the liberal left wingnuts, there are a lot of intelligent Americans who refuse to accept 4 more years of failure from the pretender-in-chief. (Montanaro 2012)
>
> I don't know if it's either cover-up or gross—the worst kind of incompetence, which doesn't allow—doesn't qualify the president as commander in chief. . . . He continued to refer, days later, many days later, to this as a spontaneous demonstration because of a hateful video. This is patently false. (John McCain on *Face the Nation*, CBS, 10/28/2012)

What exactly is the difference between calling someone a liar and saying that his statements are patently false? Not much. Yet McCain's statement is acceptable in a way that the comment forum post is not. Functionally, both communicate the same message; it is primarily the name-calling that makes the comment forum post look ugly. Ugly language does not need to be praised, but recognizing and appreciating the underlying messages communicated in comment forums is important. And some people would say that the anger and emotion expressed by character attacks and name-calling simply reflect a passionate and engaged citizenry. As Jamelle Bouie (2012) notes, "the negativity of this election is simply a sign that both sides are deeply serious about the consequences of victory or defeat." The alarm raised by this discourse seems out of proportion to its actual threat.[16]

Conclusion

It is useful to situate this discourse within the historical tension between elite and common political expression. Kenneth Cmiel (1990) says that the history of the United States has been characterized by elites' attempts to privilege a certain type of speech, namely, their own. The opening of society occasioned by increased political participation and educational opportunities in the nineteenth century, among other things, meant that the elites typically failed to establish clear boundaries between elite and common speech. This has only become more difficult over time as social hierarchies weaken, blurring the distinction between elites and the masses. As Cmiel (1990, 14) said of nineteenth-century debate about distinguishing refined and vulgar speech, "The problem was not that high and popular culture were so different; the problem was that they were so much alike." That describes well the contemporary conflict between elite political discourse and comment forum speech. Critics try to isolate and condemn the undesirable qualities of this speech, only to find that these qualities are usually found in other discourses, as well.

Efforts to privilege one type of discourse over another can be explained partly by what is at stake. In a discussion of the differences between the patricians and plebeians of the eighteenth century, Cmiel (1990, 29) observed that "language was an instrument of power, deciding who would be admitted to authoritative discourse, what words would be taken seriously." That statement is no less true now. Those who criticize comment forum speech as vulgar and shallow are implying that it is speech that should not be taken seriously. It is thus not surprising that journalists are very critical of this speech, while participants are much more supportive. Upon close examination, most of this speech, in substance at least, mirrors elite discourse. This should not be interpreted as a ringing endorsement but rather makes the point that the defects of comment forum speech are also common in elite political discussion. The following statement makes a good point: "The difference between a lot of trolls and politicians is the paycheck. With money comes identity" (Reader 2012, 504). In other words, part of our disdain for comment forum speech has to do with the lack of status of its participants. It is appropriate to consider whether the criticism of comment forums is yet another example of elite-dominated discourse dictating the rules of political debate.

"One studies ordinary democracy out of a love of democracy, and one finds little that is loveable." With this statement, Robert Hariman (2007, 220) perfectly captures elites' unease with comment forum discourse. The idea of a public space that provides the opportunity for significantly expanded citizen-generated political discourse is an exciting possibility in terms of democratic theory. Its potential seems less inspiring, however, after one reads examples of the political language found there. But as the online forum discussion about the 2012 presidential election demonstrates, this speech may not be "loveable," but it is certainly not much worse than other, more respected, political discourse. As Cmiel (1990, 63) noted in a discussion of Thomas Paine's penchant for blunt and plain language, "It was direct and rough, valuing truth over politeness, no matter how hard the language might sound. It marked the difference between saying, 'I think you're mistaken there' and 'That's stupid and you're wrong.'" There is an awful lot of "That's stupid and you're wrong" on comment forums, but perhaps that has its place in democratic discourse. As Stephen Hartnett (2002, 176) says, "democracy is nothing more than the institutionalization of a culture that cherishes public dissent." Although we commonly strive for unity and agreement, dissent between individuals, groups, and discourses is important. Perhaps the very fact of a public space that does not align with the rules of elite discourse can itself be a legitimizing force in American society as it represents the broader reach of political information. There are still more questions than answers with respect to this speech, and certainly there are areas of concern; but we should be cautious about guiding and structuring this discourse, for as the rules and limits increase, the openness and accessibility of the communicative space narrows.

Appendix A: List of Articles

Note: The *Wisconsin State Journal* articles used were from the Associated Press; therefore, they are not archived on the *Wisconsin State Journal* website. The URL addresses listed here are from the Yahoo! News website archive.

August 27, 2012

CNN—"North Carolina Moves in CNN Electoral Map," http://politicalticker.blogs.cnn
.com/2012/08/27/north-carolina-moves-in-cnn-electoral-map/
Milwaukee Journal Sentinel—"Election Offers Choice for a Generation, Ryan Says at Send-Off," http://www.jsonline.com/news/statepolitics/election-offers-choice-for-a
-generation-ryan-says-at-sendoff-ak6koic-167608595.html
NBC—"Romney's Task in Tampa: Sell Voters on Himself, Not Just against Obama," http://nbcpolitics.nbcnews.com/_news/2012/08/27/13508692-romneys-task-in
-tampa-sell-voters-on-himself-not-just-against-obama?lite

Wisconsin State Journal—"Walker in Spotlight at GOP Convention, Lauded as Hero," http://host.madison.com/news/local/govt-and-politics/walker-in-spotlight-at-gop-convention-lauded-as-hero/article_be503f1c-f058-11e1-ae57-0019bb2963f4.html

September 4, 2012

CNN—"John King: To Win, Obama Must Make History Again," http://www.cnn.com/2012/09/03/politics/king-dnc-preview/index.html
Milwaukee Journal Sentinel—"RNC's Priebus in Charlotte: Romney Would Win Today," http://www.jsonline.com/blogs/news/168391046.html
NBC—"Obama Courts Labor Voters in Auto Industry's Footprint," http://firstread.nbcnews.com/_news/2012/09/03/13640326-obama-courts-labor-voters-in-auto-industrys-footprint?lite
Wisconsin State Journal—"President Says GOP Creating 'Fictional' Obama," http://news.yahoo.com/president-says-gop-creating-fictional-obama-231359739--election.html

September 11, 2012

CNN—"CNN Poll: Obama Up by Six Points over Romney," http://politicalticker.blogs.cnn.com/2012/09/10/cnn-poll-obama-up-six-points-over-romney/
Milwaukee Journal Sentinel—"Biden to Appear in Eau Claire on Thursday," http://www.jsonline.com/blogs/news/169199636.html
NBC—"First Thoughts: After Tampa and Charlotte," http://firstread.nbcnews.com/_news/2012/09/10/13779606-first-thoughts-after-tampa-and-charlotte?lite
Wisconsin State Journal—"The Race: Both Sides Focus on Ads, Retail Politics," http://finance.yahoo.com/news/race-both-sides-focus-ads-retail-politics-163431555--election.html

September 18, 2012

CNN—"Obama Touts His Record on China," http://whitehouse.blogs.cnn.com/2012/09/17/obama-touts-his-record-on-china/
Milwaukee Journal Sentinel—"Average Family Can Expect Same Tax from Obama, Unknown from Romney," http://www.jsonline.com/news/statepolitics/average-family-can-expect-same-tax-from-obama-unknown-from-romney-im6rd6d-169974536.html
NBC—"Obama Hits Romney on China: 'I Like to Walk the Walk, Not Just Talk the Talk,'" http://firstread.nbcnews.com/_news/2012/09/17/13918770-obama-hits-romney-on-china-i-like-to-walk-the-walk-not-just-talk-the-talk?lite
Wisconsin State Journal—"Romney Receives First Intelligence Briefing," http://news.yahoo.com/romney-receives-first-intelligence-briefing-230916811--election.html

September 25, 2012

CNN—"Obama Campaign Stands by 'Overboard' Ads," http://politicalticker.blogs.cnn.com/2012/09/24/obama-campaign-stands-by-overboard-ads/

Milwaukee Journal Sentinel—"Romney of Ryan: 'I'm the Guy Running for President, Not Him,'" http://www.jsonline.com/blogs/news/171037531.html

NBC—"First Thoughts: Battleground Ohio," http://firstread.nbcnews.com/_news/2012/09/24/14067006-first-thoughts-battleground-ohio?lite

Wisconsin State Journal—"The Race: Ohio and Florida Could Be the Deciders," http://news.yahoo.com/race-ohio-florida-could-deciders-171700081--election.html

October 2, 2012

CNN—"10 Questions for Obama to Answer," http://www.cnn.com/2012/10/01/opinion/frum-10-questions-for-obama/index.html

Milwaukee Journal Sentinel—"After Debate, Obama Plans to Visit UW-Madison," http://www.jsonline.com/news/statepolitics/after-debate-obama-plans-to-visit-uwmadison-1p72h8h-172171971.html

NBC—"First Thoughts: Needing a Great October," http://firstread.nbcnews.com/_news/2012/10/01/14169015-first-thoughts-needing-a-great-october?lite

Wisconsin State Journal—"Ryan Rejects Need for Romney Breakthrough Moment," http://news.yahoo.com/ryan-rejects-breakthrough-moment-191532202--election.html

October 9, 2012

CNN—"Battlegrounds: Colorado Is 'Ground Zero' of Presidential Election," http://www.cnn.com/2012/10/08/politics/king-battlegrounds-colorado/index.html

Milwaukee Journal Sentinel—"Romney Favors Health Care Competition, Gives Few Details," http://www.jsonline.com/business/romney-favors-health-care-competition-gives-few-details-iq73n0s-173046681.html

NBC—"First Thoughts: Has the Race Changed?" http://firstread.nbcnews.com/_news/2012/10/08/14293246-first-thoughts-has-the-race-changed?lite

Wisconsin State Journal—"Obama to Backers: Time to Get 'Almost Obsessive,'" http://news.yahoo.com/obama-backers-time-almost-obsessive-024722326--election.html

October 16, 2012

CNN—"What Is President Obama's Greatest Challenge at Tomorrow Night's Debate," http://caffertyfile.blogs.cnn.com/2012/10/15/what-is-president-obamas-greatest-challenge-at-tomorrow-nights-debate/

Milwaukee Journal Sentinel—"Ryan Talks of Debt and Taxes at Carroll University," http://www.jsonline.com/blogs/news/174209751.html

NBC—"Team Romney Raises over $170 million in September," http://firstread
.nbcnews.com/_news/2012/10/15/14457492-team-romney-raises-over-170-million-in
-september?lite

Wisconsin State Journal—"Obama Out to Seize Momentum from Romney in Debate," http://news.yahoo.com/obama-seize-momentum-romney-debate-065036203
--election.html

October 23, 2012

CNN—"Obama's Foreign Policy on Trial," http://www.cnn.com/2012/10/22/opinion/
rothkopf-foreign-policy-debate/index.html

Milwaukee Journal Sentinel—"Tale of Two States: Ohio and Wisconsin Pivotal in Race for President," http://www.jsonline.com/blogs/news/175282711.html

NBC—"NBC/WSJ Poll: Obama Leads by 45 points with Latinos," http://firstread
.nbcnews.com/_news/2012/10/22/14617456-nbcwsj-poll-obama-leads-by-45-points
-with-latinos?lite

Wisconsin State Journal—"Obama Seeks to Emphasize Second-Term Agenda," http://
news.yahoo.com/obama-seeks-emphasize-second-term-agenda-153752265--election
.html

October 30, 2012

CNN—"Obama Campaign Unveils Response to Romney Auto Ad," http://political
ticker.blogs.cnn.com/2012/10/29/obama-campaign-unveils-response-to-romney
-auto-ad/

Milwaukee Journal Sentinel—"Press-Gazette Backs Romney, Wausau Daily Herald for Obama," http://www.jsonline.com/blogs/news/176168941.html

NBC—"Obama's Secret Weapon: Latinos—and New Poll Shows Them Fired Up,"
http://firstread.nbcnews.com/_news/2012/10/29/14782235-obamas-secret-weapon
-latinos-and-new-poll-shows-them-fired-up?lite

Wisconsin State Journal—"The Race: Storm Disrupts Campaigning on Both Sides," http://news.yahoo.com/race-storm-disrupts-campaigning-both-sides-155629070
--election.html

November 6, 2012

CNN—"Margin of Error: Two Candidates, Two Journeys, One Race of Lost Dreams," http://www.cnn.com/2012/11/04/politics/margin-of-error-campaign-foreman/index
.html

Milwaukee Journal Sentinel—"Obama, Springsteen Take Stage," http://www.jsonline
.com/blogs/news/177252611.html

NBC—"Obama, Romney Cap Election Eve with Rallies in States That Launched

Them," http://nbcpolitics.nbcnews.com/_news/2012/11/05/14944405-obama-romney-cap-election-eve-with-rallies-in-states-that-launched-them?lite

Wisconsin State Journal—"Obama, Romney Make Last-Minute Pleas in Close Race," http://news.yahoo.com/obama-romney-last-minute-pleas-close-race-202056291--election.html

Appendix B: Variables

Reference to issues. This variable included any reference to a political issue (following prior research that distinguishes issues from character traits, such as Geer 2006 and Lau and Pomper 2001) *Issue* was defined broadly because the purpose of the variable was to identify those comments that addressed any substantive matters, as opposed to reference to personal character attributes and name-calling. While it is true that a president's character can be viewed as a legitimate issue (Parry-Giles 2010), those references were collected elsewhere, under the more specific variable of character. The issue variable included things such as unemployment, the attack on the embassy in Libya, tax policy, campaign finance, the Electoral College, voter photo identification, Israel, and so on. Note that this variable captured any reference to an issue; the manner in which the issue was addressed was not considered. An angry statement that Obama was destroying the American economy was coded the same as a well-reasoned argument about the absence of voter fraud throughout the country.

Reference to character. This variable included any language that either criticized or praised an individual's or group's personal character traits. Speech about trustworthiness, flip-flopping, breaking one's word, or lying were common examples.

Name-calling. This variable included any language that identified a person or group with a specific critical term. Names such as "Odumbo" or "Mitt Robme" were included, as well as more generic names. The one exception is the term "liar." Because calling someone a liar is a direct attack on one's character, all references to lying and liars were coded for character. Also, certain names that were invariably intended to be derogatory were not included because they also happened to be the candidates' real names. Willard is Mitt Romney's first name, although he prefers Mitt. Barack Obama was often called Barry when he was younger, and Hussein is his middle name. Thus, Willard, Barry, and Hussein were not coded as name-calling.

Media cynicism. This variable captured language that criticized the media. Most references related to media bias, but comments about the media's profit orientation were also included.

Government cynicism. This variable included any language that suggested that the government as an entity was acting dishonestly or working against the public interest. It did not include any references to the actions of specific individuals and parties. So, for instance, language that accused Obama of covering up what happened during the attack on the embassy in Libya was coded for issue, not government cynicism. Someone accusing the Bureau of Labor Statistics of using false numbers was coded as government cynicism.

Notes

1. I am very grateful to my coders. Brandon Savage cheerfully spent his Christmas break working on this project, and Shannon McLean's work ethic resulted in painless reliability testing. Many thanks!
2. johndeagan, comment on "Report: Millions of White House Dollars Helped Pay for NYPD Muslim Surveillance," FoxNews. com, February 27, 2012, http://www.foxnews.com/politics/2012/02/27/report-millions-white-house-dollars-helped-pay-for-nypd-muslim-surveillance/#comment.
3. Arieus, comment on "Santorum Wins Kansas Caucuses as Romney Takes Wyoming," by Tom Curry, MSNBC.com, March 10, 2012, http://nbcpolitics.msnbc.msn.com/_news/2012/03/10/10634057-santorum-wins-kansas-caucuses-as-romney-takes-wyoming.
4. Zizi Papacharissi argues that the anonymity of the Internet creates a unique environment. "Identities are fluid and mobile," and "the conditions which encourage compromise are lacking in virtual discourse" (2004, 269).
5. It is important to note that while Matt Zoller Seitz describes comment speech in unflattering terms, he defends this speech because it reflects the real world.
6. Because Fox News disabled its comment forums in the spring of 2012, CNN was chosen as the largest cable site with comment forums (Holcomb and Mitchell 2013).
7. Wisconsin is a particularly good place to analyze political speech not only because of its status as a battleground state in the presidential election but also because of the tumultuous political environment in the two years leading up to the 2012 election. Since 2010, when Scott Walker led the Republicans to control of both the executive and legislative branches, Wisconsin has been involved in debates about some of the most important issues facing states across the nation, such as collective bargaining rights, photo identification for voting, gun rights, and tax cuts. The divisive quality of Wisconsin politics also mirrors national polarization as heated political battles led to a record nine legislative recall elections in the summer of 2011, as well as a gubernatorial recall election in 2012.
8. See appendix A for a list of the articles. All the articles were the election headline pieces on the home pages of the news site for that particular day. Occasionally, the state newspaper sites did not headline an election story, so it was necessary to go to the "Politics" page of the site and find the headline on that page.
9. John Geer (2006) used the distinction between issue and character references in his research on negative campaign advertisements. See also Brooks and Geer 2007 and Lau and Pomper 2001.
10. There were two main coders, one of them the author. A third coder conducted reliability testing. Intercoder reliability was calculated with ReCal at two stages of the analysis using Krippendorff's Alpha coefficient, a measure that is considered quite reliable because it takes into account the role that chance plays in coding agreement (Joyce 2013; Neuendorf 2002;

Hayes and Krippendorff 2007). Krippendorff's Alpha is known to be a conservative indicator, sometimes overly conservative, so that values of .80 and above are widely accepted as satisfactory (Lombard et al. 2010). For the initial coding of posts in terms of Obama or Romney support, the coefficient was .84. At the second stage, the coefficient was .95 for issue references, .82 for character references, and .95 for name-calling references. For reliability data, the third coder tested roughly 18% of the comments at the first stage and 10% of the comments at the second stage.

11. Susan Herbst argues that the twentieth-century trend toward public-opinion polling has had a negative effect on political discussion: "I contend that the rigid, structured nature of polling may narrow the range of public discourse by defining the boundaries for public debate" (1993, 166). Online discourse can help remedy that situation by expanding those boundaries.
12. There are several possible reasons for this. First, racist posts may be more prevalent on more ideologically narrow forums and thus less frequently encountered on general outlets such as the ones utilized in this study. Second, the occasion of a presidential election may attract participants who do not typically contribute to these forums. Third, it is possible that the prevalence of racist speech has been exaggerated.
13. Initially, the goal was to look specifically at support for Obama and Romney, but the extreme polarization of the speech means that one can just as easily equate Obama support with Democrats and Romney support with Republicans.
14. The Pew Research Center for the People and the Press reports that the credibility of both NBC and CNN is more than twice as high for Democrats as Republicans (Pew 2012a).
15. This is one of the variables that was most difficult to code for. Virtually any criticism could be phrased as a character issue, but coders were careful not to include criticism that clearly focused purely on policy disagreement as opposed to implicating a person's honesty, trustworthiness, and other personal qualities.
16. That being said, the extreme polarization found throughout political discourse more generally is alarming in its use of the language of "enemyship." Enemyship is a strategy whereby political opponents are defined as dangerous enemies, a strategy that closes off the possibility of agreement, leading to increased gridlock and stalemate (Engels 2010).

References

Baum, Matthew A., and Tim Groeling. 2008. "New Media and the Polarization of American Political Discourse." *Political Communication* 4:345–365.
Bennett, W. Lance. 2011. "What's Wrong with Incivility? Civility as the New Censorship in American Politics." Paper prepared for the 2011 John Breaux Symposium, "In the Name of Democracy: Leadership, Civility, and Governing in a Polarized Media Environment." Reilly Center for Media & Public Affairs, Manship School of Mass Communication, Louisiana State University, March 28–29.
Bouie, Jamelle. 2012. "Yes, This Campaign Is Negative and Nasty—and That's a Good Thing." *The Plum Line* (blog), *Washington Post*, August 17. http://www.washingtonpost.com/blogs/plum-line/post/yes-this-campaign-is-negative-and-nasty--and-thats-a-good-thing/2012/08/17/37b671fc-e873-11e1-9739-eef99c5fb285_blog.html.
Brooks, Deborah Jordan, and John G. Geer. 2007. "Beyond Negativity: The Effects of Incivility on the Electorate." *American Journal of Political Science* 51 (1): 1–16.
Chambers, Simone. 2009. "Rhetoric and the Public Sphere: Has Deliberative Democracy Abandoned Mass Democracy?" *Political Theory* 25:323–350.

Cmiel, Kenneth. 1990. *Democratic Eloquence: The Fight over Popular Speech in Nineteenth-Century America.* New York: William Morrow.

Coffey, Brian, and Stephen Woolworth. 2004. "'Destroy the Scum, and Then Neuter Their Families': The Web Forum as a Vehicle for Community Discourse?" *Social Science Journal* 41:1–14.

Cohen, Tom. 2012. "Obama, Romney Tone Down Rhetoric, but Campaigns Don't." CNN Online, November 1. http://www.cnn.com/2012/10/31/politics/campaign-sandy/.

Donald, Brooke. 2012. "How Low Can You Go? Stanford Experts Weigh In on the Tone of the 2012 Presidential Race." *Stanford Report*, August 8. http://news.stanford.edu/pr/2012/pr-election-campaign-nastiness-080812.html.

Engels, Jeremy. 2010. *Enemyship: Democracy and Counter-revolution in the Early Republic.* East Lansing: Michigan State University Press.

Fantana, Bernedetto, Gary J. Nederman, and Gary Remer. 2004. "Introduction: Deliberative Democracy and the Rhetorical Turn." In *Talking Democracy: Historical Perspectives on Rhetoric and Democracy*, edited by Bernedetto Fantana, Gary J. Nederman, and Gary Remer, 1–26. University Park: Pennsylvania State University Press.

Fishkin, James S. 2002. "Deliberative Democracy." In *The Blackwell Guide to Social and Political Philosophy*, edited by Robert L. Simon, 221–238. Malden, MA: Blackwell.

Garner, Andrew, and Harvey Palmer. 2011. "Polarization and Issue Consistency over Time." *Political Behavior* 33:225–246.

Geer, John G. 2006. *In Defense of Negativity: Attack Ads in Presidential Campaigns.* Chicago: University of Chicago Press.

Gilbert, Craig. 2012. "GOP Redistricting Leaves Its Stamp on 2012 Election." *The Wisconsin Voter* (blog), *Milwaukee Journal Sentinel*, December 10. http://www.jsonline.com/blogs/news/182754381.html.

Grabill, Jeffrey T., and Stacey Pigg. 2013. "Messy Rhetoric: Identity Performance as Rhetorical Agency in Online Public Forums." *Rhetoric Society Quarterly* 42 (2): 99–119.

Hariman, Robert. 2007. "Amateur Hour: Knowing What to Love in Ordinary Democracy." In *Prettier Doll: Rhetoric, Discourse, and Ordinary Democracy*, edited by Karen Tracy, 218–249. Tuscaloosa: University of Alabama Press.

Hartnett, Stephen John. 2002. *Democratic Dissent and the Cultural Fictions of Antebellum America.* Urbana: University of Illinois Press.

Hayes, Andrew F., and Klaus Krippendorff. 2007. "Answering the Call for a Standard Reliability Measure for Coding Data." *Communication Methods and Measures* 1 (1): 77–89.

Herbst, Susan. 1993. *Numbered Voices: How Opinion Polling Has Shaped American Politics.* Chicago: University of Chicago Press.

———. 2010. *Rude Democracy: Civility and Incivility in American Politics.* Philadelphia: Temple University Press.

Holcomb, Jesse, and Amy Mitchell. 2013. "The State of the News Media 2013: An Annual Report on American Journalism." Pew Research Center for the People & the Press. http://stateofthemedia.org/.

Howell, Deborah. 2007. "Online Venom or Vibrant Speech?" *Washington Post*, May 6. http://www.washingtonpost.com/wp-dyn/content/article/2007/05/04/AR2007050401904.html.

Iyengar, Shanto, and Kyu S. Hahn. 2009. "Red Media, Blue Media: Evidence of Ideological Selectivity in Media Use." *Journal of Communication* 59 (1): 19–39.

Jacobson, Gary C. 2013. "Partisan Polarization in American Politics: A Background Paper. *Presidential Studies Quarterly* 43 (4): 688–708.

Joyce, Mary. 2013. "Picking the Best Intercoder Reliability Statistic for Your Digital Activism Content Analysis." Digital Activism Research Project: Investigating the Global Impact of

Digital Media on Political Contention, Department of Communication at the University of Washington. May 11. http://digital-activism.org/2013/05/picking-the-best-intercoder-reliability-statistic-for-your-digital-activism-content-analysis/.

Kaste, Martin. 2012. "Newspaper Takes a Stand on Anonymous Commenters." NPR Online, July 31. http://www.npr.org/2012/07/31/157665460/shield-anonymous-commenters-more-papers-say-no.

Kenski, Kate, Kevin Coe, and Steve Rains. 2012. "Patterns and Determinants of Civility in Online Discussions." Report prepared for the National Institute of Civil Discourse at the University of Arizona. October 13. http://nicd.arizona.edu/research-report/patterns-and-determinants-civility.

Lau, Richard R., and Gerald M. Pomper. 2001. "Effects of Negative Campaigning on Turnout in U.S. Senate Elections, 1988–1998." *Journal of Politics* 63 (3): 804–819.

Light, Ann, and Yvonne Rogers. 1999. "Conversation as Publishing: The Role of News Forums on the Web." *Journal of Computer-Mediated Communication* 4 (4). doi:10.1111/j.1083-6101.1999.tb00103.x.

Loke, Jaime. 2012. "Public Expressions of Private Sentiments: Unveiling the Pulse of Racial Tolerance through Online News Readers' Comments." *Howard Journal of Communications* 23 (3): 235–252.

Lombard, Matthew, Jennifer Snyder-Duch, and Cheryl Campanella Bracken. 2010. "Practical Resources for Assessing and Reporting Intercoder Reliability in Content Analysis Research Projects." Matthew Lombard's website. http://matthewlombard.com/reliability/index_print.html.

Manseau, Peter. 2012. "Is This the Nastiest Election Ever?" *Campaign Stops* (blog), *New York Times*, September 27. http://campaignstops.blogs.nytimes.com/2012/09/27/is-this-the-nastiest-election-ever/?_php=true&_type=blogs&_r=0.

Montanaro, Domenico. 2012. "NBC/WSJ Poll: Obama Leads by 45 Points with Latinos. NBC News Online, October 22. http://firstread.nbcnews.com/_news/2012/10/22/14617456-nbcwsj-poll-obama-leads-by-45-points-with-latinos?lite.

Nekmat, Elmie, and William J. Gonzenbach. 2013. "Multiple Opinion Climates in Online Forums: Role of Website Source Reference and Within-Forum Opinion Congruency." *Journalism & Mass Communication Quarterly* 90 (4): 736–756.

Neuendorf, Kimberly A. 2002. *The Content Analysis Guidebook*. Thousand Oaks, CA: Sage.

O'Brien, Michael. 2012. "Romney's Task in Tampa: Sell Voters on Himself, Not Just against Obama." NBC News Online, August. 27. http://nbcpolitics.nbcnews.com/_news/2012/08/27/13508692-romneys-task-in-tampa-sell-voters-on-himself-not-just-against-obama?lite.

Papacharissi, Zizi. 2004. "Democracy Online: Civility, Politeness, and the Democratic Potential of Online Political Discussion Groups." *New Media Society* 6 (2): 259–283.

Parry-Giles, Trevor. 2010. "Resisting a 'Treacherous Piety': Issues, Images, and Public Policy Deliberation in Presidential Campaigns." *Rhetoric & Public Affairs* 13:37–64.

Pew Research Center for the People & the Press. 2012a. "Further Decline in Credibility Ratings for Most News Organizations." August 16. http://www.people-press.org/files/2012/08/8-16-2012-Media-Believability1.pdf.

———. 2012b. "Low Marks for 2012 Election." November 15. http://www.people-press.org/files/legacy-pdf/11-15-12%20Post%20Election.pdf.

"Politics of Insult Alive and Well Despite Obama's 2008 Lament." 2012. Fox News Online, October 29. http://www.foxnews.com/politics/2012/10/29/politics-insult-alive-and-well-despite-obama-2008-lament/.

Reader, Bill. 2012. "Free Speech vs. Free Speech? The Rhetoric of 'Civility' in Regard to Anonymous Online Comments." *Journalism and Mass Communication Quarterly* 89 (3): 495–513.

Rosenberry, Jack. 2011. "Users Support Online Anonymity Despite Increasing Negativity." *Newspaper Research Journal* 32 (2): 6–19.

Rothkopf, David. 2012. "Obama's Foreign Policy on Trial." CNN Online, October 22. http://www.cnn.com/2012/10/22/opinion/rothkopf-foreign-policy-debate/.

Ryan, Timothy J. 2012. "What Makes Us Click? Demonstrating Incentives for Angry Discourse with Digital-Age Field Experiments." *Journal of Politics* 74 (4): 1138–1152.

Sanders, Lynn M. 1997. "Against Deliberation." *Political Theory* 25:347–376.

Santana, Arthur D. 2011. "Online Readers' Comments Represent New Opinion Pipeline." *Newspaper Research Journal* 32 (3): 66–80.

Seitz, Matt Zoller. 2010. "Why I Like Vicious, Anonymous Online Comments." *Salon*, August 3. http://www.salon.com/2010/08/03/in_defense_of_anonymous_commenting/.

Smith, Aaron. 2013. "Civic Engagement in the Digital Age." Pew Research Center's Internet & American Life Project. April 25. http://www.pewinternet.org/~/media//Files/Reports/2013/PIP_CivicEngagementintheDigitalAge.pdf.

Sobieraj, Sarah, and Jeffrey M. Berry. 2011. "From Incivility to Outrage: Political Discourse in Blogs, Talk Radio, and Cable News." *Political Communication* 28:19–41.

Strandberg, Kim. 2008. "Public Deliberation Goes On-line? An Analysis of Citizens' Political Discussions on the Internet Prior to the Finnish Parliamentary Elections in 2007." *Javnost—The Public* 15 (1): 71–90.

Stroud, Natalie Jomini, Ashley Muddiman, Joshua Scacco, and Alex Curry. 2014. "Journalist Involvement in Comment Sections." Engaging News Project, Annette Strauss Institute for Civic Life at the University of Texas at Austin. http://engagingnewsproject.org/enp_2014/wp-content/uploads/2014/04/ENP_Comments_Report.pdf.

Thorson, Kjerstin, Emily Vraga, and Brian Ekdale. 2010. "Credibility in Context: How Uncivil Online Commentary Affects News Credibility." *Mass Communication and Society* 13 (3): 289–313.

Todd, Chuck, Mark Murray, Domenico Montanaro, and Brooke Bower. 2012. "First Thoughts: Battleground Ohio." NBC News Online, September 24. http://firstread.nbcnews.com/_news/2012/09/24/14067006-first-thoughts-battleground-ohio?lite.

Tracy, Karen. 2010. *Challenges of Ordinary Democracy: A Case Study in Deliberation and Dissent*. University Park: Pennsylvania State University Press.

Walker, Dan. 2012. "Press-Gazette Backs Romney, Wausau Daily Herald for Obama." *All Politics Blog, Milwaukee Journal Sentinel*, October 28. http://www.jsonline.com/blogs/news/176168941.html#!page=1&pageSize=10&sort=newestfirst.

Wallace, Gregory, Kevin Bohn, and Kevin Liptak. 2012. "Obama Campaign Unveils Response to Romney Auto Ad." *Political Ticker* (blog), CNN Online, October 29. http://politicalticker.blogs.cnn.com/2012/10/29/obama-campaign-unveils-response-to-romney-auto-ad/.

Zhuo, Julie. 2010. "Where Anonymity Breeds Contempt." *New York Times*, November 30.

Zickuhr, Kathryn. 2013. "Who's Not Online and Why." Pew Research Center's Internet & American Life Project. September 25. http://www.pewinternet.org/2013/09/25/whos-not-online-and-why/.

12

Sparking Debate

Campaigns, Social Media, and Political Incivility

DANIEL J. COFFEY, MICHAEL KOHLER, AND DOUGLAS M. GRANGER

The lack, or the perceived lack, of incivility in public discourse in the United States has become a subject of great concern.[1] Both participants in and observers of national politics believe that disrespectful and discourteous behavior is inhibiting the solution of pressing problems before the nation. The potential that political disagreements will spill over into civic life has led to some concerns that a breakdown of the social fabric or even violence may result. At the very least, there seems to be broad agreement that incivility is a threat to the health of the American political system.

Both theorists and empirical social scientists have argued that civility in public discourse serves as a foundation for the proper functioning of democracy. Civil debate has been linked to social and political trust, individual efficacy, and increased political participation. Constructive debate about pressing issues appears to necessitate a basic level of civility so that citizens can pursue their own interests with security and dignity through the democratic process. At the same time, social media promise new outlets for citizens to engage one another in public debates, especially to take a more participatory role in political campaigns. Certainly, there is no shortage of apostles promoting the transformative power of the Internet and Web 2.0 for finance, politics, entertainment, education, and just about any other area of life in which traditional institutions dominated (Shirky 2009; Freidman 2011). In theory, social media should allow citizens to take back campaigns from consultants and pundits and create a democratic environment in which more voices will be heard. If partisan bickering, negative campaigning, and polarization are products of an insular Washington politics, a more participatory environment should reduce the influence of the campaign industry and promote a more open discussion of political issues than the restricted set of voices that appears on the cable talk shows.

There is reason to suspect, however, in a polarized political environment, that social media may exacerbate differences and inhibit constructive debate (Hindman 2008). In this view, the influence of political elites may actually strengthen as online discussion forums serve to amplify the echo chamber of partisan politics. The social sciences have for some time shown that public attitudes are at least partially, if not mostly, influenced by elites (Key 1966; Zaller 1992). Elite influence via mass media has been shown to influence how the mass public conceptualizes issues and which issues are deemed salient by the public (Iyengar and Kinder 1982). Rather than replacing or revolutionizing how citizens acquire information, the development of social media may add volume to the messages originating with political elites.

In this chapter, we explore these questions by examining the effect of presidential campaigns on the nature of citizens' political discussions to explore how campaigns affect citizens' online discussions about politics. Most studies conceive of campaign effects on citizens in the specific sense of whether individual vote choice, engagement, or turnout is altered by communication from a candidate's campaign to a voter. In this case, however, the research concerns how campaigns affect individuals within a larger social context. Specifically, we examine whether living in a battleground state, with intense exposure to advertising, canvassing, visits, and media attention, affects the level of political incivility in online media forums.

The primary research question is whether the intense nature of political campaigns spills over into citizens' interactions. Social media provide many opportunities to enliven and open political debates. We suspect, however, that traditional dynamics are likely to still exert a force on citizens' attitudes. Although we conclude that campaign environments appear to intensify the incivility of discussions, we finish this chapter by examining a range of potential implications from this study and note that there may be several benefits from such discussions.

Defining Civility

It is valuable to consider what standards should be used to evaluate public online participation in the political campaigns. Ideally, campaigns engage citizens to participate in a vigorous debate of issues. Civility, in contrast, may coexist or even bolster these foundations but is not necessarily consistent with either the goal of participation or debate. Here, we define civility as a tone or display of respect and (or) courtesy toward other participants in public discourse (see Gutmann and Thompson 1996; Mutz and Reeves 2005; Sobieraj and Berry 2011). Such displays serve as a necessary foundation for constructive public debate about solving public-policy problems or at least advancing different views in an honest manner. On the one hand, civility is not just politeness or expressions of goodwill—as welcome as such things may be in public discourse. Rather, civility is conduct with broader public purposes of constructive debate. Indeed, to be vibrant, democracy requires substantive disagreements, vigorous advocacy of points of view, and cogent criticisms of alternative perspectives.

Civility is often identified as a core principle of democracy. Of course, democracy, almost by its very nature, brings forth disagreement among citizens, as noted by nearly every philosopher from ancient to modern theorists. Disagreement, especially partisan disagreement, however, should not be confused with a poorly functioning public sphere (Schattschneider 1960; Rosenblum 2010); the degree and tone of disagreement, however, can vary and is often taken as a sign of the health of a democracy (Huckfeldt, Johnson, and Sprague 2004). Yet many scholars agree that some parameters for disagreement must be established before the benefits of public debate can be achieved (Gutmann and Thompson 1996; Habermas 1989; Sunstein 2009).

As such, democratic societies must find ways to encourage citizens to voice different views, but in a way that will allow for mutual respect and the honest search for acceptable alternatives. This will not be easy in an era with more decentralized and open forms of participation. Even traditional political campaigns, by their very nature, tend to exacerbate the perceived differences between parties and candidates. Indeed, considerable research is now building in the field of political psychology that campaign appeals that tap into citizens' anger are more successful in producing citizens' participation than are appeals that tap into other emotions such as enthusiasm (Ryan 2012; Valentino et al. 2011). Recent research has shown that political attitudes, in an era of intense polarization, are becoming strongly linked to citizens' self-identity (Abramowitz 2011; Mason 2013). Threats to self-identity, provoked by new opportunities for interactions between citizens with different political views, should be expected to produce more hostile and less civil communication. In the next section, we discuss the opportunities and challenges provided by social media and review alternative theories that offer ways to evaluate these news forms of participation.

Democracy and Mass Online Participation

As noted earlier, social media and the Internet in general would appear to greatly expand the number of voices that can be heard in political debates. Indeed, advocates of new modes of communication, particularly online communication, often express a nearly missionary zeal for the revolutionary nature of the Internet. Campaigns have responded, finding that instead of relying on professional, top-down campaigns as they did in the 1980s, parties and their candidates can effectively use social networks to help turn out supporters, to generate contributions, and to spread campaign messages (Bai 2004; Sobieraj 2011; Issenberg 2012). Citizen-to-citizen appeals have been shown to be more effective forms of contact compared to contact by paid professionals (Green and Gerber 2008) Consequently, many political campaigns now invest heavily in developing volunteers, often through Internet-based activism (Karpf 2012).

Importantly, the development of social media means that citizens have many ways to participate in campaigns without necessarily being on a campaign.

Citizens can post their likes and dislikes on Facebook, help fundraise for campaigns online, forward important new stories to friends, tweet about campaigns, and comment on news websites.

So it is plausible that new forms of communication will alter how citizens are affected by political campaigns. Numerous studies have examined how communication is altered by a change in mode. For example, Diana Mutz (2007) found that exposure to television coverage of debates increases citizens' perceptions of policy differences and reduces their respect for the views of opponents. She found that this is the case because television tends to rely on extreme close-ups of discussants, which serves to increase viewers' attention and memory. Further, Matthew Baum and Tim Groeling (2008) found that new media such as web-based publications and blogs tend to be selective in a partisan manner, while traditional news wire services tend to be more neutral. Min analyzed face-to-face and online deliberation and found that both forms of communication increase feelings of efficacy: "Even in situations of opinion polarization or majority domination, there is some evidence that participants still learn new perspectives from others and empathize with others' views" (2007, 1382). Shanto Iyengar, Robert Luskin, and James Fishkin (2004) found that online deliberation can generate a positive effect on public opinion that is comparable to face-to-face deliberation.

Nevertheless, several studies have found that online communication loses many of the benefits of deliberation that occur in face-to-face settings. Considerable research indicates that the lack of face-to-face communication increases hostility in discussions. Kristin Byron (2008) found that emotions are much more easily misinterpreted in email compared to other forms of communication because emotional cues are often nonverbal, leading readers to misinterpret the sender's meaning. In particular, Byron found that messages were more likely to be perceived as negative even when the message was either nuetral or positive. Bryon did find that readers were more likey to correctly interpret nonemotional information. Similarly, Daniel Menchik and Xiaoli Tian (2008) found that online commmunciation tends to increase the chances for participants to misinterpret nonverbal cues. Email participants in their experiment had many problems correctly interpreting terminology and sorting the relevance of information contained in emails. The researchers did find that the use of emotional cues in writing, such as writing certain phrases in capital letters and putting quotation marks around certain phrases, improved the interpretation of emotional content. They concluded that people tend to be more aggressive when it comes to nonverbal communication than in face-to-face communication.

It is this online type of participation that we examine in this chapter. Most newspapers allow citizens to post comments online. In the past, such reactions were registered by letters to the editor. H. Christopher Cooper et al. (2009) found that letters to the editor are not a representative sample of general public opinion but that in general such letters represent general public opinion quite well. Online comments sections, though, have developed some notoriety. For example, Chmiel et al. (2011) found that user-generated comment threads for BBC News forums tended to be dominated by a relatively few discussants. The comments sections are well-known for containing rude comments and nasty exchanges. Ashley Anderson et al. (2013), in an experiment, found that readers easily polarize when discussing issues, even issues lacking political associations, and that those who are exposed to uncivil exchanges draw different interpretations of a story's meaning.

In general, newspaper editors often state that they are deeply troubled by the comments yet acknowledge that these forms of participation are valued by their readers. Many newspapers now actively moderate these exchanges, at times removing particularly vile comments and often requiring commenters to register before posting comments. *Popular Science*, for example, decided in 2013 to stop allowing readers to comment on stories (LaBarre 2013). Some research indicates that forcing commenters to register and have their names (or usernames) attached to comments increases the civility of these comments (Rowe 2013). In the next section, we explore how we might evaluate this new form of political participation.

Theories on Mass Participation and Deliberation

Existing studies and theories about democracy place great value on political participation (Dahl 1956; Pateman 1970; Rosenstone and Hansen 1993; Putnam 2000). The benefits of participation can be summarized as increasing trust and efficacy, fostering mutual respect and cooperation, and educating citizens about important issues and the political process. Carol Pateman (1970, 110) specifically claims that greater opportunities for participation in society will improve democracy:

> The existence of a participatory society would mean that [the citizen] was better able to assess the performance of representatives at the national level, better equipped to take decisions of national scope when the opportunity arose to do so, and better able to weigh the impact of decisions taken by national representatives on his own life and immediate surroundings. In the context of a participatory society the significance of his vote to the individual would have changed; as well as being a private individual, he would have multiple opportunities to become an educated, public citizen.

Democratic debates, however, are often presupposed to require more of participants than the expression of individual preferences. Amy Gutmann and Dennis Thompson (1996, 1) ask, how does (or can) a democracy deal with disagreement? They claim, "when citizens or their representatives disagree morally, they should continue to reason together to reach mutually acceptable decisions." Since Gutmann and Thompson are primarily concerned with what constitutes deliberative democracy—the content or substance of deliberation—they focus primarily on the demand of deliberative democracy to deal with moral disagreement in a pluralistic society.

The goal of deliberative democracy is not agreement but the construction of an environment in which opponents recognize the moral standing of those with whom they disagree. Gutmann and Thompson are concerned with the tendency of modern democracy to "communicate by soundbite" (1996, 12). In this state of affairs, moral conflict is either suppressed to avoid heated, complex, and often irresolvable moral debate, or it is dealt with by alternative mechanisms, such as bargaining, in which the resolution of moral conflict is reduced to deal making between self-interested parties or in which opposing sides demonize others' positions without taking those positions as moral judgments worthy of consideration.

Conversely, proponents of deliberative democracy place great faith in discussion among groups to breed the necessary mutual respect among opponents on moral issues. In their view, democratic institutions are "arenas of judgment and decision" where "individual and collective reason will converge" (Warren 1993, 212–213). Both serve to reinforce each other. Participation through reason giving increases an individual's sense of autonomy, which is produced by the affirmation of the individual's unique character and values. Reason giving produces a sense of difference from others but breeds mutual respect as individuals come to understand their own place within society by virtue of reciprocal respect.

There is tension, however, between the goals of participation and deliberation. Jürgen Habermas (1989), among others, is critical of the notion that individual preferences are fixed and argues that the conditions under which public debate takes place will affect how individual attitudes are expressed and understood. Although Habermas has generally supported participatory democracy, he notes that many of the forms of public participation have atrophied in the modern era (even prior to development of social media). Habermas places great faith on the value of open speech to help citizens publicly reason about issues, provided that speech is truly open and participants reason in good faith toward a common understanding.

Unfortunately, as Mutz (2006, 16) points out, "the best social environment for either one of these two goals [participation and deliberation] would naturally undermine the other." Even Robert Putnam (2000, 341) admits the danger of participatory democracy if participation is broken down into associational memberships:

> Voluntary organizations that are ideologically homogeneous may reinforce members' views and isolate them from potentially enlightening alternative viewpoints. In some cases such parochialism may nurture paranoia and obstruction.

In a polarized voluntary group universe, reasonable deliberation and bargaining toward a mutually acceptable compromise is well nigh impossible, as each side refuses "on principle" to give ground. Moreover, political polarization may increase cynicism about government's ability to solve problems and decrease confidence that civic engagement makes any difference.

Putnam specifically notes that studies performed by the Roper Center show that citizens with stronger ideological views are significantly more likely to participate in politics, while those with self-described "middle of the road" attitudes are significantly less likely to participate; moreover, the differences between these groups are increasing (342). Numerous other studies indicate that participation does not appear to yield the potential benefits that deliberative theorists claim should result from greater discussion. Cass Sunstein (2009), for example, cites several studies that find discussion can often produce *stronger* disagreement.

The Effect of Campaigns on Civic Discourse and the "Spillover" Hypothesis

The concerns outlined in the preceding section are amplified if citizens can isolate themselves into cocoons in which opinion homogeneity reinforces existing attitudes. The massive proliferation of information sources and discussion networks for contemporary citizens might have the perverse effect of increasing participation but reducing deliberation and mutual respect (Prior 2007; Stroud 2011). News shows frequently tap into this effect; Diana Mutz and Byron Reeves (2005) demonstrated in experiments that televised displays of incivility by politicians reduced experimental participants' political trust but that respondents rated such displays as more entertaining than did a control group that was exposed to the same disagreement but that did not witness the visual display of incivility.

The concern about incivility is in part because the increase in the number of ways for citizens to participate in politics is occurring at a time when political polarization is unusually high in the United States. Generally, there is a consensus that polarization can now be characterized as both elite and mass driven. Polarization is extensive among party activists and elected officials (Layman and Carsey 2002; McCarty, Poole, and Rosenthal 2006) and nearly equaled in the mass public (Bartels 2000; Hetherington 2001; Goren 2005; Abramowitz and Saunders 2008; Abramowitz 2011).

Citizens may seek participation in order to express different viewpoints, without an interest in compromise or reasoned deliberation; this is especially the case in an environment in which public attitudes are highly polarized. Indeed, some research indicates that individuals tend to seek disagreement and that the experience of encountering different views is psychologically rewarding (Huckfeldt,

Johnson, and Sprague 2004). The net result is that the growth of social media may spur on polarization, in turn undermining meaningful civic deliberation of issues. Studies in political science and social psychology have found that partisans, especially knowledgeable partisans, are especially adept at rejecting information that is inconsistent with their prior beliefs (Gaines et al. 2007; Taber and Lodge 2006). Political discussions are unlikely, in this environment, to promote meaningful deliberation and, in fact, may contribute to greater political incivility (Wolf, Strachan, and Shea 2012).

Campaign Effects on Social Media

Few studies have examined how new forms of Internet-based participation are affected by political campaigns. Presidential campaigns, especially in recent years, have pushed what many people feel are the limits of civil discourse and have created an environment in which vitriol is rampant and opposing sides view each other with suspicion or even hostility (Mutz 2007). Modern political campaigns frequently use attack advertising to denigrate not only the opposing candidates but the moral foundation of their beliefs, and in the heat of the campaign, campaign surrogates often disparage the supporters of the opposing candidate.[2] Indeed, recent research in social psychology finds that citizens' evaluations of opposing partisans are historically low (Hawkins and Nozick 2012).

In general, past research has found that campaigns have limited effects on individual citizens' attitudes (see Holbrook 1996 for a review of this research). In terms of social behavior, the effects of campaigns, particularly advertising, have been hypothesized, as noted earlier, but the question is a bit like the research on violent video games. It stands to reason that there should be some effect, but documenting this effect is empirically difficult. The orthodoxy of the "minimal effects model" suggests that campaigns are conducted in front of audiences that have already made up their minds or people not paying enough attention to be persuaded. Widespread inattention and limitations on the ability of citizens to conceptualize political information tends to reduce the impact of campaigns on voters' attitudes (Converse 1964).[3]

On the other hand, minimal effects are not the same as no effects, and social science research has documented examples of media and campaign effects in certain contexts. A broader definition of *effect*, beyond vote choice or single issue attitude, yields of a number of identifiable consequences. Shanto Iyengar and Donald Kinder (1982), for example, found that although media do not generally affect individual issue attitudes, media coverage of issues increases the salience of these issues in the public. In addition, some studies have found that campaigns increase citizens' knowledge about ballot issues (Smith and Tolbert 2004). In addition, advertising in particular has been linked to political engagement and vote choice. Donald Green and Alan Gerber (2008) found that campaign advertisements have strong but limited effects that dissipate within a few days without repeated exposure. Overall, then, media and campaigns have been shown to have potentially wide-ranging effects.

We can bring together our two strains of discussion on online participation and campaigns by examining how elite influence might affect discourse in social media. The belief that political elites can temper public discourse has been advocated from ancient theorists to modern social scientists. In the 1950s and 1960s, theories of opinion leadership in the fields of sociology and political science generally advocated that opinion leaders, with higher levels of education, a desire for influence, and a vested interest in the preservation of the status quo, served to interpret information from mass media for friends, family, and neighbors (Katz and Lazerfield 1955).

Campaigns largely work through media coverage, and together these have been shown to affect public perceptions of the salience of an issue and to help activate voter predispositions (Finkel 1993) by making considerations about an issue more accessible, often through issue framing (Miller and Krosnick 2000; Schneider and Jacoby 2005). Marc Hetherington (2001) identifies elite polarization as the causal mechanism for increasing partisan attachment in the public. If elites demonstrate uncivil behavior or voice intense disagreements, the extant research would indicate that the public should use these disagreements in developing their own views. We take this a step further by arguing that citizens will also respond to the tone of disagreement in a way similar to the pattern observed by Mutz and Reeves (2005). Recently, James Druckman, Erik Peterson, and Rune Slothuus showed that citizens respond to elite polarization: "When individuals engage in strong partisan motivated reasoning, they develop increased confidence in their opinions. This means they are less likely to consider alternative positions and more likely to take action based on their opinion. . . . In short, elite polarization fundamentally changes the manner in which citizens make decisions" (2013, 74). In sum, we expect elite polarization to uniquely affect citizen participants in online discussions when they participate in such discussions immediately after having read campaign messages.

Research Claim

We argue that the effects of citizens' exposure to campaign messages may spill over to their conversations and social civility in general. In a broader sense, this research addresses the question of how highly politicized environments affect citizens' interactions with each other. Campaign effects can be thought of as wider than just how citizens decide how to cast a ballot. Indeed, research indicates that social networks and interpersonal conversations have strong effects on citizens (Mutz 2007). Paul Beck et al. (2002) show that media effects are weaker than those of interpersonal discussions.[4] Consequently, we predict that citizens participating in online discussions during a political campaign will have more uncivil discussions than will citizens participating in discussions outside a campaign environment.

We further expect these effects to be greater in places where campaigns are most intense. Current research indicates that citizens are more affected by campaigns in battleground states, in comparison to citizens who do not live in battleground states. In general, citizens in battleground states are exposed to much higher levels of media, which in turn affects the acquisition of political knowledge and has been shown to lead to higher levels of interest and the likelihood of voting (McClurg and Holbrook 2009). Quin Monson, Kelly Patterson, and Jeremy Pope (2011) showed that citizens in battleground states were more likely to vote along partisan lines and that campaigns serve to strengthen partisan identities (although see Wolak 2006).

Thus, social media bring together two factors to produce the effect we hypothesize. We posit that citizens in battleground states, having absorbed more campaign messages and being primed to see the candidates as starkly different, will be more uncivil in their interactions than will citizens in less intense environments. As noted earlier, considerable research demonstrates that interpersonal discussions have strong effects on participants, more so than television and radio commercials, direct mail, or robocalls, the typical vehicles of campaign messages. So participants in online discussions, having been primed by just having read elite comments about the campaign in the newspaper, should be more willing to argue with those with whom they disagree. To make an analogy with epidemiology, the pathogen is contained in the article, and its contagious effects are passed along through the online discussion.[5]

In this way, the online discussion independently causes more heated and uncivil conversations. By contrast, citizens in less intense settings should receive fewer messages and be less likely to perceive strong differences between candidates. With less priming and less emotion (again, we stress, relative to battleground citizens), citizens are less likely to come into contact with contagion and also less likely to spread their own emotions.[6]

We acknowledge that these effects are in some ways limited to those who read the article and comment. This is, however, the heart of our research claim; in the days before social media, the causal mechanism for spreading campaign effects from person to person was limited as citizens largely acquired campaign information passively in their own living rooms through nightly news broadcasts and television commercials. A viewer might have a strong reaction to a television commercial but would have time between the viewing of the commercial and the watercooler discussion at the office the next day or the weekend soccer game. In the current environment, social media allow citizens to respond to each other directly and immediately, and thus, campaign effects are intensified through new forms of interpersonal contact.

Sample Selection and Study Design

To test the spillover hypothesis, we selected articles appearing in major newspapers in two states, Wisconsin and Ohio. Using a quasi-experimental design, we aimed to capture unfiltered citizen reactions to the campaigns in different environments, one where the campaign was intense and one where the presidential campaign was contested but not to the same degree. In October 2012, all political stories appearing in the *Cleveland Plain Dealer* and the *Milwaukee Journal Sentinel* were collected, and users' posted comments were coded.

According to the hypothesis, citizens in Ohio should show greater levels of incivility than do citizens in Wisconsin, since in Ohio, citizens were inundated with messages from campaigns, while there was less exposure in Wisconsin. We have selected Ohio because it is arguably the single most intensely contested state in presidential elections, receiving the most commercials, campaign visits, and campaign spending among the "battleground" states year after year. For the sake of comparison, we needed a state that was less contested but still had a similar demographic makeup to try to control for regional or socioeconomic differences. To provide some degree of matching, we selected Wisconsin, which is similar to Ohio in many respects; it is an industrial midwestern state along the Great Lakes with a history of balanced political competition between Republicans and Democrats. The primary difference is that in recent years, while Ohio has flipped back and forth between voting Democratic or Republican in presidential elections, Wisconsin has increasingly become a "blue" state in presidential elections, even as the state government remains in Republican hands. Ohio, then, fits our case of an intensely polarized political environment in a presidential election, while Wisconsin fits our need for a "control" in that the political environment will be relatively less contested.[7]

To be sure, with Paul Ryan on the ticket, Wisconsin was one of the final contested states. If anything, however, this provides a more difficult test of the hypothesis. In addition, earlier in the year, Wisconsin received considerable national attention when a recall effort failed to turn Republican governor Scott Walker out of office due to his support of a bill that eliminated collective bargaining for public employees. The same was true in Ohio, however; in the previous year, Ohioans had voted down a referendum on a law eliminating collective bargaining for public employees in a campaign that had also received substantial national attention.

Despite the highly politicized environment of the previous year, Ohio and Wisconsin were very different media markets during the presidential election and the time period for this study. In the presidential election, Ohio had more candidate visits, more campaign ads, and more money spent within the state than Wisconsin did by large margins. While $150 million was spent on campaign ads in Ohio, only $39 million was spent in Wisconsin. In the last month of the campaign, Ohio saw 82 visits by the candidates, their running mates, and their wives, while Wisconsin had 28. The Obama campaign had 131 field offices in the state, compared to 69 for Wisconsin. Romney had 40 offices in Ohio, compared to 24 in Wisconsin. For top events during the "peak season," Romney held 45 in Ohio, compared to just 7 in Wisconsin, and Obama held 28 in Ohio and 11 in Wisconsin. During the last week of the campaign, six Ohio markets were in the top 20 for advertising, while only two Wisconsin markets ranked in the top 20 (Wesleyan Media Project 2012).

We acknowledge that there are limitations to the findings. We do not know how much campaign information the commenters were exposed to, nor do we know much about their partisan affiliation or demographic traits. Indeed, we cannot say for certain that the commenters were living in Ohio or Wisconsin at the time. We will further explore the limitations of this study design in the conclusion. Although this research design is not perfect, it is well designed to capture the effects of the campaign in different contexts. Overall, however, this is a nonreactive observer study, and such studies provide great benefits for analysis. Although such studies often do not allow researchers to exercise direct experimental control, they allow researchers to examine individual behaviors as they occur naturally (Webb et al. 1966). As a result, the external validity of the research design is protected, and participants, unaware of their participation, do not alter their behavior or opinions due to some unintended intervention by the researcher.

Certainly, respondents to newspaper articles are a select group and may already have polarized viewpoints, as noted earlier. In addition, as also noted earlier, the nature of online discussions tends to promote more uncivil or confrontational behavior. Of course, these concerns do not differentiate the discussions in the different states, and the research hypothesis specifically predicts that one set of online discussion threads will be more heated *relative* to the other.

In addition, the research design may not fully capture the effect of the campaign. The national nature of presidential campaigns means that geographic location may not exert the same degree of control as in a typical quasi-experimental design. Consequently, the research design may underestimate the effect of living in a different campaign environment, as citizens are receiving information from national outlets and participants could be from outside the geographic area.

The quasi-experimental design is useful, however, because it specifically allows for a test of the differential effect predicted by the hypothesis. The states are both industrial midwestern states with similar demographic compositions. This allows for some measure of control to test the effect of campaigns on political civility.

Data and Analysis

We coded stories and the associated reader comments appearing in the *Cleveland Plain Dealer* and the *Milwaukee Journal Sentinel* in October 2012. We coded user comments on a 1 to 5 scale, where 1 was coded as "very civil" and 5 was coded as "very uncivil." Comments were coded as a 1 or 2 if they were noncontroversial, were factual observations, or otherwise helped to soften the tone of the discussion. In many cases, posters complimented other posts or tried to lighten the discussion thread with a joke. Statements were coded as a 3 if they contained argumentative statements or opinions but were neutral in tone. Statements were coded as a 4 if they were combative and enticed a response, were critical of another poster's comment, or contained harsh comments about political officials or public policies. Statements were coded as a 5 if they contained personal attacks, accusations, inflammatory language, or name-calling or endorsed conspiracy theories about candidates or parties.[8] Accordingly, our first hypothesis predicts that the comments posted by readers in the *Cleveland Plain Dealer* will be more uncivil than the comments posted by readers of the *Milwaukee Sentinel Journal*.

We applied the same coding scheme to comments in the story by political elites, such as government officials and officeholders, campaign consultants or spokespersons, or commentators and pundits. This allows for a more precise test of our "spillover hypothesis"; in articles in which comments by elites are more heated, we suspect we will see comment threads that are similarly more heated. Classical political science, however, also posits that elites tone down public debate. This calls for two tests to be performed; first, whether elite comments are more civil than the responses they engender by the public and, second, whether there is a correlation between the two. As a result, we have two related predictions: that comments posted by readers in both media markets will be more uncivil than are the comments of political elites quoted in the newspaper stories and that the average incivility of the quotes of political elites in the newspaper stories will be positively related to the mean incivility of the comment threads.

Finally, as a control, we took into account the overall contentiousness of the stories. Some campaign reports are on difficult topics or high-profile events, and statements should engender widespread controversy. Comment threads for these stories should be more heated than those for fluff pieces of, say, a candidate's surprise visit to a local diner. Therefore, our final hypothesis predicts that the content of the newspaper story predicts the civility of comments posted by readers.

We collected 90 articles from the *Plain Dealer* and 51 articles from the *Journal Sentinel*. On average, there were 104 comments per *Plain Dealer* article and 172 comments per *Journal Sentinel* article.[9] Not every story generated user comments, and the range of comments per story was similar, from 0 to over 1,000 for both the *Plain Dealer* and *Journal Sentinel* as seen in figure 12.1.

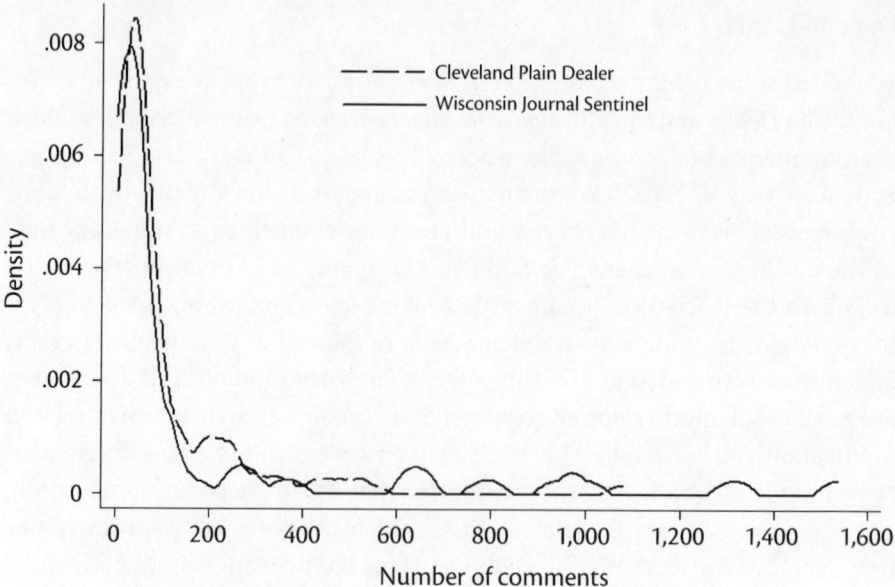

Figure 12.1. Kernell density plot of comments by newspaper

In addition, to help establish a baseline for the comments' civility level, we used the results from a similar study conducted in the spring of 2011. With the help of two research assistants, 65 stories appearing in the *Cleveland Plain Dealer* between January and April 2011 were coded. The average number of comments per story was 39, with a range of 1 to 295.

Discussion of Results

The initial results indicate support for our first hypothesis; the comments in the *Plain Dealer* are more uncivil in tone than those in the *Journal Sentinel*. The average score for the *Plain Dealer* comments was 3.29, and the average for the *Journal Sentinel* was 2.94.[10] Since each newspaper had a sample size of over 9,000 comments (18,000 overall), the 95% confidence interval is quite narrow (.01) for both papers, and it is fairly easy to reject the null hypothesis that the average for the two papers is identical. These figures surely understate the level of incivility since highly problematic posts were excluded by the website managers. Indeed, many stories were Associated Press stories that were virtually printed identically in both papers. As a result, the observed differences are particularly noteworthy in that it is difficult to claim that aspects of the stories themselves really account for the differences. Moreover, the contentiousness rating of the stories was nearly identical for the two papers, adding a further measure of confidence to the validity of the findings.

Moreover, the political campaign appears to have modestly increased the incivility of the comments among the Ohio readership; the average incivility of the *Plain Dealer* comments in the spring of 2011 was 3.171. With 2,526 comments, the standard error is .03, and so the null hypothesis that the civility level intervals overlap for the *Plain Dealer* at the two different time points can be rejected. It is, however, fairly close. I suspect a major reason for this is that during the spring of 2011, Ohio was the center of a national debate over union rights (just as Wisconsin was), and efforts to repeal Senate Bill 5 were well under way. Consequently, in this quasi-campaign environment, the incivility of the comments makes sense. Importantly, the stories in the spring 2011 sample were more contentious compared to the stories appearing in the presidential election (see table 12.1). Many of the stories in the fall of 2012 simply reported candidates' appearances (for both the *Plain Dealer* and *Journal Sentinel*), and these stories generally had muted comment threads. Since this was not the case for the spring 2011 *Plain Dealer* stories, I suspect the coding may underestimate the difference between the campaign and noncampaign environments.

The results show that the stories were similar in many respects, and so the comparisons are valid, as indicated by table 12.1. The papers had similar numbers of elite quotes, with the *Journal Sentinel* having slightly more per article. The civility of elite quotes in the news stories subject to the comment posts were much more civil in their discourse, with less than one-tenth making uncivil statements, using the same standards as used for the posts. As shown in table 12.1, readers were much more likely to make uncivil comments compared to elites quoted in the articles. Consequently, there is strong support for our hypothesis that reader comments are more uncivil than are comments made by political elites.

Table 12.1. Summary Statistics for Newspaper Comment Coding

	Cleveland Plain Dealer 2011	*Cleveland Plain Dealer* October 2012	*Milwaukee Sentinel Journal* October 2012
Stories	67	90	52
Mean number of reader comments per story	38.86 (55.53)	103.8 (153.71)	182.31 (350.45)
Mean civility of reader comments	3.17 (.56)	3.29 (.51)	2.94 (.88)
Mean number of elite quotes	1.89 (2.35)	3.89 (4.33)	5.72 (4.90)
Mean civility of elite quotes	1.95 (1.25)	2.11 (.82)	2.13 (.70)
Mean contentiousness of story	3.14 (1.60)	2.44 (1.14)	2.44 (.77)

Note: Standard deviations in parentheses

In terms of what drove different numbers of comments, an increasing level of incivility as the number of comments increases was correlated with the comments in the *Plain Dealer* but not the *Journal Sentinel*. The *Plain Dealer* pattern is consistent with the finding of Chmiel et al. (2011) that threads are driven largely by expressions of negative emotions; this pattern was true for the *Plain Dealer* in the spring of 2011. Our third hypothesis, then, cannot be confirmed, but there is some support for this claim.

To avoid comparing apples and oranges, we estimated a simple regression model using the story factors as control variables. The story was the unit of analysis, and the dependent variable was the average comment civility rating for each story. A dummy variable for the paper was added for the newspaper, with the *Journal Sentinel* serving as the baseline. This resulted in a sample of 103 total cases, as some cases were dropped due to the lack of candidate or other elite quotes.

The results show that controlling for contentiousness, elite comments, and the overall number of user comments, comments in the *Plain Dealer* were more uncivil than those in the *Journal Sentinel*. The coefficient of .26 means that the comments on a story in the *Plain Dealer* would be noticeably more uncivil than those on a story in the *Journal Sentinel* to a reader browsing or participating in the comment threads. Indeed, a qualitative review of the comments between the papers reveals a more contentious tone in many threads in the *Plain Dealer*. Posters tended to more frequently make personal comments about previous posts, relative to those posts in the *Journal Sentinel*.

In addition, the results also confirm our final hypothesis. That is, elite civility is positively related to the comment civility of the readers. This was true in both

Table 12.2. OLS Model of User Comment Mean Civility per News Article

Variable	*Plain Dealer* and *Journal Sentinel*
Contentiousness of story	−.03
	(.05)
Number of elite quotes	−.01
	(.01)
Number of comments	.00
	(.00)
Avg. quote civility	.21**
	(.08)
Plain Dealer	.40**
	(.09)
Constant	2.59
	(.22)
Adjusted R^2	.21
Sample size	102

Notes: Dependent variable is the average civility of user comments per story, where: 1 = very civil and 5 = very uncivil. Robust standard errors in parentheses: * $p < .05$, ** $p < .01$

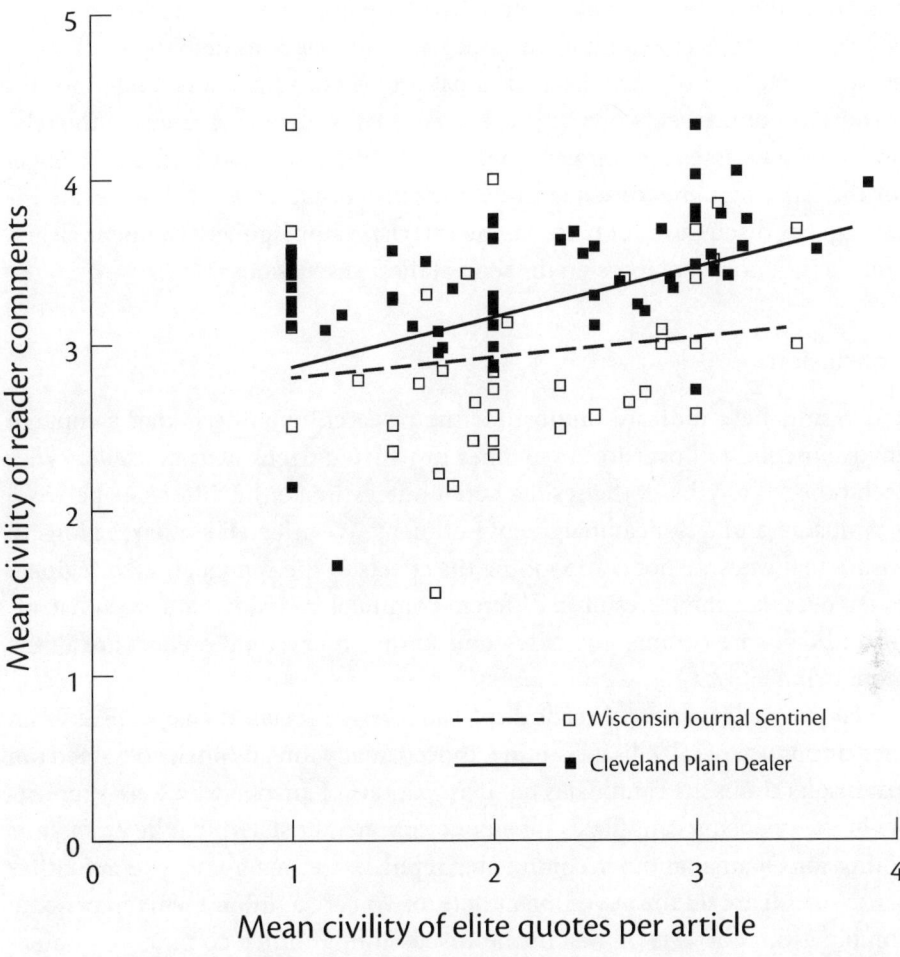

Figure 12.2. Relationship between elite civility and reader comment civility

papers. Although elite comments were more muted, they were more contentious than in the results from the 2011 study, as seen in table 12.1. As noted, this was most common in the stories reporting on the debate, in which the candidates were not particularly civil toward each other. In addition, the correlation between the overall number of comments for a story and the civility rating of the elite quotes is positively correlated, indicating support for the "spillover" hypothesis. So even if the campaigns are conducted at different levels of intensity, the underlying mechanical process proposed by the theory is that messages from the campaign influence citizens' behavior. That is, when elites were more uncivil in the tone they used, commenters were similarly more uncivil.

Evidence for this finding can be seen in figure 12.2. For the readership of both the *Plain Dealer* and the *Journal Sentinel*, an increase in the incivility of political elites is positively related to increasing incivility of the comments posted by readers of the stories. To be fair, in particularly long threads, the readers often go well beyond the content of the story and diverge into new topics. This is, however, not true of most discussion patterns. Instead, readers tended to stay within the bounds set by the article. Moreover, as shown in figure 12.2, the relationship between elite comments and reader comments is identifiably stronger for the *Plain Dealer*. Consequently, while we hypothesize that elites prime the subsequent discussions of citizens, the external campaign environment clearly also exerts a powerful force on the tone of these discussions.

Conclusion

The results here indicate support for the research hypothesis that campaign environments spill over to the manner in which citizens discuss politics with each other. If anything, the results here underestimate the difference between a campaign and a noncampaign environment. We selected similar regions to ensure that we were not confounding the effects of the campaign with regional differences that might result in different commenter civility patterns. Wisconsin and Ohio are comparable states, and so the observed differences are all the more striking.

Many of the comment threads displayed levels of incivility that were at times shocking and generally disappointing. Indeed, many threads often contained not just insults about the candidates but denigrations of anyone who were supporters of the opposing candidate. When one commenter stated that he or she was voting for Obama, another commenter replied, "Let me guess, you are either black, or you are on the government dole, or you are a union member, or some combination, correct?" Later in the discussion, another commenter stated, "Anti-American, anti-constitutional and yet the blind mice still support their leader despite the worse record in history. Given how much support they give the Muslim Brotherhood I don't don't obama is most likely a muslim. Sharia law awaits."[11] This was met with, "Although you try and project [Obama] to be something he isn't, we know what your candidate is . . . a member of a cult."

Terms such as "idiots" and "morons" were commonly used. Commenters often insulted each other, and threads frequently digressed about trivial points or claims impossible to substantiate. Many commenters expressed exaggerated fears about the consequences of the outcome of the election if the preferred candidate did not win. Many commenters reasoned that if their candidate did not win, the American people were "ignorant" or being somehow deceived.

The analysis here is somewhat pessimistic about the virtue of social media. It is important to note, however, that the comments on both websites contain examples of thoughtful discourse and civility. The presidential campaign was intense, and the greatest number of comments appeared in stories about the presidential debates when the candidates were not particularly civil themselves. Many comments, although negative in tone, contained detailed arguments about public policies. Although some facts may have been dubious, the commenters did appear to be reaching toward the deliberative goal of honest persuasion or the use of objective information to state a point. Many comments were very lengthy and contained external links to factual sources such as poll results. One comment was typical of a relatively open-minded attempt to reason in a respectful and yet passionate manner, an approach that is called for by deliberative theorists:

> It depends on where you live in this country. Some regions and job sectors are producing slow gains others are painstakingly slow. If you vote just based on what is going on outside your front door it necessarily may not be helping all of America. I have 3 grown children and they are employed in three very different job sectors. From oldest to youngest child these are their jobs. U.S. Military career/active duty; Executive Officer in Non-Profit Organization; Laborer/Consultant for a Private Landscape Construction. The youngest child working for the private company is financially doing the best. The middle child has been living on a stagnant salary for four years. Both are 2 parent-adult homes. The middle child has 2 kids & mortgage. One has no children and rents. They pay their bills and loans on time. Both have health insurance through their employers. Only the youngest makes enough to be able to save, have an IRA, and take vacations and afford to go out socially. Their college loans are paid and they have a baby fund started. The oldest child's salary is preset. Additional pay has come from promotions, 3 combat years deployment periods, boots on the ground pay, airborne supplement (jump pay). Under Obamacare their health care insurance has less coverages for theirself and their family of 4 people. Many personnel are forgoing it and buying private health insurance. The deep Defense budget cuts will affect their work and the productivity and capableness of their duty. This affect & the health insurance cuts are unacceptable to me. But I'm just the mom. The soldier never complains, they just follow orders! They all work hard but the the middle child is not equally able to save for their future & their kids college funds. The salary stagnation is completely imbalanced to the cost of the living increases that have occurred over the past years. For the next four years I will give Governor Romney a chance. My vote is for my kids & grandkids, my soon to be retired spouse, my elderly parents, and myself hanging in there approaching 58 years.

Although there is considerable angst about incivility in politics, we are reminded of James Madison's argument in *Federalist* 10. Most people remember this as an essay about humanity's factional nature, but his real point was that with carefully designed processes, democratic citizens can reason their way toward "justice and the greater good," provided there are institutional mechanisms in place to produce deliberation.

The problem posed by new forms of online media is that they may promote disagreement without providing these necessary mechanisms to find common agreement. Participants in online forums often post anonymously, and respondents, by virtue of the new technologies, can post instantly. Considerable research in social psychology demonstrates that the effect of removing face-to-face contact tends to undermine empathy and produces misunderstandings. Posting comments without further thought or interaction, without the responsibility of placing one's name next to a post, encourages recklessness and incivility. James Fishkin (1995, 146–150) argues that the promise of deliberative democracy requires "social capital" to make such an experiment reality. Without a "dense network of civic associations" (146), it is not possible to sufficiently engage citizens to care seriously enough about the mutual interest they have in solving problems collectively.

We stress, however, that there are a number of question we cannot answer through this research, and we urge some caution in interpreting any studies on the "effects" of social media usage. Due to the nature of the research, we cannot say anything about the individuals participating in the online discussions. For example, perhaps this participation is related to engagement, and those who participate in intense discussions are more likely to vote, contribute, and stay informed. What are the medium- and long-term effects? We are capturing immediate emotional responses, but perhaps those who are participating undergo some opinion change in the time after participating. Moreover, Robert Huckfeldt, Paul Johnson, and John Sprague (2004) and R. Kelly Garrett, Dustin Carnahan, and Emily Lynch (2013) document that in an age of selective media exposure, there is value to being exposed to dissonant opinions, and these forums make it clear that citizens are being exposed to a variety of viewpoints. Finally, participants may feel psychologically rewarded having blown off steam; on occasion, frequent posters often announced their presence and were welcomed by those who would then begin an immediate barrage of comments aimed at their fellow commenter.[12]

It should be noted that voter turnout is increasing through much of the nation, and while this may have as much to do with more opportunities and time to cast ballots, citizens' engagement in elections and politics does appear to be increasing. Social media does not by itself undermine deliberation, but it does have a darker side that requires attention from public-policy scholars. Perhaps with more time to become accustomed to new technology, individuals will become more judicious in their use of these technologies. Many newspapers are now requiring individuals to register to post comments, and this tends to reduce some of the most egregious cases of incivility. With time and more experience, the "social capital" needed to fulfill the hopes of participatory and deliberative democracy may be achieved by the new forms of social media.

Notes

1. The authors would like to thank John Green and Tim Hatton for assistance with various aspects of the research. Partial research support was provided by the Ralph Regula Center for Public Service, the Ray C. Bliss Institute of Applied Politics, and the Maxine Goodman Levine College of Urban Affairs.
2. There is a huge volume of research on the effects on negative advertising on citizens. The research is mixed on its effects (see Geer 2006 and Ansolabehere and Iyengar 1995). This is a different question than whether campaigns make use of attacks as part of their strategy.
3. Such findings are generalized by John Zaller (1992), whose theory of public opinion formation specifies that citizens have inverse probabilities of receiving and accepting new information.
4. Beck et al.'s study, however, specifies the question in an either/or sense. We argue instead that media and interpersonal conversations both have the potential to impact citizens and that social media combine both types of effects.
5. This is just an analogy, and the language is not meant as a commentary on the state of campaigns.
6. See Christakis and Fowler 2009 on how emotions can be spread from person to person.
7. We had considered Indiana, but none of the major newspapers would have allowed us access to reader comments. Illinois is in some ways sui generis among midwestern states because of Chicago. Minnesota has a far different political culture than Ohio and would not make a good comparison. Other midwestern states were too rural to serve as valid cases for matching.
8. Both newspapers have policies for removing especially inflammatory remarks. Such policies may lead us to underestimate the incivility of the user comments but are a threat to the research claim only if the policies are enforced differently by the papers. The papers do not release such comments, and so we cannot ascertain if their polices are enforced differently. We estimate that approximately 1 out of every 20 comments are removed from each paper.
9. We were unable to code nine articles for the *Journal Sentinel* and one for the *Plain Dealer* since the associated comments could not be found.
10. The intercoder reliability score was calculated using the SPSS Macro developed by Andrew Hayes (see Hayes and Krippendorff 2007). Ten percent (15 articles) were recoded independently. Krippendorff's alpha reliability was calculated as .65. These measures are sometimes hard to evaluate, but a more intuitive (but less rigorous) way is the correlation between the mean article civility rating between the independent coders. In this case, the Pearson correlation was .78, suggesting that the overall scores were coded in consistent manner. Another way to evaluate this is to consider the hypothesis at stake; if all the articles were switched initially between the three authors, would the civility scores for the *Plain Dealer* have overlapped with the *Journal Sentinel*? The results here strongly suggest that this is not the case that and the results do not reflect coding error.
11. Comments are reported without alteration; we are left to wonder if the greater threat to democracy is incivility or poor grammar.
12. Indeed, during Superstorm Sandy, several participants asked, with apparent genuine concern, about commenters who had not posted in a few days.

References

Abramowitz, Alan I. 2011. *The Disappearing Center: Engaged Citizens, Polarization, and American Democracy*. New Haven: Yale University Press.

Abramowitz, Alan I., and Kyle L. Saunders. 2008. "Is Polarization Really a Myth?" *Journal of Politics* 70:542–555.

Anderson, Ashley A., Dominique Brossard, Dietram A. Scheufele, Michael A. Xenos, and Peter Ladwig. 2013. "The 'Nasty Effect': Online Incivility and Risk Perceptions of Emerging Technologies." *Journal of Computer-Mediated Communication* 19 (2014): 373–387.

Ansolabehere, Stephen, and Shanto Iyengar. 1995. *Going Negative: How Political Advertisements Shrink and Polarize the Electorate*. New York: Free Press.

Bai, Matt. 2004. "The Multilevel Marketing of the President." *New York Times Magazine*, April 25.

Bartels, Larry M. 2000. "Partisanship and Voting Behavior, 1952–1996." *American Journal of Political Science* 44:35–50.

Baum Matthew A., and Tim Groeling. 2008. "New Media and the Polarization of American Political Discourse." *Political Communication* 25:345–365.

Beck, Paul Allen, Russell J. Dalton, Steven Greene, and Robert Huckfeldt. 2002. "The Social Calculus of Voting: Interpersonal, Media, and Organizational Influences on Presidential Choices." *American Political Science Review* 96:57–73.

Byron, Kristin. 2008. "Carrying Too Heavy a Load? The Communication and Miscommunication of Emotion by Email." *Academy of Management Review* 33:309–327.

Chmiel, Anna, Pawel Sobkowicz, Julian Sienkiewicz, Georgios Paltoglou, Kevan Buckley, Mike Thelwall, and Janusz A. Holyst. 2011. "Negative Emotions Boost Users Activity at BBC Forum." *Physica A* 390:2936–2944.

Christakis, Nicholas A., and James H. Fowler. 2009. *Connected: The Surprising Power of Social Networks and How They Shape Our Lives*. New York: Little, Brown.

Converse, Philip E. 1964. "The Nature of Belief Systems in Mass Publics." In *Ideology and Discontent*, edited by David E. Apter, 206–261. New York: Free Press.

Cooper, H. Christopher, Gibbs Knotts, and Moshe Haspel. 2009. "The Content of Political Participation: Letters to the Editor and the People Who Write Them." *PS: Political Science & Politics* 42:131–137.

Dahl, Robert. 1956. *A Preface to Democracy*. Chicago: University of Chicago Press.

Druckman, James M., Erik Peterson, and Rune Slothuus. 2013. "How Elite Partisan Polarization Affects Public Opinion Formation." *American Political Science Review* 107:57–79.

Finkel, Steven E. 1993. "Reexamining the 'Minimal Effects' Model in Recent Presidential Campaigns." *Journal of Politics* 55:1–21.

Fishkin, James S. 1995. *The Voice of the People*. New Haven: Yale University Press.

Friedman, Thomas. 2011. "Make Way for the Radical Center." *New York Times*, July 23.

Gaines, Brian J., James H. Kuklinski, Paul J. Quirk, Buddy Peyton, and Jay Verkuilen. 2007. "Interpreting Iraq: Partisanship and the Meaning of Facts." *Journal of Politics* 69:957–974.

Garrett, R. Kelly, Dustin Carnahan, and Emily K. Lynch. 2013. "A Turn toward Avoidance? Selective Exposure to Online Political Information, 2004–2008." *Political Behavior* 35:113–134.

Geer, John. 2006. *In Defense of Negativity: Attack Ads in Presidential Campaigns*. Chicago: University of Chicago Press.

Goren, Paul. 2005. "Party Identification and Core Political Values." *American Journal of Political Science* 49:881–896.

Green, Donald, and Alan Gerber. 2008. *Get Out the Vote: How to Increase Voter Turnout*. Washington, DC: Brooking Institution Press.

Gutmann, Amy, and Dennis Thompson. 1996. *Democracy and Disagreement*. Cambridge: Harvard University Press.

Habermas, Jürgen. 1989. *The Structural Transformation of the Public Sphere: An Inquiry into a Category of Bourgeois Society*. Cambridge: MIT Press.

Hawkins, Carlee B., and Brian A. Nozick. 2012. "Motivated Independence? Implicit Party Identity Predicts Political Judgments among Self-Proclaimed Independents." *Personality and Social Psychology Bulletin* 38:1441–1455.

Hayes, Andrew F., and Klaus K. Krippendorff. 2007. "Answering the Call for a Standard Reliability Measure for Coding Data." *Communication Methods and Measures* 1:77–89.

Hetherington, Marc J. 2001. "Resurgent Mass Partisanship: The Role of Elite Polarization." *American Political Science Review* 95:619–632.

Hindman, Matthew. 2008. *The Myth of Digital Democracy*. Princeton: Princeton University Press.

Holbrook, Thomas M. 1996. *Do Campaigns Matter?* Thousand Oaks, CA: Sage.

Huckfeldt, Robert, Paul E. Johnson, and John Sprague. 2004. *Political Disagreement: The Survival of Diverse Opinions within Communication Networks*. New York: Cambridge University Press.

Issenberg, Sasha. 2012. *The Victory Lab: The Secret Science of Winning Campaigns*. New York: Crown.

Iyengar, Shanto, and Donald Kinder. 1982. *News That Matters: Television and American Opinion*. Chicago: University of Chicago Press.

Iyengar, Shanto, Robert C. Luskin, and James S. Fishkin. 2004. "Deliberative Public Opinion in Presidential Primaries: Evidence from the Online Deliberative Poll." Paper presented at the conference "Voice and Citizenship: Re-thinking Theory and Practice in Political Communication," University of Washington, April 23–24.

Karpf, David. 2012. *The MoveOn Effect: The Unexpected Transformation of American Political Advocacy*. New York: Oxford University Press.

Katz, Elihu and Paul F. Lazerfeld. 1955. *Personal Influence: The Part Played by People in the Flow of Mass Communication*. The Free Press: New York.

Key, V. O. 1966. *The Responsible Electorate: Rationality in Presidential Voting, 1936–60*. Cambridge: Belknap Press of Harvard University Press.

LaBarre, Suzanne. 2013. "Why We Are Shutting Off Our Comments." *Popular Science*, September 24. http://www.popsci.com/science/article/2013-09/why-were-shutting-our-comments.

Layman, Geoffrey, and Thomas Carsey. 2002. "Party Polarization and 'Conflict Extension' in the American Electorate." *American Journal of Political Science* 46:786–802.

Mason, Lilliana. 2013. "The Rise of Uncivil Agreement: Issue versus Behavioral Polarization in the American Electorate." *American Behavioral Scientist* 57:140–159.

McCarty, Nolan, Keith T. Poole, and Howard Rosenthal. 2006. *Polarized America: The Dance of Ideology and Unequal Riches*. Cambridge: MIT Press.

McClurg, Scott D., and Thomas M. Holbrook. 2009. "Living in a Battleground: Presidential Campaigns and the Activation of 'Fundamental' Considerations." *Political Research Quarterly* 62:495–506.

Menchik, Daniel A., and Xiaoli Tian. 2008. "Putting Social Context into Text: The Semiotics of E-mail Interaction." *American Journal of Sociology* 114:332–370.

Miller, Joanne M., and Jon A. Krosnick. 2000. "News Media Impact on the Ingredients of Presidential Evaluations: Politically Knowledgeable Citizens Are Guided by a Trusted Source." *American Journal of Political Science* 44:295–309.

Min, Seong-Jae. 2007. "Online vs. Face-to-Face Deliberation: Effects on Civic Engagement." *Journal of Computer-Mediated Communication* 12:1369–1387.

Monson, J. Quin, Kelly D. Patterson, and Jeremy C. Pope. 2011. "The Campaign Context for Partisan Stability." In *The State of the Parties*, 6th ed., ed. John C. Green and Daniel J. Coffey, 271–288. Lanham, MD: Rowman and Littlefield.

Mutz, Diana C. 2007. "Effects of 'In-Your-Face' Television Discourse on Perceptions of a Legitimate Opposition." *American Political Science Review* 101:621–635.

Mutz Diana C., and Byron Reeves. 2005. "The New Videomalaise: Effects of Televised Incivility on Political Trust." *American Political Science Review* 99:1–15.

Pateman, Carol. 1970. *Participation and Democratic Theory*. New York: Cambridge University Press.

Prior, Markus. 2007. *Post-broadcast Democracy: How Media Choice Increases Inequality in Political Involvement and Polarizes Elections*. New York: Cambridge University Press.

Putnam, Robert D. 2000. *Bowling Alone: The Collapse and Revival of American Community*. New York: Simon and Schuster.

Rosenblum, Nancy L. 2010. *On the Side of the Angels: An Appreciation of Parties and Partisanship*. Princeton: Princeton University Press.

Rosenstone, Steven J., and John Mark Hansen. 1993. *Mobilization, Participation, and Democracy in America*. New York: Longman.

Rowe, Ian. 2013. "Civility 2.0: A Comparative Analysis of Incivility in Online Political Discussion." Paper presented at the Elections, Public Opinion, and Parties (EPOP) Conference, September 13–15, University of Lancaster, UK.

Ryan, Timothy J. 2012. "What Makes Us Click? Demonstrating Incentives for Angry Discourse with Digital-Age Field Experiments." *Journal of Politics* 74:1138–1152.

Schattschneider, E. E. 1960. *The Semi-sovereign People: A Realist's View of Democracy in America*. New York: Holt, Rinehart, and Winston.

Schneider, Saundra K., and William G. Jacoby. 2005. "Elite Discourse and American Public Opinion: The Case of Welfare Spending." *Political Research Quarterly* 58:367–379.

Shirky, Clay. 2009. *Here Comes Everybody: The Power of Organizing without Organizations*. New York: Penguin.

Smith, Daniel A., and Caroline J. Tolbert. 2004. *Educated by Initiative: The Effects of Direct Democracy on Citizens and Political Organizations in the American States*. Ann Arbor: University of Michigan Press.

Sobieraj, Sarah J. 2011. *Soundbitten: The Perils of Media-Centered Political Activism*. New York: NYU Press.

Sobieraj, Sarah J., and Jeffrey M. Berry. 2011. "From Incivility to Outrage: Political Discourse in Blogs, Talk Radio, and Cable News." *Political Communication* 28:19–41.

Stroud, Natalie J. 2011. *Niche News: The Politics of News Choice*. New York: Oxford University Press.

Sunstein, Cass. 2009. *Going to Extremes: How Like Minds Unite and Divide*. Oxford: Oxford University Press.

Taber, Charles S., and Milton Lodge. 2006. "Motivated Skepticism in the Evaluation of Political Beliefs." *American Journal of Political Science* 50:755–769.

Valentino, Nicholas A., Ted Brader, Eric Groenendyk, Krysha Gregorowicz, and Vincent L. Hutchings. 2011. "Election Night's Alright for Fighting: The Role of Emotions in Political Participation." *Journal of Politics* 73:156–170.

Warren, Mark E. 1993. "Can Participatory Democracy Produce Better Selves? Psychological Dimensions of Habermas's Discursive Model of Democracy." *Political Psychology* 14:209–234.

Webb, Eugene J., Donald T. Campbell, Richard D. Schwartz, and Lee Sechrest. 1966. *Unobtrusive Measures: Nonreactive Research in the Social Sciences*. Chicago: Rand McNally.

Wesleyan Media Project. 2012. "Presidential Ad War Tops 1M Airings." November 2. http://mediaproject.wesleyan.edu/2012/11/02/presidential-ad-war-tops-1m-airings/.

Wolak, Jennifer. 2006. "The Consequences of Presidential Battleground Strategies for Citizen Engagement." *Political Research Quarterly* 59:353–361.

Wolf, Michael R., J. Cherie Strachan, and Daniel M. Shea. 2012. "Incivility and Standing Firm: A Second Layer of Partisan Division." *PS: Political Science & Politics* 45:401–404.

Zaller, John. 1992. *The Nature and Origins of Mass Public Opinion*. Cambridge: Cambridge University Press.

13

Flaming and Blaming
The Political Effect of Internet News and Reader "Comments"

BRIAN R. CALFANO

The events of the 2012 election suggest that race and religion were salient contributors to President Obama's victory (Scheiber 2012). Obama's second win in as many presidential contests solidified the notion that identity politics can capture voters' motives as much as any other subject, including the economy (Smith 2013). Of course, identity politics are nothing new to U.S. presidential campaigns. In the modern presidency era, appeals to ingroup and outgroup identities as the basis for political judgments (see Tajfel and Turner 1979) have been strongly associated with Republican Party strategy, although Democrats have not sworn off these tactics either (Mendelberg 2001; Leege et al. 2002; Busch 2005). With the nation's demographics tilting toward a majority nonwhite electorate over next two election cycles, both parties have the motive to pursue identity politics strategies that leverage race and religious identities for their candidates' advantage (Domke and Coe 2008; Djupe and Calfano 2013). But the 2012 race was perhaps most notable for the maladroit way that Republican candidates devised and executed their group identity strategies.

Religion was arguably the most consistent and observable group battleground, with the White House catapulting the topic into campaign 2012 at a very early stage. Obama's support for a January 2012 Department of Health and Human Services ruling that required certain religious institutions to provide contraception services in employee health plans drew furor from the U.S. Conference of Catholic Bishops and a plurality of the Catholic laity. Perhaps remembering his difficulties in letting conservatives define religion for him in 2008, Obama may have been deliberately trying to get the religion question out in the open early in 2012, with the expectation that the GOP would race to defend "religious freedom" in shoring up white conservative and religious voters.

Though both Romney and Obama did well among their parties' traditional constituencies (e.g., African Americans and the nonreligious for Obama, married whites for Romney), Obama garnered a 40 point lead among Latinos and won a slim majority of Roman Catholics—despite, or perhaps because of, the dustup over contraception. Meanwhile, Romney handily outpaced the president among white Protestants (69%–30%) and white "born-again" Christians (78%–21%) (Bedolla and Haynie 2013).

Identity Politics

The common refrain from pundits following Obama's win was that the GOP had lost credibility with a litany of voter groups that, at least in particular configurations, can now deliver national victories for the Democrats. If this analysis is correct, it bears a certain irony. After all, having leveraged group identity differences to polarize former elements of the New Deal coalition as far back as the 1972 presidential campaign (Leege et al. 2002; Fiorina, Abrams, and Pope 2006; Baum and Groeling 2008), the GOP now finds itself on the wrong side of a new majority that can punish Republicans for catering to their most vocal, and ideologically unyielding, constituencies.

This may be particularly true in an era when media fragmentation has made interaction and opinion orientations within virtually bounded communities a common occurrence. Assuming the continued elite-level interest in symbolic racism and coded cues in political messages (Sears, Henry, and Kosterman 2000; Calfano and Djupe 2009, 2011; Calfano and Paolino 2010), 2012 is probably not the last election in which identity politics along racial and religious lines will be linked to the provision of political information. And given the media's interlocutor role between campaigns and identity groups (Bennett and Entman 2000; Norris 2000), it is reasonable to expect that information provision through media determines the future success of identity politics for either party.

The GOP's 2012 troubles aside, conventional wisdom might suggest that political strategists would be wise to exploit the incivility, polarization, and intergroup conflict that media messages provide campaigns—despite their negative effect on trust and government legitimacy (Forgette and Morris 2006; Fridkin and Kenney 2008). Interestingly, negative political content has also been found to increase some forms of political participation, including information use (Brader 2006; Geer and Lau 2006), which lends some credence to the "rough and tumble" style of contemporary American politics. But scholars have been slow in assessing the direct effects of political communication that is *not* offered from candidates or political parties. The problem, of course, is that candidates and campaigns are hardly the only purveyors of political messages. As disenchantment with the political coverage offered by news organizations continues to sort along partisan lines (Crawford 2006; Prior 2007; Stroud 2011), many people are moving away from older media platforms in favor of the Internet. Indeed, social media, blogs, YouTube, and Internet-based news products offer information for public deliberation and political engagement along identity group boundaries (Johnson and Kaye 2002; Benkler 2006). What is more, the relative ease that users have in moving between information sources and formats over the web means that the public may encounter a diet of political messages unimaginable just two decades ago. This is especially true in the case of online "hard" news when it is paired with elements of "soft" news or infotainment (see Baum 2002, 2003, 2005; Yang 2007; Heaney, Newman, and Sylvester 2011).

The computer-human interaction at the core of online political communication is, itself, a collection of separate subjects, including foci on visual user cues (Pirolli 2003), cognitive processing (Chaiken 1987), elite agenda setting (McCombs and Shaw 1972), alternative information sources (Farrell and Drezner 2008), selective exposure (Stroud 2008), emotion (Brader 2006), and political tolerance (Stouffer 1955). This presents many unique possibilities for the study of Internet news, identity politics, and political behavior. One that has lacked attention is the proximal combination of "hard" and "soft" news elements from a single source or platform. Though Internet users can manually shift their gaze between websites offering different political messages (and editorial and professional standards), they can frequently encounter this same type of contrast on single websites. The most common example is arguably the Internet-based "hard" news article followed by a reader "comments" section. The readers offering comment are often anonymous in attribution and positioned just below the hard-news story itself. This provides the cloaked commentators a sense of legitimacy by their proximity to the hard-news product on the same platform that "soft" news sources do not enjoy. Though some media outlets may consider anonymous comments an effective way to encourage public deliberation, it is more likely that these organizations permit comments as a way to draw attention to their news product so as to increase readers and revenue—making the comments much closer to serving a commercial or "soft" news purpose. And while some media outlets have begun limiting online reader comments to people with verified Facebook or other social media accounts (Rieder 2013), this is hardly a standard practice across the news industry.

Since these reader comments are usually not subject to real-time monitoring by the "hard" news organization posting the story, the section is a prime vehicle for the kind of offensive and hyperbolic content that exacerbates group identities in ways Republicans have tried to leverage for decades. But in addition to strengthening a sense of intergroup difference, these reader comments may also work to remove public sensitivity to the importance of domain-specific expertise in understanding and evaluating public policies. In the increasingly complex policy realm, and assuming a politically disinterested public (Capella and Jamieson 1997), scholars have come to distinguish between "easy" and "hard" issues (Carmines and Stimson 1980). The expectation is that, when the public perceives that certain issues require less effort to understand, people are more likely to join in the partisan battle—spurred by elites in the process (Oldmixon 2005). Conversely, the public is not so motivated when political issues seem more complex. Yet this dichotomy may be undergoing substantial revision. As seen in the rise of the Tea Party movement (Skocpol and Williamson 2010), the unedited social media dimension that online reader comments provide users can function as an effectual highway for those who might otherwise encounter barriers to opinion articulation on "hard" issues. And with online social networks reaching into local, interpersonal social networks, there is ready encouragement for people to adopt ingroup perspectives about specific political outgroups (Koger, Masket, and Noel 2010)—exactly the development that Republican candidates played into between 2008 and 2012.

The problem, of course, is that the effect of online reader comments and social network encouragement may produce outcomes far afield of the common assumptions about civic trust, social capital, and democratic deliberation (Dewey 1927; Putnam 2000). Though increased political participation is a normative democratic goal, Booth and Richard's (1998) distinction between helpful and harmful social capital suggests that online comments are not supportive, a priori, of traditional democratic values when filtered through sociocognitive impacts of the media equation (Nass and Moon 2000).

One especially notable form of reader comment is the phenomenon termed *flaming and blaming* (see Oegema et al. 2008). In its most strident form, flaming and blaming is a conduit of discrimination, abuse, and misinformation for political extremists against targeted outgroups (Tajfel and Turner 1979; Lohman 1993; Stryker 2000; Farrell and Drezner 2008). The term itself is fairly self-explanatory. Oegema et al. (2008, 333), drawing on Kayany (1998), define flaming "as an uninhibited expression of hostility, such as swearing, calling names, ridiculing, and hurling insults towards another person, his/her character, religion, race, intelligence, and physical or mental ability." The "blaming" portion serves as justification for the flaming maltreatment and is meant to establish some form of intergroup superiority on behalf of the ingroup aggressors (Finch 2000).

This brings to bear aspects of the group identity literature including group prototypes (Hogg and Reid 2006), individual status within groups (Hogg, Fielding, and Darly 2005), and individual exclusion from groups (Theiss-Morse 2009). It also revises the traditional agenda-setting role of media to one of a partial guide on topical concerns rather than an omnipotent determiner of issue salience for the public (McCombs and Shaw 1972; Dearing and Rogers 1996). Stepping into this breach are individual media consumers—the public audience, who, depending on motive, may utilize the freedom to engage in online commentating as a realization of their own agenda-setting power. While the "hard" news information associated with the so-called mainstream media will likely maintain its first-order agenda-setting influence (dealing with frequency of topical coverage), those who engage in flaming and blaming have the potential to play a strong second-order role in attribute assignation and intergroup perceptions (see McCombs et al. 1997).

Perhaps what several 2012 campaigns were hoping is that a range of media users beyond those with a core interest in online commentary would be drawn in by the flaming and blaming comments. Here, and unlike standard political blogs or social media pages, the "hard" news product provides a broad-based credibility for the general public. Then, in scrolling below the story to engage reader comments, flaming and blaming establishes the narrative for how the story topic should be viewed. In the absence of strong predispositions and specific identity group preferences, most people could be significantly influenced by this new form of opinion making (Converse 2006; Zaller 1992; Marcus, Neuman, and MacKuen 2000).

But there is an additional layer of complexity presented by this combination of "hard" news and unbridled reader reactions. Since the public accesses these reader comments via legitimate or "mainstream" news sources, there is a ready potential for the news product to interact with reader comments in affecting audience response. An especially intriguing possibility is that the controversy offered in the reader comments leads to an enhanced information search on the topic originally featured in the news article (Brader 2006). Since people are inclined to process information heuristically (Chaiken 1987; Popkin 1991; Lau and Redlawsk 2001), this raises the question of selective exposure among audiences (Chaffee and McLeod 1973; Gunther 1988; Huckfeldt and Sprague 1991; Redlawsk 2002).

And though the literature is mixed on whether selective exposure is a reliable occurrence, audiences may be most likely to look to preferred information sources when social identity and emotion are activated (Valentino et al. 2011). Of the salient intergroup emotions, anger has dominated much of the recent literature (see Bang-Petersen 2010). Anger is considered demonstrably different from the social emotions (e.g., pride and shame) that situate perception of oneself from the perspective of another (Scheff 1990) and from largely internal reactions to perceived threats (e.g., anxiety) (Marcus 2002). But while offensive reader comments may beget negative intergroup reactions, it is not clear what effect exposure to a larger "hard" news information environment might have.

Using three separate Internet-based experiments in which the nature of the reader comments varied as assigned treatments between civil discourse and an offensive, often irrational, scapegoating of a targeted political outgroup, I find that subjects exposed to flaming and blaming have statistically higher rates of perusal of "hard" news stories, selective exposure to a specific media source, reported anger, and expressed intolerance toward identity groups related to the treatment comments. The following sections detail both my research design and data analysis.

Treating the Online Flame Unobtrusively

One of the lingering challenges for social science experiments is the use of obtrusive outcomes (e.g., nonsurvey measures). Not only would these help with the obvious desirability bias problems encountered in self-reporting about sensitive topics, but researchers can gain insight into how subjects behave in as "real life" an environment as possible. Admittedly, achieving such realism has been a bugaboo of political science experiments since the earliest randomized designs of news-based influence (Iyengar and Kinder 1987). Though field experiments leveraging media platforms are becoming more popular in political science (see Green, Calfano, and Aronow 2014 for a review), there can be difficulty in ensuring treatment compliance, stable unit treatment values, and nonattrition—especially when the subject pool has little or no direct supervision from the researcher.

Perhaps the happy medium is a design emphasis in which subjects are recruited and monitored by the researcher as to their compliance with the random assignment, but the experiment's intervention calls for activities that mirror real-world behaviors while relying on unobtrusive measurement to the extent possible. Essentially, this rules out the on-campus laboratory given the heightened expectation that one is being tested or otherwise observed. An inherent advantage of social media and related Internet-based studies, however, is that treatment delivery and subject response occur online as part of the natural use of the Internet itself. Though the popular expectation is that all online activity is subject to third-party observation, this public perception is in keeping with the overall context of contemporary Internet use—it is not an artifact of the Internet-based experimental design itself.

The two experimental designs using this blend of online treatment and unobtrusive measurement for the present study were administered through Qualtrics in December 2012 and January 2013. All three featured a one-by-three design with the same "hard" news story randomly paired with reader comments modeled after flaming and blaming (flaming treatment), modeled after civil discourse (nonflaming treatment), or presented without reader comments (control). Through a series of JAVA modifications to the Qualtrics software, I created a mock Google News search page complete with a series of "hard" news articles related to the original story in the treatment and control conditions. In addition to capturing any latent influence of topic-congruent "hard" news stories, the Google search provides an unobtrusive measure of selective exposure in subjects. And in keeping with the preceding discussion about the GOP's difficulty with minority voting groups along racial and religious lines, both of these issues are featured in a separate experiment with discrete subject pools.

First, the racial experiment features an article on a new policy by the Los Angeles County Sheriff to no longer process illegal immigrants committing low-level offenses through to federal immigration authorities (Gaynor 2012). I use the flaming treatment to target "Mexicans"—who are not referred to in the actual Reuters article itself. Following the nature of flaming and blaming, in which comments about targeted outgroups are not based in reality (or are not necessarily germane to an actual news story or event), the mention of "Mexicans" approximates the kind of leap in intergroup appraisal that these types of comments typify. Thus, discussion of "Mexicans" is limited to the comments section of the flaming treatment. It does not appear in the nonflaming comments. Meanwhile, the article in the religion experiment describes the efforts of a high school student to block proposed changes to the Louisiana public education curriculum that would teach creationism in school science classes (Dvorsky 2013). The reader comments offered in the religion experiment kept to the general style and form used in the immigration story.

The mock Google News search page followed each subject's randomly assigned condition and varied in search box names between "illegal immigration" and "creationism," though none of the Google articles contained mention of "Mexicans" or pejorative terms related to creationism. Each subject's click of a specific news story, and the order of the stories viewed, was recorded unobtrusively, and the original order of the Google News stories was randomized per subject. However, since actual Internet news search results (including those offered by Google) are based on a type of Markov chain model (Langville and Meyer 2004), it is unlikely for the stochastic selection process in real Google searches to result in an even number of stories from the specific media sources. Thus, and for ease of detecting selective exposure patterns, I include a mix of fifteen "hard" news stories attributed to Fox News or MSNBC, with a distribution of eight stories to six in favor of Fox News. This source ratio is helpful considering the general population characteristics of the area in which the subject pools were drawn (see later). And note that all story content was taken from actual news stories available from both Fox and MSNBC (although some dates were changed to reflect the period in which the experiments were fielded). Figures 13.2 through 13.5 contain representations of the flaming and nonflaming online reader comments sections for both the two "hard" news articles used in the experiments. A summary visual of the Google News search page used in the immigration study can be found in the appendix.

During the second week of December 2012, 199 subjects were recruited for the immigration experiment from the undergraduate student and local adult population in southwest Missouri. In January 2013, 115 subjects were recruited from these same populations for the creationism experiment. Southwest Missouri is significant as a location for subject recruitment in studies of flaming and blaming and GOP political strategy, as the region is recognized as a center of both secular and religious conservatism (see Chinni and Gimpel 2010). It also has a strong contingent of Tea Party identifiers—exactly the kind of audience that may be predisposed to target political outgroups though online comments (Skocpol and Williamson 2010).

Regarding general procedure, and because Qualtrics uses a randomization algorithm after subjects have clicked on an active survey-access link, there was no pretreatment subject blocking on specific covariates. Subjects were told that they would receive a Qualtrics link at their email address on a specific day and time within the five-day study period used for each of the experiments. Once the link was sent, subjects had a 24-hour period to log on and complete the assigned tasks on the Qualtrics pages. Subjects were not allowed to save responses and return to complete or amend their answers at a later time—a policy made clear in a preliminary series of email announcements. Subjects were not told anything more about the nature of the study than that they would be completing a series of online tasks.

The Qualtrics randomization algorithm ensures that the SUTVA requirement—treatment assignment for one subject does not depend on the assignment of another—was fulfilled, but it cannot guard against willful contamination of the control or treatment groups. Neither can it guard against subject attrition, the nature of which can lead to substantial bias in treatment effect calculations. Because of the unobtrusive nature of the design itself, subjects were left to interact with the software at unsupervised physical locations. To guard against the possibility of fraud or other response misrepresentations, subjects were informed prior to receiving the email link that the Qualtrics tracks URLs and prohibits multiple log-ons from the same address (which are true statements). In examining the list of URLs generated by subject activity, none were duplicated across any of the three experiments. In addition, and because of the timing rollout over the five-day study periods used for each design (cohorts of 35 to 45 subjects were emailed the link at a given time), only a handful of subjects were found to participate in the survey at exactly the same time. Given the generally unobtrusive nature of the main outcome measures I use, it is unlikely that subjects would have been clued in to the precise nature of the design. They would, therefore, be less likely to engage in discussion with subjects who had yet to receive their email link. Perhaps because of the relatively small number of subjects involved and/or the consistent contact made with subjects concerning the participation protocols and expectations, there were no instances of subject attrition across the three experiments.

Figure 13.1 is a representation of the major design elements to which subjects were exposed. Recall that random assignment to a treatment or the control group was determined by the software when subjects selected a link within the email they received.

Flaming Effect: Selective Exposure, Anger, and Group Intolerance

As seen in the design flow in figure 13.1, balancing between unobtrusive behavioral measures, while still capturing valid indicators for use in the statistical models, means that some of the outcomes were recorded "downstream" from the initial random assignment and treatment exposure. Since it is possible that the Google News search and subject emotion measures exert a type of

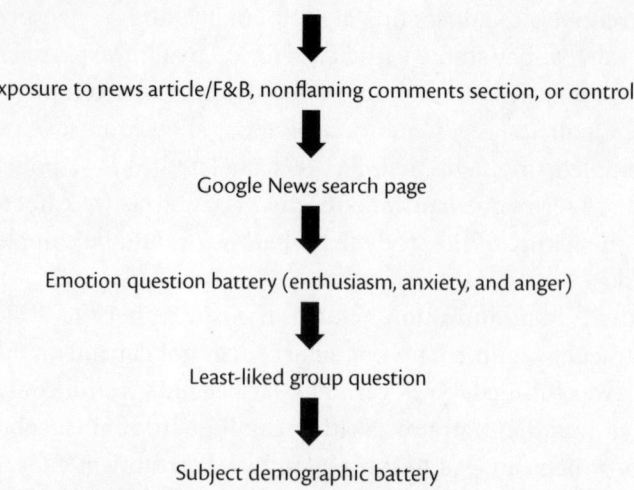

Figure 13.1. Treatment/control assignment (random via Qualtrics)

question-order effect on subsequent outcomes (e.g., intergroup tolerance), I use a series of modeling approaches later in this section that report both direct and indirect effects of the treatment and follow-on items.

Table 13.1 contains basic descriptive information about the two experimental subject pools, including random assignment percentages to treatment and control groups. Subjects' demographic difference according to sex, ideology, and political interest is fairly consistent with general population parameters for southwest Missouri. The exception, of course, is the subjects' age. The ongoing methodological debate over the inferences drawn from student convenience samples (Sears 1986; Druckman and Cam 2011) suggests that it is best to underscore the obvious—these subjects are not a parametric sample of the Missouri or U.S. populations. Yet because of the subject recruitment procedures used in the design, 17% of the subject pool falls outside the traditional undergraduate age in the immigration experiment, 36% does so in the creationism experiment, with 34% doing the same in the pay-gap study—making these pools much less "convenient" than many other experimental studies in psychology and political science. And since the research question and treatment interventions are online in nature, this study does not suffer from criticisms over mundane realism in lab experiments (see McDermott 2002).

Google News Story Search

The first testable outcome in the design sequence regards whether subjects, upon viewing the Google News search page, elected to do anything with the stories presented to them. Table 13.2 contains binary logit model results with a dependent variable coded 1 for subjects who clicked on at least one of the randomly

Table 13.1. Descriptive Statistics of Subject Pool

	Immigration frequency (%)	Creationism frequency (%)
Flaming treatment	59 (30)	38 (33)
Nonflaming treatment	59 (30)	40 (35)
Control group	81 (60)	37 (32)
Female	103 (52)	69 (60)
Male	96 (48)	46 (40)
Strongly liberal	3 (2)	3 (3)
Liberal	42 (21)	23 (20)
Moderate	94 (47)	54 (47)
Conservative	50 (25)	28 (24)
Strongly conservative	10 (5)	5 (6)
Not interested in politics	55 (28)	24 (21)
Somewhat interested in politics	122 (61)	64 (55)
Very interested in politics	22 (11)	27 (24)
18–24	165 (83)	74 (64)
25+	34 (17)	41 (36)
N	199	115

Table 13.2. Logistic Regression with Odds Ratios: Subject Story Search

	Immigration odds ratio (bootstrap SE)	Creationism odds ratio (bootstrap SE)
Flaming treatment	4.52 (1.82*)	5.51 (3.23*)
Nonflaming treatment	.686 (.281)	.889 (.522)
Subject female	2.44 (.857*)	1.10 (.529)
Subject ideology	1.43 (.326)	.720 (.193)
Subject nonundergrad	1.32 (.622)	2.50 (1.25)
Intercept	.099 (.079*)	.585 (.731)
χ^2	.000	.020
N	199	115
Bootstrap replications	5,000	5,000

> **Comments (35)**
>
> **Zaichik** wrote:
> I understand why they might want to focus their efforts on thigns other than illegal immigration but it is part of the law and it would probably decrease crime better than just letting illegal immigrants go unpunished.
> Dec 05, 2012 7:33pm EST – Report as abuse
>
> **Johne37179** wrote:
> I'm not sure that's exactly what's happening here. I'm pretty sure they're still being charged for crimes they commit within the district, they're just not reporting every single person they arrest that is an illegal immigrant to the federal government. I think that's perfectly reasonable.
> Dec 05, 2012 7:37pm EST – Report as abuse
>
> **usagadfly** wrote:
> They are enforcing the laws, but are no longer reporting every illegal immigrant to the federal government adn working with federal authorities to create records.
>
> Instead of wasting their time filling out paperwork about an illegal immigrant who gets arrested for traffic violations or some crap they're focusing on violent offenders and protecting the citizens they serve.
>
> It is the federal government's job to deal with illegal immigration. Our states and cities don't have the resoureces to deal with the massive problem. It's not a secret that immigration is an agenda item that needs to be addressed - Obam and Bush both tried. The problem is partisan gridlock in Washington and politicians that would rather express ignorant opinions than solve problems.
>
> Yes, it is sad that the police can't enforce the laws because they don't have the resources. But on the other hand they shouldn't have to choose between writing reports to the federal government on illegal immigration and wasting resources instead of protecting people.
>
> I'm all for this decision – it is definitely a good example of local and state governments forcing the issue with the federal government. Maybe we can finally get something done if the issue becomes big enough they'll have to deal with it.
> Dec 05, 2012 7:39pm EST – Report as abuse
>
> **xcoldbeer** wrote:
> I agree, but I sure wish it wasn't this way. They need more money so they can encforce the law's like they're supposed to.
> Dec 05, 2012 7:46pm EST – Report as abuse

Figure 13.2. Nonflaming comments (immigration)

ordered stories in the Google search and 0 for subjects who clicked on none of the stories. Though this and subsequent tables contain covariates for subjects' sex, ideology, and age (which is a binary measure of whether subjects are over the 18–24 age window), all tests are first reported as differences between the treatment and control group values, reported as odds ratios (Mutz 2011). All significantly signed (*) standard errors in the following tables are at the Bonferroni-adjusted threshold of $p < .017$, which, for this design, is the standard .05 significance threshold divided by three (representing the number of randomly assigned subject groups). Also, given the relatively small and nonparametric nature of the subject pool, all models are reported with bootstrapped standard errors using 5,000 replications with replacement (see Guan 2010). I report the odds ratios for just the flaming and nonflaming treatment dummies in the text. The full models, including the relevant covariates, are reported in the tables.

There is clear evidence to support the expectation that exposure to flaming comments from the online audience spurs subjects' information use in the form of viewing at least one news story. In the treatment-only models, flaming subjects in the immigration experiment show a 4.56 increase in the odds, versus control subjects, of clicking on at least one of the Google News stories ($p < .017$). Meanwhile, flaming subjects in the creationism experiment show a 4.63 increase

Comments (35)

Zaichik wrote:
fucking mexicans now were not even going to send them back when they break the laws this is how america ends. blame the democrats ruining the country especially that one in the white house.
Dec 05, 2012 7:33pm EST – Report as abuse

Johne37179 wrote:
illegal immigration will ruin the country. we're spending out citizen's money to pay for illegal immigrants to break the laws, rot in jail, and take jobs from americans that want them... we have a huge debt but mexicans are getting social security buying drugs then getting sent back on the taxpayers dollar what bullshit
Dec 05, 2012 7:37pm EST – Report as abuse

usagadfly wrote:
I'm sure that they're just trying to do their bets with limited resources. This isn't somebody saying "don't enforce the laws." They are trying to keep the most violent people off the streets and stop the worst crimes.

I think that rather then spending all of their time on paperwork and all the crap they have to do for illegal immigrants they're choosing just not to focus on that issue. The cops are trying to keep people safe. It's not a secret that the federal government is way behind on addressing illegal immigration - even Obama said he would do something about it and Bush before him said the same thing.

If the partisan gridlock in Washington would let up for even a second I'm sure our country could figure somethign out that would make unfortunate situations like this one not be necessary. If they're breaking the laws they SHOULD be prosecuted but something you have to focus on what is most important. The police in this instance have decided it's more important to spend their time stopping violence and other stuff from happening rather than waste it reporting every single illegal immigrant they find.

Are there illegal immigrants being arrested? Of course. But why waste time sending reports to the government when they basically don't do anything about it anyway? I think this is a reasonable and useful way of addressing illegal immigration and crime.
Dec 05, 2012 7:39pm EST – Report as abuse

xcoldbeer wrote:
Shut the fuck up usagadfly you sound like an idiot. The cops are blatantly not enforcing the laws. That's just wrong.
Dec 05, 2012 7:40pm EST – Report as abuse

Figure 13.3. Flaming comments (immigration)

> **Comments (35)**
>
> **Zaichik** wrote:
> Whatever happened to religious freedom? Students shouldn't have to learn something their parents feel is against their religious beliefs.
> Dec 05, 2012 7:33pm EST – Report as abuse
>
> **Johne37179** wrote:
> I'm not sure the issue is religious freedom. Religious students are not being FORCED to abandon their religion or their beliefs. And what about the students who do not want to be taught creationism? Why would the standard or religious freedom not apply to both groups equally?
> Dec 05, 2012 7:37pm EST – Report as abuse
>
> **usagadfly** wrote:
> Religious tolerance is NOT an argument that applies here to defend creationism.
>
> The US has, since its inception, protected the rights or religious groups to practice their religion as they want. This right is not absolute; it disappears when their rights infringe upon the rights of others.
>
> Essentially, you can practice your religion, but if your religion says you should steal from other people or kill people you can't do that. If your religion says that you should force other people to practice your religion, you can't do that.
>
> Christians have to respect other religions (and people with no religion) just as they want to be respected - isn't that in the Bible as well? The best option here is to set up their own schools.
>
> While I'm not sure about the voucher system being unconstitutional on these grounds (that's a hard argument to win, in my opinion) it is much simpler to say that creationism shouldn't be taught in public schools.
> Dec 05, 2012 7:39pm EST – Report as abuse
>
> **xcoldbeer** wrote:
> Good point about the way that people's rights disappear when they affect other people.
> Dec 05, 2012 7:46pm EST – Report as abuse

Figure 13.4. Nonflaming comments (creationism)

in the odds, versus control subjects, of clicking on at least one news story ($p < .017$). Importantly, these treatment effects maintain relatively similar magnitudes when the covariates are included in the table 13.2 models. Though it is a blunt measure of information use, accessing even a single news story related to the original "hard" news article is basic confirmation that the flaming treatment spurred general subject interest in additional "hard" news stories, as featured in the Google search.

Table 13.3 offers greater precision in capturing subjects' responses to the Google News stories. This model features a count estimator for the number of unique stories subjects clicked on while engaging in their information search. These "unique" views measure the total number of different news stories subjects clicked on, rather than the total of stories viewed. Though count models are often assumed to follow the Poisson distributions assumptions, these data are overdispersed, which recommends a negative binomial regression. Note that negative binomial coefficients, not odds ratios, are reported for this model.

Looking first at the treatment-only results, flaming subjects in the immigration experiment show a significant increase in stories viewed versus the control (coef. 1.12, $p < .017$, versus $-.048$ for the nonflaming subjects). Subjects in the creationism experiment also exhibited an increase in the number of stories viewed when exposed to the flaming treatment versus the control, but this coefficient (.864 versus $-.250$ for nonflaming) is just outside the $p < .017$ threshold. As seen table 13.3, the flaming treatments remain consistent motivators of subjects' engagement in the "hard" news environ. At the least, then, we can conclude that online reader comments of a flaming nature spur engagement with information sources—even those that do not reflect the flaming content in the reader comments. But what of the news sources that subjects prefer?

Insular Information via Selective Exposure

Recall that subjects were able to select Google stories that were attributed to either MSNBC or Fox News. This design was premised on the notion that flaming and blaming would encourage subjects to engage in an insular use of available media information (i.e., selective exposure). In this case, source insularity is operationalized as a subject viewing only stories that were credited to Fox News and is coded as the number of unique Fox News stories viewed on

Table 13.3. Negative Binomial Regression: Subject Unique Story Views

	Immigration coefficient (bootstrap SE)	Creationism coefficient (bootstrap SE)
Flaming treatment	1.00 (2.59*)	1.38 (.495*)
Nonflaming treatment	−.179 (.337)	−.259 (.582)
Subject female	.661 (.253*)	1.10 (.529)
Subject ideology	.324 (.141)	−.452 (.263)
Subject nonundergrad	.476 (.360)	1.23 (.386*)
Intercept	−1.40 (.521*)	.462 (.976)
γ	1.98 (.392*)	3.18 (.700*)
χ^2	.000	.001
N	199	115
Bootstrap replications	5,000	5,000

> **Comments (35)**
>
> **Zaichik** wrote:
>
> They want our guns and they want our God. This is how America will end.
>
> Dec 05, 2012 7:35pm EST – Report as abuse
>
> ---
>
> **Johne37179** wrote:
>
> Typical rednecks: guns and god. Lol you think your story book with some made up stories told by sheep herders is science? You are writing your comments on a computer that was made with SCIENE on the internet made with SCIENCE not with the BIBLE. You probably fuck your sister.
>
> Dec 05, 2012 7:37pm EST – Report as abuse
>
> ---
>
> **usagadfly** wrote:
>
> Typical liberals - going to hell just with the rest fo your atheist scumbag friends.
>
> GOD sent his son JESUS to save us and if you reject that youare going to to burn in hell, its in the Bible.
>
> you are such a small person, making fun of these beliefs it doesnt matter i know what i believe and i know its true you try to make me stop believing in my god and my country you can be damn sure ill use my guns to defend my rights!!!!
>
> these liberals scum are brainwashign our kids with "facts' that are just what they believe how is it any different than what i beliefe in the Bible? I could go on but your too stupid for this to make any sense lol
>
> this country was founded on crhistian beliefs. it says right in our pledge one nationa UNDER GOD the founding fathers wouldnt have put it there if they didnt mean it. All mean created equal by GOD dumbass.
>
> God will destroy the nation when we turn away from him but those who believe will be saved thats for sure. i will be in heaving with Him when that time comes and then youll wish you had listend better to peopel who are smarter than you
>
> Dec 05, 2012 7:39pm EST – Report as abuse
>
> ---
>
> **xcoldbeer** wrote:
>
> its what hitler did they took away their rights and their guns and then the nazis took over. 1776 will happen again!!!!
>
> Dec 05, 2012 7:40pm EST – Report as abuse

Figure 13.5. Flaming comments (creationism)

the Google search page. In the treatment-only models reporting odds ratios, the odds of insular reliance on Fox News stories increases by 5.21 ($p < .017$, versus 1.0 for the nonflaming subjects) for immigration subjects exposed to the flaming treatment versus the control. Meanwhile, the odds increase a sizeable 40.0 ($p < .017$, 4.0 for nonflaming subjects) for flaming subjects in the creationism experiment versus the control.

Subject Anger

Moving away from the unobtrusive measures of subjects' reactions, I now consider their affective responses to the assigned treatments, with anger the specific focus. Recall that anger, as an emotion associated with aggression toward social outgroups, required measurement using a standard survey item that followed the Google News search exercise. In testing the possibility that the availability of selectively preferred media information affects subjects' emotion, it is important not to lose sight of the fact that the randomized treatments are theorized to have "downstream" influence on response items appearing after the Google News search. In other words, subjects' anger may be the product of both the assigned experimental conditions and Google News search content. Hence, the survey response question measuring anger asked subjects to refer back to what they had "just read"—without differentiating between the original news article and the Google search.

In the treatment-only models, immigration subjects receiving the flaming comments had a 2.94 increase in the odds, versus the control ($p < .017$, versus 1.07 for the nonflaming subjects), of indicating anger toward the information they viewed in the "hard" news article and/or follow-on Google News search. Though the flaming subjects in the creationism experiment show a 2.41 increase in the odds of indicating anger versus the control (versus .73 for nonflaming subjects), this finding is just outside the accepted significance threshold ($p < .017$).

Use of typical multiplicative variables to determine interaction effects between the treatment and Google search is problematic due to the inherent endogeneity in combining dependent and independent variables from prior models (e.g., the flaming treatment with Fox News insularity). A standard path analysis using OLS is problematic in this case because the anger measure is ordinal. Hence, as a partial solution, I employ Karlson, Holm, and Breen's (2010) method of effect decomposition. The authors' KHB estimator, which is specifically designed for maximum likelihood, avoids the effect comparison problem caused by rescaling in logit and similar models. KHB allows for comparison of mediator effects between "full" and "reduced" models by using mediator variable residuals from regression of the mediator on the indicators of interest.

Using the Fox News insularity measure as the mediating variable, tables 13.4 through 13.6 report effect decomposition on subject anger (as scaled 0–4 by Marcus 2002). Table 13.6 is the most instructive in comparing the "full" and "reduced" effects. There, notice that the full model for flaming subjects in the immigration experiment (which includes the insularity measure) shows the odds of increased levels of subject anger are 1.31 versus the control when insularity is in the model and 1.57 versus the control when insularity is excluded—a between-model difference statistically significant at $p < .017$. A similar reduction in odds between the full and reduced models among flaming subjects is seen in the creationism experiment—1.23 versus 1.84 (difference significant at $p < .017$).

This general trend in anger reduction may reflect the comforting effect of selective exposure on flaming subjects, but it is not necessarily in keeping with the expectation that selective exposure of media sources encourages an

Table 13.4. Ordered Logit Decomposition: Subject Anger (Full Model)

	Immigration coefficient (bootstrap SE)	Creationism coefficient (bootstrap SE)
Flaming treatment	.564 (.173*)	.210 (.242)
Nonflaming treatment	.082 (.170)	−.258 (.250)
Fox News insularity	.633 (.170*)	1.02 (.285*)
Subject female	.138 (.313)	.485 (.453)
Subject ideology	.385 (.174)	−.118 (.252)
Subject nonundergrad	−.676 (.390)	−.139 (.444)
Cut 1	.904 (.636)	−.151 (1.20)
Cut 2	1.00 (.638)	.014 (1.20)
Cut 3	1.72 (.652*)	.459 (1.20)
Cut 4	3.30 (.666*)	2.31 (1.14*)
χ^2	.000	.001
N	199	115
Bootstrap replications	5,000	5,000

echo-chamber effect. Reconciling these findings to the wider literature might recommend source insularity as a phenomenon separate from online audience comments and related entities. Indeed, Berry and Sobieraj (2011) make a strong case for treating the elements of "outrage" in blogs, talk radio, and cable news as distinct from "hard" news content and even incivility (19). "Outrage," as the authors operationalize it, includes the kind of insulting language and misrepresentative intergroup exaggerations that are flaming and blaming hallmarks. Therefore, source insularity, when represented as "hard" media content, may not push the public in the same responsive direction as intentionally offensive and hyperbolic flaming comments.

The Group Liked Least

In extending this analysis to how subjects perceive outgroup members, I consider expressed levels of group tolerance using an adapted version of the standard "least liked" group measure (Stouffer 1955). Of the response variables assessed, this is the most directly related to political outcomes in the identity politics context. Given the findings on subject anger via the source insularity mediator, it is worth asking whether subjects' characterization of a group as "least liked" is itself mediated by a combination of source insularity and anger.

Following the hyperbolic leaps in group attribution that article comments feature, the groups offered for subjects to select from do not exactly match those mentioned in the assigned "hard" news article or comments sections. Instead, the groups are proximate options for the "least liked" distinction and include American Nazis, Mexicans, illegal immigrants, the KKK, atheists, environmental activists, and gay-rights activists. Though one might quibble with this list, it mixes direct and indirect intergroup associations that subjects might make. In the context of political campaigns, in which subtlety in cueing intergroup intolerance is a well-documented goal (e.g., Mendelberg 2001), any effects from the randomly assigned content and/or mediating variables will be noteworthy.

Since Mexicans were the target of the flaming treatment in the immigration experiment, either Mexicans or illegal immigrants should be selected if this

Table 13.5. Ordered Logit Decomposition: Subject Anger (Reduced Model)

	Immigration coefficient (bootstrap SE)	Creationism coefficient (bootstrap SE)
Flaming treatment	.791 (.159*)	.611 (.225*)
Nonflaming treatment	.037 (.171)	−.129 (.246)
(Insularity)	.633 (.172*)	1.02 (.293*)
Subject female	.443 (.294)	.615 (.448)
Subject ideology	.449 (.172*)	−.213 (.253)
Subject nonundergrad	−.671 (.391)	−.199 (.433)
Cut 1	1.26 (.631*)	−.263 (1.20)
Cut 2	1.36 (.635*)	−.098 (1.21)
Cut 3	2.08 (.651*)	.347 (1.21)
Cut 4	3.66 (.661*)	2.19 (1.15*)
χ^2	.000	.001
N	199	115
Bootstrap replications	5,000	5,000

Table 13.6. Ordered Logit Decomposition: Subject Anger (Effect Comparison)

	Immigration odds ratio (bootstrap SE)	Creationism odds ratio (bootstrap SE)
Flaming treatment		
Reduced model	1.57 (.122*)	1.84 (.414*)
Full model	1.31 (.143*)	1.23 (.299)
Difference	.260 (.111*)	1.49 (.261*)
Nonflaming treatment		
Reduced model	.629 (.329)	.879 (.217)
Full model	.450 (.405)	.773 (.194)
Difference	.179 (.267)	1.14 (.159)
Pseudo R^2	.11	.12
N	199	115
Bootstrap replications	5,000	5,000

treatment has a statistical impact on subjects' response. This is the most direct of the associations between the flaming comments and group selection of the three experiments. And with the flaming treatment in the creationism experiment targeting conservative Christians (who are well represented in southwest Missouri), atheists should be the least-liked group in that instance (although there is a less direct connection between opposing creationism in the classroom and negative affect toward atheists).

As with the prior models, I examine the treatment-only effects before reporting the full model results, this time using a multinomial logit estimator. American Nazis are the excluded group category. Largely unsurprising given the flaming treatment's content in the immigration experiment, subjects randomly assigned to this condition show a significant trend versus the control in selecting Mexicans as their least-liked group (coef. 2.13, $p < .017$). In the creationism experiment, meanwhile, flaming subjects show a significant trend in choosing environmentalists as their least-liked group versus the control (coef. 3.61, $p < .017$).

Left to explore, then, are any moderating effects from the "downstream" components of the experiment—news source insularity and subjects' anger, particularly for subjects in the immigration and creationism experiments. Using the KHB method with a multinomial logit estimator allows for this assessment, the results of which are reported in tables 13.7 through 13.9.

Table 13.7. Multinomial Logit Decomposition: Least-Liked Group (Full Model)

	Immigration coefficient (bootstrap SE)	Creationism coefficient (bootstrap SE)
American Nazis	(Base outcome)	(Base outcome)
Mexicans		
Flaming treatment	2.98 (.623*)	3.27 (1.99)
Nonflaming treatment	.222 (.528)	−17.74 (54.6)
Fox News insularity	−1.36 (.538)	−18.52 (91.94)
Subject anger	−.705 (.471)	.588 (.710)
Subject female	.649 (.438)	−1.02 (1.66)
Subject ideology	.025 (.253)	−.931 (1.09)
Subject nonundergrad	−.356 (.570)	2.24 (1.77)
Intercept	−.748 (.853)	−.243 (4.16)
Illegal immigrants		
Flaming treatment	.245 (1.20)	.114 (2.22)
Nonflaming treatment	.080 (.655)	−21.90 (26.07)
Fox News insularity	−16.89 (15.57)	6.12 (6.17)
Subject anger	.193 (.646)	−1.36 (1.59)
Subject female	−.352 (.657)	−2.83 (1.83)
Subject ideology	.481 (.388)	1.90 (1.06)
Subject nonundergrad	.545 (.755)	−16.52 (40.68)
Intercept	−2.50 (1.34)	−2.46 (4.04)
KKK		
Flaming treatment	1.39 (.820)	−14.90 (32.26)
Nonflaming treatment	−.461 (.695)	−.117 (.977)
Fox News insularity	−2.32 (.917*)	−16.37 (35.78)
Subject anger	−.184 (.624)	−.446 (.318)

(*continued*)

Table 13.7 (*continued*)

	Immigration coefficient (bootstrap SE)	Creationism coefficient (bootstrap SE)
Subject female	.382 (.598)	.882 (1.18)
Subject ideology	.157 (.350)	.676 (.530)
Subject nonundergrad	.119 (.767)	2.62 (1.04)
Intercept	−1.52 (1.19)	−4.88 (3.23)
Atheists		
Flaming treatment	1.73 (.685*)	1.12 (1.21)
Nonflaming treatment	.160 (.538)	−.098 (.650)
Fox News insularity	−1.78 (.630*)	.919 (1.00)
Subject anger	−.248 (.503*)	−.257 (.202)
Subject female	.374 (.479)	−.309 (.639)
Subject ideology	.200 (.284)	−.089 (.341)
Subject nonundergrad	−.357 (.666)	−1.80 (.941)
Intercept	−1.27 (.956)	1.98 (1.66)
Environmental activists		
Flaming treatment	.879 (1.24)	4.36 (1.39*)
Nonflaming treatment	−.612 (.920)	−.679 (.946)
Fox News insularity	−16.83 (17.48)	.165 (.109)
Subject anger	−1.10 (.914)	.106 (.259)
Subject female	−.051 (.824)	−.064 (.811)
Subject ideology	.339 (.502)	.212 (.440)
Subject nonundergrad	.252 (.948)	2.61 (.993)
Intercept	−2.05 (1.67)	−2.59 (2.30)
Gay-rights activists		
Flaming treatment	.879 (1.24)	2.30 (.1.91)

Table 13.7 (*continued*)

	Immigration coefficient (bootstrap SE)	Creationism coefficient (bootstrap SE)
Nonflaming treatment	−.612 (.920)	−2.43 (1.73)
Fox News insularity	−16.83 (17.48)	2.40 (1.73)
Subject anger	−1.10 (.914)	−.621 (.462)
Subject female	−.051 (.824)	−3.37 (1.53)
Subject ideology	.339 (.502)	.465 (.750)
Subject nonundergrad	.252 (.948)	19.68 (20.88)
Intercept	−2.05 (1.67)	−14.68 (20.88)
Pseudo R^2	.12	.41
N	199	115
Bootstrap replications	5,000	5,000

Table 13.8. Multinomial Logit Decomposition: Least-Liked Group (Reduced Model)

	Immigration coefficient (bootstrap SE)	Creationism coefficient (bootstrap SE)
American Nazis	(Base outcome)	(Base outcome)
Mexicans		
Flaming treatment	2.35 (.546*)	−2.43 (31.24)
Nonflaming treatment	.217 (.528)	−19.82 (55.56)
(Insularity)	−1.36 (.538*)	−18.59 (95.15)
(Anger)	−.705 (.471)	.588 (.710)
Subject female	.419 (.430)	−1.68 (47.59)
Subject ideology	−.113 (.250)	−.325 (35.12)
Subject nonundergrad	−.267 (.567)	2.65 (22.08)
Intercept	−.800 (.852)	−1.12 (85.42)
Illegal immigrants		
Flaming treatment	−5.46 (42.97)	1.20 (2.19)

(*continued*)

Table 13.8 (*continued*)

	Immigration coefficient (bootstrap SE)	Creationism coefficient (bootstrap SE)
Nonflaming treatment	.300 (10.90)	−20.92 (26.06)
(Insularity)	−16.90 (12.62)	6.12 (6.17)
(Anger)	.193 (.646)	−1.34 (1.59)
Subject female	−2.82 (18.47)	−3.15 (1.87)
Subject ideology	−.231 (54.77)	1.85 (1.03)
Subject nonundergrad	.082 (32.04)	−16.59 (40.68)
Intercept	−2.11 (27.83)	−3.72 (4.19)
KKK		
Flaming treatment	.555 (.750)	−20.59 (34.37)
Nonflaming treatment	−.446 (.694)	.063 (.641)
(Insularity)	−2.32 (.917*)	.919 (1.00)
(Anger)	−.184 (.624)	−.257 (.202)
Subject female	.035 (.591)	−.382 (.636)
Subject ideology	.036 (.348)	−.086 (.341)
Subject nonundergrad	.093 (.753)	−1.81 (.945)
Intercept	−1.49 (1.18)	1.72 (1.64)
Atheists		
Flaming treatment	1.07 (.614)	1.25 (1.17)
Nonflaming treatment	.169 (.538)	.063 (.640)
(Insularity)	−1.78 (.630)	.919 (1.00)
(Anger)	−.248 (.503)	−.257 (.202)
Subject female	.103 (.473)	−.382 (.636)
Subject ideology	.095 (.278)	−.086 (.341)

Table 13.8 (*continued*)

	Immigration coefficient (bootstrap SE)	Creationism coefficient (bootstrap SE)
Subject nonundergrad	−.358 (.658)	−1.81 (.945)
Intercept	−1.26 (.953)	1.72 (1.64)
Environmental activists		
Flaming treatment	−5.12 (59.54)	4.49 (1.34*)
Nonflaming treatment	−.494 (15.10)	−.689 (.938)
(Insularity)	−16.83 (17.48)	.165 (.109)
(Anger)	−1.10 (.914)	.106 (.259)
Subject female	−2.56 (25.58)	−.007 (.811)
Subject ideology	−.515 (75.88)	.192 (.439)
Subject nonundergrad	.017 (44.39)	2.60 (.995)
Intercept	−1.80 (38.55)	−2.44 (2.26)
Gay-rights activists		
Flaming treatment	.155 (.803)	2.66 (1.93)
Nonflaming treatment	−.835 (.747)	−2.03 (1.65)
(Insularity)	1.13 (.760)	2.40 (1.73)
(Anger)	.360 (.671)	−.621 (.462)
Subject female	1.03 (.666)	−3.53 (1.53)
Subject ideology	−.067 (.366)	.462 (.749)
Subject nonundergrad	−.031 (.866)	19.65 (20.99)
Intercept	−1.64 (1.24)	−15.29 (20.88)
Pseudo R^2	.12	.41
N	199	115
Bootstrap replications	5,000	5,000

Table 13.9. Ordered Logit Decomposition: Subjects' Anger (Effect Comparison)

	Immigration odds ratio (bootstrap SE)	Creationism odds ratio (bootstrap SE)
Flaming treatment		
Reduced model	2.35 (.546*)	4.49 (1.34*)
Full model	2.92 (.623*)	4.37 (1.38*)
Difference	−.634 (.265*)	.126 (.347)
Nonflaming treatment		
Reduced model	.217 (.528)	−.689 (.934)
Full model	.222 (.528)	−.679 (.946)
Difference	−.006 (.175)	−.010 (.163)
Pseudo R^2	.12	.41
N	199	115
Bootstrap replications	5,000	5,000

In terms of actual mediated difference between subjects as a result of insularity and anger, only flaming subjects in the immigration experiment are significantly impacted in terms of odds differences between the "full" and "reduced" models. Yet, unlike the anger models earlier, the mediating effect in the "full" model here actually increases outcome odds. Specifically, with news source insularity and subjects' anger in the model as mediators, the odds of flaming subjects naming Mexicans as their least-liked group increases by 2.92 versus the control ($p < .017$), while the odds increase is only 2.35 versus the control ($p < .017$) in the reduced model. This suggests that, while source insularity may dampen anger in some cases, the emotion itself is a strong motivator in intergroup appraisals stoked by flaming and blaming.

Implications and Conclusions

I began this chapter with consideration of the identity-based politics that campaigns and candidates—particularly Republicans—have pursued in recent election cycles. Different from prior work in the area of media-driven campaign message effects, however, the analysis presented herein has examined the effect of politically oriented messages as presented through another common mode of media-driven messages—the online reader comments positioned below "hard" news articles on Internet websites. In applying the literature on flaming and blaming reader comments—which has become a ubiquitous way to advance group conflict narratives on Internet and social media sites—to an experimental design assessing outcome effects along an array of media use, emotion, and group perception indicators, I find general confirmation that exposure to flaming and blaming comments spurs engagement with "hard" news sources, increases reported levels of anger in those who are exposed to the flaming and blaming comments, and pushes exposed audience members toward targeting outgroups generally associated with those comments.

There are, however, some less straightforward findings that may be cause for reflection about the assumptions that both scholars and campaign strategists hold regarding selective exposure to media sources. Though additional research using subjects culled from a different geographic area will provide additional clarification, it is worth noting that the flaming comments did not drive subjects toward articles sourced to Fox News in the Google search to a different degree than the control group. While it is perhaps evidence of a ceiling effect on Fox News preference among these subjects, it is also possible that "hard" news products—even those with generally congruent ideological attributes—do not necessarily reinforce the effects associated with online flaming and blaming and are not seen as "go to" necessities after one encounters flaming content.

The mediated relationship between the flaming treatment, source insularity, and subjects' anger supports this contention. In the anger model decomposition, insularity toward the Fox News stories significantly decreased subjects' anger, which is the exact opposite of what is generally considered to be a reinforcing relationship between information media sources on the political right. In this instance, however, the nature of online flaming and blaming comments might constitute an entirely different factor of media use separate from "hard" news—even that which is sourced to Fox. Notice also that, while source insularity did not significantly reduce the odds of flaming subjects targeting an outgroup as "least liked," reliance only on the Fox News stories did not increase those odds either. In the broader context of new media and presidential campaigns, these results should be considered as a general guidepost concerning the need for a continued drilling down into the complex relationships between not only political communication and media but specific media platforms and environments. Just as with the established assumptions about identity politics that the GOP used to its detriment in 2012, there may be several established assumptions about media effects on audiences that campaigns maintain to their detriment.

Appendix: Google News Search (Immigration) from Study

(*Note*: clicking on the article title opened a text box containing the full story content for each.)

This page displays Internet search results of news stories dealing with illegal immigration. Read as many stories as you want by clicking on the article title.

When you're done reading the stories you want, click the "end news search" button at the bottom of the screen to proceed to just a few more questions.

Illegal Immigration >>
Fired Workers Say Chipotle Was Soft on Immigration
October 14, 2012
Reported by FoxNews.com
Minneapolis: The hundreds of illegal immigrants recently fired

Illegal Immigration >>
Business Groups Can't Stop Immigration Bills
October 10, 2012
Reported by FoxNews.com
Tallahassee: Neither tears, nor prayer nor opposition

Illegal Immigration >>
Farmer Ordered to Pay $150,000 in Immigration Suit
October 24, 2012
Reported by FoxNews.com
Des Moines: A dairy farmer and his company will pay $150,000

Illegal Immigration >>
Faith, Immigration, and the Law
October 19, 2012
Reported by MSNBC.com
Atlanta: A new study, conducted by the Human Economics Institute,

Illegal Immigration >>
Pastor Voices Concern on Immigrants' Use of Government Resources
October 20, 2012
Reported by MSNBC.com
Los Angeles: A new report links illegal immigration and economic growth.

Illegal Immigration >>
Clergy Says Immigrants Worthy of Respect
October 22, 2012
Reported by FoxNews.com
Philadelphia: A new study, conducted by the Human Economics Institute,

Illegal Immigration >>
Colorado Illegal Immigrants Pay Enough Taxes to Offset Cost of Their Social Services, Study Says

October 20, 2012
Reported by FoxNews.com
Denver: Colorado's undocumented immigrants pay as much in taxes

Illegal Immigration >>
Some Businesses Fear Impact of Immigration Law
October 27, 2012
Reported by MSNBC.com
Atlanta: Some Georgia business owners and farmers say

Illegal Immigration >>
Immigration Report Stirs Debate
October 23, 2012
Reported by FoxNews.com
Denver: Pastor John Stead, who leads the progressive Congregation of Hope in
    suburban

Illegal Immigration >>
Study Shows Immigration a Spiritual Issue
October 24, 2012
Reported by MSNBC.com
Charlotte, NC: Pastor John Prague, leader of North Carolina's Evangelical Covenant
    Church

Illegal Immigration >>
Companies Eager to Show Compliance on Immigration Employment Rules
October 16, 2012
Reported by MSNBC.com
Washington, DC: More than 1,000 companies have volunteered

Illegal Immigration >>
Georgia Legislature Passes Controversial Anti-immigrant Law
October 27, 2012
Reported by FoxNews.com
Atlanta: The Georgia state legislature passed anti-immigrant legislation

Illegal Immigration >>
Border Patrol Weekend Activities Report
October 27, 2012
Reported by MSNBC.com
Tucson: The following is a rundown of arrest activities

Illegal Immigration >>
Illegal Immigrants Arrested
October 23, 2012
Reported by FoxNews.com
San Diego: Seven illegal immigrants were arrested Sunday after docking

References

Bang-Petersen, M. 2010. "Distinct Emotions, Distinct Domains: Anger, Anxiety and Perceptions of Intentionality." *Journal of Politics* 72:357–365.

Baum, M. A. 2002. "Sex, Lies and War: How Soft News Brings Foreign Policy to the Inattentive Public." *American Political Science Review* 96:91–109.

———. 2003. *Soft News Goes to War: Public Opinion and American Foreign Policy in the New Media Age*. Princeton: Princeton University Press.

———. 2005. "Talking the Vote: Why Presidential Candidates Hit the Talk Show Circuit." *American Journal of Political Science* 44:213–234.

Baum, M. A., and T. Groeling. 2008. "New Media and the Polarization of American Political Discourse." *Political Communication* 25:345–365.

Bedolla, L. G., and K. L. Haynie. 2013. "The Obama Coalition and the Future of American Politics." *Politics, Groups, and Identities* 1:137–142.

Benkler, Y. 2006. *The Wealth of Networks: How Social Production Transforms Markets and Freedom*. New Haven: Yale University Press.

Bennett, W. L., and R. Entman, eds. 2000. *Mediated Politics: Communication in the Future of Democracy*. New York: Cambridge University Press.

Berry, J. M., and S. Sobieraj. 2011. *The Outrage Industry: Political Opinion Media and the New Incivility*. New York: Oxford University Press.

Booth, J. A., and P. B. Richard. 1998. "Civil Society, Political Capital, and Democratization in Central America." *Journal of Politics* 60:780–800.

Brader, T. 2006. *Campaigning for Hearts and Minds: How Emotional Appeals in Political Ads Work*. Chicago: University of Chicago Press.

Busch, A. 2005. *Reagan's Victory: The Presidential Election of 1980 and the Rise of the Right*. Lawrence: University Press of Kansas.

Calfano, B. R., and P. A. Djupe. 2009. "God Talk: Religious Cues and Electoral Support." *Political Research Quarterly* 62:329–339.

———. 2011. "Not in His Image: The Moderating Effect of Candidate Religious Appeals." *Politics and Religion* 4:338–354.

Calfano, B. R., and P. Paolino. 2010. "An Alan Keyes Effect? Examining Anti-Black Sentiment among White Evangelicals." *Political Behavior* 32:133–156.

Cappella, J. N., and K. H. Jamieson. 1997. *Spiral of Cynicism: The Press and the Public Good*. New York: Oxford University Press.

Carmines, E. G., and J. A. Stimson. 1980. "The Two Faces of Issue Voting." *American Political Science Review* 74:78–91.

Chaffee, S., and J. M. McLeod. 1973. "Interpersonal Perception and Communication." *American Behavioral Scientist* 16:483–488.

Chaiken, S. 1987. "The Heuristic Model of Persuasion." In *Social Influence: The Ontario Symposium*, edited by M. P. Zanna, J. M. Olson, and C. P. Herman, 3–39 Hillsdale, NJ: Erlbaum.

Chinni, D., and J. Gimpel. 2010. *Our Patchwork Nation: The Surprising Truth about the "Real" America*. New York: Gotham.

Converse, P. 2006. "The Nature of Belief Systems in Mass Publics (1964)." *Critical Review: A Journal of Politics and Society* 18:1–74.

Crawford, C. 2006. *Attack the Messenger: How Politicians Turn You against the Media*. Lanham, MD: Rowman and Littlefield.

Dearing, J. W., and E. Rogers. 1996. *Agenda Setting*. Thousand Oaks, CA: Sage.

Dewey, J. 1927. *The Public and Its Problems*. New York: Holt.

Djupe, P. A., and B. R. Calfano. 2013. *God Talk: Experimenting with the Religious Causes of Public Opinion*. Philadelphia: Temple University Press.

Domke, D., and K. Coe. 2008. *The God Strategy: How Religion Became a Political Weapon in America*. New York: Oxford University Press.

Druckman, J., and C. D. Cam. 2011. "Students as Experimental Participants: A Defense of the 'Narrow Data Base.'" In *Cambridge Handbook of Experimental Political Science*, edited by D. P. Green, J. H. Kuklinski, and A. Lupia, 41–57. New York: Cambridge University Press.

Dvorsky, G. 2013. "How 19-Year-Old Activist Zack Kopplin Is Making Life Hell for Louisiana's Creationists." io9, January 15. http://io9.com/5976112/how-19-year-old-activist-zack-kopplin-is-making-life-hell-for-louisianas-creationists.

Farrell, H., and D. W. Drezner. 2008. "The Power and Politics of Blogs." *Public Choice* 134:15–30.

Finch, L. 2000. "Psychological Propaganda: The War of Ideas on Ideas during the First Half of the Twentieth Century." *Armed Forces and Society* 26:367–386.

Fiorina, M. P., S. J. Abrams, and J. C. Pope. 2010. *Culture War? The Myth of a Polarized America*. New York: Pearson.

Forgette, R., and J. Morris. 2006. "High Conflict Television News and Public Opinion." *Political Research Quarterly* 59:447–456.

Fridkin, K. L., and P. Kenney. 2008. "The Dimensions of Negative Messages." *American Politics Research* 36:694–723.

Gaynor, T. 2012. "Los Angeles Sheriff to Stop Turning Over Low-Level Offenders to Immigration." Reuters, December 5. http://www.reuters.com/article/2012/12/06/us-usa-california-immigration-idUSBRE8B504L20121206.

Geer, J., and R. Lau. 2006. "Filling in the Blanks: A New Method for Estimating Campaign Effects." *British Journal of Political Science* 36:269–290.

Green, D. P., B. R. Calfano, and P. M. Aronow. 2014. "Field Experimental Designs for the Study of Media Effects." *Political Communication* 31:168–180.

Guan, W. 2003. "From the Help Desk: Bootstrapped Standard Errors." *Stata Journal* 3:71–80.

Gunther, A. 1988. "Attitude Extremity and Trust in Media." *Journalism Quarterly* 65:279–287.

Heaney, M. T., M. E. Newman, and D. E. Sylvester. 2011. "Campaigning in the Internet Age." In *The Electoral Challenge: Theory, Meets Practice*, 2nd ed., ed. S. C. Craig and D. B. Hill, 165–193. Washington, DC: CQ.

Hogg, M. A., S. K. S. Fielding, and J. M. Darly 2005. "Fringe Dwellers: Processes of Deviance and Marginalization in Groups." In *The Social Psychology of Inclusion and Exclusion*, edited by D. Abrams, M. A. Hogg, and J. M. Marques, 191–210. New York: Psychology Press.

Hogg, M. A., and S. A. Reid. 2006. "Social Identity, Self-Categorization, and the Communication of Group Norms." *Communication Theory* 16:7–30.

Huckfeldt, R., and J. Sprague. 1991. "Discussant Effects on Vote Choice: Intimacy, Structure, and Interdependence." *Journal of Politics* 53:122–158.

Iyengar, S., and D. R. Kinder. 1987. *News That Matters*. Chicago: University of Chicago Press.

Johnson, T. J., and B. K. Kaye. 2002. "Webelievability: A Path Model Examining How Convenience and Reliance Predict Online Credibility." *Journalism and Mass Communication Quarterly* 79:619–642.

Karlson, K. B., A. Holm, and R. Breen. 2010. "Total, Direct, and Indirect Effects in Logit Models." Centre for Strategic Research in Education, Working Paper Series, No. 0005.

Kayany, J. M. 1998. "Context of Uninhibited Online Behavior: Flaming in Social Newsgroups on Usenet." *Journal of the American Society for Information Science* 49:1135–1141.

Koger, G., S. Masket, and H. Noel. 2010. "Cooperative Party Factions in American Politics." *American Politics Research* 33:33–53.

Langville, A. N., and C. D. Meyer. 2004. "Deeper Inside PageRank." *Internet Mathematics* 1: 335–380.

Lau, R. R. and D. P. Redlawsk. 2001. "Advantages and Disadvantages of Cognitive Heuristics in Political Decision Making." *American Journal of Political Science* 45:951–971.

Leege, D. C, K. D. Wald, B. S. Krueger, and P. D. Mueller. 2002. *The Politics of Cultural Differences: Social Change and Voter Mobilization in the Post–New Deal Period*. Princeton: Princeton University Press.

Lohmann, S. 1993. "A Signaling Model of Informative and Manipulative Political Action." *American Political Science Review* 87:319–333.

Marcus, G. E. 2002. *The Sentimental Citizen: Emotion in Democratic Politics*. University Park: Pennsylvania State University Press.

Marcus, G. E., W. R. Neuman, and M. MacKuen. 2000. *Affective Intelligence and Political Judgment*. Chicago: University of Chicago Press.

McCombs, M. E., J. P. Llamas, E. Lopez-Escobar, and F. Rey. 1997. "Candidate Image in Spanish Elections: Second-Level Agenda-Setting Effects." *Journalism and Mass Communication Quarterly* 74:703–717.

McCombs, M. E., and D. L. Shaw. 1972. "The Agenda-Setting Function of Mass Media." *Public Opinion Quarterly* 36:176–187.

McDermott, R. 2002. "Experimental Methodology in Political Science." *Political Analysis* 10:325–342.

Mendelberg, T. 2001. *The Race Card: Campaign Strategy, Implicit Messages, and the Norm of Equality*. Princeton: Princeton University Press.

Mutz, D. C. 2011. *Population-Based Survey Experiments*. Princeton: Princeton University Press.

Nass, C., and Y. Moon. 2000. "Machines and Mindlessness: Social Responses to Computers." *Journal of Social Issues* 56:81–103.

Norris, P. 2000. *A Virtuous Cycle: Political Communication in Postindustrial Societies*. New York: Cambridge University Press.

Oegema, D., J. Kleinnijenhuis, K. Anderson, and A. M. J. Van Hoof. 2008. "Flaming and Blaming: The Influence of Mass Media Content on Interactions in On-line Discussions." In *Mediated Interpersonal Communication*, edited by E. A. Konijn, M. Tanis, and S. Utz, 331–358. Mahwah, NJ: Erlbaum.

Oldmixon, E. A. 2005. *Uncompromising Positions: God, Sex, and the U.S. House of Representatives*. Washington, DC: Georgetown University Press.

Pirolli, P. 2003. "Exploring and Finding Information." In *HCI Models, Theories, and Frameworks: Toward a Multidisciplinary Science*, edited by J. Carroll, 157–191. San Francisco: Morgan Kauffmann.

Popkin, S. 1991. *The Reasoning Voter: Communication and Persuasion in Presidential Campaigns*. Chicago: University of Chicago Press.

Prior, M. 2007. *Post-broadcast Democracy: How Media Choice Increases Inequality in Political Involvement and Polarizes Elections*. New York: Cambridge University Press.

Putnam, R. D. 2000. *Bowling Alone: The Collapse and Revival of American Community*. New York: Simon and Schuster.

Redlawsk, D. P. 2002. "Hot Cognition or Cool Consideration? Testing the Effects of Motivated Reasoning on Political Decision Making." *Journal of Politics* 64:1021–1044.

Reider, Rex. 2013. "Anonymous Comments Banned Because They're So #*!% Rude." *USA Today*, February 15, 4B.

Scheff, T. J. 1990. *Microsociology: Discourse, Emotion, and Social Structure*. Chicago: University of Chicago Press.

Scheiber, N. 2012. "Exclusive: The Internal Polls That Made Mitt Romney Think He'd Win." *The Plank* (blog), *New Republic*, November 30. http://www.newrepublic.com/blog/plank/110597/exclusive-the-polls-made-mitt-romney-think-hed-win.

Sears, D. O. 1986. "College Sophomores in the Laboratory: Influences of a Narrow Data Base on Social Psychology's View of Human Nature." *Journal of Personality and Social Psychology* 51:515–530.

Sears, D. O., P. J. Henry, and R. Kosterman. 2000. "Egalitarian Values and Contemporary Racial Politics." In *Racialized Politics: The Debate about Racism in America*, edited by D. O. Sears, J. Sidanius, and L. Bobo, 75–117. Chicago: University of Chicago Press.

Skocpol, T., and V. Williamson. 2010. *The Tea Party and the Remaking of Republican Conservatism*. New York: Oxford University Press.

Smith, Rogers. 2013. "Identity Politics and the End of the Reagan Era." *Politics, Groups, and Identities* 1:129–136.

Stouffer, S. A. 1955. *Communism, Conformity, and Civil Liberties: A Cross-Section of the Nation Speaks Its Mind*. New York: Doubleday.

Stroud, N. J. 2008. "Media Use and Political Predispositions: Revisiting the Concept of Selective Exposure." *Political Behavior* 30:341–366.

———. 2011. *Niche News: The Politics of News Choice*. New York: Oxford University Press.

Stryker, Sheldon. 2000. "Identity Competition: Key to Differential Social Movement Participation?" In *Self, Identity, and Social Movements*, edited by S. Stryker, T. Owens, and R. White, 21–40. Minneapolis: University of Minnesota Press.

Tajfel, H., and J. C. Turner. 1979. "An Integrative Theory of Social Conflict." In *The Social Psychology of Intergroup Relations*, edited by W. G. Austin and S. Worchel, 33–47. Chicago: Nelson-Hall.

Theiss-Morse, E. 2009. *Who Counts as an American?* New York: Cambridge University Press.

Valentino, N. A., T. Brader, E. W. Groenendyk, K. Gregorowicz, and W. L. Hutchings. 2011. "Election Night's Alright for Fighting: The Role of Emotions in Political Participation." *Journal of Politics* 73:156–170.

Yang, C. C. 2007. "Factors Influencing Internet Users' Perceived Credibility of News-Related Blogs in Taiwan." *Telematics and Informatics* 24:69–85.

Zaller, J. R. 1992. *The Nature and Origins of Mass Opinion*. New York: Cambridge University Press.

Conclusion

Message Control at the Margins

VICTORIA A. FARRAR-MYERS AND JUSTIN S. VAUGHN

In the introduction, we identified four key themes that would guide the series of independent yet intersecting analyses that would follow. As those themes were explored and answers were provided to the questions being asked, a series of lessons for operating in the social-media-driven political environment emerged. These lessons shape the larger conclusions that can be derived from the collective efforts of the analyses herein.

The first important lesson that candidates and others must remember is that the fundamentals of running a campaign—developing a message that voters will buy into, targeting potential voters who will be the most amenable to support the candidate, reaching those voters, and then getting them to turn out and vote for the candidate—are just as critical in this new media age as they have always been. Certainly the context that candidates, campaigns, interest groups, and others offering a different message face requires them to try to distinguish themselves via an increasing array of new outlets so that their voice will stand out from the competing forces. What the various conclusions of the analyses presented in this volume show, however, is that success is far more likely to come to those who blend traditional campaign fundamentals with modern social media than to those who ignore or underemphasize the former while focusing on the latter.

The seemingly revolutionary nature of new and social media causes people to forget a simple fact about them: new and social media are tools to convey a message, not the message itself. To be sure, social media affect how information is structured and delivered, the speed with which it can be delivered, and the rawness of the information with no spin and no editing. Often, though, as the preceding studies show, political actors utilize the new tools of social media simply to present information in the exact way in which it was originally disseminated, without assessing the greater impact that new media could have in promoting the content of the message.

By contrast, consider the Coffin Handbill discussed in this book's first pages. In its day, the use of printed posters constituted an advanced technological media tool. Yet it was the content, especially the striking visual of the six black coffins, that made the handbill such an effective campaign advocacy tool against Andrew Jackson. The 2012 presidential election's version of the Coffin Handbill may have been an advertisement called "Stage," run only in Ohio during the period between Mitt Romney's securing of the Republican nomination and the Republican convention. The ad was produced and run by Priorities USA, a Super PAC formed to promote President Barack Obama's reelection. The ad recounted the experience of a worker who helped erect a stage in the factory where he worked. The stage was set up to announce that the worker's employer had been acquired by Romney's company, Bain Capital, which was shutting down the factory and firing all the employees. The effect of this advertisement resonated with Ohio voters; indeed, a Republican strategist concluded early into the general election phase of the election, "that ad alone has killed Mitt Romney in Ohio" (Blumenthal 2012). As was the case with the Coffin Handbill, the impact of the "Stage" advertisement demonstrates that no matter what form of media outlet is utilized, the person delivering the message must have meaningful content to convey for consumers to be interested in the message.

A second important lesson that the chapters in this volume demonstrate is that in many ways the effects of social media usage occur at the margins. For example, both perceptions derived through social media mechanisms and the relationship between online and offline participation is conditioned by numerous factors. Further, social media usage in the political realm seems concentrated among the attentive publics and governing elites. Although such usage provides another mechanism to reach out and disseminate information to the mass public, social media has not, at least yet, had a substantial impact on the nature of the mass public's involvement in the political process. As a result, the emphasis on social media in the political context may not seem proportional to the effects it has.

The better way to frame this impact, though, and the true lesson to be learned, stems from the fact that many key political victories are earned at the margin. For example, the 2012 presidential election was almost entirely waged in nine key battleground states, which together constituted only about 20% of the nation's population, and with even greater concentration on a mere handful of counties that were seen as potentially swinging the election in those states. Or in the legislative process, the signature piece of President Obama's first term in office, the Patient Protection and Affordable Care Act (Obamacare), passed the House of Representatives by only seven votes (219–212). In this highly divided, partisan political context, the smallest sway in support or opposition for one's point of view can make the difference between winning and losing the most important political battles. If there is a factor that has been shown to have an effect at the margins, it is not something to be dismissed but to be emphasized. The consequences of social media in the political context fall into this category and thus do in fact warrant the level of interest and inquiry it has and will continue to receive. Moreover, if a person or group can identify ways to utilize social media more effectively, to more efficiently incorporate social media usage into its overall political operations, to better tailor its message in a way that is enhanced when delivered through new and social media outlets, or to better mobilize even a small portion of the mass public, that person or group stands to reap the political benefits of doing so.

Another important lesson harks back to the normative questions concerning the allegedly negative effects that new media's democratization of political discourse has facilitated by lowering the barriers to entry to the social media marketplace of ideas. As a starting question, is democracy enhanced simply by summing up the amount of political expression and participants in the process? In many ways, a greater quantity of expression—with its related increase in the number of issues discussed, the depth of their exploration, and the size of the audience reached—is not just a worthy goal but a fundamental component on which our nation's political structure rests. Indeed, the crux of the Supreme Court's basis for striking down many campaign finance regulations on First Amendment grounds relates back to this very notion.[1] In this light, the ease with which citizens can add their voice and ideas to the ongoing political discourse, even if doing so expands the breadth of political discourse but not the depth, can be nothing but a democratically positive outcome.

A reasonable criticism of this position can be made, however, by asking whether the qualitative nature of that increased public engagement matters, too. That is, should *more* democracy be as valued as *better* democracy? Should we treat the negative, hostile, and personal attacks often found in mass political discourse in social media outlets as a "plus" for democracy so long as it means that an additional person who might not be doing so otherwise is expressing him- or herself within the context of a political discussion? This volume does not attempt to answer those questions directly, but it does offer the lesson that such matters need to be considered when assessing the impact of social media.

The potential of enhanced participation of ordinary citizens in the political discourse through means of new and social media leads to one final thought with which we want to leave readers and future researchers to consider. Over the decades, scholars have continued to observe a transition from *party*-centered campaigns, in which the political parties and their leaders direct their candidates' campaigns, to *candidate*-centered campaigns, in which candidates are in control of their own campaigns (Maisel and Brewer 2011). As seen in this volume, though, social media promote the importance of the individual within the context of the political process generally and in campaigns specifically. Individual citizens can add their thoughts to the political dialogue just as easily as anyone else. Moreover, the ease of obtaining information could help close the gap between attentive and mass publics, meaning that political appeals may need to go to a broader base of individuals. Candidates and campaigns, for their part, have already started to design social media tools and to implement social media strategies to target and reach individual voters (Scherer 2012; Shear 2012).

All this leads us to our final question, one that can only be answered with the passage of time: will the advent of social media in the political context usher in yet another era, that of *voter*-centered campaigns? Voter-centered campaigns are ones in which voters can be part of the campaign dynamic instead of being passive receivers of information—in which voters can inject themselves into the campaign process, candidates proactively reach out to individual voters to develop voters' loyalty to that candidate, or as with the Romney 47% comment, a bartender in his late 30s with a video recorder or smart phone and the luck of being in the right place at the right time to capture a comment not meant for widespread dissemination and consumption could help determine who becomes the next president of the United States. Since all these events have already taken place, the foundation for a voter-centered campaign system may well have already been laid. Although individuals may not be able to control campaigns in the same way as parties and candidates have done in the previous systems, the widespread incorporation of social media in our daily and political lives may allow individual voters to affect political outcomes at the margins, which as we all know is where key political victories are earned.

Notes

1. See *Buckley v. Valeo*, 424 U.S. 1, at 19 (1976) ("A restriction on the amount of money a person or group can spend on political communication during a campaign necessarily reduces the quantity of expression by restricting the number of issues discussed, the depth of their exploration, and the size of the audience reached").

References

Blumenthal, Paul. 2012. "Super PACs, Outside Money Influenced, but Didn't Buy the 2012 Election." Huffington Post, November 7. http://www.huffingtonpost.com/2012/11/07/super-pacs-2012-electionoutside-money_n_2087040.html.

Maisel, L. Sandy, and Mark D. Brewer. 2011. *Parties and Elections in America: The Electoral Process*. 6th ed. Lanham, MD: Rowman and Littlefield.

Scherer, Michael D. 2012. "Friended: How the Obama Campaign Connected with Young Voters." *Swampland* (blog), *Time*, November 20, 2012. http://swampland.time.com/2012/11/20/friended-how-the-obama-campaign-connected-with-young-voters/.

Shear, Michael D. 2012. "Obama Campaign Releases iPhone App for Canvassing." *The Caucus* (blog), *New York Times*, July 31, 2012. http://thecaucus.blogs.nytimes.com/2012/07/31/obama-campaign-releases-iphone-app-for-canvassing/.

ABOUT THE CONTRIBUTORS

Julia R. Azari is Assistant Professor in the Department of Political Science at Marquette University. She received her Ph.D. from Yale University. She is the author of *Delivering the People's Message: The Changing Politics of the Presidential Mandate* and coeditor of *The Presidential Leadership Dilemma: Between the Constitution and a Political Party*. Her work has also appeared in *Social Science Quarterly, Social Science History, Presidential Studies Quarterly,* and *Perspectives on Politics*.

Todd L. Belt is Professor of Political Science at the University of Hawai'i at Hilo. He is the coauthor of the books *Getting Involved: A Guide to Student Citizenship, We Interrupt This Newscast: How to Improve Local News and Win Ratings, Too,* and *The Presidency and Domestic Policy: Comparing Leadership Styles, FDR to Obama,* as well as the author of more than two dozen peer-reviewed journal articles and book chapters.

Brian R. Calfano is Associate Professor of Political Science at Missouri State University. His work appears in *Political Communication, Political Research Quarterly, PS: Political Science & Politics, Political Behavior,* and other journals. His is the coauthor (with Paul Djupe) of *God Talk: Experimenting with the Religious Causes of Public Opinion*.

Daniel J. Coffey is Associate Professor of Political Science at the University of Akron and a Research Fellow in the Ray C. Bliss Institute of Applied Politics. He coauthored *Buckeye Battleground* and has published several other edited volumes, book chapters, and journal articles.

Meredith Conroy is Assistant Professor in the Department of Political Science at California State University–San Bernardino. She earned her Ph.D. in political science from the University of California–Santa Barbara. Her work has appeared in journals such as *International Journal of Communication* and *Computers in Human Behavior*.

Matthew Eshbaugh-Soha is Associate Professor of Political Science at the University of North Texas. He has authored numerous articles on the presidency, media, and public policy and is coauthor of *Breaking through the Noise: Presiden-*

tial Leadership, Public Opinion, and News Media. He earned his Ph.D. in political science at Texas A&M University in 2002.

Victoria A. Farrar-Myers is Full Professor and Distinguished Teaching Professor of Political Science at the University of Texas at Arlington. Among her many publications, Farrar-Myers is the author of *Scripted for Change: The Institutionalization of the American Presidency*, coauthor of *Legislative Labyrinth: Congress and Campaign Finance Reform* and *Limits and Loopholes: The Quest for Money, Free Speech, and Fair Elections*, and coeditor of *Corruption and American Politics*. Farrar-Myers has garnered multiple campus and statewide teaching awards, was inducted into UT Arlington's Academy of Distinguished Teachers in 2011, and in 2012 received the UT System Regents' Outstanding Teaching Award. During 1997–1998, she served as an American Political Science Association Congressional Fellow and in 2014 was a Fulbright Distinguished Chair in Australia.

Jessica T. Feezell is Visiting Assistant Professor at the University of New Mexico. Her work on new media and civic engagement has appeared in the *Journal of Information, Technology, and Politics*, *New Media and Society*, and the *International Journal of Communication*.

Douglas M. Granger is Project Manager at the Center for Marketing and Opinion Research located in Akron, Ohio. He holds a master's degree in applied politics from the University of Akron and is a graduate of the University of Mount Union, where he studied comparative politics.

Mike Gruszczynski is Assistant Professor of Political Science at Austin Peay State University, where he teaches courses in political psychology, research methods, and American politics. His research has been published in journals including *Policy Sciences* and *Political Behavior*.

Mario Guerrero is Assistant Professor of Political Science at California State Polytechnic University, Pomona. His research has appeared in journals including *Computers in Human Behavior* and *Journal of Political Science Education*. He received his Ph.D. from the University of California–Santa Barbara.

Girish J. Gulati is Associate Professor of Political Science at Bentley University. He earned his Ph.D. from the University of Virginia. His recent work has appeared in *New Media & Society*, *Telecommunications Policy*, *Social Science Computer Review*, and *Electronic Government: An International Journal*. He also is an elected member of the executive board for the Informational Technology & Politics section of the American Political Science Association and serves on the editorial boards of the *Journal of Information Technology & Politics* and the *Journal of Political Marketing*.

Joshua Hawthorne is a doctoral student in communication at the University of Missouri. His research on social media and politics has been published in several journals, including *Communication Studies, Argumentation & Advocacy,* and *American Behavioral Scientist*. His work has also won several awards, notably including the Central States Communication Association's J. Jeffrey Auer Award.

Karen S. Hoffman is Director of Undergraduate Studies and Visiting Assistant Professor in the Department of Political Science at Marquette University. She is the author of *Popular Leadership in the Presidency: Origins and Practice*. She has also published articles on the presidency, presidential rhetoric, and political communication in *Rhetoric & Public Affairs* and *Congress and the Presidency*.

Robert J. Klotz is Associate Professor of Political Science at the University of Southern Maine. He is the author of *The Politics of Internet Communication*. His articles on Internet politics have appeared in *Political Communication*, the *Journal of Information Technology & Politics, PS: Political Science & Politics, Women & Politics,* and *Social Science Computer Review*.

Michael Kohler is a master's candidate in political science at the University of Akron, where he is also a research assistant for the Ray C. Bliss Institute of Applied Politics. He has conducted survey research on the Tea Party and, most recently, faith-based nonprofits in the state of Ohio, and his work has previously appeared in the book *Financing the 2012 Election*.

Daniel Kreiss is Assistant Professor in the School of Journalism and Mass Communication at the University of North Carolina at Chapel Hill. In *Taking Our Country Back: The Crafting of Networked Politics from Howard Dean to Barack Obama*, Kreiss presents the history of new media and Democratic Party political campaigning over the past decade. Kreiss is an affiliated fellow of the Information Society Project at Yale Law School and received a Ph.D. in communication from Stanford University.

Regina G. Lawrence holds the Jesse H. Jones Centennial Chair in the School of Journalism and directs the Annette Strauss Institute for Civic Life at the University of Texas at Austin. Her books include *When the Press Fails: Political Power and the News Media from Iraq to Katrina* and *Hillary Clinton's Race for the White House: Gender Politics and the Media on the Campaign Trail*. She earned her Ph.D. at the University of Washington.

Benjamin A. Stewart holds an M.A. in international affairs from Marquette University and is a Ph.D. candidate in policy and strategic management at York University's Schulich School of Business. His previous work has appeared in *Critique: A Worldwide Student Journal of Politics*. He is the recipient of several fellowships and awards, including the 2012 Pi Sigma Alpha Award for the best paper at the 20th Annual Illinois State University Conference for Students of Political Science.

Justin S. Vaughn is Assistant Professor of Political Science at Boise State University. He has published several studies of presidential politics, including *Women and the White House: Gender, Presidential Politics, and Popular Culture* and *The Rhetoric of Heroic Expectations: Establishing the Obama Presidency*, as well as articles in journals including *Presidential Studies Quarterly*, *Political Research Quarterly*, and *Social Science Quarterly*.

Benjamin R. Warner is Assistant Professor of Communication at the University of Missouri. His research has been published in several outlets, including *Communication Quarterly*, *Communication Studies*, *American Behavioral Scientist*, and the *Atlantic Journal of Communication*.

Creighton Welch received an M.A. from the University of Texas at Austin and was a Roy H. Park Fellow in the School of Journalism and Mass Communication at the University of North Carolina at Chapel Hill. Welch has worked in Washington, DC, as a communications director for two U.S. representatives and took part in all aspects of both offline and online communications and campaign strategies at a local and national level. Welch also has been a reporter and blogger at the *San Antonio Express-News* and is currently a senior account executive with KGBTexas.communications in Houston, where he manages public relations and public affairs for clients.

Christine B. Williams is Professor of Political Science in the Global Studies Department at Bentley University. She serves as North American Managing Editor of the *Journal of Political Marketing* and as Associate Editor and on the senior editorial board of the *Journal of Information Technology & Politics*. She edited and contributed to the book *Political Marketing in Retrospective and Prospective* (2012), and her work has appeared in academic journals and conference proceedings, trade and professional association publications, and news media outlets worldwide.

INDEX

1992 presidential election, 147, 148
2000 presidential election, 144
2004 presidential election, 16, 19, 27n3, 143–144, 216n4
2006 midterm elections, 32, 33, 37
2008 presidential election, 17, 18, 19, 20, 138, 144, 147; Republican primary, 18, 136, 201
2010 midterm elections, 17, 20, 32, 34, 37, 149n7
2012 Republican nomination contest, 79, 93, 100, 119, 125, 142, 143, 303

ABC News, 132n5, 149n5
Abramoff, Jack, 32
Abramson, Jill, 105
Adams, John Quincy, 1
Akin, Todd, 59, 86, 162
Alexander, Ryan, 50n2
Allen, George, 137
Althaus, Scott, 140, 149n4
America Blog, 118
American Crossroads, 55–56, 62, 63
American National Election Studies (ANES), 166, 204
Americans for Prosperity, 55–56
America Online, 19, 21
Anderson, Ashley, 249
Anderson, Chris, 115
Arizona Daily Star, 223
Associated Press (AP), 140, 235, 258
audience fragmentation, 53
Azari, Julia, 6

Bachman, Michelle, 79
Bad Lip Reading, 83, 87, 212
Bain Capital, 56, 229, 303
Balz, Dan, 105–106, 108n7
BaracksDubs, 83, 87
Baum, Matthew, 248
Bayh, Evan, 50n2
BBC News, 249
Beck, Paul, 254
Belt, Todd, 7–8
Benghazi, Libya, attacks in, 56, 60, 61–63, 64, 65, 68, 118, 120, 121, 122–123, 125, 126, 128, 129, 131–132, 132n7, 149n10

Bennett, W. Lance, 224
Berry, Jeffrey, 286
Biden, Joe, 63, 229
Bieber, Justin, 77
big data, 15–19, 26
Biggert, Judy, 50n14
Blake, Aaron, 106
Blogger (software), 156
bloggers, 81, 94, 101, 108n5, 223, 225
blogging. *See* blogs
blogosphere. *See* blogs
blogs, 7, 55, 83, 97, 98, 99, 100, 107, 113–118, 119, 120–121, 123, 125–132, 132nn3–4, 136, 139, 140, 142, 143, 144, 145, 146, 149n1, 150n14, 156, 221, 222, 248, 271, 274, 286
Blue State Digital, 18
Boczkowski, Pablo, 107, 108n3
Booth, John, 273
Bouie, Jamelle, 234
Boulianne, Shelley, 138, 149n1
Branstetter, John, 77, 81
Breen, Richard, 285
Buckley v. Valeo, 305n1
Burns, Alexander, 109n24
Bush, George W., 27n3, 64, 143, 144, 201, 216n4, 280
BuzzFeed, 104
Byron, Kristin, 248
Bystrom, Dianne, 157

Cain, Herman, 79, 86, 149n10
Calahan, Ezra, 50n3
Calfano, Brian, 9
Capella, Joseph, 149n3
Carnahan, Dustin, 264
CBS / CBS News, 118, 132nn5–6, 233
Chalmers, Matthew, 99
Chambers, Simone, 224
Chesnut, Tim, 37
Chmiel, Anna, 249, 260
Christie, Chris, 59, 229
Cillizza, Chris, 106
citizenship norms, 182–184, 189–192, 195
civil discourse. *See* civility
civility, 221, 223–224, 227, 245–247, 249,

311

civility (*continued*)
  251–264, 265n8, 265nn10–11, 271, 274, 275, 286
Cleveland Plain Dealer, 255, 257–262, 265nn9–10
Clinton, Hillary, 139
Cmiel, Kenneth, 234
CNN, 97, 132n6, 201, 226, 228, 230–232, 233, 240n6, 241n14
Coffey, Daniel, 8, 9
Coffin Handbill, 1–2, 302–303
comment forum discourse, 221–235, 272–273
Conference of Catholic Bishops, U.S., 270
congressional elections, 5, 32–52, 74, 79, 80, 83, 84, 86, 88
Congress, U.S., 5, 32, 47, 54, 67
Conroy, Meredith, 7, 186, 197n3
conventions, 123, 143, 144, 156
Cook, Charlie, 39
Cook Political Report, 39
Cooper, H. Christopher, 248–249
Corn, David, 104
Crigler, Ann, 200
Crimson Hexagon, 142
Crooks and Liars (blog), 118
Crouse, Timothy, 94, 102, 108n2
Cutter, Stephanie, 25–26

Daily Beast, The (blog), 103, 104, 118
Daily Kos (blog), 55, 60, 62, 118, 132n3
Daily Show, The, 76
Dallas Morning News, 101, 105
Dalton, Russell, 182–184, 195, 197n1
Dashboard (software), 25–26
Dean, Howard, 1, 16, 47, 181
debates: presidential, 23, 56, 63–64, 65, 140, 144, 212; 2008 primary debates, 201; 2012 foreign-policy debate, 63; 2012 presidential debate, first, 7, 24, 63, 143, 144, 146, 155, 156, 161, 162, 164–165, 166, 167, 168–169, 171–174; 2012 vice presidential debate, 56, 63, 164
DeFranco, Philip, 83
DeLay, Tom, 32
DeLong, Gary, 39
Democratic National Committee (DNC), 55, 58, 60–61, 62, 63
Democratic National Convention, 143, 144
Democratic Party / Democrats, 13, 15–16, 17, 26, 27n3, 32, 37, 38, 39, 44, 48, 64, 65, 86, 141, 144, 163, 166, 168–174, 201, 229–232, 241nn13–14, 255, 270–271, 281
Department of Health and Human Services, 270

Des Moines Register, 104
Deuze, Mark, 107
diffusion of innovation, 16, 34, 35–37, 42, 48–49, 155
Dimitrova, Daniela, 157
Dingell, John, 40
DNC. *See* Democratic National Committee
Don't Ask, Don't Tell, repeal of, 58–59
Dovere, Isaac, 102, 103
Druckan, James, 253
Dutta-Bergman, Mohan, 149n4
duty-based citizenship. *See* citizenship norms
Dylko, Ivan, 77, 78

easy issues, 272
eBizMBA, 50n1
Economist, 102
election narratives, 1, 53–63, 65–66, 87–88, 158–162, 174
Ellen DeGeneres Show, The, 22
Enderle, Lance, 50n10
engaged citizenship. *See* citizenship norms
Entman, Robert, 160
Eshbaugh-Soha, Matthew, 7, 140
Essig, Alisia, 50n15, 50n20
Experian Hitwise, 22

Facebook, 2, 5, 7, 13, 14, 18, 21, 22, 23, 24, 25–26, 32, 33–35, 37–49, 50n1, 50n3, 54, 78, 100, 102, 136, 137, 139, 140, 141, 143, 144, 145, 146, 147, 149n1, 149n4, 155, 156, 158, 161, 166, 167, 173, 181–182, 186–187, 189, 193–196, 248, 272; adoption of, by candidates, 5, 34–35, 37–38, 41–43, 44, 45, 47–49; usage by candidates, 4, 5, 38–39, 40, 43–45, 46–49; usage by citizens, 187–188
Face the Nation, 233
Farhi, Paul, 99, 101, 106
Fealy, Gerard, 78
Federal Communications Commission, 216n4
Federal Election Commission, 22
Feezell, Jessica, 7, 186
Fey, Tina, 86
Fishkin, James, 248, 264
FiveThirtyEight (blog), 165
flaming and blaming, 273–278, 281, 283–284
Flickr, 156
Focus on the Family, 67
Foley, Mark, 32
Fowler, Erika, 77, 81
Fox Nation, 55–56, 59, 62, 64, 65
Fox News, 118, 132n1, 132n6, 138, 141, 149n3, 226, 233, 240n6, 276, 283–284, 285, 295

FoxNews.com, 140, 149n3
Frankel, Glenn, 108n7
Frerking, Beth, 104, 108n7
Frum, David, 103

Gallup, 59, 63, 146
Garcia, Joe, 39
Garrett, R. Kelly, 173, 264
Geer, John, 240n9
gender, 23–24, 36, 40, 41, 43, 44, 45, 59, 64, 68
Gerber, Alan, 253
Ghonim, Wael, 75–76
Gilman, Todd, 105
Gingrich, Newt, 79, 102, 109n24, 119
Goes, James, 35
Goode, Sigi, 35
Goodman, Nicole, 184
Goldberg, Jonah, 65
Google, 78, 280, 282, 283–284, 285, 295; Google Hangouts, 23; Google News, 275–276, 277–285
GOP. *See* Republican Party / Republicans
Gore, Albert, 37
Granger, Douglas, 8
Green, Donald, 253
Greider, Erica, 102, 103
Griffith, Morgan, 50n9
Groeling, Tim, 248
Gruszczynski, Mike, 7, 117
Gueorguieva, Vassia, 76
Guerrero, Mario, 7, 186
Gulati, Girish, 5
Gutenberg, Johannes, 221
Gutmann, Amy, 249–250

Habermas, Jürgen, 250
Hamby, Peter, 97, 99, 101
Hamilton, Bill, 102
Hanabusa, Colleen, 50n8
Hannity, Sean, 61
hard issues, 271, 272, 273–274, 275–276, 282, 283, 285, 287, 294–295
Hargittai, Eszter, 118
Hariman, Robert, 235
Hartnett, Stephen, 235
Hawthorne, Joshua, 7, 157, 166
Hayes, Andrew, 265n10
Haynes, Audrey, 139, 140
Herbst, Susan, 241n11
Heritage Foundation, 55–56, 65
Hermida, Alfred, 97–98, 107
Hetherington, Marc, 253
Himelboim, Itai, 173

Hindman, Matthew, 81
Hirschbiel, Paul, 50n16
Hoffman, Karen, 8, 9
Holm, Anders, 285
Holton, Avery, 97, 99
Hong, Se-Joon, 36
Hoppe, Christy, 101
Hot Air (blog), 118
House of Representatives, U.S., 32, 37, 38, 47–48
Houston, Brian, 139, 157
Huckfeldt, Robert, 264
Huffington Post, 116, 140
Hughes, Chris, 50n3
Hulu, 20, 21
Huntsman, John, 79
Hurricane Sandy, 150n11, 265n12

Incivility. *See* civility
Ingraham, Laura, 55–56, 59, 62, 65
Instagram, 23, 156
Instapundit, 118
Iowa caucuses, 79
Iraq, 68
Iyengar, Shanto, 248, 252

Jackson, Andrew, 1, 302
Jamieson, Kathleen Hall, 149n3
Jay-Z, 59
Jepsen, Carly Rae, 212
Jimmy Kimmel Live, 202, 211
Johnson, Paul, 264
Jones, Jeffrey, 63
Judd, Nick, 24–25

Kaid, Lynda Lee, 157
Karlson, Kristian Bernt, 285
Kayany, Joseph, 273
Keitzmann, Jan, 6
Kelly, Jacinta, 77
Kennedy, John F., 136–137
Kerry, John, 143
Kim, Jin, 77
Kinder, Donald, 252
King, Angus, 80
King, Gary, 142
Kirkpatrick, Ann, 50n12
Klotz, Robert, 6, 8
Kohler, Michael, 8
Krauthammer, Charles, 65
Kreiss, Daniel, 5
Krugman, Paul, 55
Kushin, Matthew, 139
Kwon, T. H., 35

Larry Sabato's Crystal Ball, 39
Lasorsa, Dominic, 96, 97, 98, 99
Latinos, 21, 270
Lawrence, Regina, 7
Lewis, Seth, 97, 99
LexisNexis, 119, 132nn5–6
Libya. *See* Benghazi, Libya, attacks in
Liebovich, Mark, 107
Limbaugh, Rush, 64–65
LMFAO, 212
Loke, Jaime, 223
Los Angeles County Sheriff, 275
Love, Mia, 50n15, 50n20
Lowe, Evan, 140
Lugar, Richard, 121
Lukach, Mike, 50n14
Luskin, Robert, 248
Lynch, Emily, 264

Madden NFL 13, 22
Maddow, Rachel, 55, 62
Madison, James, 263
Malkin, Michelle, 55–56, 59, 61, 65, 118
Matthews, Chris, 86
May, Albert, 77
McCain, John, 19, 27n3, 233
McCreery, Stephen, 173
McKain, Aaron, 76
McKinney, Mitchell, 157
meetup.com, 181
Menchik, Daniel, 248
Mencken, H. L., 76
Messenger, Leslie, 39
Messina, Jim, 18
Meyer, Alan, 35
Michaels, Lorne, 203
microblogging, 93, 99, 156
microtargeting, 16, 22
Milwaukee Journal Sentinel, 222, 226, 227, 228, 230–232, 255, 257–261, 265nn9–10
Min, Seong-Jae, 248
Mitchelstein, Eugenia, 107
Monson, Quin, 254
Moore, Michael, 64
Mother Jones, 86, 104, 123
Moulitsas, Markos, 55
Mourdock, Richard, 58, 86, 121
MoveOn.org, 216n4
MSNBC, 55, 118, 132n1, 132n6, 141, 276, 283
MTV, 147
Mutz, Diana, 248, 250, 251, 253
MyBarackObama.com, 181
MySpace, 139, 156

Nahon, Karine, 117
Nation, 55, 64
National Council of La Raza, 55
National Institute for Civil Discourse, 223
National Review, 55–56, 62, 64, 65
NBC / NBC News, 132n5, 226, 228–232, 241n14
Neuhardt, Sharen, 39
Newsweek, 103
New York Times, 55, 63, 95, 102, 103, 105, 107, 118, 132n4, 233
NGP VAN, 18
Nichols, Bill, 109n19
Nisbet, Erik, 149n2
Nisbet, Matthew, 185
Nixon, Richard, 136–137
Norris, Chuck, 206
notions of citizenship. *See* citizenship norms
NPR, 22

Obama, Barack, 1, 3, 13, 14, 40, 47, 56, 59, 60–61, 62, 63, 64, 68, 74, 79, 80, 86, 87, 89, 114, 118, 119, 120–121, 125, 126, 127–128, 136, 141, 143, 145, 146, 149n10, 150nn12–13, 155, 161, 162–163, 164–166, 167–174, 181, 204, 206, 211–212, 222, 227, 229–233, 241n10, 241n13, 256, 262, 270, 271, 280, 281, 303; administration of, 56, 62, 66, 120, 121, 123, 131, 132n7; AMA on Reddit, 181; as Bronco Bamma, 82, 216n2; and economic performance/policy, 59, 60, 64, 68, 239; and foreign policy, 61, 62, 63, 230; "private sector is doing fine" comment, 118, 120, 121, 122–123, 126, 128, 129, 132n7; supporters of, 13, 18, 19, 20, 22, 25, 61, 86, 181, 227, 228, 229, 230, 262; 2008 presidential campaign of, 1, 13, 17, 18, 19, 21, 144, 181; 2012 presidential campaign of, 13, 15, 16, 17, 18, 23, 24, 26, 55, 56, 58, 59, 60–61, 62, 119, 129, 161, 181, 256; and 2012 victory, 23, 61, 63, 64, 155, 165, 166, 270; "you didn't build that" comment, 23, 118, 120, 121–122, 126, 129, 132n7
Obama, Michelle, 155
Obamacare, 68, 263, 303
Obama for America, 25–26
Obama Girl, 137
Oegema, Dirk, 273
online advertising, 14, 19–22, 24, 201
Operation Fast and Furious, 59
Organizing for America, 17

Paine, Thomas, 235
Palin, Sarah, 55–56

Papacharissi, Zizi, 240n4
Partisan Voting Index, 39–40
party conventions. *See* conventions
party networks, 15, 16, 18
Pateman, Carol, 249
Patient Protection and Affordable Care Act, 68, 263, 303
Paton, Jonathan, 50n18
Patterson, Kelly, 254
Patterson, Thomas, 128
Paul, Ron, 47, 87
PayPal, 78
PBS, 63, 80, 161
Pearce, Katy, 149n2
Perry, Katy, 206, 212
Perry, Rick, 79, 86
Peterson, Erik, 253
Pew Research Center, 99, 108n1, 149n5, 221, 241n14; Internet and American Life Project, 77, 155; Project for Excellence in Journalism (PEJ), 137, 142, 146, 147, 149n1, 149n4, 149n6, 149nn8–9, 150n11, 150n14
Pinterest, 23
Pitts, Brian, 139, 140
Planned Parenthood, 55, 59, 64
Politico, 50n5, 100, 102, 103, 104, 105, 109n19, 109n24, 203
politics51.com, 50
Pope, Jeremy, 254
Popular Science, 249
Prior, Markus, 139
PROCESS, 167
Project Houdini, 17, 27n4
Project ORCA, 17, 27n4
Proposition 8 (California), 140
Psy, 74, 77
Putnam, Robert, 250–251

Qualtrics, 275, 276–277

Rachel Maddow Show Blog, 55, 60
Raese, John, 86
Rainie, Lee, 149n5, 156
RAND, 165
Real Clear Politics, 39
ReCal, 240–241n10
Reddit, 181
RedState (blog), 118, 132n3
Reeves, Byron, 251, 253
Republican National Committee, 55–56, 59, 61, 62–63, 64, 65, 68
Republican National Convention, 121, 123, 143, 226, 303

Republican Party / Republicans, 16, 17, 18, 27n3, 37, 38, 60, 65, 68, 121, 141, 162, 163, 166, 168–174, 201, 229–232, 241nn13–14, 255, 270–273, 275–276, 294–295
Reuters, 175
Richard, Patricia Bayer, 273
Ridout, Travis, 20, 77, 81
Romney, Mitt, 1, 3, 7, 27n3, 56, 58–59, 62, 63, 68, 79, 80, 82, 87, 102–103, 109n24, 114, 119, 121, 125, 126, 127, 128, 130, 136, 141, 143, 144, 145, 146, 149n10, 150nn12–13, 162–163, 164–166, 167–174, 181, 204, 206, 211–212, 216n2, 227, 229–232, 241n10, 241n13, 256, 263, 271, 303; "Big Bird" comment, 24, 63, 136, 137, 161; "binders full of women" comment, 23–24, 27n5, 136; 47% comment, 7, 56, 60–61, 64, 65–66, 86, 119, 120, 123–124, 126–127, 129, 132, 132n7, 144, 156, 162, 163, 164, 165–166, 167, 170–172, 174, 175, 305; "I like firing people" comment, 103; strapping dog (Seamus) to roof of car, 119, 120, 121, 123–125, 127, 129, 132n7; supporters of, 86, 136, 227, 228, 230; trip to Europe in summer 2012, 119, 120, 121, 123–124, 126–127, 129, 132n7; and 2012 loss, 61, 64–66; 2012 presidential campaign of, 15, 16, 17, 18, 21, 23, 55–56, 59, 61, 62, 64, 65, 66, 79, 119, 123, 126, 165
RNC. *See* Republican National Committee
Roper Center, 251
Rosen, Jay, 95, 106
Rucker, Philip, 104, 105
Ryan, Paul, 63, 255
Ryan, Timothy, 224

Sabato, Larry, 39
Salon, 55, 60, 64
Sanders, Lynn, 224
Santorum, Rick, 79, 222
Saturday Night Live, 202, 203, 211
Sayre, Ben, 140
Scherer, Michael, 25
Scheufele, Dietram, 185
Senate, U.S., 32, 37, 47, 57, 59, 79, 80, 84, 86, 88, 162
Sensata Technologies, 229
Serrano, Jose, 50n13
Sesame Street, 63
Sheldon, Christopher, 50n11
Silver, Nate, 165
Simpsons, The, 188
Singer, Jane, 97, 98, 107, 108n5
Slater, Wayne, 105
Slothuus, Rune, 253

Smith, Marc, 173
Smith, Tom, 86
Smooth-E, 83
Sobieraj, Sarah, 286
social media targeting, 19–22
Sparrow, Bartholomew, 95, 96, 106
Spotify, 23
Sprague, John, 264
Stanford Report, The, 233
Stevens, Kenneth, 35
Stewart, Ben, 6
Stoycheff, Elizabeth, 149n2
Strandberg, Kim, 223–224
Stromer-Galley, Jennifer, 46
Stroud, Natalie, 131
Summers, Juana, 102, 104, 105
Sunstein, Cass, 131, 251
Superstorm Sandy, 150n11, 265n12
Supreme Court, U.S., 57, 304
Susan B. Anthony List, 55–56, 59, 65
Swalwell, Eric, 39

Talking Points Memo (blog), 118
Tam, Kar Yan, 36
targeted sharing, 24–25
targeting, 5, 13, 14, 19, 20, 21, 22, 26, 46, 48, 78, 288, 295, 302
Tau, Byron, 102, 105
Tea Party, 66, 272; members/identifiers, 103, 276
Technorati.com, 118, 132n2
Tedesco, John, 185
Tewksbury, David, 141, 149n4
TheTruthLaidBear.com, 132n2
ThinkProgress (blog), 118
Thompson, Clive, 76
Thompson, Dennis, 249–250
Tian, Xiaoli, 248
Townhall.com, 55–56, 59, 65
Tracy, Karen, 225
Tuchman, Gaye, 107
Tumblr, 156
Tumulty, Karen, 105
Turner-McGowen, Sarah, 166
Turow, Joseph, 22
Twitter, 2, 7, 18, 22, 23–24, 26, 45, 53, 54, 55, 57, 59, 60, 62, 64, 65, 66–67, 68, 93–94, 96–107, 107–108n1, 136, 137, 139, 140, 141, 142, 143, 144, 146–147, 149n1, 149n4, 155, 156, 158, 161, 166, 167, 173, 181–182; Firehose Data Feed, 142

Uppal, Jack, 50n19
USA Today, 59

Van Dongen, Rachel, 103
VoteBuilder, 16
voter matching, 21
voter modeling, 13, 14, 17
Voter Vault, 16

Wagner, Michael, 117
Walker, Scott, 240n7, 255
Wallsten, Kevin, 117, 118
Wall Street Journal, 86, 165
Warner, Benjamin, 7, 166
Washington Post, 65, 100, 103, 104, 105, 108n6, 109n19, 222
Wasserman Schultz, Debbie, 50n17
Watson, Roger, 8
Web 2.0, 98, 245
Welch, Creighton, 5
Whedon, Joss, 83
Williams, Christine, 5
Williams, Juan, 109n24
Wired, 76
Wisconsin State Journal, 226, 227, 228, 230–232, 235
women. *See* gender
Wordpress, 156

Yahoo!, 21
Yamamoto, Masahiro, 139
Young Turks, 55, 63, 86
YouTube, 3, 6, 21, 23, 74, 76–89, 136, 139, 146, 147, 149n1, 156, 200–202, 203–205, 208, 211–212, 271

Zaller, John, 95, 265n3
Zeleny, Jeff, 103, 105
Zmud, Robert, 35
Zoller Seitz, Matt, 225, 240n5

Printed in the United States
By Bookmasters